ASA DI VAR

MANESHWAR S. CHAHAL

FINGERPRINT!

Published 2025

FINGERPRINT!
Prakash Books

Fingerprint Publishing
@FingerprintP
@fingerprintpublishingbooks
www.fingerprintpublishing.com

ISBN: 978 93 5856 425 9

Dedicated to all those who
seek the One True Lord

THANKS AND ACKNOWLEDGEMENTS

Five years ago, freshly retired, I and wife were in the USA to meet our dear daughters, Guneet and Puneet, both bright and busy Doctors of whom we are really proud.

Interaction with the Sikh Diaspora during that visit helped concretize a long cherished thought, and I spent the next three years on a detailed commentary on the *Japji Sahib*, the *Bāṇi* that best encapsulates the essentials of Sikh Philosophy.

That book was published by Prakash Books in Sept. 2006, and has had kind reviews from scholars, as also readers here and in the USA. I was encouraged thus to take up the daunting, yet pleasurable, task of a similar commentary on the *Āsa Di Vār*. It has been two very grueling years, but the task was made easier by many, to some of whom I must here offer my gratitude.

Above all I must thank Simrat, my soul mate for nearly four happy decades, a gentle helpful soul, ever kind and careful never to hurt anyone. It was her constant and unfussing support that kept me functional through the tough days of researching and writing this book.

Thanks are due to S. Darshan Singh, Chief Engineer (Rtd), a true follower of the Guru with a deep understanding of Sikh tenets, for his invaluable help in finalizing the draft. He spent many days going over each word of the draft, and offered many valuable suggestions. If errors still persist in this book the fault is entirely mine.

Thanks are also due to S. MP Singh, an old colleague from the Pb. & Sind Bank, a sincere and upright human. His familiarity with the publishing world and his helpful nature ensured that the lengthy drill of the publishing process sat lightly on me.

Last, but not the least, I must thank Priyanka Dey, the young and knowledgeable editor who helped put the book into final shape.

Contents

Foreword 9
Preface 11
Introduction 17
The Structure and Theme 21
Mool Mantra & Title 25
Pauṛi 1 33
Pauṛi 2 44
Pauṛi 3 63
Pauṛi 4 79
Pauṛi 5 93
Pauṛi 6 108
Pauṛi 7 122
Pauṛi 8 135
Pauṛi 9 144
Pauṛi 10 154
Pauṛi 11 165
Pauṛi 12 178
Pauṛi 13 190
Pauṛi 14 202
Pauṛi 15 211
Pauṛi 16 223
Pauṛi 17 234
Pauṛi 18 242
Pauṛi 19 251
Pauṛi 20 260
Pauṛi 21 269
Pauṛi 22 275
Pauṛi 23 285
Pauṛi 24 290
Select Bibliography 296
Key to Pronunciation 298

FOREWORD

The *Sri Guru Granth Sahib* (*SGGS*) was installed at the Harmandir Sahib in Amritsar, in AD 1604, by the fifth Nanak after collecting and compiling the compositions of the Gurus, and of mystics whose vision of the Lord was as clear and in tune with that of the Gurus. A century later, in AD 1708, the tenth Nanak formally anointed the *SGGS* as the Guru incarnate for the Sikh nation. It has continued since then to be the only source from where a true Sikh can seek guidance on the path to enlightenment. Richly strewn across its 1430 pages are to be found invaluable pearls of divine wisdom. All it requires of the seeker is diligence, disciplined application of mind and a true desire to be uplifted.

In seeking to approach the *SGGS* there are a few practical problems the seeker will face. The Gurus while presenting this new philosophy have quite naturally employed the language and the idiom with which their audience would have been familiar. This causes for many readers of today some difficulty in comprehending the true message, made even harder by the use of the verse form for these compositions. Some learned ones have attempted translations of the *SGGS* and of some important compositions. These however are necessarily brief and leave little space for elaborating on and discussing the terms used. Fortunately for us, learned men of high spiritual attainments, like Bhai Vir Singh and Prof. Sahib Singh, have given their lifetime creating detailed commentaries explaining the terminology and even the most abstruse references. These are quite illuminating, but being in Punjabi again pose some difficulty for the ones not familiar with Gurmukhi, especially those settled outside India. Thus, a pressing need existed for a detailed commentary in English. This humble effort seeks to fill that gap.

While the proper study of any part of the *SGGS* is fruitful, some compositions explain the philosophy more succinctly, more pointedly. In this category is the *Japji Sahib*, rightly called the 'key to the *SGGS*, which explains the central theme of the Guru's message most clearly. The basic formula laid down there, in the first *pauṛi*, was **"ਕਿਵ ਸਚਿਆਰਾ ਹੋਈਐ ਕਿਵ ਕੂੜੈ ਤੁਟੈ ਪਾਲਿ ॥ ਹੁਕਮਿ ਰਜਾਈ ਚਲਣਾ ਨਾਨਕ ਲਿਖਿਆ ਨਾਲਿ ॥੧॥**" – "Kiv sachiāra hoīai kiv kūṛai tuttai pāl. Hukam rajāi chalṇa Nanak likhiya nāl." This translates as "How shall the veil of this illusion, this falsehood be removed?" And the answer added in the same line is, 'We must surrender to the Lord and run our lives in accordance with His Will or **ਹੁਕਮ** (*Hukam*). Throughout the *SGGS* has this message been reiterated, and driven home through different illustrations and examples from everyday life familiar to the common man.

The central theme remaining the same, there is slight change in emphasis in the various *bāṇis*. Thus, while the *Japji Sahib* concentrates more on the spiritual aspects, some *bāṇis* refer also to certain aspects of everyday living, and of worship; to teach us the true spiritual aspect of these activities. In this category the *Āsa di Vār* can be especially counted. The *Āsa di Vār* calls on us to eschew formalism and to enter into the real spirit of the various religious observances, and this message continues to be as powerfully relevant today.

It is a repeatedly stressed injunction in the *SGGS* that for molding our lives to His way we will need the help and guidance of the true Guru, the Satguru. The Guru says in this baṇi the very first *slok*, "Balihāri Gur āpṇay diuhaṛi sadvār. Jin māṇas te devtay kiye karat na lāgi vār meaning "I would be a sacrifice hundredfold to the Guru because he is the one who will, in a trice, elevate us from the human to the stage of the *Devta*, the supra human, the divine." This can be called the central theme of this composition.

The *Āsa di Vār* also teaches a seeker to avoid the trap of falling into the practices of superficial religiosity. The Sikh can learn the vital importance of following the path delineated for us by the true Guru, the *SGGS*. Followers of other paths or belief systems would also greatly benefit from the universally applicable injunction to eschew formalistic practices and to develop in the heart a genuine love and awe for the Lord, which is an essential ingredient on the road to God-realization.

Since the *Japji Sahib* spells out the central theme of the Guru's message, it may be fruitful if this commentary is read along with the first book in the series 'Way to God in Sikhism', the author's commentary on the *Japji Sahib* (published by Prakash Books India Pvt. Ltd., New Delhi, September 2006).

This volume on the *Āsa di Vār* is, however, complete in itself, and should help the seeker understand more about the Guru's message as contained in this divine composition. It is presented in full awareness of the mightiness of the task. It is entirely possible that your humble interlocutor may have at places erred in his interpretation of the Divine Word. The many learned scholars and achieved souls who may be reading this would no doubt have done better justice to this task. May this endeavour be of at least some avail to some of my fellow seekers.

PREFACE

The Sikh faith is the youngest of the major religions, yet is it as old as human existence on this Earth.

It is ancient because it but restates the eternal verities and it speaks to all mankind of the one Reality, the one Truth known since the ages to the achieved souls. It can, in another sense, be called the youngest of the major world religions, having come into existence in the 16th century AD. It is certainly the most egalitarian, recognizing no differences on the basis of sex, caste or status and treating all mankind as the children of the one Lord. It was in AD 1469 that the world was lucky enough to receive a great Master, Guru Nanak Dev. As his ministry progressed, the power and the majesty of his teachings soon succeeded in attracting a sizeable following, and the Sikh religion took shape. It was to be given its final form gradually over the next couple of centuries. The true Sikh, today, is one who accepts the Sri Guru Granth Sāhib as the only Guru. In everyday life he observes the practices laid down in the *Rehat Maryāda*, code of conduct, drawn up with the help of learned men, and approved by the Sikh Gurdwaras Prabandhak Committee (SGPC). This code lays down how a Sikh shall conduct himself in everyday life and in his social interactions. It can broadly be summed up that a Sikh is required to follow three basic tenets; these being *kirat karna* (earning an honest living through hard work), *vand chhakṇa* (sharing with others what the Lord has granted to you), and *Nām japna* (reciting the Name of the Lord).

Guru Nanak Dev ji was no aggressive proselytizer and his message was one of love and understanding towards all created things, all humans. Above all it prescribed total surrender and unquestioning, single-minded devotion to the One Lord. His simple, easy to understand message was presented in beautifully composed hymns teaching humanity the lesson that the passage to the Lord is to be found through righteous living, and above all, the one single device of *Nām Simran*. His message is universal, for all mankind, and for the ages. He couched his compositions in the most elegant language, yet employing very often the everyday idiom of the common man that would be easily comprehensible to the simplest among his audience.

What was the situation prevailing in the area where these eternal verities were thus being restated by him? The majority community, the Hindus, were in a particularly pitiable state, but the times were hard for everyone. In the religious sphere the world was deeply sunk in empty formalism and worse. In everyday life the rulers had turned rapacious and oppressive. As the *SGGS* says, in *Rāg Malhār*, page 1288, "**ਰਾਜੇ ਸੀਹ ਮੁਕਦਮ ਕੁਤੇ**" – "rājay sīh mukadam kutay", meaning "kings have become rapacious predators and the dispensers of justice are like dogs." Bhai Gurdas, the great mystic and the contemporary of the fourth to sixth Nanaks, in his monumental and highly respected work, the *Vārs*, also depicts the same picture. In *vār* 1, *pauṛi* 30, he says, "**ਰਾਜੇ ਪਾਪ ਕਮਾਵਦੇ ਉਲਟੀ ਵਾੜ ਖੇਤ ਕਉ ਖਾਈ**" – "rājay pāp kamāvday ulti vāṛ khet kau khāi", meaning, "kings have become sinful and the protectors eat up their own protectees". Justice and fair play was not thus the mark of that age.

It was in such times that the Guru came to us. From his earliest childhood the Guru exhibited extraordinary charisma, and showed amazing spiritual insights. As he grew so did his appeal to whosoever interacted with him. Such was the force of his persona and such the attraction of the new path propounded by him that very soon large numbers, both Hindu and Muslim, were flocking to him. These disciples came to be called 'Sikhs'. The term has its root in the Sanskrit 'Shishya' meaning student or learner. The Sikh by the very definition is thus forever an aspirant for the knowledge of the Divine, a seeker of truth.

Guru Nanak was born in AD 1469, in village Talwandi Bhoe, located in the present day Pakistan in Punjab. His father Mehta Kalyan Dass, popularly called Mehta Kālu, was a revenue official with Rai Bular, son of Rai Bhoe, who ruled the principality in which this village fell. Rai Bular was an open-minded individual who could appreciate the spiritual gifts of the young Guru. Numerous stories are told in the *Janam Sākhis* penned by various authors, of the Guru's precocious spiritual talents. It is uniformly accepted that the Guru as a child exhibited a wisdom and knowledge well beyond the capacity of a normal human being.

While his spiritual stature and attainments were recognized soon enough, it is also recorded that the young Nanak showed an absence of enthusiasm for worldly commerce. His father tried hard to get him to take up any suitable job or vocation. These exertions were however in vain. After many failed efforts to settle him it was decided to send him to Sultanpur Lodhi where his sister Nanaki, his sole sibling, was married to Jai Ram, an employee of the Nawab Daulat Khan Lodhi of Sultanpur. According to Prof. Sahib Singh this move happened on 30 October 1504. The young Nanak, through the intercession of

Jai Ram, was soon given an important assignment as the person in charge of the *modikhāna* (the stores) of the Nawab. He remained in that position in Sultanpur Lodhi for nearly three years till AD 1507. During this period it is said that the Guru set up a routine of religious discourses and *kīrtan* (singing of devotional hymns). He was also joined here by Bhai Mardana, son of one Mir Badra, a Muslim of the 'Mirāsi' caste belonging to Talwandi. Mardana was about nine years older than the Guru and was an accomplished *rabāb* (rebec) player, and he was to be an inseparable companion to the Guru from then on. He was an important part of the religious congregations and the singing of *kīrtan*, which regularly took place around the Guru.

In AD 1507, there occurred the famous incident of the Guru's immersion in the *Bein*, which is a rivulet flowing close to the city and was commonly used by the populace for bathing. Therefore, when the Guru entered the water on that fateful day, said to be in the month of August, there was nothing unusual about it.

The Guru however soon after entering into the water disappeared from sight. Naturally, his companions thought him drowned. There was uproar and the town people, who loved him dearly turned out in large numbers to look for him. He was however not to be found and after some frantic searching was given up as lost. There was general mourning among the populace who were deeply grieved by the loss of their much admired and deeply respected companion. A miracle, however, then occurred when suddenly, three days later, the Guru reappeared from the *Bein*. The *Purātan Janam Sākhi* says that the Guru spent these three days in the physical presence of the *Akāl Purakh* – the Lord Himself. Some may argue that the Lord is formless and so could not be said to be holding court like a human being where the Guru could appear in His presence. To understand this fondly held belief we must here bear in mind that the Lord is not merely Transcendent, but is also the Immanent, all pervasive Reality that permeates the Universe. For the Lord to manifest Himself as a ruler holding court is therefore not anomalous. He could well so have appeared for His special devotee. The *Sākhi* describes in detail the manner in which the Guru was received in the Divine presence and the events that transpired there.

The details of the occurrence are of course a matter of personal faith. The devout will insist on the veracity of each detail recorded in the *Purātan Janam Sākhi*, while others may seek to impart a different metaphysical significance to the matter. The evidence however is unanimous that after his disappearance in the *Bein*, the Guru was away from human eyes for those three days, and that he as suddenly reappeared at the end of that period.

The reappearance of the Guru occasioned great rejoicing. It is said that his first words after he reappeared were, "There is no Hindu, there is no Mussalmān." This was not by any chance meant to negate or condemn the belief systems followed by the adherents of these religions. Rather was it a reassertion of the universality of the spiritual experience. It spoke of a religion beyond mere sectarianism. The Guru when he spoke these words was indirectly indicating to the world the contours of the one true religion he was to propagate, the religion that had less to do with the material human form but was to concentrate on the spirit. This moment is said to mark the formal beginning of Guru Nanak's ministry on this earth.

During the next many years he was to travel extensively, undertaking four long journeys to the four quarters of the Asian landmass. These journeys are called the *Udāsīs*, and spanned nearly fourteen years. The Guru thereafter settled down in a new township set up by him at Kartārpur, on the western banks of the river Ravi in the year AD 1521. There he was to stay for the rest of his sojourn on this Earth, till he passed on to the Divine Realms in September 1539. He had before then passed on the torch, during his lifetime, to his most devoted follower, Bhai Lehṇa.

The second Nanak was born as Lehṇna, in the village of Mattay di Sarāi on Baisākh *vadi* 1, 1561 *Bikrami*, corresponding to 31st March 1504. The village, located in the district of Faridkot in Punjab, is today better known as Sarāi Nāga. His mother was Sabhirai who was, as was the custom, named as Rāmo in her in-laws' house. His father, Bhai Pheru, a Trehan Khatri by caste, was a trader and also for some time served as factotum to a landlord named Takht Mal. The daughter of Takht Mal, named Veerāi, treated Bhai Pheru like a brother, and was very fond of young Lehṇa. Through her intervention he was married in AD 1521, to Bibi Khivi, daughter of Devi Chand Marwaha of village Sanghar, located near Khadur Sahib in what is today Amritsar district. According to Principal Satbir Singh, he had two sons, Dās and Dāt, more commonly called Dāsu and Dātu; and in between, two daughters, Amaro and Anokhi. His father was a devotee of *Devi Durga* and regularly used to lead a group from his area to her shrine at *Jwālāmukhi*, presently in the state of Himachal Pradesh.

The young Lehṇa was a spiritually gifted child and was well recognized as a kind-hearted soul. Rather unusually for a child, he was known to serve food to passing *sadhus* and to set up *chhabeels* (roadside stations) for serving cold water to passersby on hot days. He had to take up the family responsibilities after his father passed away in AD 1526. He also became the leader of the group that used to go to *Jwālāmukhi*. On one such trip he heard about Guru Nanak and the desire arose in him to meet the Guru. There was a Jātt named Jodha of the Khehṛa caste, from the same village, who was a follower of Guru Nanak and lived in Kartaarpur. Once, when he was on a visit to his old village Lehṇa happened to hear him singing the Guru's *Bāṇi*. The desire to see the Guru was rekindled stronger in his heart, and on his next trip to *Jwālāmukhi* he did visit the Guru. He was so impressed with what he saw that he gave up all old associations and decided to stay at Kartarpur. There are many stories that narrate his total devotion to the Guru and to the new path the Guru was delineating. Bhai Lehṇa's humility, total dedication and his spiritual attainments were so above those of any other devotee that Guru Nanak named him 'Angad', meaning 'a part of', 'ang' being the Hindi word for limb. Bypassing his own sons, Guru Nanak set a new tradition and on 13th June 1539, anointed him as the Guru. A few months later, on 7th September, Guru Nanak departed this world.

Guru Angad had within the few years he spent with him imbued himself totally in Guru Nanak's colours, so much so that even his hymns are hard to distinguish in style or content from Guru Nanak's compositions. Truly had he become the second Nanak

Guru Nanak throughout his lifetime and especially during this period composed hymns, which were preserved and finally incorporated by the fifth Nanak, Guru Arjan Dev into the *Sri Guru Granth Sahib* (*SGGS*) and formally installed in August 1604 in the Harimandir Sahib at Amritsar, popularly called the Golden Temple these days. The *SGGS* apart from Guru Nanak's hymns also contains the compositions of the 2nd, the 3rd, the 4th, the 5th, and the 9th Nanak; and the compositions of *Bhagats*, mystics and men of God, whose message was in consonance with the message of Guru Nanak. The tenth Nanak later added some compositions of the ninth Nanak at the appropriate places under different *Rāgas*.

Guru Gobind Singh, before leaving this mortal abode in AD 1708 also anointed the *Guru Granth Sahib* and bestowed on it the title of 'Guru'. Since that day the

SGGS has been the only Guru for the Sikhs and is viewed as the manifest body of the spirit of the Gurus. It is therefore accorded respect and honour as due to a preceptor, and has been the guide and the spiritual support of the Sikh nation since then. The *SGGS* governs the daily life and for a true Sikh provides answers to all questions, whether of the spirit or mundane. Much more importantly it delineates the roadmap, the discipline that anyone can follow for purifying the spirit and making it worthy of receiving the Lord's grace.

INTRODUCTION

Among the many sublime hymns in the *SGGS*, the seeker will find the *Āsa Di Vār*, on pages 462 to 475. This *Vār* comprises 24 *pauṛis* and 59 *sloks*, of which 44 are by Guru Nanak Dev and 15 by the second Nanak.

The *Vār* form has often been used by the Gurus, there being 22 *Vārs* in the *SGGS*, in 17 different *Rāgs*. In addition to the *Āsa di Vār,* Guru Nanak himself composed *Vārs* in *Rāg Mājh* and *Rāg Malhār*, each comprising 27 *pauṛis*. This total count of the 22 comprises: one *Vār* each in *Sri Rāg, Rāg Mājh, Rāg Āsa, Rāg Bihāgṛa, Rāg Vadhans, Rāg Soratth, Rāg Jaitsari, Rāg Sūhi, Rāg Bilāwal, Rāg Basant, Rāg Sārang, Rāg Malhār, Rāg Kānṛa; two each in Rāg Gauṛi, Rāg Gūjri, Rāg Māru;* and three in *Rāg Rāmkali*. Out of these only the *Vār* in *Rāg Rāmkali* by two Muslim Bards, Satta and Balwand, and the *Vār* in *Rāg Basant* have no *sloks* attached. To all the other *Vārs* varying numbers of *sloks* have been attached.

The *Vār* form was at that time commonly employed by bards, typically for narrating stirring tales of popular warriors and heroes. As such it had wide acceptability and enjoyed easy recognition among the general public. The Gurus probably for this reason, having adapted it to matters spiritual, utilized it for many of their compositions to convey to the world their message of the spirit, and of righteous living.

In its essence the *Vār* requires two protagonists, a hero and the antihero. The narration then describes the conflict between the two with usually the hero coming out triumphant. The Gurus subtly altered the content and form and substituted the mundane with the spiritual. In doing so they made the inner good and the evil within us the two protagonists. The struggle here is thus for overcoming the dark and evil tendencies within ourselves. The narration then proceeds to tell us how to strengthen the good within us and to win the battle within, and ultimately realize God by following the right spiritual path under the guidance of the right preceptor.

There has been never been any question that the *Āsa di Vār* was composed by Guru Nanak Dev himself. The precise date, however, when it may have been composed is difficult to establish. Bhai Vir Singh narrates in his *Panj Granthi* that according to the *Purātan Janam Sākhi* the first nine *pauṛis* are said to have been spoken to Sheikh Ibrahim Farid Sāni, named in that *Sākhi* as Sheikh Brahm. The remaining 15 *pauṛis* were, according to the 37th *Sākhi*, spoken to one Duni Chand in Lahore.

This view however is not universally accepted. Many learned ones opine that most of the Guru's *bāṇi* was composed after he had settled in Kartarpur after AD 1521. Prof. Sahib Singh, in his *Sri Guru Granth Sahib Darpan* (Volume 4, page 604), argues quite convincingly that these stories of the Gurus having composed their *Bāṇi* on special occasions or for special purposes are not based on reality. He says that even where the *shabads* or *sloks* do pertain to, or refer to, an historical or actual event, the lesson these convey is always universal and applicable to all mankind for all times. As the Guru says, in *Rāg Sūhi*, *Mahla* 3, *SGGS,* page 755, **"ਮਹਾ ਪੁਰਖਾ ਕਾ ਬੋਲਣਾ ਹੋਵੈ ਕਿਤੈ ਪਰਥਾਇ ॥ ਓਇ ਅੰਮ੍ਰਿਤ ਭਰੇ ਭਰਪੂਰ ਹਹਿ ਓਨਾ ਤਿਲੁ ਨ ਤਮਾਇ ॥੮॥"** "maha purkha ka bolṇa hovai kitai parthāye, oye amrit bharay bharpūr haih ona til na tamāye", meaning that the words of the great souls uttered in any context are like nectar and are not tainted by any desire for themselves. These are never intended for any individual but are meant to be a message to all seekers for all times. It also seems hardly likely that the Guru would have produced a composition addressing some individual, and that somebody would also have been around to record it immediately for posterity. Quite possibly this and many other of these divine hymns would have been composed in moments of inspiration and at comparative leisure. These could then have been jotted down by the companions of the Gurus, or by the Guru himself.

There is a long-standing tradition of the *Āsa di Vār* being sung in the early morning hours. There is, however, no clear reference to this *Bāṇi* having been part of the Sikh liturgy, the daily prayers, in the earliest days of Sikhism. As the great savant and scholar, Bhai Gurdas, says, **"ਸੋਦਰ ਆਰਤੀ ਗਾਵੀਐ ਅੰਮ੍ਰਿਤ ਵੇਲੇ ਜਾਪ ਉਚਾਰਾ"** "Sodar Ārti gāvīai amrit velay jāp uchāra".

This translates as, "The *Sodar* and the *Ārti* were sung, and in the ambrosial hour of the morning the *Jāp* was recited." He makes no specific mention of the *Āsa di Vār*. According to Dr. Jaggi (introduction to the commentary on the *Āsa di Vār* by Swami Anandghan, Punjabi University, 1990), the *Purātan Janam Sākhi* shown to have been written in AD 1588, 16 years prior to the installation of the *SGGS*, records the first nine *pauṛis* with *sloks* attached. Bhai Vir Singh also says in the *Panj granthi* that the fifth Nanak probably allowed the *sloks* being already attached by the bards to stand as such. *Encyclopedia of Sikhism* (Volume 1, page 203) also confirms that the custom of reciting the *Āsa di Vār* at morning time can be traced to the days of Guru Nanak himself. The Encyclopedia says that Bhai Lehṇa (later, Guru Angad) was the first to sing it in the presence of Guru Nanak Dev and that the *Vār* then comprised twenty-four *pauṛis* (stanza) by Guru Nanak and some *sloks* which were also his compositions.

Thus, the tradition of singing this composition in the morning hours may well have originated in Guru Nanak Dev's time. That certain *sloks* were sung before each *pauṛi* can also reasonably be inferred. What we do know for sure is that the Sri Guru Granth Sahib, as formally installed in AD 1604 included the *Āsa di Vār* comprising 24 *pauṛis* and 59 *sloks*, 44 by Guru Nanak Dev and 15 by the second Nanak, Guru Angad Dev, and it is since then being sung as *Kīrtan* in Gurdwaras and in the homes of the devout every morning in the early hours.

Another tradition, and for this there is no clear guidance to be found even in the SGGS, but which is also age-old, is to affix one quatrain, a *Shabad*, in the *chhant* form by the fourth Nanak, Guru Ramdas before the *sloks* with each *pauṛi*, while performing the *Kīrtan*. These *chhants* are, however, separately placed in the *SGGS* on pages 448 to 451.

It is for a seeker, of course, not so vital as to when and how the hymn was composed. What really matters is the lesson it contains, the message the Guru wanted to communicate to us through the medium of this sublime composition.

THE STRUCTURE AND THEME

The *SGGS* is the word of God brought to us by the Gurus. It lays down for each Sikh the roadmap for reaching the only destination worth striving for: God-Realization. This theme runs through, and is common to, all *bāṇis* in the SGGS. Each hymn, each composition speaks to all mankind of what should be the single focus of all our endeavours – how to succeed in the struggle to reach from here to the Divine. Naturally the theme of the *Āsa di Vār* is no different.

Thus, we have the *SGGS* telling us that this soul was granted this human form as a great reward by the Lord, and that was for the sole purpose of enabling us to break through the veil of illusion that blinds us. This invaluable opportunity has been granted us so that by overcoming the besetting sin of man – *haumai* – the sense of selfness, of being separate from the Lord, the soul can achieve God-realization. The simple device prescribed for achieving that purpose is the device of *Nām Simran* (reciting His Name). In the course of this lesson the Guru tells us how easily man is diverted away from this vital goal and how readily he starts chasing the false glitter of *Maya* that pervades this world. The path to salvation, he tells us, will be found through the auspices of and under the guidance of the right Guru. This Guru will teach us how by devotedly and single-mindedly focusing on the recitation of the 'Name' we are purified enough to realise that all that exists and the only Reality is the Lord Himself. When we become aware that He is the only power, that He underpins all that exists, and permeates all that we see and all events that occur, then will we be fit to receive His Grace. This state, of course, will come only as a measure of His grace, when and where He so wills. It is not within any created being's power to claim it as a right, however deserving we may deem ourselves.

As we noted above, attached with the *pauṛis* are attached *sloks*, 44 by Guru Nanak and 15 by the second Nanak which are placed as follows: one each before *pauṛis* 1, 2, 7, 24; two each before *pauṛis* 12, 21, 23; and 5 before *pauṛi* 22. The title of this *Bāṇi* on page 462 does not mention specifically that the *sloks* of the second Nanak are included. This aspect has not been discussed by most of the learned commentators. Only Bhai Vir Singh in his commentary in the Panj Granthi, and Prof. Darshan Singh in his audio-commentary offer a view. Prof. Darshan Singh says that the *sloks* of the second Nanak included here can conceptually be seen as addenda to the *sloks* of Guru Nanak, elaborating and reinforcing the point made in those and therefore no separate mention may have been considered necessary. Bhai Sahib offers the view that mention may not have been made of these sloks specifically in the title because these were few in number. Both views have some force but neither seems clinching enough. The Guru alone knows why he chose not to mention this aspect in the title. Within the bani, of course the indication is clear enough where a slok is by the second Nanak.

There is no strict linkage of concept discernable between *sloks* and the *pauṛi* with which it is attached. The thrust of the lesson in each composition, in different ways, is, however, consistent and conveys the same message of how to reach the Lord through true devotion.

Learned commentators have explained that there was a body of hymns left over after the compilation of the *SGGS*, and the Guru decided to incorporate these by adding some *sloks* with most of the *Vārs*. As we have discussed earlier, only the *Vār* by Satta and Balwand, and the *Vār* in *Rāg Basant* have no *sloks* attached. Some *sloks* still left over were then incorporated at one place in the *SGGS* from page 1410, under the heading *slok vāra(n) to vadhīk*, meaning that these are *sloks* in addition to those that have been added with the *Vārs*.

The number of *sloks* added with each *pauṛi* ascribed to Guru Nanak, *Mahla* 1, and to the second Nanak, Guru Angad, is as follows:

Pauṛi	***Mahla 1***	***Mahla 2***
1	2	1
2	2	1
3	2	nil
4	2	nil

5	2	nil	
6	2	nil	
7	1	1	
8	2	nil	
9	2	nil	
10	2	nil	
11	3	nil	
12	2	2	(some count 3 sloks by Guru Nanak)
13	2	nil	
14	2	nil	
15	4	nil	
16	2	nil	
17	2	nil	
18	3	nil	
19	2	nil	
20	2	nil	
21	0	2	
22	0	5	
23	0	2	
24	1	1	
	44	**15**	

The *pauṛis* are uniform in structure, each consisting of four lines with a short pithy concluding the 5th line except for *pauṛi* 22, which has 6 lines. Also, in *pauṛi* 23, the 5th line is slightly different, being longer than in the other *pauṛis*. The *sloks* however are of widely varying lengths and different in style and structure. These pertain to different issues, both spiritual and those pertaining to the everyday life and practices of the common man. Many of these relate to and offer sharp commentary on the socio-political conditions prevalent at that time.

The number of *sloks* can be counted as 44 by the first Nanak and 15 by the second Nanak. Some differences on this can be seen among respected commentators. For instance Prof. Teja Singh in his commentary (1968, fifth edition, January 1998), puts this number at 46 by Guru Nanak and 14 by the second Nanak. The *Encyclopedia of Sikhism* (Volume 1, page 203), puts the number of *sloks* as 45 by *Mahla* 1 and 14 by *Mahla* 2. This may possibly be because the first *slok* in *pauṛi* 12, starting with "**ਦੁਖੁ ਦਾਰੂ ਸੁਖੁ ਰੋਗ ਭਇਆ**" – "dukh dāru sukh rog bhaya" – has been counted as one for the portion before the pause, and as a separate slok for the part after the "**ਰਹਾਉ**" – pause – starting with "**ਜਾਤਿ ਮਹਿ ਜੋਤਿ**". Another issue is about *pauṛi* 22 where the second *slok* which says, "**ਜੋ ਜੀਇ ਹੋਇ ਸੋ ਉਗਵੈ**" – "jo jee hoye so ugwai" has been ascribed to *Mahla* 2 in the text of the Asa di Var in the *SGGS* but assigned to *Mahla* 1 in commentaries as highly respected as the ones by Prof. Sahib Singh and Prof. Teja Singh, possibly because the same slok at page 1353 has been ascribed to Mahla 1. These are minor details and are mentioned only to put the record straight, having no significant relevance to a study of this Bāṇi.

MOOL MANTRA & TITLE

The *Āsa di Vār* commences on page 462 of the *SGGS* with the *Mool Mantra*, followed by the Title which runs as "*Āsa Mahla 1. Vār* sloka nāl slok bhi mahle pehle ke likhay. Tunday Asrājay ki dhuni", which means that the composition is by Guru Nanak and has attached *sloks*, the *sloks* being also the composition of *Mahla 1*, to be sung to the tune of the maimed king *Asrāj*." Let us discuss this in more detail.

It has been since ancient days a practice in India to commence any holy or otherwise important task with an invocation to a deity. This is meant to ensure the blessings of that deity for the unimpeded completion of the task. The most usual invocation in Hinduism is to Lord Ganesha, also called *Vighneshwara, meaning* remover of obstacles. The Gurus, however, in keeping with Guru Nanak's new vision always chose instead to invoke the Timeless One, the Creator Himself. The invocation is in the form of what has come to be popularly called the *Mool Mantra*, meaning the 'basic creed'. It runs as, *"Ik Onkār Satnām Kartāpurakh Nirbhau Nirvair Akālmūrat Ajūni Saibhang Gurprasād."* This invocation in this form is to be found at the very commencement of the *SGGS*, at the head of the first composition recorded therein, the *Japji Sahib*. It has been repeated at the beginning of many compositions, usually in its full form but also at some places in shortened form. The full form of the invocation is said to occur 33 times in the *SGGS*; and 26 of the 31 *rāgs* open with this. A somewhat shorter form – *Ik Onkār Satnām Kartāpurakh Gurprasād* – occurs nine times. A much shorter form – *Ik Onkār Satguru Prasād* – has been used nearly 520 times. The briefest form – *Ik Onkār* – has also been used in the concluding hymns. The use of this invocation is meant to reiterate that the Guru's message was universal and not confined to any one religion or belief system. This was a new path that saw nothing but the One Lord in all that exists.

The *Mool Mantra* can be said to be an effort by a realized soul to communicate to the rest of us a vision of the Eternal One. Here is a master seeking to put into words a mystical insight that he has personally experienced. The task is obviously daunting, and akin to describing colour to the blind. So he attempts to do it by stressing some of the main attributes we humans can ascribe to the One Lord, though it is really trying to describe that which is beyond all description. The foremost of these attributes is that He is *Ik Onkār*. This term needs to be understood first.

Ik Onkār literally means that there is but One God. The Guru is saying that He is 'One', and He is the 'Word'. The concept of the 'Word' as Creator is prevalent in many belief systems. Thus, we have in Hinduism the concept of 'AUM' or 'OM' as the underlying principle of the Universe. Even ancient Greek thought postulated 'LOGOS', the Creative Word. This is the divine power that directs and sustains the creation, both within and without. Guru Nanak modified and added to this when he affixed the word *Ik* with the term *Onkār*. The Guru in coining this new word annunciated his new philosophy, which postulated a Lord over and above the various Trinities and powers that were then worshipped. Implicit in *Ik Onkār* is a Creator who is unique all by Himself, and permeates His creation as the Immanent Lord. The Lord is thus not merely the Prime Cause but is Himself within that creation. The Guru, in short, is telling us that the Lord is transcendently the Creator, the Sole Reality; but He is also the Immanent Presence within that creation.

The next attribute is that He is *Satnām* – the only Truth, the sole Reality. This is not meant to convey that the Universe is unreal or an illusion. The Lord's creation is real too, and that is so because He is Himself within it. All that we see is thus the Lord manifest. Without Him this material world can have no existence, but because He permeates it the material world is real. The Prime Cause behind it all is He Himself. Thus is He the only Reality, the cause that gives materiality to all creation. He is the *Satnām*.

He is the *Karta Purakh*, the Creator who is Immanent in His creation. This reiterates the nature of the Lord as both Transcendent and Immanent. He is not a distant Maker who having brought the Universe into existence then watches as an outsider from afar. The creation comes from within Him, and then He resides within.

The Guru, after telling us of the relationship between the One Lord and this creation, then describes for us the Lord in terms of traits with which humans could from personal experience relate. He says the Lord is *Nirbhau* – the One without fear – and *Nirvair* – the One without rancor. Since the Lord is the sole Reality the question of Him knowing fear cannot arise. Whom could He be afraid of? The question of enmity or rancor is similarly answered. The One without any equals obviously can hold no enmity with anyone. This is also in tune with Guru Nanak's concept of the Lord as the ever benevolent, the ever loving.

The terms *Akāl Mūrat*, *Ajūni* and *Saibha[ng]* are the other attributes that at least partially make clear the concept of the Creator. *Akāl Mūrat* refers to the Lord as free from the limitations of Time. All that exists is under the sway of Time, and will one day wither away or cease to exist. It is only the Lord who is not thus bound. Put differently, this means He is Deathless, while all else is ruled by Death. *Ajūni* again, means not born, not incarnated, and therefore by implication not subject to death. Lastly, He is *Saibha[ng]* or self-created. Obviously the Prime Cause – the One, by definition cannot have someone else to create Him.

The last words in the *Mool Mantra* – the invocation – are *Gur Parsād*, meaning by the grace of the Guru. The thought behind this is that the Lord is to be realized through the guidance of the Guru, through his grace. We will see throughout the *SGGS* this stress on the importance of the Guru as the guide who will show us the way to the Lord. Because the Guru laid down this formulation, many are there for whom it has become a convenient handle to present themselves as the Guru, and acquire their personal set of followers. In Sikhism, let there be no doubt that this Guru is none else but the *Sri Guru Granth Sahib*. This was so prescribed by the tenth Nanak in AD 1708 before he passed from this world.

The *Mool Mantra* is then followed by the title that says, "*Rāg Āsa, Mahla 1. Vār* with *sloks*, the *sloks* added being also those of the *Mahla 1*. To be sung to the tune of the maimed king *Asrāj*".

The title of the *Āsa di Vār* says that it is by *Mahla 1*, which is how Guru Nanak is referred to. It is set to the *Rāg* (musical measure) called *Āsa*. The *Encyclopedia of Sikhism*, page 230, Volume 1, says that this *Rāg* is prescribed for use in the predawn hours; and adds that the custom of singing this *Vār* at early morning hours is traceable to the days of Guru Nanak himself, Bhai Lehṇa, later installed as the second Nanak by the name Guru Angad, being the first to sing it in the presence of Guru Nanak.

The definition of the term *Vār* has been rendered varyingly by learned scholars as 'Ode' or 'ballad'. Bhai Vir Singh explains that the root of the word is *Vārta*, meaning news, narration, and talk. Bhai Sahib Bhai Kahan Singh has given as many as 31 different meanings of this word. At serial number 4 among these, he defines it as "a poem about battles describing valorous deeds". He also defines it as a type of *chhant*. At serial number 6 he defines it further as, "the *Bāṇi* in praise of the Lord, in the *SGGS*". Bhai Vir Singh also says that this form was mostly used to give detailed information about battles and wars. Gradually these narrations were reduced in the form of quatrains, or *chhants*, by the bards for ease of recollection. These quatrains then came to be sung in public performances to the accompaniment of simple instruments like the *sārangi* (lute) and the *dhad* (tabor). These *chhants* came to be called *pauṛis*, and to these were added in due course some *sloks* to illustrate and elucidate the tales being narrated in the *pauṛis*. Thus was born the *Vār* form. It remained therefore, essentially a form used for describing heroic tales and events; stories of struggle where the valiant hero faced strong adversaries and triumphed against the most forbidding and tough odds. It obviously needed two protagonists – the good and heroic figure versus the powerful evil one.

If we consider the above background, describing this form as an 'Ode' or a 'ballad' does not therefore quite define it accurately. A ballad is defined by Webster's *Encyclopedic Unabridged Dictionary* as: "A simple, often crude, narrative poem of popular origin composed in short stanzas, especially one of romantic character and adapted for singing." Another definition given is: "Any light, simple song especially one of sentimental or romantic character having the same melody for each stanza." Chamber's *Twentieth Century Dictionary* describes it as: "A simple, straightforward narrative poem in short stanzas." It would usually be 'a slow sentimental popular song', according to Webster's *New World Dictionary*, which also defines an Ode as 'a lyric poem characterized by lofty feeling and dignified style'. The term ode is defined by the *Twentieth Century Dictionary* simply as a poem intended to be sung. The Webster's dictionary also gives it the same meaning, but adds that it is a "lyric poem typically of elaborate or irregular metrical form and expressive of exalted or enthusiastic emotion".

We can now see that these definitions do not quite do justice in describing fully the *Vār* form. The *Vār* does have short, simple stanzas; it also has often a lofty feeling and dignified style, especially when used by the Gurus in the *SGGS*. The essence of the *Vār* in Punjabi, however, is the pulsating throb of the beat, and the narration of the underlying strife. This is typically suited for martial occasions, when it is necessary to rouse emotions, and for paying tribute to valiant heroes. It is safer therefore to avoid translating it either as an 'Ode' or 'Ballad'. It deserves to be simply called the *Vār*, a unique Punjabi contribution to poetic literature.

As we see, the element of strife and conflict between the hero and the anti-hero is an inherent part of the *Vār*. Adapting it for use in a mystical, spiritual milieu therefore required special ability; and the *Gurbaṇi* amply demonstrates the very successful application of that skill. In fact, as we have already noted above, the *Purātan Janam Sākhis* also touch on this aspect of the unusual application of the *Vār* form to spiritual compositions. It is said that when Sheikh Brahm heard that Guru Nanak had composed a *Vār* to the Lord himself, he was deeply intrigued and is reported to have asked, "Let me see how you could compose a *Vār* to God who is uniquely One, while the *Vār* cannot exist without two protagonists". The *Sākhi* does not record the Sheikh's reaction after he had heard the composition, or, as the *Purātan Sākhi* says, the first nine *pauṛis* thereof. Apparently, he must have been fully satisfied with the success of this adoption of the martial poetic form to matters spiritual by the Guru. That is because the Guru while composing the *Vār* did use two protagonists; one could call these the 'good' and the 'evil' within us. The struggle to overcome the evil and to attain enlightenment is indeed the theme of this *Vār*.

The *sloks* adduced to the *pauṛis* may not always strictly conform to the thought expressed in the *pauṛi*. This is because the *sloks* have been used also as a vehicle for social comment, and these express the Guru's views on the many social evils, and the cant and hypocrisy that were the hallmark of those times. The *pauṛis* adhere more strictly to the conveying of the spiritual message, which of course is by no means absent from the *sloks* also. Thus, unlike the *Japji Sahib* where the Guru has strictly concentrated on the shaping of the inner self into a divine form, which can then merge completely with the Lord, the *Āsa di Vār* while ultimately carrying the same message contains also a large measure of social comment. It, in that context, can be said to prescribe some practical rules of conduct to govern the daily life of men as social beings existing in an imperfect world.

It incidentally also becomes, for this reason, a valuable source of information about the social conditions prevailing at that time, and highlights some serious weaknesses that had crept into the social fabric. Thus, the lesson in the *sloks*, though essentially spiritual is not restricted to the purely spiritual, as it is in the 24 *pauṛis*. The Guru has through the medium of these *sloks*, also given a social and practical everyday dimension to the lesson through comments on diverse social evils and hypocrisies.

Having made clear in the title that the *Bāṇi* entered therein is not only the *Vār* as composed by Guru Nanak but also contains some *sloks* composed by him, the fifth Nanak then prescribes the tune, called *Tunday Asrājay ki dhuni*. It is easy to infer that this must have been a popular folk tale at that time, and the tune to which it was usually sung must have been well known. Bhai Vir Singh, referring to Dr. Charan Singh who had researched this matter, says that the story went that one King Vichitra Virya got married at an advanced age to a young wife, when he already had grown sons. Prince Asrāj, one of the sons, who was a handsome youth, became the target of lascivious attentions of this new queen. He quite properly repulsed her advances; she out of a sense of frustration viciously accused him of having made improper advances to her. The infuriated king for this reason ordered the young Asrāj slain, but through the intervention of a wise vazir he was let off in the jungle after cutting off one of his hands. Fate later gave him the rulership of another nearby realm. Meanwhile, his old country happened to suffer a drought and sought help from other states. As chance would have it, it was none other than Asrāj who came to the rescue. Subsequently, he was invited back by the now chastened king who was being oppressed by his other sons. Asrāj then fought against his brothers and rescued his father. This story was set to a martial tune describing mainly the battle scenes of the war between the brothers.

It is interesting to note the striking similarities this narration has with the story of Potiphar's wife in the *Bible*, and the famous story of *Puran Bhagat* still well known in the Punjab. As the *Bible* says in Genesis 39, Joseph, son of Jacob, was sold by the Ishmaelites to Potiphar, one of the pharaoh's officers in Egypt. It so transpired that Potiphar took a liking to him and appointed him on his personal staff. The master's wife was smitten by his good looks and pestered him to go to bed with her. Joseph said that would be immoral, and kept refusing her for many days. The officer's wife driven to frustration accused him of attempting to rape her. Joseph was jailed. Being a man of God, he ultimately won the pharaoh's confidence and was in due course even made Governor of Egypt. It will be seen how similar this is to the famous tale of Puran Bhagat, who also was the subject of improper attentions from his young step-mother and had to similarly suffer unjust punishment. In his case he became intensely spiritual and was later to earn great renown as a *Bhagat*.

Like many legends the story of the maimed Asrāj has many versions. For instance, Prof. Sahib Singh and Bhai Vir Singh mention the name of the father of Asrāj as king Sārang. Master Mehtab Singh, in his *Nāwān tay thāwān da kosh*, says that the name of the father was either Sārang or Chitrbīj. Macauliffe mentions the name of the father as Chitra Bir. Some have called him Vichitra Virya.

His brothers are named Sardūl Rai and Sultān Khān. The anomaly of a king with a patently Hindu name, having sons with Muslim names such as Sultān Khān, is not explained. The sequence of events as narrated also differs in the details in the various versions.

The essence of the tale however is clear enough, and according to most of the versions, *Asrāj* regained his old kingdom after a battle, probably against his stepbrothers. This event formed the basis of a *vār* and the Guru found that martial tune suitable for the singing of this composition. Bhai Vir Singh says that the *Vār* runs as, "Bhakkio Sher Sardūl Rai raṇ main bajjay. Sultān Khān bad sūrmay vich ran day gajjay. Khat likhay tunday Asrāj nū patshāhi Ajjay. Tikka sārang bāp nay dita bhar lajjay. Fateh pāye Asrāj ji shāhi par sajjay."

In this background we can now look at the message of the *Vār* in detail.

PAUṚI 1

The first *pauṛi* has been assigned three *sloks*, two by Guru Nanak and one by the second Nanak. The first *slok* is by Guru Nanak, and it is as follows:

ਸਲੋਕ ਮਹਲਾ: ੧ ॥	Slok Mahla: 1
ਬਲਿਹਾਰੀ ਗੁਰ ਆਪਣੇ ਦਿਉਹਾੜੀ ਸਦ ਵਾਰ ॥	Balihāri gur āpṇay diuhaṛi sad vār.
ਜਿਨਿ ਮਾਣਸ ਤੇ ਦੇਵਤੇ ਕੀਏ ਕਰਤ ਨ ਲਾਗੀ ਵਾਰ ॥੧॥	Jin māṇas te devtay kīye karat na lāgi vār. 1.

Glossary:

ਦਿਉਹਾੜੀ	Diuhaṛi	Each day
ਸਦ ਵਾਰ	Sad vār	A hundred times
ਮਾਣਸ	Māṇas	From a human
ਕਰਤ	Karat	Shaping; making
ਨ ਲਾਗੀ ਵਾਰ	Na Lāgi Vār	Without delay, instantly

In this, the opening *slok*, the Guru lays down what can be called the central theme of this *bāṇi*. He salutes his master and says that not merely once but he would sacrifice himself to his Guru a hundred times a day. It is the Guru who shapes *Devtas* out of humans and for so doing he takes not a moment.

In the *Japji Sahib* the central theme of that *Bāṇi* is to be found in *Pauṛi* 1, in the line "ਕਿਵ ਸਚਿਆਰਾ ਹੋਈਐ ਕਿਵ ਕੂੜੇ ਤੁਟੈ ਪਾਲਿ" – "kiv sachiāra hoīai kiv kūṛay tuttai pāl", meaning 'how is one to realize the Godhead within oneself, remove the veil of illusion and thus become True'. In a similar way, this *slok* here could be said to epitomize this *Bāṇi*. Throughout the *Āsa di Vār* the Guru will tell us how the crass material of the worldly human form is to be transmuted into the divine form; and how for this purpose we need the right Guru. The transformation of the *Māṇas* (humankind), into the *Devta* (the divine form), or in other words from the mundane level of consciousness to the suprahuman consciousness, can be said to be the central theme of this composition.

As the *Gurbāṇi* tells us repeatedly, the passage from the spiritually base stage to enlightenment becomes possible only through the auspices of a Guru, a master. For Guru Nanak here in this *slok*, the Lord himself is that Master. He is therefore rendering homage to the Lord and in doing so he says, in the first line, that such is the glory of the Lord and such the depth of his love for Him that he would be a sacrifice to the Lord repeatedly. Using slightly different terminology the Guru had conveyed the same sentiment in the *Japji Sahib*. There, in *pauṛi* 16 to 19 he had used the refrain, "Kudrat kawan kaha vichār, vāriya na jāva[n] ek vār", meaning such is the greatness of the Lord that the Guru does not deem himself fit to even once be a sacrifice to Him. Thus we see that the Guru repeatedly says that he would very much want to sacrifice himself to the Lord but he is diffident about his worthiness to even be a sacrifice. He is saying here in the same vein, that a hundred times a day would he sacrifice himself to the Lord – his Guru.

In the second line he says the Lord can metamorphose mere humans into divine creatures and for doing so it takes Him no time at all. Implicit in the words is the thought that such transformation will occur only when the Lord so wills. This is again a thought that repeatedly occurs in the *SGGS*. The message is that it is our duty to constantly strive to be worthy of His grace and benediction, but that being worthy does not create an entitlement. The Lord reserves to Himself the sole right to bestow His glance of grace and none may demand it by right. The movement from the mundane to the divine will occur only when the Lord so wills. And when He does so will it will not be a lengthy, slow process but that "**ਕਰਤ ਨ ਲਾਗੀ ਵਾਰ**" – "karat na lāgi vār", the moment of enlightenment will be instantaneous.

This stress on the importance of the Guru can be found throughout the *Gurbāṇi*. For Guru Nanak the Lord Himself is the Guru. For the rest of us it has been ordained by the Tenth Nanak that the *Sri Guru Granth Sahib* shall be the living Guru for all times. It is in fact the Word enshrined in the *SGGS* that is coterminous with God. As the *SGGS*, on page 982, *Rāg Nat Nārāyaṇ, Mahla* 4, says, "ਬਾਣੀ ਗੁਰੂ ਗੁਰੂ ਹੈ ਬਾਣੀ ਵਿਚ ਬਾਣੀ ਅੰਮ੍ਰਿਤ ਸਾਰੇ॥" – "bāṇi guru guru hai bāṇi vich bāṇi amrit sāray", meaning that the Word is the Guru and the Guru is the Word, and within the Word is all Nectar.

This command from the tenth Nanak becomes the last word for the follower of the Sikh faith, and this means we can find salvation by sincerely following the message of the *SGGS*. Others are of course at perfect liberty to make their own choices. For the Sikh a great amount of time and effort is saved because a Sikh has the good fortune to be blessed with an ever-present Guru the moment he is born. He can seek learning within the *SGGS* and make his way out of this morass of the cycle of birth and rebirth. For many who choose other paths, time will inevitably have to be spent seeking the true Guru and only a lucky few will find one. Some may waste a whole lifetime just in the search. Those who are staunch followers of any other true master would therefore be well advised to sincerely follow the path they have chosen, but make a firm choice as early as possible, for the time allotted to us on this earth is but brief.

The Guru is for the seeker the key to the passage from here to the Divine, said the Guru in this first *slok*. The next *slok*, which is by the second Nanak, further stresses the same point in another way. It runs as follows:

ਮ: ੨ ॥	M: 2
ਜੇ ਸਉ ਚੰਦਾ ਉਗਵਹਿ ਸੂਰਜ ਚੜਹਿ ਹਜਾਰ ॥	Jay sau chanda ugveh sūraj chaṛeh hajār
ਏਤੇ ਚਾਨਣ ਹੋਦਿਆਂ ਗੁਰ ਬਿਨੁ ਘੋਰ ਅੰਧਾਰ ॥੨॥	Etay chānaṇ hodiā[n] gur bin ghor andhār. 2.

Glossary:

ਸਉ	Sau	Hundred
ਏਤੇ ਚਾਨਣ	Etay chānaṇ	With this much light
ਘੋਰ ਅੰਧਾਰ	Ghor andhār	Pitch dark

Literally translated, this means that were a hundred moons and a thousand suns to rise the light they shed would be as nothing. Without the Guru we will be in a state of spiritual darkness, notwithstanding the light all these suns and moons can shed. The importance of the Guru is being underlined further here.

The reference obviously is to the enlightenment that we are all seeking, the spiritual enlightenment that would lead the soul from out of the morass of ignorance that marks our existence on this earth. The light that these heavenly bodies shed is for the outside. The light that will reach inside us and banish the dark from within our souls is not the material light of this world. The light that is really required is that which will touch the spirit inside all humans; and that light is the light of the knowledge of the Divine. The source for this mystical light can be none but the Guru. Only he can set our feet on the path, only he can tell us how to move forward and only he can tell us which pitfalls to avoid. Only by listening to the word of the Guru, acquiring full faith in him and obeying strictly the prescription that he may lay down for our daily conduct, can we hope to reach that enlightened state. The Suns and Moons of this world are irrelevant to that inner illumination. Only the Guru will light up that dark space; for it is the Guru only who can provide the spiritual light needed for it.

Continuing on the subject of the vital importance of the Guru, the third *slok*, again by Guru Nanak, says:

ਮ: ੧ ॥	M: 1
ਨਾਨਕ ਗੁਰੂ ਨ ਚੇਤਨੀ ਮਨਿ ਆਪਣੈ ਸੁਚੇਤ ॥	Nanak Guru na chetni mann āpṇay suchet
ਛੁਟੇ ਤਿਲ ਬੂਆੜ ਜਿਉ ਸੁੰਞੇ ਅੰਦਰਿ ਖੇਤ ॥	Chhuttay til buāṛ jiu sunjhay andar khet
ਖੇਤੈ ਅੰਦਰਿ ਛੁਟਿਆ ਕਹੁ ਨਾਨਕ ਸਉ ਨਾਹ ॥	Khetai andar chhutia kahu Nanak sau nāh
ਫਲੀਅਹਿ ਫੁਲੀਅਹਿ ਬਪੁੜੇ ਭੀ ਤਨ ਵਿਚਿ ਸੁਆਹ ॥੩॥	Phaliye phuliye bappuṛay bhi tann vich suāh. 3.

Glossary:

ਨ ਚੇਤਨੀ	Na chetni	Think not of
ਬਪੁੜੇ	Bappuṛay	Wretches
ਬੂਆੜ	Buāṛ	A spurious weed growing in sesame crops

Referring to the large number of people in this world who think they are in no need of any guidance, the Guru in this *slok* says they care not for the Guru and deem themselves fully aware and knowledgeable. Such ones are like spurious sesame thrown in a barren field. Without a master they are in the field and they falsely seem to bloom while inside they are only dust and ashes. The Guru is speaking of something we would have all experienced often in our lives. He speaks of those who think they know all they need to, and see not the need for a Guru to guide them. Such a state of mind is obviously indicative of a highly exaggerated sense of self-importance, of an inflated ego. In the previous two *sloks* the importance of the Guru has been explained and stressed. Here he speaks of those unfortunate ones who deceive themselves into the belief that they are too smart and do not need any guidance. Let us now study the *slok* in detail.

The Guru says in the first line that there are some who bother not for the Guru because they are so 'full' of themselves that they think they do not need to be educated. Puffed up with the sense of their own importance they deem it unnecessary, nay beneath their dignity, to deign to pay any attention to the Guru, or even the need for a Guru.

The Guru states in the 2nd to 4th lines what he thinks of the plight of these unfortunate ones. He says they are like unfruited sesame in a lonely field. The allusion is to a common practice in rural India at that time. The populations then were sparser than today and agricultural fields were not always cultivated. Some fields would be left fallow intentionally, others would lie untilled because there was no owner, or the farmer did not have the capacity to sow anything for that season. The Guru says the condition of these unfortunate ones is like sesame seed thrown wild in an untenanted field. Not only, he says, are these cast into this inhospitable terrain but even these seeds thus cast are spurious, leaving no chance whatever for any fruitful outcome. The term ਬੁਆੜ (*Buāṛ*) refers to a form of weed that grows usually in unhusbanded sesame crops. The irony is that such seeds outwardly look healthy enough and they even seem to ripen normally and give every appearance of having borne fruit. However, when opened they yield no healthy oilseed. So the appearances are here entirely deceptive. The seemingly healthy growth has produced nothing but a black inedible mess. The same, implies the Guru, is the plight of these self-centered ones, who refuse to believe there is anything they need to learn. They may in real life appear to be fruiting but what they produce in reality is nothing. Their spiritual attainments in this situation will be zero.

The Guru says further that the field in which these seeds have been dropped is not only untilled, but it also has no master. Learned commentators have interpreted the phrase sau nāh in line 3 in two different ways. The term *sau* can mean a hundred, as in the first line where the Guru speaks of *sau* (hundred) moons. It also is used to describe 'master' except that the pronunciation would then be *sauh*. Prof. Sahib Singh says the term should properly be rendered as 'hundred', and therefore it would mean 'a hundred masters'. He quotes the example of say, a field of gram spoiled by weather, which is then ignored for that reason by the farmer. What happens thereafter is that this neglected field will attract, and will soon then be denuded by, hundreds of poor villagers seeking firewood. Thus the field, by reason of being neglected will have suddenly found a hundred masters, but yet it is in reality without any real master. He says that the situation of the human who ignores the need for a master, a Guru, is like this neglected field. He becomes susceptible to attack by hundreds of evils born of his own uncontrolled senses. Such a mind is then overwhelmed and becomes denuded by these evils. Thus the golden opportunity that this human birth had made available is tragically lost.

Bhai Vir Singh in his commentary offers three alternate explanations for the phrase *sau nāh*. The first is 'a hundred masters', which really implies 'no master at all'; the second meaning is 'no master'. A third possible meaning takes the word *sau* as *suād*, meaning enjoyment. In this rendering the phrase would then translate as 'no joy'.

Most commentators, however, have adopted the rendering as 'hundred masters', and this seems the more appealing interpretation. The sense of course remains broadly unaltered in either of these interpretations. What the Guru is telling us is that such unfortunate, self-centered ones without a Guru, are in the position of sesame seeds that do not yield the fruit and lie useless, and are at the mercy of everyone. Such will be their plight before the Lord also and the precious gift of this human birth would have been wasted. These unfortunate ones may often be giving the false impression of being in bloom but within them will be nothing but spiritual emptiness, the ashes of their spiritual potential.

In the *pauṛi* that follows, these three *sloks*, the Guru speaks to us of the process of creation and of the Lord Himself. The Guru says:

ਪਉੜੀ ॥	Pauṛi
ਆਪੀਨ੍ਹੈ ਆਪੁ ਸਾਜਿਓ ਆਪੀਨ੍ਹੈ ਰਚਿਓ ਨਾਉ ॥	Āpīnay āp sājiyo āpiney rachiyo nāo
ਦੁਯੀ ਕੁਦਰਤਿ ਸਾਜੀਐ ਕਰਿ ਆਸਣੁ ਡਿਠੋ ਚਾਉ ॥	Dui kudrat sājīai kar āsaṇ dittho chāo
ਦਾਤਾ ਕਰਤਾ ਆਪਿ ਤੂੰ ਤੁਸਿ ਦੇਵਹਿ ਕਰਹਿ ਪਸਾਉ ॥	Dāta karta āp tu[n] tus devai karhe pasāo
ਤੂੰ ਜਾਣੋਈ ਸਭਸੈ ਦੇ ਲੈਸਹਿ ਜਿੰਦੁ ਕਵਾਉ ॥	Tu[n] jāṇoyi sabhsai dey laiseh jind kavāo
ਕਰਿ ਆਸਣੁ ਡਿਠੋ ਚਾਉ ॥੧॥	Kar āsaṇ dittho chāo [1]

Glossary:

ਆਪੀਨ੍ਹੈ	Āpīnai	By himself
ਨਾਉ	Nāo	Name; here, the Divine laws, the Lord's manifest form
ਸਾਜੀਐ	Sājīai	Has created
ਤੁਸਿ	tus	From his pleasure
ਪਸਾਉ	Pasāo	Prasād, benediction
ਸਭਸੈ	sabhsai	Of all
ਲੈਸਹਿ	laiseh	Will take
ਜਿੰਦੁ ਕਵਾਉ	Jind kavāo	The soul's dress; the body

Simply translated the *pauṛi* tells us that the Lord created Himself of His own Will. He then created the *nāo*, His Name, in the form of the visible Universe, in which He resides and which is therefore the Lord manifest. With it came into existence also the set of inexorable Divine Laws, which were to be the governing principles of all creation. He then created Nature in which He resides and fondly watches what He has wrought. He is the Bestower, the Creator and gives when He is so pleased to do. He knows all and He gives and takes away life at His will. With fondness He watches from His seat. Let us now look at the *pauṛi* in more detail.

The Guru says in the first line that the Lord created Himself of His own will. He created thereafter His ਨਾਉ (*nāo*), His Name. The term here is used in the sense that the Guru has used it in *pauṛi* 19 of the *Japji Sahib*, where he says,

"Jeta kīta teta nāo, viṇ nāvai nāhin ko thhāo", meaning all that He has created is His Name, there being no place in the entire creation where His Name is not. The term thus becomes coterminous with all creation. In other words, it refers to the Lord manifest in His Immanent form. For doing so the Lord has put into place a system of Divine Laws that would govern this creation. Thus is *nāo* to be understood both as the set of Divine Laws, and also the Lord's visible form. Again we can see in the *Sukhmani Sahib, astpadi* 5/16, where the Guru says, "Nām ke dharay saglay jant, nām ke dharay khand brahmand", meaning it is the Lord's Name that sustains all beings, it is the Name that is the underpinning to the Universe and all parts thereof. In this sense the word denotes the governing principle of the universe, of the entire infinity of worlds. The Guru is here telling us that He is self-created and from Him alone has sprung the underlying principle that determines the existence of all that is material. Prof. Sahib Singh therefore translates this term as 'greatness', 'grandeur'.

Bhai Vir Singh also refers to it in this sense, and quotes from *Rāg Sūhi, Mahla* 3, "Nāmai hee tay sabh kichh hua, bin satgur nām na jāpai", meaning that the Name is the primal Cause for all that exists. He further says that the Semitic religions hold that the 'the Word' is God and co-exists with him. The Guru wants to stress here the uniqueness of the Lord and therefore says that firstly the Lord created His Own Self, and thereafter He also created the 'Word'. It is not therefore only co-existent with the Lord but is also His creation. Only the Lord is self- created. There is nothing that exists or can exist without Him.

In short the Lord exists outside of Time or Space and is in that form Transcendent. Then at His will he chooses to assume the immanent form and, for want of a better phrase, we say He creates Himself. The reality is that He just is and does not create or uncreate Himself. The reference here in this line is to His assuming this particular form, the Immanent, the visible. When He does assume this form, He also brings into existence His Name, the underlying governing principle of the material universe. This action is assumed to be simultaneous and thus the Guru has not indicated a time lag between the two when he says that the Lord created Himself as also His name. The thought *āpinay āp sājio*, here, is a paraphrasing or explanation of the term *Saibha[ng]* used in the *Mool Mantra.*

In the 2nd line the Guru now clearly spells out the sequentiality of the action of creation of the material Universe. He says having first created Himself and

His Name, He proceeded next to create Nature and having done so He pervades all that He created and thus exists in each particle thereof. This is of course a reference to the Immanence of the Creator. He is not a distant maker who then is to be deemed separate from His creation. No, rather is He an inseparable part of all that exists. This is referred here as "kar āsaṇ dittho chāo", meaning he resides within the creation, and not just resides but watches with pleasure, with fondness His creatures at play. He is *karta purakh*, the creator who lives within His creation. This thought we also see in the *Japji Sahib*, *pauṛi* 37, where the Guru says "vekhai vigsai kar vīchār", meaning the Lord sees, He ponders on it and is filled with joy. The idea is quite in consonance with the concept of a Lord who loves His creation and showers His blessings eternally on His creatures. This is a God of love, full of beneficence and mercy.

In the 3rd line the Guru refers to the Lord as the Benefactor and the Creator who from His pleasure bestows gifts as a measure of His grace. Bhai Vir Singh says that the term *Karta* (Creator) carries in it the implication of creation being effected from the same material. For example, the potter creates pottery for which he will need to procure clay. But by putting together the terms *Dāta* (donor, bestower) and *Karta*– (Creator), the Guru is telling us that the Creator here did not need any outside material. The matter from which He fashioned this creation did not exist independent of Him, but it is of His own Self that this matter comes into being. He from His own Self brings into existence the entire manifested phenomenon that we call the Universe. From the Lord's pleasure, His will, has this event occurred. The creation is His *prasād* (His gift). Thus the concept here is that because He is *tus* (pleased) to so do, He gives this *prasād*, and the manifested Universe comes into existence, made by an act of His will, from His own Self. Various learned commentators have rendered this line in a similar fashion. For instance, the Lord is "solely the Bestower and Creator, and grants boons and shows grace", to quote Prof. G.S. Talib. Macauliffe, Dr. Gopal Singh and others have adopted similar rendering.

Thus, the 3rd line can in one way be seen as a straight- forward statement conveying the sense of the Lord being merciful and the bestower of gifts on all that He has wrought from a sense of fondness for His creation. It can also be viewed as not just a simple statement but at a deeper level, as an explanation of the nature of creation. In this sense the stress is on all creation as being fashioned by Himself, from His own Self. In other words, the material from which the material universe is shaped is the Lord Himself; and He is also the one who does the shaping. No difference can thus be said to exist between creation and the Lord, its Creator.

In line 4 the Guru says the Lord is Omniscient and is the giver of life, which He also takes away when He so deems fit. The formulation of the Lord as All Knowing, as Omniscient is common to all religious belief systems; it being axiomatic that the Power above all powers necessarily has to be cognizant of all that is below Him. Since everything that exists is under the Lord, He can see all and know all, nothing can be hidden. The view of the Lord as the bestower of life, and consequently as also the one who takes it away, is also common to all religions. *Day* (gives) here refers to the Lord's function as the source from which all life emanates. *Laiseh* (will take away) refers to His power to take back the life that He has bestowed. Implicit herein is the thought that these events occur at His sole pleasure. We will assume existence in this universe when He wills, and that existence will cease only when it so pleases Him. The phrase *Jind kavāo* is rendered in two ways by learned commentators. One rendering takes the word *kavāo* as meaning "the word of God", the sense in which it has been used by the Guru in the *Japji Sahib, pauṛi* 16 where it says "Kīta pasāo eko kavāo", meaning He created everything with one word. This comes from the Punjabi root where *kavāo* means 'speaking'. In this way the phrase would mean that with one word He will take away the life which He gave.

In the other sense, the word *kavāo* is rendered as 'dress', from *kuwa* (*kuba*) meaning attire. *Jind* means life or soul, and the phrase *Jind Kavāo* would then translate as "the soul's dress", which of course means this human form, this body. In this rendering the translation becomes "He will take away this soul's dress". The sense of the Guru's message does not materially get altered in either rendering. Viewed either way what the Guru is saying is that life is a gift from the Lord, and that the moment of death is also determined by the Lord and it will come instantaneously when the Lord so wills.

The final, the 5th, line is a repetition of the main point made in the 2nd line. It is typical of the *Vār* form and we will see in almost all the *pauṛis* the last line either repeating the main point already given in one of the previous lines; or in a pithy, short line summing up the central idea of the *pauṛi*. In this *pauṛi* the idea reiterated in the concluding line is that the Lord resides, or to put it literally "has His seat", in His creation. He watches in fondness and is pleased with what He has wrought. The concept brings to mind the image of a parent watching over his children. There is concern; there is love and perhaps a little bit of amusement in that glance at the children's antics. The Lord has created, the Guru is saying, and He loves what has come into existence. Things material, things living or non-living are all equally the object of His fond glance.

The Guru tells us that it is only to humankind however that the freedom to choose between evil and good has been granted. Therein lies the secret of why we are here, and therein lies also the clue to how this soul separated from the Lord because of its own actions, is to achieve reunion with the Divine. This reunion, says the Guru repeatedly in the *SGGS*, will come from choosing the right path. The purpose of our existence will be fulfilled when we have learnt to choose good over evil. The disciplining of the inner self for fighting this battle is a struggle that we all have to undergo in our own ways. How to proceed, and how optimally to utilize our limited time on this earth, will be learnt by listening to and following the path that the Guru prescribes for us.

We have seen in the three *sloks* that preceded this *pauṛi* how much stress the Guru has laid on the importance of finding the right Guru and then observing the discipline he may prescribe for us. Ignoring the Guru will leave us in a plight similar to those seeds of sesame which are grown in a field untilled and with no real owner, and which have not the capacity to yield anything useful. The Guru warns us that the fruit of following an ego-centered path will, like those sesame seeds, be nothing but ashes. If we follow the Guru we will learn the way to reach that One Lord from whom we are separated by the veil of falseness cast over us by our *haumai*, our pride and our false sense of being separate from the Lord. When we learn the correct lesson, and start to correctly obey and follow the Guru's path, we will become *Gurmukh* (Guru-centered). At that stage the love and beneficence, the grace of the Lord, which is forever available to all souls will start reaching us. This will happen because the vessel, our own inner selves, will have now become worthy of receiving His grace. Here it may be repeated that for the Sikh the Guru is none but *Sri Guru Granth Sahib*. For others of course the prescription may be found in their own belief systems, but the *SGGS* will for anybody provide the correct path. It is vital, however, that whatever path has been chosen should then be sincerely followed, with love and kindness in the heart and with the mind fixed strictly on the one Lord.

PAUṚI 2

In this, the second *pauṛi* also, the fifth Nanak has added three *sloks*. Two of these are by the *Mahla* 1, Guru Nanak and one is by the second Nanak. The first *slok* says:

ਸਲੋਕ ਮ: ੧ ॥	Slok M: 1
ਸਚੇ ਤੇਰੇ ਖੰਡ ਸਚੇ ਬ੍ਰਹਮੰਡ ॥	Sachay teray khand sachay brahmand
ਸਚੇ ਤੇਰੇ ਲੋਅ ਸਚੇ ਆਕਾਰ ॥	Sachay teray loew sachay ākār
ਸਚੇ ਤੇਰੇ ਕਰਣੇ ਸਰਬ ਬੀਚਾਰ ॥	Sachay teray karṇay sarab bīchār
ਸਚਾ ਤੇਰਾ ਅਮਰੁ ਸਚਾ ਦੀਬਾਣੁ ॥	Sacha tera amar sacha dībāṇ
ਸਚਾ ਤੇਰਾ ਹੁਕਮੁ ਸਚਾ ਫੁਰਮਾਣੁ ॥	Sacha tera hukam sacha phurmāṇ
ਸਚਾ ਤੇਰਾ ਕਰਮੁ ਸਚਾ ਨੀਸਾਣੁ ॥	Sacha tera karam sacha nīsāṇ
ਸਚੇ ਤੁਧੁ ਆਖਹਿ ਲਖ ਕਰੋੜਿ ॥	Sachay tudh ākheh lakh karoṛ
ਸਚੈ ਸਭਿ ਤਾਣਿ ਸਚੈ ਸਭਿ ਜੋਰਿ ॥	Sachai sabh tāṇ sachai sabh jor
ਸਚੀ ਤੇਰੀ ਸਿਫਤਿ ਸਚੀ ਸਾਲਾਹ ॥	Sachi teri sipht sachi sālāh
ਸਚੀ ਤੇਰੀ ਕੁਦਰਤਿ ਸਚੇ ਪਾਤਿਸਾਹ ॥	Sachī teri kudrat sachay pātsāh
ਨਾਨਕ ਸਚੁ ਧਿਆਇਨਿ ਸਚੁ ॥	Nanak sach dhiyāyan sach
ਜੋ ਮਰਿ ਜੰਮੇ ਸੁ ਕਚੁ ਨਿਕਚੁ ॥੧॥	Jo marr jammay su kach nikach. 1.

Glossary:

ਸਚੇ	Sachay	True, real (because eternal)
ਬ੍ਰਹਮੰਡ	Brahmand	Universe
ਲੋਅ	Loew	Worlds

Pauṛi 2

ਆਕਾਰ	Ākār	Shapes, forms
ਅਮਰੁ	Amar	Rule, reign
ਦੀਬਾਣੁ	Dībāṇ	Courts
ਕਰਮੁ	Karam	Blessing, Grace, Benediction
ਸਚੈ	Sachai	of the sachey (the Lord)
ਕੁਦਰਤਿ	Kudrat	Creation
ਕਚੁ ਨਿਕਚੁ	Kach Nikach	Totally unripe

In this *slok Guru Nanak* tells us that the Lord is the sole Truth. All that exists is a manifestation of the One Lord and by that reason it is true and real. Those who fix their mind on that Lord also become true. Simply translated this *slok* says that true are the Universes and regions created by the Lord. These are true for the reason that the Lord resides within His creation and they are all part of His grand scheme of things. This is meant here to remove doubts existing in some belief systems that the universe is mere illusion. The Guru continues in the same vein here and says that true are the created worlds, and true are the forms. True are His doings and true the contemplation. True is His edict, His rule and true His courts. True is His Benediction and true the mark thereof. Uncounted numbers call Him True. True are the might, the power, the force and strength of the Lord. True is His laudation and His praise. O True Lord, says the Guru, true indeed is your Nature, and those who fix their minds on the Lord are rendered true. Those who do not are doomed to the circle of rebirths and are the unbaked, the unripe ones. The Guru is telling us that all that happens is part of the Lord's inexorable ordinance. All the material parts of creation are underpinned by His force, His might. In other words, it is the fact that all these exist strictly as per the Lord's ordained system that makes all of these things true and real. We can now look at the *slok* in more detail.

In the 1st and 2nd lines of this *slok* the Guru says, "True are Your regions, Your universes. True are the worlds and the forms that exist thereon." The implicit thought here is that the entire creation is the One Lord's doing, and He permeates every atom of it. Since the Lord is the only Reality, therefore whatever He has wrought, this entire creation is also true and real. Having made this basic statement the Guru then describes the various components of this infinite creation. He says the universes, the galaxies, the regions, and the worlds that He has created, being inseparable from His own eternal Self, are therefore all real and true.

In lines 3, 4 and 5 the Guru refers now to the principles that govern this creation. The created universes, being true and real, are also regulated in the real world by the rules, the laws of governance, the edicts laid down by the same Eternal One. Therefore, says the Guru, real and true is His reign and true the courts where He judges the doings of His created beings. The Guru adds further in line 5 that true are His commandments and true His edicts. In line 3 he has said true are all His doings and true His purposes. Since the Lord himself is the underlying Cause of all creation, and all that exists is nothing but the Lord Himself, therefore the Guru sees the entire created matter as the Lord's visible form, the Lord manifest. In this sense are these components of the created universe spoken of as being true. The divine laws, the principles put in place for regulating the operation of this vast and mysterious structure also therefore bear the same stamp. All this exists in accordance with the Lord's command. The Guru seeing the Lord as the ruler of this infinite realm says the orders, the commands, the Divine Court that regulates this realm are true and real. This re-stressing of the real nature of the creation and its governing laws is to be seen in the context of some belief systems that held the World to be but an illusion. The Guru's belief is that it is not an illusion, but is a reality; and it exists as the arena, the field of action where human souls can strive to win back their place by the Lord's side.

In lines 6 and 7 the Guru says, "True is His beneficence, true the mark thereof. Countless are the ones who speak of Him as the ultimate Reality." The Guru uses the term *karam* here in the Persian sense of "blessing, grace". The term *nīsāṇ* refers to that mystical mark of His grace which those fortunate enough to have earned it are said to be carrying on their foreheads. The concept has been referred elsewhere also in the *SGGS*. Some believe that there is in fact a real mark of such approval visible to the mystic eye. It could also be said to metaphorically indicate that those who have been blessed enough to order their lives and to discipline themselves sufficiently, in accordance with the path laid down by the Guru will have earned the Lord's approval and on their souls the Lord's mark of approval will, so to say, have been stamped. This will in everyday life manifest itself through goodness of conduct and the very soothing nature of the proximity of those thus blessed. The Guru further says, in line 7, that there are countless those who praise Him as the one True Reality. The number used is *Lakh karoṛ* meaning literally a thousand billion. But it is not intended here to put a definite number on those who recognize Him as the sole Reality, but to convey that those who do so are uncountable. After all in an infinite multi-verse those blessed enough to sing of the Lord must also be beyond count. All those innumerable ones who fix their minds on the Lord are, says the Guru, all saying that He is the only Truth.

In line 8 the Guru says all power, all the force existing in the universe emanates from, and therefore belongs to the Lord. The term used is *Sachai*, meaning "of, or belonging to, *sachay*". The term *sachay* (the True One) is used to describe the Lord. Dr. Gopal Singh renders this line as, "For in Thee, the True one is all Power and all Majesty." Most learned ones have adopted this view with minor changes in terminology. The sense here is that all that exists, all creatures that are, and also all their actions are underpinned by the one Reality. As Prof. Teja Singh says, "all energies and forces are from that Reality".

In lines 9 and 10 the Guru says true are His praises, His eulogies. True is His Nature, He is the True King. The underlying theme of course continues to be that the Lord is the only Truth, the only Reality. All that exists is because of Him. If that is so, then whatever is said in praise or eulogy of Him is also true. There can thus be no flattery, no over-praise of the Lord. As Guru Nanak says on page 795 of the *SGGS*, in *Rāg Bilāwal,* "Tu sultān kaha[n] hau miya[n]", meaning "you are emperor and I call you merely a chieftain"; thus implying that such is His great stature that no words are sufficient to really describe Him. This is because we just do not have the vocabulary sufficiently lofty to fully laudate Him. On the other hand, to whatever extent we may attempt His praises; the description of His greatness will not be untrue. Taken another way Prof. Sahib Singh has sought to explain it by saying that the praises and eulogies to the Lord are as eternal as creation itself, and these in that context are everlasting and hence true. This is an interpretation trying to take a consistent approach to the term *sacha* (True) in the sense of that which will always be as against that which is ephemeral. The term *kudrat* in line 10 is interpreted as 'creation' by Prof. Sahib Singh and as 'Nature' by Dada Chellaram, as 'Might' by Macauliffe and as 'Creative Might' by Prof. Talib. Dr. Gopal Singh calls it 'Play'. The more appealing rendering of the term here is 'creation'. We saw in the previous *pauṛi* that *kudrat* is referred to as something separate from the Lord, as something created by Him. This was in stark contrast to the view taken by some of the belief systems which treat creation as having, independently of the Lord, originated from *Shakti, Maya* or *Prākriti*. Some learned ones in some belief systems have, says Bhai Vir Singh (page 403,

Panj Granthi, note), propounded the concept that the creation was wrought by the Creator but it is thereafter independent of Him. In Sikhism however, as Bhai Sahib also clarifies; the Oneness of the Creator and His creation is a basic tenet. To clarify this aspect the Guru has used this term here to express that the creation also is 'True', because He brought it into existence and He resides in it.

In the last two lines, the 11th and 12th, the Guru says those who meditate on this Truth themselves become, or merge into, the Truth. The others are subject to birth and death and are the unbaked, the unripe. This detailed listing in this *slok* seems to be intended to convey that their existence is real and tangible only because the Real Truth, the Lord Himself permeates them. Thus is *kudrat*, even though separate and subordinate to the Lord, yet a Reality. Distinct but owing its existence only to Him, and therefore 'True'. So in these concluding lines the Guru says that meditating on Him can raise you to the level where you become one with Him. All others are subject to the tyranny of transmigration and are therefore not 'True'; rather are they the most unripe of all. The concept of ripeness here is in the context of the state of spiritual attainment. Single- minded meditation and full faith in Him raises this level to such loftiness that the devotee eventually becomes one with Him. Those unwilling or unable to thus fix their minds will remain unripe, meaning not yet ready to be acceptable to the Lord. The term *kach nikach* is used to describe a state of total unripeness, in other words total unworthiness.

Prof. Sahib Singh has rendered this *slok* on the lines that the universes and regions, the worlds (reckoned as fourteen in some belief systems), the forms of beings, the Lord's court, His grace, His beneficences and their mark are all part of His grand scheme of things. The myriads that are meditating on Him are all doing so because it is part of the Lord's inexorable ordinance. All the material creation visible to us is underpinned by but one force, the might of the One Lord. In other words it is the fact that all these exist strictly as per the Lord's ordained system that makes all of these things true and real. *Sach* is the form of Sanskrit *satya* meaning real. So the Guru is here saying that the things enumerated in the *slok* are not illusion, as the followers of some systems of philosophy hold. Rather are they real, by virtue of being His creation, with His Immanent form giving it all its right to be called 'true', with His presence permeating every atom that exists. This rendering though adopting a slightly different approach does not materially alter the overall sense.

These last two lines have also been rendered by some learned commentators in a more direct sense as saying, “those who meditate on the Lord are true, and those who are still subject to the cycle of births and death are the falsest of the false”. There are minor differences in language even among these translations. The explanation of this concept given by Bhai Vir Singh and Prof. Sahib Singh however is more appealing, that those fully meditating on Him will gradually rise to the level where they are like Him, while those who do not are doomed to the cycle of death and rebirth and are thus the unripest of the unripe. Bhai Vir Singh says that the *slok* is meant to further elucidate the concept of ‘One’ as given in the *pauṛi* and says that the *slok* is meant to tell us that *kudrat* (Nature) though separate from the Lord, is yet not independent of Him. Rather is *kudrat* sustained by the fact that He permeates it.

In the next *slok*, the 2nd in this *pauṛi*, Guru Nanak speaks to us further on the question of the Lord and of His creation. The Guru says:

ਮ: ੧ ॥	M: 1
ਵਡੀ ਵਡਿਆਈ ਜਾ ਵਡਾ ਨਾਉ ॥	vaddi vaddiāyi ja vadda nāo
ਵਡੀ ਵਡਿਆਈ ਜਾ ਸਚੁ ਨਿਆਉ ॥	vaddi vaddiāyi ja sach niāo
ਵਡੀ ਵਡਿਆਈ ਜਾ ਨਿਹਚਲ ਥਾਉ ॥	vaddi vaddiāyi ja nihchal thhāo
ਵਡੀ ਵਡਿਆਈ ਜਾਣੈ ਆਲਾਉ ॥	vaddi vaddiāyi jāṇai ālāo
ਵਡੀ ਵਡਿਆਈ ਬੁਝੈ ਸਭਿ ਭਾਉ ॥	vaddi vaddiāyi bujhai sabh bhāo
ਵਡੀ ਵਡਿਆਈ ਜਾ ਪੁਛਿ ਨ ਦਾਤਿ ॥	vaddi vaddiāyi ja puchh na dāt
ਵਡੀ ਵਡਿਆਈ ਜਾ ਆਪੇ ਆਪਿ ॥	vaddi vaddiāyi ja āpay āp
ਨਾਨਕ ਕਾਰ ਨ ਕਥਨੀ ਜਾਇ ॥	Nanak kār na kathni jāye
ਕੀਤਾ ਕਰਣਾ ਸਰਬ ਰਜਾਇ ॥੨॥	kīta karṇa sarab rajāye. 2.

Glossary:

ਵਡੀ	vaddi	High, lofty
ਜਾ	Ja	Whose
ਨਾਉ	Nāo	His Name, the governing principle of the Universe
ਨਿਆਉ	Niāo	Justice
ਨਿਹਚਲ	Nihchal	Permanent, unmovable

ਆਲਾਉ	Ālāo	Speaking, here prayers
ਭਾਉ	Bhāo	Innermost feelings
ਪੁਛਿ	Puchh	Asking (any one), taking permission
ਕਾਰ	Kār	Doings
ਕੀਤਾ ਕਰਣਾ	Kīta Karṇa	His creation
ਰਜਾਇ	rajāye	As per Lord's Will

The Guru tells us here how immeasurably mighty and beyond human ken is the Lord. Simply translated this *slok* says great is His glory because His Name is great. Great is His glory because His justice is true. Great is His glory because His abode is unshakable, everlasting. Great is His glory because He knows the prayers of all. Great is His glory because He knows the inner thoughts and feelings of all. His glory is great also because He need ask none when bestowing His beneficence. Great is His glory because He is the sole Reality. His doings are beyond our power to describe and all that He does is by His own will. We will now look at the *slok* in more detail.

In the first two lines of this *slok* the Guru says, "Great is His glory whose Name is great. Great is His glory whose justice is true." According to Bhai Vir Singh, the term *nāo* is used here in the sense of "the Lord's Name" as used by the Guru in "Nām tul kichh avar na hoye", meaning nothing exists except His Name. In a similar vein the Guru has said in the *Sukhmani Sahib* in *astapadi* 16, "**ਨਾਮ ਕੇ ਧਾਰੇ ਸਗਲੇ ਜੰਤ॥ ਨਾਮ ਕੇ ਧਾਰੇ ਖੰਡ ਬ੍ਰਹਮੰਡ॥**" – "Nām kay dhāray saglay jant. Nām ke dhāray khand brahmand", which translates as, "By His Name are sustained all creatures. By His Name are the universes and regions supported." In this sense 'Name' is intended here to describe the governing principles of the Universe that the Lord has set in place after the act of creation so that all things move in an orderly, pre-ordained manner. Bhai Vir Singh in his commentary has also said that in the first line of this *slok* the Lord's Name is called great because it is only through the remembrance of His Name that humans can hope to reach the Divine. Prof. Sahib Singh in his commentary renders this line as "It is beyond human capacity to praise the Lord because His Name is so great." Giani Sant Singh Maskin, in rendering these two lines says in his audio-commentary, that the first line is intended to convey that so great is the Lord's glory that no words can be uttered which could over-state it. That is the extent of how great, and beyond human understanding, is His Name. He renders the 2nd line as, "Great is His glory because His justice is perfect."

Other learned commentators have adopted a simpler and more straightforward rendering of these lines as, "Great is the Lord's glory (or exaltation) because His name is great." The rendering by Bhai Vir Singh as also by Prof. Sahib Singh, are both quite illuminating in their own way. While the simpler meaning as above assigned by many other learned ones also seems here quite appropriate, but the more appealing interpretation is that the Guru is referring to the fact that the Lord is great because His Name is great, for the reason that it sustains all that exists.

The concept contained in the second line of the *slok* where the Guru lauds the Lord's justice, is also to be found in *Rāg Bihāgṛa*, *Mahla* 5, page 541 of the *SGGS*, where it says, "Har ka ek achambhau dekhya meray lāl jīo jo karay su dharam niāye rām", meaning "it is wonderful to see that whatever the Lord ordains is just and right." The justice that humans can render can only be expected to be flawed, because of the very fact that those dispensing it are themselves subject to all the flaws and weaknesses that humanity is heir to. The Lord is Immaculate, free of any taint and perfect in all possible aspects. The justice He renders is therefore nothing but perfect justice.

In lines 3 and 4 the Guru says great is the Lord's glory because His abode is unshakeable, immovable, ever lasting. His glory is great also because he knows the *ālāo* (prayers) of all. In other words, he is ever aware of whatever we say. All other places, abodes and seemingly impregnable citadels that exist in this world, all things in fact, are mutable. The elements are in a constant state of flux, ringing in change in every thing and in every material condition. The human abodes, the realms of great kings, the tiny hovels of the poorest, are all here today and gone tomorrow. It is only the abode of the Lord that stays ever the same. This is the abode the Guru spoke of in the first *pauṛi*, when he said, "duyi kudrat sajīai, kar āsaṇ dittha chāo." This, as we saw, means that after He chose to assume form as the Immanent Lord, the *sargun* Creator, His Name came into existence with Him, and thereafter He created *kudrat* (this creation). Having completed this task

He then took residence within it and He ever watches with fond love what he has wrought. This concept of the Lord loving His creation is also to be seen in the *Bible* which says in Genesis 1:31: "And God saw everything He had made, and, behold, it was very good." The Lord's *āsaṇ* (abode) according to the Guru is in His very creation. This abode is for that reason indestructible until the day He chooses to take all creation back into His own formless, *nirgun*, Self. Therefore is His abode called *nihchal*– (unshakeable and eternal). Further, says the Guru, He also knows the content of every prayer addressed to Him, and the intent of every word which humans address to Him. Their prayers He hears and He knows what they want in all their myriads. Of course He also knows which prayers deserve fulfillment and in what fashion. In this manner is His dialogue with the countless number of beings in this universe going on. The Guru says, great is His glory because of it.

In lines 5 to 6 the Guru says the Lord knows the *bhāo*, the inner thoughts, of all creatures and therefore is His glory great. And it is great also because He is not required to seek anyone's consent before giving His benedictions. In the 5th line the term *bhāo* has been rendered both by Bhai Vir Singh and Prof. Sahib Singh in this manner, taking it to mean 'thoughts, feelings'. Principal Teja Singh renders it somewhat similarly as, "understands all that we feel within our hearts". Dr. Gopal Singh also puts it as "… thou Divinest our inmost thoughts". The term *bhāo* in line 5 is however also capable of being rendered as love and affection. Some learned commentators have rendered it in that sense also. Thus Macauliffe renders this line as, "who knoweth all our feelings". Dr. Sant Singh Khalsa has used the same phrase, as also has Bhai Manmohan Singh. Prof. Talib puts is as, "Great is the Lord's exaltation, who creation's love for Himself knows." The more appealing rendering seems to be the one adopted by Bhai Vir Singh, and other learned ones, and the rendering would be, "He knows our inmost thoughts or feelings." The Guru here is stressing the aspect of the Lord's omniscience, and this rendering is much closer to that concept. The reference here has to be construed as being to the Lord knowing the unexpressed inner thoughts and feelings of His creatures. Giani Maskin in his commentary says that Bhai Gurdas has rightly said that he is shaken when he recognizes that the Lord knows even our unspoken thoughts because human thoughts are often less than lofty and tend more to evil. Bhai Gurdas says in his *kabit* number 503, "**ਭਗਤ ਵਛਲ ਸੁਨ ਹੋਤ ਹੋਂ ਨਿਰਾਸ ਰਿਦੈ, ਪਤਿਤ ਪਾਵਨੁ ਸੁਨਿ ਆਸਾ ਉਰਧਾਰ ਹੋਂ॥ ਅੰਤਰਜਾਮੀ ਸੁਨ ਕੰਪਤ ਹੋ ਅੰਤਰਗਤਿ, ਦੀਨ ਕੌ ਦਆਲ ਸੁਨ ਭੈ ਭ੍ਰਮ ਟਾਰ ਹੋਂ॥**" – "Bhagat vacchal sunn hote ho[n] nirās ridai, patit pāvan sunn āsa urdhār ho[n]. Antarjāmi sunn kampat ho[n] antargat, dīn ko dayāl sunn bhai bhram tār ho[n]." Bhai Gurdas is saying that when he hears that the Lord loves His true devotees he is disheartened [because he feels his devotion is not sufficiently true] but his hopes are renewed when he hears that the Lord uplifts the fallen. Knowing that the Lord knows the inner thoughts shakes him [because he is aware his thoughts are far from pure] but he is reassured when he hears that the Lord is compassionate and kind to the lowly and the humble. The knowledge that the Lord can read our innermost thoughts should indeed, for all of us act as a powerful deterrent to letting any wrong thoughts enter our minds. Human weaknesses however are overpowering. Bhai Gurdas adds in this context that he knows he is going to keep on succumbing but takes solace in the fact that the Lord is also ever forgiving.

In line 6 the Guru says great is the Lord's glory also because He gives to us unstintingly, as and when He wishes. This line has been rendered in two ways, one view being that "the Lord bestows His gifts without our having to ask". The other view is that it refers to the Lord not having to seek any permission before He gives His gifts. Thus, Prof. Talib puts it as, "Great is the Lord's exaltation who, of his own will, confers boons." In the same vein Bhai Manmohan Singh and Dr. Sant Singh Khalsa put it as, "He gives without being asked." Dr. Gopal Singh also renders it as, "… Thou givest unasked." However, Bhai Vir Singh renders it slightly differently. He says that, "When the Lord gives us His gifts there is none whom He need consult." Prof. Sahib Singh has also rendered it on similar lines. Dada Chellaram also says, "… Thou showerest gifts, consulting none" and Macauliffe says, "… Who giveth without consulting others". The latter view seems here the more appropriate rendering for the reason that it stresses the Lord's uniqueness as the One, without a peer, who need ask none when He wishes to do something for His creation. As the fifth Nanak says in *Rāg Gond*, page 863 of the *SGGS*, "**ਬੀਓ ਪੂਛਿ ਨ ਮਸਲਤਿ ਧਰੈ॥ ਜੋ ਕਿਛ ਕਰੈ ਸੋ ਆਪੇ ਕਰੈ॥**" – "bīo pūchh na maslat dharai. Jo kicch karai so āpay karai", meaning that He need ask none before acting and does whatever He Himself wills. The first rendering stresses more on the Lord as the eternal giver, in the sense of "Denda day Lainday thhakk pāhay", as was said by the Guru in *Japji Sahib*, *pauṛi* 3. Here, in this *slok*, the stress is more on the various aspects of His greatness, His glory. The rendering by Bhai Vir Singh and others, as we have discussed above, stresses the aspect of the Lord being Unique, and in this context seems more appealing. His being peerless and above every other entity is much better brought out in this rendering.

In line 7 the Guru says great is His glory because He is unique, or in other words is the sole basis of all that exists. He is 'all in all' as Dr. Gopal Singh, Prof. Teja Singh and many others have put it. Dada Chellaram also says, "Thou art all by thyself" and Prof. Talib puts it "Who is the sole existence." Prof. Sahib Singh renders it as "There is none like Him" and Bhai Vir Singh also uses the same phrase. This would seem the more appealing view because the 7th line, the last of this *slok* could be said in a way to be summing up the previous lines, which enumerated some of the various reasons why we humans deem Him to be great. The interpretation put forth by Bhai Vir Singh and Prof. Sahib Singh seems to put the concept exactly and succinctly when they say, "His greatness is because there is none like Him."

In the last two lines, nos. 8 and 9, the Guru says the Lord's doings are beyond description and beyond human capacity to express. All that He does is as per His own will. The Guru is again emphasizing the unique peerlessness of the Lord here. His creation, the device through which He brought these infinite universes into existence and the method He uses to sustain it, are all matters much beyond human capacity to comprehend. This, the Guru has told us elsewhere also in the *SGGS*. For instance, in *slok* later in the *Āsa Di Vār*, on page 469 he says, "Jo kuchh karna so kar rahiya," meaning whatever He wishes to do He does. Also in the *Japji Sahib*, *Pauṛi* 16, on page 2 of the *SGGS*, we have "kartay kay karṇai nāhi sumār", meaning there is no estimation possible of the extent of His actions.

This last line, the 9th, endorses and strengthens the above concept by saying, "whatever He has wrought and whatever He has in store for the future is by His own will alone". There is no other agency, no other entity He needs to take into confidence or whose help He may need to seek. There is no other planner telling Him, advising Him or assisting Him in the execution of His grand design. His will alone is the instrument by which all that has happened and all that will happen in the future is determined. The fourth Nanak tells us in *Rāg Bhairon, Mahla* 4, page 1135 of the *SGGS*, "Har jo kichh karay su āpay āpay, ohh pūchh na kisai karay bīchār", meaning that whatever the Lord does is by His own will and he does not consult anyone before deciding what He wants to do. Therefore, His *kīta* (the past creation) and His *karṇa* (the future actions) are governed solely by His own will.

We now come to the third *slok* attached with this *pauṛi*. The Guru says:

ਮਹਲਾ ੨ ॥	Mahla 2
ਇਹੁ ਜਗੁ ਸਚੈ ਕੀ ਹੈ ਕੋਠੜੀ ਸਚੇ ਕਾ ਵਿਚਿ ਵਾਸੁ ॥	Eh jagg sachai kī hai kotthṛi sachay ka vich vās
ਇਕਨ੍ਹਾ ਹੁਕਮਿ ਸਮਾਇ ਲਏ ਇਕਨ੍ਹਾ ਹੁਕਮੇ ਕਰੇ ਵਿਣਾਸੁ ॥	Ikna hukam samāye laye ikna hukamay karay viṇās
ਇਕਨ੍ਹਾ ਭਾਣੈ ਕਢਿ ਲਏ ਇਕਨ੍ਹਾ ਮਾਇਆ ਵਿਚਿ ਨਿਵਾਸੁ ॥	Ikna bhāṇai kadh laye ikna maya vich niwas
ਏਵ ਭਿ ਆਖਿ ਨ ਜਾਪਈ ਜਿ ਕਿਸੈ ਆਣੇ ਰਾਸਿ ॥	Ev bhe ākh na jāpyi je Kisai āṇay rās
ਨਾਨਕ ਗੁਰਮੁਖਿ ਜਾਣੀਐ ਜਾ ਕਉ ਆਪਿ ਕਰੇ ਪਰਗਾਸੁ ॥੩॥	Nanak Gurmukh jāṇiai ja kau āp karay pargās. 3.

Glossary:

ਸਚੈ ਕੀ	Sachai ki	Of the true Lord
ਕੋਠੜੀ	Kotthṛi	Dwelling place, room
ਵਿਣਾਸੁ	Viṇās	Destruction
ਨਿਵਾਸੁ	Nivās	Residence
ਆਣੇ ਰਾਸਿ	Āṇay rās	Puts on the right path
ਜਾਣੀਐ	Jāṇiai	To understand

This *slok*, by the second Nanak, speaks about the power of the Lord and how we must know that only He can grant to humans the release from this cycle of transmigrations. Simply translated, this *slok* says this World is the abode of the True Lord and He resides therein. To some He grants the boon of reaching Him while others face destruction. Some are rescued from the coils of *Maya* (worldly attachments) by His grace while others remain entangled. None may question as to who will be put on the right path and why. The 'Gurmukh' is one on whom His divine grace is bestowed. We will now look at it in more detail.

The Guru, in the first line speaks to us of this world, this earth we dwell on. He says it is the abode of the True One, who Himself dwells therein as the Immanent Lord. Most prevailing belief systems at that time generally held to the concept of a Lord separate from, and above and beyond, His creation. It is in this context that the Guru iterates here the oneness of the Lord with this creation. The Lord is not outside of, or distant from, His creation. He resides therein, permeating every atom and it is because of this that the stamp of being real can be put on creation. The *kudrat* (creation) is real only because the Lord resides in it, permeates it. The *slok* now proceeds to elaborate this relationship between the Creator – the *sachā* – and His creation, called here the kotthṛi. Literally this term is used to describe a small room. The Guru intends perhaps in this way to put in perspective the relationship between the Creator and us. We are the dwellers of this small room and that is the extent of our importance. Yet are this small room and its occupants not insignificant, because all of it is real and is sanctified by the reason that the L1ord Himself also resides within it.

In the second line the Guru further elaborates on this relationship. He says the Lord's Will is at work unhindered. He, by His own grace and at His will grants to some the boon of becoming part of Him. There are others who fail to reach that fortunate state and are destroyed, again as per His will. This is not to say that the Lord is capricious or whimsical in granting such favors. Rather it is meant to tell us that only He knows the criteria by which such judgement is rendered upon His beings. It is beyond the capacity of humans to determine these, or even learn as to how these operate. These events are determined purely by His will and the reasons are known to, or even knowable by, none other than Him. Then, the question will arise what is a human to do. The implied lesson here is that total acceptance of the Lord's Will without demur, without question is the wise man's choice. His *hukam* is paramount and all events occur in accordance with it. Man's choice is limited to either accepting it of his own choice, or to cavil. In either case the event that is destined to happen will occur; His edicts will prevail. Thus is it wiser to accept whatever He chooses to give us. From such acceptance will follow righteous living and purification of the soul. In this way will occur the cleansing of the vessel so that it becomes fit to receive the Lord's eternally showered Grace.

In lines 3 and 4, the Guru further elaborates the same thought. Some, says the Guru, are rescued from the coils of *Maya*, while some others continue to live entangled in this world of illusion. In other words, according to His own will, at His own choice, the reasons for which none may know and none may question, He will grant enlightenment, and salvation from this cycle of death and rebirth. The escape from the coils of *Maya* will mean that the illusion of separateness from the Lord has been destroyed. What follows inevitably is a glimpse of the Reality – God realization, salvation. How He will make the selection, only he knows which ones are to be the recipients of His grace. This veil of illusion will continue to fool the rest of us, blinding us from seeing Him who permeates this entire creation and thus lives within our very selves. The Guru says in line 4 that it cannot be said, or be known to us, as to on whom He will confer this blessing; whom He will put on the right path. The 4th line has been rendered with little difference in approach by learned commentators. Thus, Dr. Gopal Singh says, "And, who of us can say whom in his mercy he will bless." Macauliffe renders it as, "It cannot be even told whom he will regenerate." Prof. Talib puts it as, '[It is] Impossible to say whose endeavour He shall approve." Prof. Teja Singh renders it as, "One cannot even tell whom he may reform." Dada Chellaram says, "… On whom he might confer fulfillment". As can be seen the sense is the same with minor changes in terminology. What the Guru is telling us is that many are the humans constantly making the effort to reach Him, to break through the veil of illusion. The fruit of such effort is however entirely in the Lord's hands. He alone will determine who deserves His grace. The rest of us will have to keep up the endeavour till we have been able to remove the taint of *haumai* from within us and have become worthy of receiving His grace.

In the 5th and concluding line the Guru sums it up. He says the Gurmukh is the one on whom He Himself bestows the Divine Grace, the illumination of true knowledge. This line has been rendered in two different ways by learned commentators. Prof. Sahib Singh says "the lucky person on whom the Lord bestows the light will be able to understand Him through the medium of the Guru". Bhai Vir Singh, on the other hand, says, "The person on whom He bestows inner light will be known as the Gurmukh." This difference in perception is because Prof. Sahib Singh renders Gurmukh as 'from the Guru', and so he says the knowledge will come through the Guru. Bhai Vir Singh on the other hand sees Gurmukh as a state of enlightenment, in the sense of one who is 'facing the Guru'. Prof. Talib takes the latter line and says, "Such alone are the God-directed as by Himself are enlightened." So does Prof. Teja Singh who says, "He alone is Gurmukh (divinely charged) whom God reveals Himself." Macauliffe also renders it the same way and says, "He to whom God revealeth Himself, is known as holy." Dr. Gopal Singh follows Prof. Sahib Singh and says, "Turns Guruward but he whose mind He Himself illumines". The *Shabdarth* takes it another way and says, "We cannot say whom he will reform; we can only recognize the Guru whom the Lord has illumined." It quotes from *Sri Rāg, Mahla* 1, *SGGS*, page 72, "Nanak gurmukh pargat hoiya, ja kau jot dhari kartār jiyo". Bhai Vir Singh's rendering is the one most commentators have adopted, and seems here more appropriate. It is also consistent with the previous lines where the Guru was telling us that all events are governed by the Lord's Will alone.

We now come to the second *pauṛi* to which these three *sloks* were added. The *pauṛi* goes as follows:

ਪਉੜੀ ॥	Pauṛi
ਨਾਨਕ ਜੀਅ ਉਪਾਇ ਕੈ ਲਿਖਿ ਨਾਵੈ ਧਰਮੁ ਬਹਾਲਿਆ ॥	Nanak jīa upāi kai likh nāvai dharma bahāliya
ਓਥੈ ਸਚੇ ਹੀ ਸਚਿ ਨਿਬੜੈ ਚੁਣਿ ਵਖਿ ਕਢੇ ਜਜਮਾਲਿਆ ॥	Othhai sachay hi sach nibṛai chuṇ vakh kaddhay jajmāliya
ਥਾਉ ਨ ਪਾਇਨਿ ਕੂੜਿਆਰ ਮੁਹ ਕਾਲ੍ਹੈ ਦੋਜਕਿ ਚਾਲਿਆ ॥	Thhāo na pāyen kūṛiyar muh kālai dojak chāliya
ਤੇਰੈ ਨਾਇ ਰਤੇ ਸੇ ਜਿਣਿ ਗਏ ਹਾਰਿ ਗਏ ਸਿ ਠਗਣ ਵਾਲਿਆ ॥	Terai Naye ratay se jiṇ gaye hār gaye se tthaggaṇ vāliya
ਲਿਖਿ ਨਾਵੈ ਧਰਮੁ ਬਹਾਲਿਆ ॥੨॥	Likh nāvai dharma bahāliya. 2.

Glossary:

ਜੀਅ ਉਪਾਇ ਕੈ	Jīa upāye kai	Having created beings
ਧਰਮੁ	Dharam	Dharamraj, the judge appointed by the Lord
ਨਿਬੜੈ	Nibṛai	Is resolved, is settled
ਓਥੈ	Othai	Before Dharamraj

ਜਜਮਾਲਿਆ	Jajmāliya	Leperous ones, low beings
ਸਚੇ ਹੀ ਸਚਿ	Sachay hi sach	Nothing but the truth
ਜਿਣਿ	Jiṇ	Having won

Simply translated this *pauṛi* says the Lord having created the beings has installed the Dharamraj to judge them. In that process of judgement the sole criterion is the truth. The bad ones will be separated out during that judgement, and these false ones will go to Hell with faces blackened. Those immersed in the Lord will win the battle and the deceivers will be losers. Let us now see the *pauṛi* in more detail.

In this *pauṛi* the Guru speaks to us of the Lord's justice. In line 1, he says the Lord created all beings and then installed Dharamraj for the purpose of judging their actions. There are slightly different ways this line is interpreted by learned scholars. Bhai Vir Singh renders it as, "The Lord after creating the beings, established Dharam to record their deeds." Prof. Sahib Singh says roughly the same except that he says Dharamraj has been placed over the beings. The *Shabdarth* says the Lord has created the Name inside of His beings, which acts as the Dharamraj, a sort of inner censor. Prof. Darshan Singh in his audio-commentary, as also Dr. Gopal Singh has followed the view taken by the *Shabdarth*. Macauliffe says, "God having created animals recorded their names and appointed Dharamraj to judge their acts." He seems to take the phrase *likh nāvay* as meaning 'having given names'. Dharamraj is of course a concept from Hindu mythology where he is reckoned as the god charged with the duty of judging the actions of the souls after their passage from this world. The Guru has often made use of concepts from Hindu mythology to make his message clear to his audience, since a majority of them happened to be the followers of that belief system. The Guru has thus, naturally alluded to this belief here. Some learned ones argue that in Sikhism the sole power is the Lord Himself and He is therefore Himself the Judge also. It is true that the Lord is indeed in all religious systems viewed as the overall power, the Real Cause of all that happens. However, in the material universe He operates through His appointed agents. Since the Guru was addressing a mainly Hindu audience he has used extensively a terminology that they could relate to and understand. Thus, throughout the SGGS the Guru speaks of Brahma as the agent to whom the Lord has assigned the task of overseeing creation, Vishnu as the empowered representative who has the duty to see that the created worlds function smoothly in strict accordance with the Lord's design, and so on. In the same way the Guru is saying that the Lord has assigned to Dharamraj the duty of judging the souls, of course in accordance with the Divine Law, and merely as His agent. The more direct interpretations as by Prof. Sahib Singh and Bhai Vir Singh, therefore, seem more appropriate in this light.

In line 2 the nature of that process of justice is now explained to us. The Guru says the sole criterion by which Dharamraj is permitted by the Lord to decide about our fate is the truth. Prof. Talib renders this line as, "There truth alone is determined." Macauliffe says, "At his own court the real truth is adjudged." Prof. Teja Singh says, "Before whom (Dharamraj) only Truth prevails". Dr. Gopal Singh and Dada Chellaram both follow the same line. The rendering by Bhai Vir Singh is on the lines of "Before Dharamraj truth gets by itself determined." Prof. Sahib Singh renders it as, "Truth alone is the determinant before the Dharamraj." As will be seen there are some minor differences in the rendering, but the sense of the message remains clear, that the truth is the only criterion relevant in that forum. No false pretences, no dissimulation, no camouflage will work; our real selves will transparently be exposed, and only where we have in reality done well will any credit be given to us. The righteous will there be picked out for just reward, and the evil ones will be separated for a different treatment. About the second part of the line Giani Sant Singh Maskin has rendered *jajmāliya* as those liable to *Jaziya*, the tax levied on non-Muslims by some Muslim rulers. Prof. Sahib Singh renders it as leprous or the evil ones. Bhai Vir Singh says in his *Panj Granthi* that *jajmāliya* is from the Persian root **'ਜਜ਼ਮ'** (*jazam*) meaning those cut-off (from the good), though he says another meaning could be leprous ones, from the Arabic **'ਜੁਜ਼ਿਮ'** (*juzim*) meaning leprosy. He renders it as the 'the ones cut off', and refers to *Rāg Gauṛi Vār, Mahla* 4, page 304, "jin andar kapat vikār jhūth oye āpay sachai vakkh kadhay jajmālay", meaning that those who have deceit, immorality and falsehood inside are *jajmālay* whom the Lord will segregate. The 'ones cut off' seems the more appealing interpretation, though the leprous one also indirectly indicates an unclean person who is shunned.

In line 3 the Guru says the bad ones will find no place before the Lord and will go to hell with faces blackened. Almost all commentators have rendered it along the same lines. Here we need to see what the Guru is really telling us because the concept of a hell where tortures are inflicted on the Lord's creatures is alien to Sikhism. In this belief system the Lord is seen as the ever merciful, ever forgiving and has been likened to a fond parent watching over his children. Yet the Guru has employed this essentially Semitic concept of hell here. This is designed to make the message clear and has to be viewed together with the first two lines of this *pauṛi*. We have been told that the Lord creates His beings, and then installs Dharamraj, whether we see him as an entity apart or as residing within each man, who is enabled by the Lord to be aware of all we do, all we think. The record of all these overt and hidden thoughts and actions is the living account of our real selves, and will ineluctably expose our reality. No simulation will be possible here, and only if our actions have been pleasing to the Lord we will find acceptance in the Divine Court. If these acts have been contrary to the path prescribed by the Guru, then our souls will be more and more besmirched by the evil we do. The blackened face spoken of here in this line is not by way of punishment by Dharamraj but is a mere recounting of our true worth. Our bad deeds are the cause of our soiled visage. With such a face we cannot rightly even aspire to face the Lord. We will remain enmeshed in the harsh cycle of transmigrations and will have to stay away from Him, distanced or even exiled from that Divine Glory. What greater hell could there be.

In the 4th line the Guru says those who were immersed in the Lord emerged victorious, while the deceivers lost the battle. The message sums up the concept that by living a life of obedience to the Lord, we will be able to achieve the goal for which we were given this invaluable human form. Those persons, says the Guru, who chose to follow this path and immersed themselves in Him, won the battle which we all fight against the evil within us, for which we were sent to this world. The soul is given human form and sent to this earth, this *karma bhūmi* (arena of action) to fight the war within, to overcome the evil in us and to mould our existence in strict accordance with His will. Our actions during this struggle are constantly under watch and the Lord's agents record all that we do, and even that which we contemplate. Those who measure up to the Lord's expectations end up victorious and will be rewarded in accordance with the value of their devotion, their observance of His law. Those ego-centered ones who thought they needed no guidance, relied on their own selves and cared not for the Lord's path will find that on the day of reckoning all their worldly smartness cannot fool the all-seeing Power. Their efforts at trickery will only backfire, their real face will be unmasked, and in the final reckoning they will have lost the game, says the Guru. Prof. Sahib Singh renders this line as "Those in pursuit of worldly wealth and who tried to trick would find no place before Him." Dr. Gopal Singh says, "They who were imbued with thy Name, O Lord, won (the Game of life), and, and the Deceivers were Deceived." The stress here is on the need to be truly and really pure and to remember that we can fool the world but when we go before the Lord there will be no cover available to our innermost selves. The good and the evil within us will be laid bare, and on that basis will our worth be determined.

In the last line, the 5th, the point of the first line has been reiterated. The Guru says, "To keep accounts of our actions Dharamraj has been installed." We have of course already discussed this concept above. Dharamraj has been created by the Lord to keep record of the actions of humans, in fact of all created beings. Then to each is justice meted strictly in accordance with the merit of their deeds and none of these is hidden at the time of rendering justice.

Elsewhere the *SGGS* will tell us that Dharamraj is the Lord's agent for meting out justice, and in performing this job he is assisted by Chitragupta, the scribe who does the actual recording of our deeds and our thoughts.

PAUṚI 3

This, the third *pauṛi*, has attached with it two two *sloks*, both by Guru Nanak. The first of these says:

ਸਲੋਕ ਮ: ੧ ॥	Slok Mahla 1
ਵਿਸਮਾਦੁ ਨਾਦ ਵਿਸਮਾਦੁ ਵੇਦ ॥	Vismād nād vismād ved
ਵਿਸਮਾਦੁ ਜੀਅ ਵਿਸਮਾਦੁ ਭੇਦ ॥	Vismād jīa Vismād bhed
ਵਿਸਮਾਦੁ ਰੂਪ ਵਿਸਮਾਦੁ ਰੰਗ ॥	Vismād rūp Vismād rung
ਵਿਸਮਾਦੁ ਨਾਗੇ ਫਿਰਹਿ ਜੰਤ ॥	Vismād nāgay phireh jant
ਵਿਸਮਾਦੁ ਪਉਣੁ ਵਿਸਮਾਦੁ ਪਾਣੀ ॥	Vismād pauṇ Vismād pāṇi
ਵਿਸਮਾਦੁ ਅਗਨੀ ਖੇਡਹਿ ਵਿਡਾਣੀ ॥	Vismād agni kheddeh viddāṇi
ਵਿਸਮਾਦੁ ਧਰਤੀ ਵਿਸਮਾਦੁ ਖਾਣੀ ॥	Vismād dhartī Vismād khāṇi
ਵਿਸਮਾਦੁ ਸਾਦਿ ਲਗਹਿ ਪਰਾਣੀ ॥	Vismād sād laggeh prāṇi
ਵਿਸਮਾਦੁ ਸੰਜੋਗੁ ਵਿਸਮਾਦੁ ਵਿਜੋਗੁ ॥	Vismād sanjog Vismād vijog
ਵਿਸਮਾਦੁ ਭੁਖ ਵਿਸਮਾਦੁ ਭੋਗੁ ॥	Vismād bhukh Vismād bhog
ਵਿਸਮਾਦੁ ਸਿਫਤਿ ਵਿਸਮਾਦੁ ਸਾਲਾਹ ॥	Vismād sipht Vismād sālāh
ਵਿਸਮਾਦੁ ਉਝੜ ਵਿਸਮਾਦੁ ਰਾਹ ॥	Vismād ujhaṛ Vismād rāh
ਵਿਸਮਾਦੁ ਨੇੜੈ ਵਿਸਮਾਦੁ ਦੂਰਿ ॥	Vismād neṛai Vismād dūr
ਵਿਸਮਾਦੁ ਦੇਖੈ ਹਾਜਰਾ ਹਜੂਰਿ ॥	Vismad dekhay hājra hajūr
ਵੇਖਿ ਵਿਡਾਣੁ ਰਹਿਆ ਵਿਸਮਾਦੁ ॥	Vekh vidāṇ rahiya vismād
ਨਾਨਕ ਬੁਝਣੁ ਪੂਰੈ ਭਾਗਿ ॥੧॥	Nanak bujhaṇ pūrai bhāg. 1.

Glossary:

ਵਿਸਮਾਦੁ	Vismād	Wonder, awe
ਭੇਦ	Bhed	Difference
ਨਾਦ	Nād	Sound
ਵੇਦ	Ved	Knowledge, the Hindu scriptures
ਅਗਨੀ ਖੇਡਹਿ	Agni kheddeh	The Agnis (fires) that play wonderful games
ਵਿਡਾਣੀ	Vidāṇi	Wonderful
ਖਾਣੀ	Khāṇi	A category of created beings (there are four)
ਸੰਜੋਗੁ	Sanjog	Humans joining together
ਵਿਜੋਗੁ	Vijog	Humans parting
ਭੋਗੁ	Bhog	Enjoyment of things material
ਉਝੜ	Ujhaṛ	Wrong path
ਵਿਡਾਣੁ	Vidāṇ	Miracles
ਬੁਝਣੁ	Bujhaṇ	Understanding, realisation

In this *slok* the Guru expresses his great awe and wonder at the manifestations of the Lord in the form of His creation that are visible around all of us. It is the spontaneous outburst of a devotee in a state of exaltation who sees nothing but the Lord Himself in all that exists. Simply translated, the lines of this *slok* say that wondrous are His sounds and wondrous the knowledge; wondrous the beings and their distinctive varieties. Wondrous are the forms and types, and the fact that many roam unclad. Wondrous are the winds, wondrous the waters. Wondrous are the various fires playing sportively. Wondrous are the Earth and the sources of creation. Wondrous are the tastes to which created beings are addicted. Wonderful are the meetings and the separations. Wondrous are the hungers and their fulfillment. Wondrous are the laudations of the Lord. Wondrous it is how some wander in the barren lands while others are on the right path. Wondrous it is how some are near and some far from the Lord. Wonderful is the fact that the Lord is ever present. Seeing all these wonders Nanak is amazed and he says that only if we are truly lucky can understanding and true realisation of these wonders come to us.

When a true devotee contemplates the Infinite he goes into a state of ecstasy where all that he sees is the Lord Himself manifest in each of His wondrous creations. The ordinary man seeing the same things will perhaps see only the material aspects; the true devotee sees much deeper and goes ecstatic. We can see an example of this in this *slok* where Guru Nanak expresses his awe at the many manifestations of Nature that he sees around him. It is the expression of a true devotee, someone who sees the Lord in anything and everything. He says all these things seem so wonderful to him that he is a state of *Vismād*. Let us consider what exactly *Vismād* here means.

In the Hindu scriptures the theory of *Rasa* (aesthetic flavours) is attributed to Bharata, a sage-priest who probably lived about AD 500. This theory was further developed by Abhinavagupta (c. AD 1000), who applied it to all varieties of theatre and poetry. The *Rasas* are divided into nine categories evoking in us nine different types of emotions. These aesthetic flavours and the states of mind that are our responses to these have been listed in the Hindu *shastras* as: 1. *Shringār* (ornamentation) relating to the sensous, 2. *Hāsya* (humorous), relating to the comic, 3. *Karuṇa* (empathy) relating to pathos, 4. *Raudra* (fury) relating to the furious, 5. *Vir* (valour) relating to bravery and courage, 6. *Bhyānak* (horror) relating to the terrible or fearsome, 7. *Bibhast* (revulsion) relating to the odious, 8. *Adbhut* (wonder), relating to the marvelous, and 9. *Shānt* (peace), relating to the quietst and the serene (*Encyclopedia Brittanica*, Vol. 13, page 23). *Vismād* is the state of mind that is evoked within us in response to the input into our senses of stimuli relating to the *Adbhut Rasa*. When we see something we find wondrous, and great, and beyond human ken, when we can only but marvel at a phenomenon, then are we said to be in the state of *Vismād*. This is a state where awe at the grandeur is mingled with love and joy at the beauty of what we see. The Guru, ecstatic at some of the manifestations of the Lord that he sees around him, exclaims repeatedly that he is in *Vismād* at these great wonders the Lord has wrought.

In lines 1 and 2 the Guru says He finds wonderful the *Nād* (sounds) the Lord has created – the *Ved* (knowledge), *jee* (beings), and the *bhed* (their distinctions). The term *Nād* literally means sound but is also used to refer to the mystic primal sound, the *Anahat Nād*. *Ved* is used generically for knowledge but also refers to the four holy books of Hinduism, the *Vedas*. From these differing meanings of these words there follows the slightly differing rendering of this line by learned ones. Thus, about the first line Prof. Talib says, "Marvelous are the varied forms of speech in the universe; marvelous the scripture recorded." Dr. Gopal Singh says, "Wonderful is sound, wonderful is wisdom." Prof. Teja Singh puts it as, "Wonderful is the word spoken and the word recorded." Bhai Vir Singh renders it as, "The various types of sounds existing, the music that exists and is being sung, and the written word, *Veda*, etc. create *Vismād*." As can be seen, the differences in interpretation are minor and the broad sense remains the same. The Guru is expressing his *Vismād* at the Sound that resonates in the ear of the mystic as also at the more mundane sounds of the world. He refers to the sum of the recorded knowledge as also to the books of wisdom he sees among the humans around him.

The second line similarly lends itself to slightly differing views. Almost all learned commentators are agreed regarding the word *jee* which means created beings. However, the word *Bhed* is taken by Bhai Vir Singh as referring to the difference between men, animals, vegetable kingdom, etc. while Prof. Sahib Singh says it refers to the different types of creatures and things. Prof. Teja Singh renders these words as, "animated beings and their distinctions". Dr. Gopal Singh puts it as, "Wonderful is life, wonderful its distinctions." Prof. Talib renders it as, "Marvelous the multiplicity of creation, wonderful their distinctions." We have to keep in mind here what the Guru has told us; that the Universe is infinite and so is the variety of beings and things existing therein. The Guru, as one gifted with the Divine sight was here seeing not merely the beings on this earth but through all infinity. So, appropriately his sense of wonder is to be seen as a response to the infinite variety of created beings that his mystic eye shows him. The distinctions between them visible to that eye must also seem truly startling. Their myriad types of shapes and forms are amazing in their variety and their functional utility; all this great variety is truly wondrous, the Guru tells us.

In the 3rd and 4th lines the Guru, in the same vein, says he is in *Vismād* at the *rūp* and *rung* (forms and the variety) of these beings. These strike him with awe and wonder. Some, he says in line 4, are clad while so many others go about unclothed. The reference is probably to humans on the one hand as the ones who wear clothing as against the large numbers of the animal kingdom who need wear nothing. Macauliffe, Prof. Teja Singh, Dr. Gopal Singh, Bhai Manmohan Singh and Dada Chellaram have used 'colours' for the word *rung* in line 3, which is of course, literally the correct meaning. Prof. Talib however sees it differently and renders it as 'variety', which is also a commonly accepted rendering of the word *rung*. This certainly seems in the present context the more appropriate view. The term *rūp rung*, meaning 'shape and colour', is quite commonly used to describe the difference between various entities, and the usage here seems to be intended in that sense.

In lines 5 and 6 the Guru expresses his *Vismād* (sense of wonder) at the different forms of winds, waters and fires that he sees. Again we must visualize the Guru as seeing across an infinite expanse of worlds, the different forms of creation of which he calls wonderful. The Guru would have noted the infinite variety of forms that water, air and fire – the essential elements supporting the various forms of life – can take in these myriad worlds. He says he is wonderstruck at what he sees. Even considering only our Earth, the belief among Hindus has been that fire is of various kinds. Prof. Sahib Singh has in his commentary on the *Āsa di Vār*, listed some of these as, 1. *Barwa agni* which rises from within the Earth into the oceans, 2. *Dāwa agni* which is of the jungles, and 3. *Jatthar agni* which is in the human stomach. He further lists some other forms of *agni*, such as *kop agni*, *chinta agni*, *gyān agni*, *rāj agni*, etc. There are also, he says, three types of *agnis* of the *havan*, a Hindu worship ritual. He calls these *gārh patya, ahnīya* and *dakhin*. How many more must exist elsewhere is beyond the limits of human knowledge, but the Guru with His divine vision sees it all. He says the sight of it leaves him in *Vismād* at how *agni*, in all its forms is playfully interacting with the other created things.

In lines 7 and 8 the Guru says *Vismād* overtakes him when he sees the world, the types of creation; and the tastes and things to which humans are addicted. The traditional sources of birth in ancient times were reckoned as four – from the egg, from the womb, from the sweat, and from the earth. So the Guru here is also referring to these four *khaṇīs* (sources). Sweat is referred to as a source of birth because things such as lice and other small parasites are apparently born of sweat. This is so because their eggs are developed and nurtured on the skin of the body, and the sweat thereon which provides the conducive medium. On other worlds, in other universes what sources of birth may exist, only the Lord and the Guru can know. The Guru seeing with his divine eye all the infinite earths and sources of birth of various beings, exclaims that all of it is awesome and wonderful. It leaves him in a state of *Vismād*. He also speaks here how, many of the created beings are attached to things purely material, some others to evil, and yet some others only to the good and pure. How variegated, he says, are the things to which humans are attached and how diverse the sources of enjoyment. The variety of all this leaves him in wonder.

Lines 9 and 10 refer now to what happens in this universe to these created beings, the different experiences they go through. The Guru says it is wonderful how chance brings some into union, and causes others to be separated. How wonderful, he says, are the types of hunger and the indulgences of these beings. The paths that the human beings follow in their brief sojourns on this planet involve numerous partings and many reunions. The fate that brings about a joining is called *sanjog* and where a loss or a parting occurs is called *vijog*. How these two situations are constantly happening simultaneously strikes the Guru as wonderful, and leaves him in *Vismad.* How varied is the range of human tastes while pandering to their senses, how wide the range of human behaviour, falling between the very evil and the extremely good, is again to the Guru a manifestation of the Lord's Will. It is wonderful, says the Guru, how men keep themselves continuously engrossed thus.

In lines 11 and 12 the Guru says he is in *Vismād* at the praise and laudation of the Lord that goes on among the created beings at all times. He is also in *Vismād* at how some creatures choose the barren lands of an ego-centered existence, while others are forever progressing on the right path. These lines have been rendered by Dr. Gopal Singh as, "Wonderful the path, wonderful the straying away", meaning that the good that humans do as also their straying into evil emanate from the same one source, the Lord Himself. Prof. Talib puts it as, "Strange the way some are straying, wonderful the sight of others following the straight path." Macauliffe is more literal and puts it as, "Wonderful the desert, wonderful the road" which is also roughly how Dada Chellaram has rendered it. Prof. Teja Singh combines the two and says, "Wonderful is man's going astray in the wilderness, or his finding out the true path." Bhai Vir Singh in his rendering combines the two lines and says, "It is wonderful how some follow the right path of singing the Lord' praises, while others forgetting it go astray in the wilderness." This interpretation would seem to come closest to explaining the idea and is more appealing.

In line 13 and 14 the Guru says it is a marvel how some are near Him and others are distanced. He is wonderstruck when he sees that the Lord is ever present and always with us. Macauliffe renders these lines as, "Wonderful Thy nearness, wonderful Thy remoteness; wonderful to behold Thee present." Dr. Gopal Singh uses roughly the same terminology. Prof. Talib puts it yet another way when he says, "Wonderful that some are close to God; strange others though far off. To see such marvels with wonder am I struck." Bhai Vir Singh renders these lines beautifully as, "The wonder of wonders is to see the Lord in one's presence and feel oneself to be in the Lord's presence." Prof. Sahib Singh renders it as, "Some are saying He is near, some say He is far away. Others say He is present everywhere." This, he says is a wonder. This explains the line succinctly and would seem the more appealing rendering.

In the concluding lines, numbers 15 and 16, the Guru says seeing all these wonders he is in *Vismād*. The ability to experience in the spirit and to understand these marvels however can come only as a grace from Him. *Vidāṇ* means a wonderful feat, a miracle. The last line has been translated in different ways by the learned ones. Thus, Dr. Gopal Singh says, 'It is through Perfect Destiny that one knows its answer." Prof. Talib similarly renders it as, "By supreme good fortune only is this mystery resolved." Macauliffe puts it on the other hand as, "They who understand (these wonderful things) are supremely fortunate." Dada Chellaram taking *pūrai* to mean 'previous', instead of 'complete', which is how most others have taken it, says, "To know it all, requireth pre-writ fortune." The idea stressed by the Guru here is that these numerous wonders exist throughout this created Universe. They strike the observer, even an achieved soul like Guru Nanak, as marvels beyond human understanding, as wonderful awe-inspiring miracles. The knowledge of these, the understanding of why all this is the way it is can however not come from our own efforts. So deep are these mysteries that any enlightenment of these can come to us only as a gift from the Supreme Power who alone knows the reasons behind these.

In the next *slok* Guru Nanak says:

ਮ: ੧ ॥	M: 1
ਕੁਦਰਤਿ ਦਿਸੈ ਕੁਦਰਤਿ ਸੁਣੀਐ ਕੁਦਰਤਿ ਭਉ ਸੁਖ ਸਾਰੁ ॥	Kudrat dissai kudrat suṇiai kudrat bhau sukh sār
ਕੁਦਰਤਿ ਪਾਤਾਲੀ ਆਕਾਸੀ ਕੁਦਰਤਿ ਸਰਬ ਆਕਾਰੁ ॥	Kudrat pātāli ākāsi kudrat sarab ākār

ਕੁਦਰਤਿ ਵੇਦ ਪੁਰਾਣ ਕਤੇਬਾ ਕੁਦਰਤਿ ਸਰਬ ਵੀਚਾਰੁ ॥	Kudrat Ved purāṇ kateba kudrat sarab vichār
ਕੁਦਰਤਿ ਖਾਣਾ ਪੀਣਾ ਪੈਨ੍ਣੁ ਕੁਦਰਤਿ ਸਰਬ ਪਿਆਰੁ ॥	Kudrat khaṇā peeṇa painaṇ kudrat sarab pyār
ਕੁਦਰਤਿ ਜਾਤੀ ਜਿਨਸੀ ਰੰਗੀ ਕੁਦਰਤਿ ਜੀਅ ਜਹਾਨ ॥	Kudrat jati jinsi rungi kudrat jee jahān
ਕੁਦਰਤਿ ਨੇਕੀਆ ਕੁਦਰਤਿ ਬਦੀਆ ਕੁਦਰਤਿ ਮਾਨੁ ਅਭਿਮਾਨੁ ॥	Kudrat nekiya kudrat badīa kudrat mān abhimān
ਕੁਦਰਤਿ ਪਉਣੁ ਪਾਣੀ ਬੈਸੰਤਰੁ ਕੁਦਰਤਿ ਧਰਤੀ ਖਾਕੁ ॥	Kudrat pauṇ pāṇi baisantar kudrat dhartī khāk
ਸਭ ਤੇਰੀ ਕੁਦਰਤਿ ਤੂੰ ਕਾਦਿਰੁ ਕਰਤਾ ਪਾਕੀ ਨਾਈ ਪਾਕੁ ॥	Sabh terī kudrat tū[n] kadir karta pāki nayi pāk
ਨਾਨਕ ਹੁਕਮੈ ਅੰਦਰਿ ਵੇਖੈ ਵਰਤੈ ਤਾਕੋ ਤਾਕੁ ॥੨॥	Nanak hukmai andar vekhai vartai tāko tāk. 2.

Glossary:

ਕੁਦਰਤਿ	Kudrat	The Lord's creation, his Will, Power, Nature
ਦਿਸੈ	Dissai	Whatever is visible
ਸੁਖ ਸਾਰੁ	Sukh sār	The basis, the essence of joy
ਕਤੇਬਾ	Kateba	Scriptures of Muslim and Christian faiths
ਜੀਅ ਜਹਾਨ	Jee jahān	In the beings of the world
ਾਕਭ।	Mān	Respect, honour
ਅਭਿਮਾਨੁ	Abhimān	Pride, vanity
ਬੈਸੰਤਰੁ	Baisantar	Fire
ਪਾਕੀ	Pāki	Pure, unattached
ਨਾਈ	Nāi	Greatness
ਵੇਖੈ	Vekhai	Sees, looks after
ਤਾਕੋ ਤਾਕੁ	TākoTāk	Unattached, expert, watchful
ਵਰਤੈ	Vartai	Operates in, exists
ਕਾਦਿਰੁ	Kādir	Creator, Lord of creation

The Guru in this *slok* now speaks to us of the things the Lord has created. The sense of wonder, which he expressed at the Lord's doings, as we saw in the previous *slok*, is now supplemented by the listing of things the Lord has wrought. Simply translated this *slok* says that whatever we see or hear is His creation, as are the fears we face and the joys we experience. The *pātāl* (nether regions) and *ākās* (heavens) are all His creation, and have been wrought by His will. All knowledge, the *Vedas*, *Puranas*, the *kateba[n]* – Semitic scriptures – are part of His created Nature, His manifest might. Our eating, drinking, our apparel, the power of love within us are part of His Nature. All species, types, genera and forms of creatures are but the manifestation of His Nature. All virtues, the good, the evil, the honours, the disgrace that we get are part of His Nature. The winds, the fires, the soils of this earth, are also part of His Nature, His might manifest. He the creator of all these things and His greatness is the holiest of the holy. The Lord is the one and only Power, existing within and permeating His creation, yet untouched by it. Let us now look at these concepts in more detail.

The *Shabdarth* explains that in the previous *slok* the Guru had spoken of the wonder aroused in the beholder when he witnesses the Lord's wondrous doings. Such a response is in a way necessary also, says the *Shabdarth*, so as to engender in us the proper sense of awe and love for the Lord. However, there is the danger that such an emotional state could also give birth to superstitions and unreasoning beliefs. To save us from that error the Guru now in this *slok* explains that all *Kudrat* (creation) functions according to the rules and systems He has prescribed and that our actions are viewed, governed and judged accordingly. Bhai Vir Singh renders *Kudrat* here as meaning creation, that which has been brought into existence by Him and which then functions in strict accordance with His will. He says that in Arabic *Kudrat* is used to convey various meanings such as creation, universe, power, might, Divine Power, but that here it refers to creation.

In the first line of the *slok* the Guru says whatever we see or hear is His creation. The word *Kudrat* is more often used for 'Nature', but here in the context of the Lord that meaning becomes coterminous with the other meaning as 'creation'. The fears we face and the essence of our joys, says the Guru, are also *Kudrat* because these are governed by His will. Learned commentators have rendered this line essentially in two ways. Bhai Vir Singh, Prof. Sahib Singh, Prof. Teja Singh and Prof. Talib render it as, "Whatever is seen and whatever heard is all

His might or His nature." Dr. Gopal Singh, Macauliffe, Bhai Manmohan Singh, Dada Chellaram slightly alter it and say, "By His Power we see and hear." In this sense it would mean that the human ability to experience His creation is His gift. However, the first interpretation, that all that exists and happens is a manifestation of the Lord, seems definitely more in tune with the Guru's message and is more appealing. The Guru adds that the *bhāo* (fear) and the *sukh sār* (essence of joy) are also a function of the Lord's might. Prof. Talib renders this line as, "By His might is inspired fear and the essence of joy." A similar interpretation is echoed by Dada Chellaram, Bhai Manmohan Singh and Dr. Gopal Singh. Bhai Vir Singh puts it as, "Fear and happiness under which the world functions are also part of His Nature." Prof. Sahib Singh slightly alters it and says that, "The *bhāo* (fear) of God is the basis of all our happiness and this is part of His Nature." Prof. Teja Singh renders it as, "Whatever is seen or heard is in the order of Nature; so is the consciousness of fear and comfort." All these slightly varying interpretations have their own strength but the view adopted by Prof. Sahib Singh here seems more appealing. The *bhāo* here could not possibly be meant to refer to our common everyday fears. The term here has to be taken appropriately as referring to the fear of the Lord. This fear is that one positive, uplifting emotion that removes all fears of any earthly threats, and is hence the very basis of true happiness and of freedom from all fear for the devotee.

Line 2 refers to the nether regions, the heavens and all the various forms that exist in this created Universe. The Guru is saying that the entire creation with its so-called nether regions (*pātāl*) and the *Ākās* – which literally translates as skies but here refers to heavens – along with the other shapes, things and forms created by the Lord are all part of His Nature. All these have come into existence through His will, His might, His creative power.

In line 3 the Guru adds that all *Vedas* or knowledge, *Puranas* Hindu religious books, or 'Kateba - Semitic scriptures, and all the wisdom that exists anywhere is part of His *Kudrat*. *Veda* means knowledge and is also used to refer to the Four *Vedas*, the four ancient Hindu scriptures. In the context it seems more probable that the term has here been used for the *Vedas*, because reference is also here made to the Semitic scriptures, called *kateba* (books), and also to the *Puranas* which are also a form of ancient scriptural literature of the Hindu religion. The Guru says that all the thoughts, the wisdom, contained in these are His '*Kudrat*,

His Nature. These are all but a part of His manifest power, part of the Divine Order under which the universe operates.

In Line 4 the Guru says all our eating, drinking and our apparel are part of His Nature, and so is the power of love within us. Since the Guru is enumerating the various practical aspects of the Lord's power manifest in the everyday life, he has added here these human activities that occupy all humans constantly.

In line 5 the Guru says the species, types, genera and forms of creatures, and all living thing in the world are but the manifestation of His Nature.

Line 6 adds another category. The Guru says the virtues, the good, the evils, the honours, the disgrace that comes to us is all part of His Nature. As Prof. Sahib Singh puts it, "It is His own Divine play that somewhere good deeds are being done, and elsewhere there is evil. Some are earning great honours and others are arrogant (thus likely to suffer disgrace)."

In line 7 the Guru says the waters, the winds, the fires and soils of this earth are all part of His Nature. Some commentators have rendered this thought as, "By His might are created the waters, the winds, etc." The sense obviously doesn't change much in these two renderings, but the former rendering seems more consistent with the message in the previous lines.

In line 8 the Guru says that all the various things and qualities that have been listed are part of His Nature and He is the Creator of all of those, and the holiest of the holy is He in His greatness. The term *pāk* is Persian, meaning pure or untainted. Bhai Vir Singh explains that *Pāki Nāi* is from *pāk*, meaning pure and untainted, and *nayi* meaning greatness, *pāki* being the feminine of *pāk* necessitated by the term *nayi* being feminine gender. He further says in his commentary that the term has been used here to express that the Lord, even while He is the Creator and permeating every part of this *Kudrat* (creation) is yet untainted by it. In other words, He is beyond and above this creation even while He is Immanent in it, and is the Creator who wrought it and the Doer, the Sustainer who ensures its existence. Dada Chellaram has translated it as, "All is in Thine Power. Thou art the Power source, the creator, the doer, O Thou the Holy Lord of unblemished Glory." The rendering by Bhai Vir Singh seems more appealing here.

In the 9th and concluding line the Guru says the Lord keeps within His *Hukam* this entire creation, watches over all and everywhere is He all by His Divine

Self. This line lends itself to slightly differing interpretations. The word *vekhai*, says Bhai Vir Singh, is from the Sanskrit *vartanay*, meaning existing, abiding in the sense of a fixed presence. The word *tāk* according to him is from the Arabic meaning one, sole, only. Prof. Sahib Singh also translates *tāko tāk* as meaning only He Himself. However, the *Shabdarth* renders *tāk* as 'expert, highly skilled', and so *tāko tāk* would then be rendered as the highest, most perfect expert. Both meanings would fit in with the message here. Let us see what some other learned ones say about it. Prof. Talib puts it as, "All creation operating under His ordinance He watches, yet from it is He separate, sole." Macauliffe says, ".... Thou art altogether unrivalled". Bhai Vir Singh's view comes out as: "He resides within His Nature, His creation, while yet is He separate all by Himself." Prof. Sahib Singh says, "The Lord keeps all this creation, or Nature, within His ordinance, sustains it and solely throughout it all is Omnipresent." Dr. Gopal Singh has another take on it and says, "The Lord acts according to His law: But lo, works also with discrimination He." Prof. Teja Singh follows the view of the *Shabdarth* and says, "God looks to everything with His will, and works most intelligently." Dada Chellaram also renders it as, "Nanak wert man to see God's nature as working under God's Will, he shall find that His working is in absolute perfection." So he also takes the term *tāko tāk* in the sense of 'expert, perfect' but changes the meaning of the line as not being a statement by the Guru explaining the Lord's relationship to His creation, but as an exhortation to man to see how Nature works under God's will and how the working is perfect. Both interpretations will fit the concept adequately, but on the whole the view taken by Prof. Talib and some other learned ones seems here more appropriate referring as it does to the Lord as the one and only Power, under whose ordinance all creation operates which he watches over but is yet untouched by it.

Now we come to the 3rd *pauṛi* to which these two *sloks* are attached. The Guru speaks to us here of the fate of the human when he passes from this world. He says:

ਪਉੜੀ ॥	Pauṛi
ਆਪੀਨੑੈ ਭੋਗ ਭੋਗਿ ਕੈ ਹੋਇ ਭਸਮੜਿ ਭਉਰੁ ਸਿਧਾਇਆ ॥	Āpīnai bhog bhog kai hoey Bhasmaṛ bhaur sidhāia
ਵਡਾ ਹੋਆ ਦੁਨੀਦਾਰੁ ਗਲਿ ਸੰਗਲੁ ਘਤਿ ਚਲਾਇਆ ॥	Vada hoa dunidar gull sangal ghat chalāia

Pauṛi 3

ਅਗੈ ਕਰਣੀ ਕੀਰਤਿ ਵਾਚੀਐ ਬਹਿ ਲੇਖਾ ਕਰਿ ਸਮਝਾਇਆ ॥	Aggai karṇi keerat vāchīyai baih lekha kar samjhāia
ਥਾਉ ਨ ਹੋਵੀ ਪਉਦੀਈ ਹੁਣਿ ਸੁਣੀਐ ਕਿਆ ਰੂਆਇਆ ॥	Thhāo na hovi paudīyi huṇ suṇīyai kiya rūaia
ਮਨਿ ਅੰਧੈ ਜਨਮੁ ਗਵਾਇਆ ॥੩॥	Mann andhai Janam gavāia. 3.

Glossary:

ਭੋਗ	Bhog	Enjoyment of material things
ਭਸਮੜਿ	Bhasmaṛ	Ashes
ਭਉਰੁ	Bhaur	Soul, the spirit
ਵਡਾ ਹੋਆ	Vadda hoa	Become great; also, died
ਦੁਨੀਦਾਰੁ	Dunīdār	The worldly man
ਕਰਣੀ	Karṇi	Deeds, acts
ਵਾਚੀਐ	Vachīyai	Is spoken
ਬਹਿ	Baih	Sitting down
ਥਾਉ ਨ ਹੋਵੀ	Thau na hovi	Can find no refuge
ਪਉਦੀਈ	Paudīyi	Is hit or beaten

Simply translated this *pauṛi* says that having enjoyed the pleasures of this world the human dies, the body is reduced to ashes and the spirit departs. When a man deeming himself big thus departs, chains are put around his neck and he is marched off. After we leave this world the criterion for judging us is nothing but our deeds, which are carefully read out to the soul facing judgement. The results of our actions will then become very clear to us. As our due punishment is meted out the regrets for a life ill spent will start hitting us. Let us now discuss it in more detail.

In the first line the Guru speaks of the man who having enjoyed to the limit the joys of this material world died. What ensues then is that after the spirit within departs the body is soon enough reduced to ashes. According to the *Shabdarth*, this line refers to the man who was a materialist and deeming himself to be his own support indulged in revelries. Then one day, like all human flesh his body turned to ashes and he departed this world. The term *āpīnai* (himself) is used in this sense as referring to the spirit, the soul animating this human form, which the

Guru says will depart from this mortal world after the body, which indulged in all enjoyment, dies and is reduced to ashes. However, Prof. Sahib Singh has taken the word as referring to the Lord as was the case in the first *pauṛi* earlier, where *āpīnai* referred to the Lord having from His own Self created Himself and then created Nature. Bhai Vir Singh has, however, in his *Panj Granthi*, taken the view that *āpīnai* here is used in reference to the man whose soul departed the world. Many other learned commentators have also used it in this sense. Thus Prof. Talib says, "After bearing the consequences of deeds, the self turning dust leaves this world," thus interpreting *āpinai* as referring to a human. He has though, rendered the term *bhog bhogke* to mean not as 'enjoying material things' but in its other sense as 'suffering the consequences of deeds'. Dr. Gopal Singh says, "Having abandoned oneself to the self, one revels and, then becoming ashes, his soul departs." Macauliffe, Bhai Manmohan Singh and Dada Chellaram have rendered it along the same lines as Prof. Teja Singh who says, "Led by himself man enjoys his lusts, until his soul departs and he is reduced to a heap of ashes." The view taken by these learned ones seems more appealing.

In the 2nd line the Guru says when the man who deemed himself big departs the world, chains are put round his neck and he is marched off. The idea here is that a man who fixes not his mind on the Lord will deem himself to be the doer. As the Guru says in the first line, such a man will indulge himself in all worldly pleasures. He may sometimes even achieve a position he deems to be mighty in the world of men, but a day will come when inevitably his time will be up. His soul will depart, and as is the custom in much of India, his body, which is all that is left behind, will then be burnt to ashes. The soul, the spirit, will now have to face the day of reckoning. The imagery used here by the Guru is the popular one of the agents of the Yamaraj, the Lord of Death, catching the soul and putting a chain around the neck. They will then drag him and produce him for justice. The 'chains' here are to be understood as those forged by our own actions where they transgressed the Lord's inexorable law, which requires each soul to answer for itself. The term *vadda hoa* is used to show worldly greatness and in this vein Macauliffe says, "However great and wealthy a man may be". Dr. Gopal Singh follows the same view. Bhai Vir Singh also renders *vadda hoa* as referring to worldly greatness. However, Prof. Sahib uses it in the other meaning of the word common in the vernacular, which is 'Dead'. Prof. Talib takes the first alternative but in the footnotes also refers to this alternate meaning. Gyani Maskin, in the first line, takes *āpīnai* to mean 'the Lord', in the sense that the soul sitting within is but a separated portion of the Lord. However, in the second line he renders *vadda* as meaning, 'having high worldly position'. The more appealing rendering is of *āpīnay* as meaning the person, and *vadda hoa* as referring to his worldly status.

In the 3rd line the Guru says that after we depart this world the criterion for judging us is nothing but our own deeds, which are carefully and in detail read out to the soul facing judgement. Gyani Maskin in his audio-commentary says that the norms for judging a man's worth undergo drastic change after death. Things that are taken to be a good measure of a man's worth in this world would lose all relevance before Dharamraj. How high or important the worldly achievements were is of no relevance and the only currency that could avail him there are his good deeds. The account of these deeds, says the Guru, is with great deliberation and in detail read out. There is at that time no scope for prevarication or camouflage. We will know for certain that the account read out will be true and accurate. Justifications and rationalizations with which we fooled ourselves while in this world will no longer in that forum work. The real worth of our accumulated actions will now get judged in the court where no error in imparting justice ever occurs. Such will be the accuracy of that judgment that we will also know that we got exactly what we deserved.

In lines 4 and 5, the Guru tells us that the results will be known and the consequences will be also glaringly clear. As our due chastisement is visited upon us the regrets for a life ill spent will start hitting us. The Guru says that, because of indulgence in the material world and having not earned any spiritual merit, such a man will now be suffering the blows and it would at that time be too late for him to cry out for help. There will now be no place for him to escape from the punishment he must face. Such a blind fool will have wasted the human birth that God had so graciously bestowed on him.

The Guru has often stressed the invaluable worth of the human state. As we read daily in the *Nitnem*, the daily prayers, the hymn from the fifth Nanak *Rāg Āsa*, "Bhaī prapt manukh dehuria, Govind Milan ki eh teri bariya", meaning "You have been granted the human form for the purpose of utilizing this birth to achieve union with the Lord." The way towards this end is also clearly prescribed by the

Guru, as the *SGGS* repeatedly tells us. The *Japji Sahib* summarizes the steps that a Sikh needs to take. Other religious systems have similarly prescribed paths that are followed by millions of humans who have the upliftment of their souls as their aim. Many are the unfortunate ones, however, who deem themselves the masters of their own fate, who are filled with pride at their own brilliance, or wealth or power. They throw themselves wholeheartedly into enjoying all those things of this world that may pander to the senses. They indulge and satisfy every lust, and amass wealth and power. They wield their strength for themselves, and all through this they deem unimportant the most important message that the masters, the achieved souls have been trying to pass to this world. They deem such spiritual lessons unimportant and not relevant to their lives. If at all they give it a thought it is as something they will either ignore or postpone for a later day, usually for the day when they are grey haired and close to their end. In this *pauṛi* the Guru speaks to us of the fate of such unfortunate souls. Their passage may seem transiently joyful while they are sunk in the pleasures of the world. However, the consequences of their actions will hit them hard in their faces when they appear for justice before Dharamraj. The chains of attachments to woldly wealth that they have forged with their own wrong actions will now bind them. They will be condemned to go from one birth to the next, and are hence big losers. Such a lowly fate awaits them, however great they may have deemed themselves in the material world. Their arrogance forgotten they will now try to seek shelter from the blows that their own evil actions will cause them to face; but by then, says the Guru, it will be much too late. The purpose for which they come to this world would have been defeated.

PAUṚI 4

In this *pauṛi* the Guru tells us further about the relationship of the Lord with His created things. There are two *sloks* attached with it, both by Guru Nanak. The first one of these goes thus:

ਸਲੋਕ ਮ: ੧ ॥	Slok M: 1
ਭੈ ਵਿਚਿ ਪਵਣੁ ਵਹੈ ਸਦਵਾਉ ॥	Bhai vich pavaṇ vahai sadvāo
ਭੈ ਵਿਚਿ ਚਲਹਿ ਲਖ ਦਰੀਆਉ ॥	Bhai vich chaleh lakh darīāo
ਭੈ ਵਿਚਿ ਅਗਨਿ ਕਢੈ ਵੇਗਾਰਿ ॥	Bhai vich agan kaddhai vegār
ਭੈ ਵਿਚਿ ਧਰਤੀ ਦਬੀ ਭਾਰਿ ॥	Bhai vich dharti dabī bhār
ਭੈ ਵਿਚਿ ਇੰਦੁ ਫਿਰੈ ਸਿਰ ਭਾਰਿ ॥	Bhai vich ind phirai sirr bhār
ਭੈ ਵਿਚਿ ਰਾਜਾ ਧਰਮ ਦੁਆਰੁ ॥	Bhai vich raja dharma duār
ਭੈ ਵਿਚਿ ਸੂਰਜੁ ਭੈ ਵਿਚਿ ਚੰਦੁ ॥	Bhai vich sūraj bhai vich chand
ਕੋਹ ਕਰੋੜੀ ਚਲਤ ਨ ਅੰਤੁ ॥	Koh karoṛi chalat na unt
ਭੈ ਵਿਚਿ ਸਿਧ ਬੁਧ ਸੁਰ ਨਾਥ ॥	Bhai vich sidh budh sur nāth
ਭੈ ਵਿਚਿ ਆਡਾਣੇ ਆਕਾਸ ॥	Bhai vich āddāṇāy ākās
ਭੈ ਵਿਚਿ ਜੋਧ ਮਹਾਬਲ ਸੂਰ ॥	Bhai vich jodh mahabal sūr
ਭੈ ਵਿਚਿ ਆਵਹਿ ਜਾਵਹਿ ਪੂਰ ॥	Bhai vich āveh jāveh pūr
ਸਗਲਿਆ ਭਉ ਲਿਖਿਆ ਸਿਰਿ ਲੇਖੁ ॥	Saglia bhau likhiya sirr lekh
ਨਾਨਕ ਨਿਰਭਉ ਨਿਰੰਕਾਰੁ ਸਚੁ ਏਕੁ ॥੧॥	Nanak nirbhau nirankār sach ek.1.

Glossary:

ਭੈ ਵਿਚਿ	Bhai vich	In obedience to the Lord's ordinance
ਸਦ	Sad	Always
ਕਢੈ ਵੇਗਾਰਿ	Kaddhai vegār	Works for (gratis)
ਇੰਦੁ Ind	Lord	Indra; here, clouds
ਰਾਜਾ ਧਰਮ ਦੁਆਰੁ	Raja dharma duar	At Dharamraj's door
ਕੋਹ	Koh	A distance of a *kos*, about two miles
ਸਿਧ	Sidh miraculours powers)	An adept (in some
ਬੁਧ	Budh	The learned
ਆਡਾਣੇ	Āddāṇey	Taut, stretched
ਪੂਰ	Pūr	The entire lot (of beings)
ਸਿਰਿ	Sirr	On their heads
ਲੇਖੁ	Lekh	Writing

In this *slok* the Guru tells us further about the relationship of the Lord with His created things. The Guru says that all created entities like the Sun, the Moon, etc. function strictly according to the role assigned to them and none of them can ever go beyond the limits set by the Lord for them. In obedience to His inexorable ordinance does every created thing function. This is the *bhai* (fear spoken) of here. It is the fear that keeps every component of this vast creation working in cohesion and co-operating to fulfill the Lord's ordinance. Simply translated this *slok* says that in obedience to the Lord do Winds and numerous rivers flow. In obedience to Him do the fires serve and the Earth carry its load. In obedience to Him does Indra in the form of clouds scurry overhead, and in compliance to His ordinance does Dharamraj function. Similarly, do the Sun and the Moon run endlessly long distances. In compliance to His command are the *Sidhs* (adepts), the *Budhs* (enlightened ones), the *Surs* (minor gods), and the *Nāths* (heads of the *Jogi* sects). In obedience to Him stretch the skies. In obedience to Him do the warriors and men of valour function. Under His ordinance are the multitudes born and die. Every created thing is fated to live within the ambit of the Lord's ordinance. The reference here is to that ennobling, liberating fear that removes all earthly fears. The Guru says that only the Lord Himself is beyond the domain of this *bhai* (fear). Let us now examine it in more detail.

In the first two lines the Guru says the winds blow and the numerous rivers flow in fear of the Lord, in obedience to His edict. The term *bhāo* used in the conclusion of this *slok* here is used in the sense of *bhai* (fear) of the Lord. Used in the context of the Lord the meaning of this word needs to be clearly understood. This *bhai*, this fear, is a fear distinct from the fears of this world. While the worldly fears are a source of tension and trouble and create terror in the mind, the fear of the Lord is an ennobling, liberating and, therefore, also a protective fear. When a human fears the Lord his steps automatically move on the right path and he will hesitate to do wrong. He will live within the limits prescribed by the Lord as explained to us by the masters, which for a Sikh is the *SGGS*. Anyone who follows this path, and has in his heart the fear of the Lord, will in fact soon lose all his fears of the things and powers of this world. Thus is that lucky man liberated from his petty fears, protected from doing wrong; and thus does he learn to follow the right path taking his soul upwards to godliness. Here the Guru is also using the term *bhai* to make clear that this fear governs all created things, so that the entire universe functions according to the order prescribed by Him. Things move in accordance with and under His ordinance, or in other words in fear of Him. The winds and the rivers flow without ever deviating from their prescribed courses. It is not open to them to choose some different ways of functioning. His order has prescribed their functioning and only in strict compliance with it do they proceed.

In lines 3 and 4 the Guru in the same context refers to the fire and the earth. He says the fire works for Him *vegār* – a term used in India for free unpaid labour. In the feudalistic social system that prevailed in the Guru's time certain serfs were required to render free service to their liege lord for a certain prescribed time. The *agni* which functions in this world performing diverse tasks, and referred to as a god in the Hindu pantheon, is according to the Guru a mere serf working in accordance with the Lord's commands. The Earth, on which these winds and rivers and the fires are existing, and which is said to carry the *bhār* (weight) of all things created on it by the Lord is also functioning in compliance with the Lord's Will. This is another way of saying that the fire and the Earth which were deified in many religious belief systems are in fact in comparison to the Lord's might mere servants and their powers are no more than the Lord chooses to grant them in His vast scheme of creation.

Lines 5 and 6 refer to Indra and Dharamraj, the two major powers believed in the Hindu pantheon to be most powerful. They are also, says the Guru, functioning under the Lord's Will. Lord Indra is believed in Hinduism to be the king of all the created *Devtas*, the gods and godlings said to number thirty-three crores which means three hundred and thirty millions. He is also the god of rains, wielding the thunderbolt and controlling the clouds. Here the reference to him is as the rain god and he is viewed as the personification of the clouds scurrying overhead. The Guru says Indra in the form of the clouds, scurries headlong in the skies. In the sixth line the Guru refers to Dharamraj and says that he also functions under the Lord's Will. Dharamraj is believed in the Hindu pantheon to be the arbiter of the soul's fate. Thus is he a very important god, and in fact could be called the most important of all gods, because he has been granted power over the human soul after it leaves the body. In the Hindu pantheon he has the power to consign the soul to hell or grant it residence in heaven. His limitations are pointed out here and the Guru says he is no independent authority, but is only a subordinate carrying out the Lord's commandments. His role of arbiter is also thus within the strict confines of what the Lord has prescribed. He is thus in Sikhism not an independent power but a delegate to whom the Lord has assigned the task of keeping track of the deeds of men and giving his judgement within the confines of the Lord's commandments and prescriptions. He functions, says the Guru, in fear of the Lord. Dharamraj's *duār* (court) is also not to be seen as a seat of an independent authority. It also functions under the Lord's writ and thus is in fear of the Lord in the same way.

In lines 7 and 8 the Guru says the Sun and the Moon are in fear of, or in obedience to, His command as they move over *koh karoṛi*– (millions of miles) or in other words over an uncountable distance. *Karoṛ* is an Indian number equal to ten million, while *koh* is a form of *Kos*, an old measure of distance usually equal to a little over two miles. The Sun and the Moon are also considered to be very important gods in the Hindu belief system. In their physical presence on this earth we of course see them moving everyday across the skies, and this process goes on endlessly. This movement, their regular appearance in this world is also in strict accordance with the Lord's ordinance, and is not an expression of their own volition. Over their long, unending paths they move as the Lord has ordered them.

In lines 9 and 10 the Guru says, in fear of God are the *Sidhs*, the *Budhs*, the *Surs*, and the *Nāth*. The skies, the firmament stretching over the earth, are in fear of Him. *Sidh* is a term used for classes of adepts who through yogic practices achieve control over certain mystical powers, which enables them to perform miracles. These powers are called *sidhis* and so the one who has achieved such powers is called a *Sidh*. The heads of the Jain belief system are also called *Sidhs*. *Budh* is a term commonly used to refer to the founder of Buddhism. The term, however, also denotes any enlightened man, a learned man. *Surs* is another name for the *Devtas*, gods and minor godlings in the Hindu belief system. *Nāth* is the term used for the heads of the sects of yogis, or as they are called in the *SGGS*, *jogis*. All these respected and spiritually powerful creatures are not independent powers, says the Guru, but all exist in accordance with His will. The sky overarching the Earth is there in accordance with His will. Since the vault of the sky is another phenomenon that universally evokes wonder and fear among men, the Guru tells us that this too is no independent entity but is there as per His will.

Lines 11 and 12 the Guru says in fear of Him are the warriors and men of great valour; the multitudes being born and dying are all within His ordinance. The movement of living things on this universe is governed strictly by what He has prescribed. We all come when He wills it and we depart this world when He so decides, going the same way without independent volition. In the previous lines the Guru had spoken of many creatures and humans considered powerful. In the same context the category of warriors and heroes is also listed here, because they are also reckoned in ancient times to be as highly exalted in their own way among human beings, as were the *Sidhs*, *Budhs*, *Nāths*, etc.

In line 13 and 14, the Guru concludes by saying that for everyone is this *bhāo*, this fear, prescribed; it is only the Lord Himself who exists outside its domain. This is another way of telling us that in this Universe there is only one Power, the Lord Himself. He underpins all existence, every component of it. All the beings that exist, all the divine ones we imagine to be powerful and as controlling us are nothing but puppets in the hands of that Supreme Power. The Lord has created everything and has then set in place His ordinance, His *Hukam*, the eternal Divine Order. All created beings, and this includes the *Devtas*, as also the supervisory *Devtas*, the holy trinity in Hinduism, Brahma, Vishnu and Mahesh, are now required to function within this ordinance. All of these entities and powers function strictly according to the role assigned to them and none of them can ever go beyond the limits set by the Lord for them. This is the *bhāo*, the *bhai*, the fear spoken of here. It is the fear that keeps every component of this vast creation working in cohesion and co-operating to fulfill the Lord's purpose.

These is of course only one power that falls outside of this set of rules, this *Hukam*, this fear, and that is but the Lord Himself.

Let us now look at the next *slok* where the Guru says:

ਮ: ੧ ॥	M: 1
ਨਾਨਕ ਨਿਰਭਉ ਨਿਰੰਕਾਰੁ ਹੋਰਿ ਕੇਤੇ ਰਾਮ ਰਵਾਲ ॥	Nanak nirbhau nirankār hor ketay rām rawāl
ਕੇਤੀਆ ਕੰਨ੍ ਕਹਾਣੀਆ ਕੇਤੇ ਬੇਦ ਬੀਚਾਰ ॥	Ketīya kanh kahāṇiya ketay beid bīchar
ਕੇਤੇ ਨਚਹਿ ਮੰਗਤੇ ਗਿੜਿ ਮੁੜਿ ਪੂਰਹਿ ਤਾਲ ॥	Ketay nacheh mangtay giṛ muṛ pūreh tāl
ਬਾਜਾਰੀ ਬਾਜਾਰ ਮਹਿ ਆਇ ਕਢਹਿ ਬਾਜਾਰ ॥	Bājāri bājār meh āye kaddheh bājār
ਗਾਵਹਿ ਰਾਜੇ ਰਾਣੀਆ ਬੋਲਹਿ ਆਲ ਪਤਾਲ ॥	Gaveh rajay rāṇīya boleh āl patāl
ਲਖ ਟਕਿਆ ਕੇ ਮੁੰਦੜੇ ਲਖ ਟਕਿਆ ਕੇ ਹਾਰ ॥	Lakh takiya key mundṛay lakh takiya ke hār
ਜਿਤੁ ਤਨਿ ਪਾਈਅਹਿ ਨਾਨਕਾ ਸੇ ਤਨ ਹੋਵਹਿ ਛਾਰ ॥	Jit tann pāīeh Nanka say tann hoveh chhār
ਗਿਆਨੁ ਨ ਗਲੀਈ ਢੂਢੀਐ ਕਥਨਾ ਕਰੜਾ ਸਾਰੁ ॥	Gyan na galīyi ddhūddhīyai kathhna karṛa sār
ਕਰਮਿ ਮਿਲੈ ਤਾ ਪਾਈਐ ਹੋਰ ਹਿਕਮਤਿ ਹੁਕਮੁ ਖੁਆਰੁ ॥੨॥	Karam milai ta pāīai hor hikmat hukam khuar. 2.

Glossary:

ਰਵਾਲ	Rawāl	Dust (hence, insignificant)
ਕੇਤੀਆ	Ketīya	Many
ਕੰਨ੍ ਕਹਾਣੀਆ	Kanh kahāṇiya	Stories of Lord Krishna
ਗਿੜਿ ਮੁੜਿ	Giṛ muṛ	Wheeling, revolving
ਬਾਜਾਰੀ	Bājāri	Mummers, street actors
ਆਲ ਪਤਾਲ	Āl Patāl	Literally, of heavens and nether worlds Hence meaningless babble
ਮੁੰਦੜੇ	Mundṛay	Earrings
ਗਿਆਨੁ	Gyān	Knowledge of the divine
ਗਲੀਈ	Galiyi	Through mere talk, with words

Pauṛi 4

ਸਾਰੁ	Sār	Iron
ਕਰਮਿ	Karam	By Lord's grace
ਹਿਕਮਤਿ	Hikmat	Device; cleverness

The Guru here speaks to us of the uniqueness of the Lord, and of the uselessness of superficial religiosity like performing street plays on religious or mythological subjects as a form of worship. Simply translated this *slok* tells us that only the Formless One is without fear; others, even the likes of Lord Rama are insignificant before Him. The Guru refers to the *Rāslīla* – plays enacted on the lives of the various *Avatārs* in Hinduism – and says that in these are depicted many stories of Lord Krishna and many thoughts from the *Vedas*. Many put on dances for money. Many are the mercenaries who come to the bāzār. Many dress up as kings and queens and babble meaninglessly. They wear ornaments worth lakhs, but forget that the body that they are adorning is destined to be dust. Real knowledge of the Lord will not come through such prattle, because trying to explain it is as tough as chewing on iron. God-realization can come only through His grace and all other devices are of no avail. Let us now look at the lesson in more detail.

The Guru in this *slok* carries forward the message from the previous *pauṛi* which ended with "Nirbhau Nirankār Sach Ek", meaning that only the *Nirankār*, the formless One, the only real Truth, is outside the confines of that fear, that command under which the entire created Universe functions. Now here in the 1st line he says again that the *Nirankār*, the One who is not in need of any one form, is the only one without fear. All others such as the incarnations worshipped on this earth, like Lord Rama, are insignificant in comparison to Him. The Guru is stressing again the uniqueness of the Lord. Elsewhere we have been told that Brahma, Vishnu and Mahesh, the divine trinity who are believed as per the Hindu pantheon to create, maintain and destroy the universe, are the Lord's creations and work in strict obedience to His law. In this context then, Lord Rama who is seen as an incarnation of Lord Vishnu on this earth during the *Treta Yuga* can obviously not be viewed as greater than Vishnu himself. Compared against the ultimate Creator such incarnations then have to be viewed as insignificant. It is never the Guru's style to denigrate anybody's beliefs. Here also he is not trying to run down anybody's belief system, but is only stressing something that is in fact present even in the *Vedas*, that there is but one *Brahm*, the spirit, the Power that becomes the source of all creation. The Guru is only making it clearer and as he has consistently done in the *SGGS*. He says again that only the One, the

Nirankār – the Transcedent, Formless, Unmanifest – is outside of the Divine Command under which the Universe functions. All others, the worshipped deities like Rama, etc. are but dust before Him.

In lines 2 and 3 the Guru says many are the stories of *Kānh*, and many the thoughts in the *Vedas*. Many are the dancers wheeling and whirling as they put on shows with some dressed up as *Kānh*; but in fact they all seek money. As such these performers are no better than beggars. *Kānh, or Kāhan,* is the popular name for Lord Krishna, the *avatār* of Lord Vishnu who came in the *Dwāpar Yuga* and with whose departure that *Yuga* (age) is said to have come to an end and *Kali Yuga* to have commenced. The Guru in these lines is referring to the popular practice where tales from Lord Krishna's life were enacted on the streets by actors dressed up as characters from the life of Lord Krishna, or *Kānh* as he is also called. This was considered a way of worshipping the Lord. The Guru says numerous are such stories of *Kānh*, and many the Vedic thoughts, that are thus enacted by street performers twirling and dancing. The usual method of enacting was that the actors would dress up as mythological characters and perform these religious plays dancing vigorously with steps that involved whirling around. *Pūreh tāl* therefore refers to the beating of the cadence, dancing to a rhythm. The reference to *ketay ved vīchār* (Vedic thought), could have been included, says Bhai Vir Singh, because while enacting these plays the stories from the life of Krishna were often embellished with philosophical observations taken from the *Vedas* and the *Upanishads*. Some learned commentators have however rendered it as referring to the "many systems of Vedic thought", as Prof. Talib has put it; or as Dada Chellaram says, "several the thoughts in the Veda". Macauliffe puts it as, "how many Veds and religious compositions", or alternately as, "how many expound the Veds". In the context here the more appealing interpretation seems to be the more direct one, that the actors recited thoughts from the *Vedas* along with the tales of *Kānh*.

In lines 4 and 5 the Guru says these mercenaries come to the market, the bāzār. They dress up as kings and queens and babble about tales of the heavens and the nether worlds, which is another way of rendering this phrase to say that their talk makes no sense. This is really a continuation of the previous two lines. The actors performing all those elaborate plays are spoken of as *bāzāri* (traders) who have come to the market with their wares, the plays about *Kāhn*, and are trying to earn some money by putting up these plays. There is no real devotion involved and the entire show is but a drama at the end of which the members of the cast would in fact ask for cash from the audience. It was for them merely a way of earning their livelihood. The devotional exercise had turned entirely mercenary. These actors in the course of these displays would dress up as kings and queens and other august characters. This is why the Guru says, "gavay rājay rāniya", meaning kings and queens sing. The Guru adds that they speak *āl patāl* (senseless babble), which is how most learned ones have interpreted it. Prof. Sahib Singh, however, takes *āl* to mean a trick or ruse, and renders *āl patāl* as meaning the deepest trickery. In the context here the rendering of the phrase as 'babble' or 'senseless' seems more appropriate.

In lines 6 and 7 the Guru speaks more on the same theme. He says these actors and role players dress up in what looks like jewellery worth lakhs of rupees, meaning lots of money. But while flaunting this finery they forget that the bodies that are adorned by these expensive jewels worth millions, are fated to soon be ashes. Bhai Vir Singh renders it to say that the reference here is to the jewellery being artificial, because in a street play real jewellery is unlikely to be used. Bhai Sahib further adds that not only is the jewellery false but even the body which is adorned by these is also false or, in other words, ephemeral. Very soon it will be reduced to ashes. The essence of the reference however is that the body is fated to die and this necessary truth is often forgotten by all of us when we become engrossed in pandering to the senses, and the false glitter of worldly wealth.

The message that the Guru is giving us in these lines from 2 to 7 is that this sort of play-acting and such superficial forms of worship so often indulged in, is a false trail and in no way can it take us to God-realization. Bhai Vir Singh, the great mystic, poet, writer and commentator, has a slightly different rendering of these lines that would be useful to look at. As we noted above, Bhai Vir Singh says about line 2 that these actors used to narrate not only stories from the *Purānas* but also would quote the *Upanishads*, which is why the phrase "ketīya kanh kahāṇiya ketay ved vīchār" has been used. The phrase "bāzāri bāzār meh", in line 4 is an allusion, he says, to the practice where traders would gather periodically and a *bāzār* would temporarily come up. According to him the Guru is comparing these actors to the itinerant traders who come briefly only to make some money and then go away. The term *Āl patāl*, in line 5 has also been rendered slightly differently by Bhai Sahib, who says it refers to talking of 'heavens and nether worlds'. However, he also says that this implies that the talk may entertain but is essentially meaningless. Just as the heavens can never meet the nether worlds, in the same way is their talk disjointed. The *rājay rāṇiya* in the same line have been spoken of here because these players, says Bhai Sahib, included tales of religious kings like King Rasāloo, King Bharthari, Queen Loona or Indumati, etc. and these tales were dragged into the plays regardless of whether these were relevant or not. We have of course already discussed the concept in each line already above, including the views of Bhai Sahib here. These do not materially alter the inferences we have drawn for each line, because these are broadly in consonance.

In the last two lines, the 8th and 9th, the central idea of this *slok* has been summed up. The Guru says God-realization will come not from such prattle, saying further that even the describing of it is as difficult as trying to chew iron. Realization will come only through His Blessing and all other devices are of no avail. This is a lesson we have repeatedly been told by the Guru to imbibe, that the Lord is not to be attained through effort or actions; He will only be known to us when He Himself chooses to give us that gift. Having described a commonly pursued practice, of staging religious plays and enacting the roles of ancient kings or mythical *avatārs*, the Guru says all this is pointless prattle. The moment of God-realization is not going to follow from such games and mummery. The realization of the Lord is not to be had, but is a gift that will only come as a measure of grace, as and when He so chooses to bestow it on us. Mere talk of religious things is going to bear no fruit, because even to discourse on the Lord is as difficult as attempting to chew on iron. The Lord alone will determine when to grant to us that moment of enlightenment. His grace is therefore what we must patiently and faithfully wait for, praying for it and striving within our limits to make ourselves ready and worthy of receiving that grace. That requires constant cleansing of the inner self, and strict self-discipline in following the path the Guru prescribes for us. All other *hikmats* (devices, clever ruses) and *hukam* (exercise of our own will, any show of our own strength material or spiritual) is of no avail whatsoever on this path. As Prof. Talib nicely puts it, "All clever devices and forces bring only ignominy."

In the 4th *pauṛi* the Guru says:

ਪਉੜੀ ॥	Pauṛi
ਨਦਰਿ ਕਰਹਿ ਜੇ ਆਪਣੀ ਤਾ ਨਦਰੀ ਸਤਿਗੁਰੁ ਪਾਇਆ ॥	Nadar kareh je āpṇ tā nadri Satgur pāia

Pauṛi 4

ਏਹੁ ਜੀਉ ਬਹੁਤੇ ਜਨਮ ਭਰੰਮਿਆ ਤਾ ਸਤਿਗੁਰਿ ਸਬਦੁ ਸੁਣਾਇਆ ॥	Eh jeeo bahutey janam bharmia ta Satgur sabad suṇāia
ਸਤਿਗੁਰ ਜੇਵਡੁ ਦਾਤਾ ਕੋ ਨਹੀ ਸਭਿ ਸੁਣਿਅਹੁ ਲੋਕ ਸਬਾਇਆ ॥	Satguru jevad dāta ko nahi sabh suṇioh lok sabāia
ਸਤਿਗੁਰਿ ਮਿਲਿਐ ਸਚੁ ਪਾਇਆ ਜਿਨੀ ਵਿਚਹੁ ਆਪੁ ਗਵਾਇਆ ॥	Satgur miliai sach pāia jini vichoh āp gavāia
ਜਿਨਿ ਸਚੋ ਸਚੁ ਬੁਝਾਇਆ ॥੪॥	Jin sacho sach bujhāia. 4.

Glossary:

ਨਦਰਿ	Nadar	His glance of grace
ਨਦਰੀ	Nadari	By His glance of grace
ਭਰੰਮਿਆ	Bharmia	Went on wrong paths
ਸਬਾਇਆ	Sabāia	Entire, all
ਸਚੁ	Sach	Truth, the eternal Lord
ਜਿਨ੍ਹੀ	Jini	Those
ਆਪੁ	Āp	The self, ego
ਬੁਝਾਇਆ	Bujhāia	Explained
ਜਿਨਿ	Jinn	Who (the Guru)

The Guru in this *pauṛi* stresses for us the great importance of the Guru through whom are we going to find the way to the Lord. Simply translated, this *pauṛi* says that if the Lord so blesses us we will find the true preceptor. This soul wandered many births before this grace was granted us to hear the true Guru's word. Let everyone know that there is no greater benefactor than the true Guru. Through good fortune do we find the 'Satguru', and his guidance helps remove the sense of *haumai* from within us, which leads us to the Lord. After we have found the Guru the sense of separateness from the Lord is shed from within and the knowledge of the Truth descends on us. Let us now look at it in more detail.

Having in the *sloks* told us that the Lord will Himself decide when to shower His glance of grace on us and that our efforts, or cleverness or elaborate charades will not reach us to Him, the Guru now in the 1st line recapitulates the concept and restates it for our better understanding. He says that only when the Lord turns His glance of grace on us will we find the true Guru. According to the *Mool Mantra*,

Gur prasād means 'as a benediction from the Guru'. This has repeatedly been reiterated in the *SGGS*. For being put on the correct path we all need a true Guru, a preceptor. The Guru in this line is saying that even finding the true Guru is a blessing from the Lord.

Let us look at this a little more in detail. Since the *SGGS* stresses that the requirement of a Guru is mandatory, there are to be found many in this world claiming to be such Gurus and inviting humans to become their disciples. It is of course not written on anyone's face if the one making such claims is bogus or indeed a true Guru. Sometimes, such true Gurus do indeed exist and those who are lucky enough to find them will be set on the path to making a real success of their human existence. Unfortunately such true ones are few indeed and pretenders are very numerous. This is only to be expected in this material world, because there is power and prestige to be gained in this game. If many adherents are acquired, impressive establishments will soon follow. Large offerings will start pouring in bringing wealth and power. Networks of the financially and politically powerful get created and it all becomes a big business.

There is unfortunately no easy criterion available to determine the real worth of such claimants. Valuable time is, therefore lost by any sincere seeker before reality dawns. At that stage the search starts anew for another Guru. Sometimes an entire lifetime could thus get wasted. As it is, human beings are only too easily beguiled by the glitter of *maya* and the urge towards the spiritual is only rarely to be found. How tragic it is if out of these very few spiritually inclined ones, many are left floundering for want of a true Guru. In the case of a Sikh the Gurus themselves have forever resolved this problem. It has been enjoined upon the Sikh to seek his guidance from the *Shabad*, the word of the Guru, the *Bāṇi*, enshrined in the *Sri Guru Granth Sahib*. The tenth Nanak made this eminently clear to the Sikhs in AD 1708, before he departed from this earth. He prescribed that the *Granth Sahib* shall henceforth, after him, be the Guru. The Sikh, therefore, knows this book by the title *Sri Guru Granth Sahib*. The *Granth* and the Word of the Guru therein, is the Guru for a Sikh. As the Guru says in the *SGGS*, *Rāg Nat Nārāyaṇ*, *Mahla* 4, page 982, "bāṇi Guru, Guru hai bāṇi, vich bāṇi amrit sāray", meaning the *Bāṇi* (Word) is the Guru and the Guru is the Word, contained wherein are all divine qualities and the Name of the Lord. A child born to a Sikh family is thus extremely fortunate in that he need never have to go seeking for Gurus or waste precious time in a morass of sundry religious and spiritual doubts. His Guru is present from the day he comes into this world to the day he departs. It is now up to him to go to this Guru and seek from the word therein the roadmap to salvation. But let there be no doubt, as has been restated in the first line of this *pauṛi*, that the true Guru is a real necessity and such a Guru is to be found only through the Lord's grace.

In the 2nd line the Guru says this soul had wondered through many births before this grace descended and the true Guru's word could be heard. The very fact that we are still in the midst of this cycle of birth and rebirth is proof that we haven't yet heard the true Guru's message. This wandering can end only when we do hear the true Guru and we act on the path he prescribes and thus make ourselves fit and worthy. The moment of salvation will of course still come only when, and if, the Lord so wills. Regarding our own efforts, however strenuous, there are no guarantees that He will deem them worthy. However, if we do not make the effort we will not even be able to come within the zone of consideration, so to say. Without that effort the inner self will never be pure enough to receive the Lord's grace. In that situation we will have to keep moving through the cycle of death and rebirth. At best we may succeed in achieving birth of a superior level, in accordance with the prescription "karmi āvay kapṛa" laid down in the *Japji Sahib* in *pauṛi* 4. Or, of course the opposite could happen and the life we are reborn into could also be worse depending on our *karma* (deeds).

In line 3 the Guru says there is no greater benefactor than the true Guru, and he says "suniyo lok sabāia", meaning let all people know this truth. The Guru is thus proclaiming to the whole world the importance of the true Guru. As Gyani Maskin says, the importance of the Guru is much higher than that of the parents. Parents only bring us into this world, he says, but it is the Guru who finishes this raw material into the shape where it is capable of reaching the Lord, it is worthy enough to receive His grace.

In lines 4 and 5 the Guru says after we have met the true Guru our *haumai*, our sense of self that keeps us separated from the Lord, will vanish. It will be gone because the true Guru sets us on the right path, such that we become worthy of being given the glance of grace by the Lord. The Guru says in this way is the sense of the self lost and the realization of the true Lord dawns upon us. These lines have been rendered in different ways by learned ones. One rendering puts it that when we find the Lord, it follows that we lose the sense of the self. The second view holds, conversely, that because we lose the sense of self through the intermediation, the advice, of the true Guru, the Lord is realized. Thus Bhai Vir Singh says "those who on meeting the true Guru lose their sense of self, their *haumai*, have attained the *Sach* – the Lord. Prof. Sahib Singh says on the other hand, "Those who have lost the sense of self reach the Lord after meeting the true Guru."

Macauliffe has another view of the matter and says, "By meeting the true Guru who hath removed pride from his heart; and who preacheth the Truest of the true, the True one is obtained." Thus he takes a third line and says that the true Guru has eradicated this sense of self from within himself, and so through Him the True One is obtained. Prof. Talib also similarly says, "By touch of the holy Preceptor is obtained Truth. By such as the ego have discarded." Dr. Gopal Singh on the other hand says, "Receiving the Guru, we attain to the Truth and lose our self." Prof. Teja Singh says, "We get the truth by meeting the true Guru who removes all vanity of self from our souls." Dada Chellaram also says the *Satguru* will eradicate all ego from within us. Bhai Manmohan Singh adopts the view that it is the *Satguru* who has removed the 'self-conceit' from within.

Thus, we have three different interpretations; first that on meeting the *Satguru* our *haumai* is destroyed through his guidance and the Lord is realized. Secondly, those who lose the sense of self, reach the Lord through the *Satguru*; and thirdly that the *Satguru*, one who has eradicated the sense of self from within himself, is our medium for reaching the Lord. The more appealing interpretation would seem to be that through good fortune is the *Satguru* found by us, and his guidance helps remove the sense of *haumai* from within us, thus making us suitable to receive the grace of the Lord, which of course will only come when He so chooses. The Guru's prescription that we need a preceptor to set us on the right path would imply that only through the preceptor is the *haumai* lost and not before.

The last line clearly states that the *Satguru* is the one who awakens in us the realization of the Truest of the True, the Lord Himself. As Dr. Gopal Singh says, "Yes, through Him, the Essence of the God's Truth is revealed to us." Though terminology varies yet almost all learned ones have adopted a similar view of this line. It is of course also true that a true preceptor will have shed his own sense of the self, his *haumai*, before he can be a guide to others.

PAURI 5

There are added with this *pauṛi*, two *sloks*, both by Guru Nanak. Both these *sloks* expound further, especially in the second of these, on the subject already referred to in the *sloks* attached with the previous *pauṛi*. The subject is the street shows staged to depict tales of kings and supernatural beings, such as gods and demons. In the first *slok* the Guru says:

ਸਲੋਕ ਮ: ੧	Slok M: 1
ਘੜੀਆ ਸਭੇ ਗੋਪੀਆ ਪਹਰ ਕੰਨ੍ਹ ਗੋਪਾਲ ॥	Ghaṛia sabhay gopīya pahar kanh gopāl
ਗਹਣੇ ਪਉਣੁ ਪਾਣੀ ਬੈਸੰਤਰੁ ਚੰਦੁ ਸੂਰਜੁ ਅਵਤਾਰ ॥	Gahṇay pauṇ paṇi baisantar chand sūraj avatār
ਸਗਲੀ ਧਰਤੀ ਮਾਲੁ ਧਨੁ ਵਰਤਣਿ ਸਰਬ ਜੰਜਾਲ ॥	Sagli Dharti māl dhan vartaṇ sarab janjāl
ਨਾਨਕ ਮੁਸੈ ਗਿਆਨ ਵਿਹੂਣੀ ਖਾਇ ਗਇਆ ਜਮਕਾਲੁ ॥੧॥	Nanak musai gyan vihūṇi khāye gaia jamkāl. 1.

Glossary:

ਘੜੀਆ	Ghaṛīa	Sixtieth part of the day; 24 minutes
ਗੋਪੀਆ	Gopīya	Milkmaids, girls of Vridāvan who were Lord Krishna's friends and playmates
ਪਹਰ	Pahar	Eighth part of the day; 3 hours
ਕੰਨ੍ਹ	Kanh	A name for Lord Krishna

ਗੋਪਾਲ	Gopāl	Keeper of cows, also a name for Lord Krishna
ਬੈਸੰਤਰੁ	Baisantar	Fire
ਮੁਸੈ	Musai	Is being cheated
ਵਿਹੂਣੀ	Vihūṇi	Empty

In this *slok* the Guru alludes to the street plays he had spoken of in the previous *sloks* and says that there is a real play being enacted by the Lord, implying that there is no need to waste time on these dramas and amusements. The real actors putting up this Divine Play are the entities and powers the Lord Himself has created. Simply translated, this brief *slok* says that the quarters of the day are the *Kānhs* and *Gopāls*. The ornaments being used in these plays are the winds and waters. The Sun and the Moon are the real life incarnations, as opposed to the actors donning the costumes of Lord Krishna or Rama. This entire earth is the stage and the things placed on it by the Lord are the stage scenery. Guru Nanak says that all this exists but we are blind to this grand display and for lack of knowledge is the entire world beguiled and led astray. Let us now see it in more detail.

In the 1st and 2nd lines the Guru says that the *gharīs* and the *pahars* – the quarters and the divisions of time – are *Kānhs* and *Gopāls*. The reference is in continuation of the previous *pauṛi* where the *sloks* referred to the incarnations of Lord Vishnu, Rama and Krishna, and then in the next *slok* to *Kānh*, which is another name for Lord Krishna, and Rama. Here continuing to refer to the incarnations, the Guru says in the 2nd line that the Moon and the Sun are the Lord's incarnations. The Guru is in this manner telling us that instead of the street plays where actors enact the roles of divine incarnations we should pay attention to the divine drama being daily played out under the Lord's dispensation. In this play the Sun and the Moon who are marking out the periods of time for us on this earth, act as the *Avatārs* and the hours and quarters of the day act as the other members of the cast. The Guru adds to the above picture by saying that these actors, placed b[illegible]ord on this earth, are adorned by the jewellery consisting of the winds, the w[illegible]nd fire. Thus is this divine, regularly enacted play, which should rightly engro[illegible] and within it must we look for the Lord.

In the 3rd line the Guru says this Earth itself provides the stage on which this entire divine drama takes place. The things placed by the Lord on this earth are the accoutrements, the background scenery, and the stage properties that are being used for that play. The drama inherent in the everyday dealings between humans provides the screenplay, the script for this drama.

In the concluding, the 4th line, the Guru says when they lack the knowledge of the Lord then is entire mankind beguiled and led astray. The Guru further says that Time, acting as the agent of Death, eats up all that exists.

Thus, we will note that the Guru speaks here to us of the meaningless dramas and plays depicting the ancient kings and avatars being enacted by professional actors for the amusement of the public. He is telling us that the true knowledge of the Divine, the inner enlightenment cannot come from such mummery. He then compares this play-acting with the actual Divine drama that all of us are witness to every day of our lives. The play of Time, with those major markers of its passage the Sun and the Moon dividing up our days and nights, is now brought home to us. In this Divine play the hours and the passing *ghaṛīs* and *pahars* are the actor playing the role of Kahan and of his famous playmates the *gopāls* – cowherds, and the *gopīs* - milkmaids. The endowments the Lord has gifted to all beings in the form of the Winds, the Waters, the Fire and all the other precious things of this earth constitute the stage scenery, the costumes for the characters. Beguiled by all this entrancing play of nature and of time, and with human interactions providing the story line; the human beings can be truly lost, says the Guru, if they do not seek the only really important goal, the knowledge of the Lord. In the absence of this enlightenment the life of the beguiled human is wasted and is just eaten up by Time, the agent of Death.

Prof. Talib renders the concluding lines as, "The whole world is wealth and property – Attachment to it leads to involvement in Yama's snare, saith Nanak. Mankind bereft of enlightenment is being robbed by Yama, agent of death, who destroys it." Dr. Gopal Singh renders it as, "And all the earth dances with myriads of men embellished with their riches, playing many, many parts. But without wisdom, one is beguiled, and the Yama of Time wastes one's life away." Macauliffe puts it as, "The whole earth your stage properties and vessels which are all entanglements. Nanak, they who are devoid of divine knowledge are robbed, the minister of death hath devoured them." Thus, the learned commentators, while differing slightly in their approach, are essentially agreed on the interpretation of the concept here, that the Divine Play enacted by the forces of Nature will remind us of the Lord much more convincingly and the street plays are nothing but means of mere passing enjoyment for the audience, and a livelihood for the cast. The only difference in interpretation is regarding the term *vartaṇ* which most have taken to mean 'interaction' but Macauliffe views it as 'vessel' from the Punjabi word *Bartan*. This however does not seem very convincing. Interaction is the more appropriate rendering for *vartaṇ*.

The Guru in the next *slok* reverts to the theme of the plays regarding the *avatārs*, which formed the subject matter of the second *slok* of the previous *pauṛi*. Here he says:

ਮ: ੧ ॥	M: 1
ਵਾਇਨਿ ਚੇਲੇ ਨਚਨਿ ਗੁਰ ॥	Vayin chelay nachan gur
ਪੈਰ ਹਲਾਇਨਿ ਫੇਰਨਿ੍ ਸਿਰ ॥	Paer halāyan pheran Sirr
ਉਡਿ ਉਡਿ ਰਾਵਾ ਝਾਟੈ ਪਾਇ ॥	Udd udd rāva jhātai pāye
ਵੇਖੈ ਲੋਕੁ ਹਸੈ ਘਰਿ ਜਾਇ ॥	Vekhai lok hasai ghar jāye
ਰੋਟੀਆ ਕਾਰਣਿ ਪੂਰਹਿ ਤਾਲ ॥	Rottīya kāraṇ pūreh tāl
ਆਪੁ ਪਛਾੜਹਿ ਧਰਤੀ ਨਾਲਿ ॥	Āp pachhāreh dharti nāl
ਗਾਵਨਿ ਗੋਪੀਆ ਗਾਵਨਿ ਕਾਨ੍ ॥	Gāvan gopīya gāvan kānh
ਗਾਵਨਿ ਸੀਤਾ ਰਾਜੇ ਰਾਮ ॥	Gāvan sīta rājay rām
ਨਿਰਭਉ ਨਿਰੰਕਾਰੁ ਸਚੁ ਨਾਮੁ ॥	Nirbhau nirankār such nām
ਜਾ ਕਾ ਕੀਆ ਸਗਲ ਜਹਾਨੁ ॥	Ja ka kīya sagal jahān
ਸੇਵਕ ਸੇਵਹਿ ਕਰਮਿ ਚੜਾਉ ॥	Sevak seveh karam chaṛāo
ਭਿੰਨੀ ਰੈਣਿ ਜਿਨ੍ਾ ਮਨਿ ਚਾਉ ॥	Bhinni raiṇ jinha mann chāu
ਸਿਖੀ ਸਿਖਿਆ ਗੁਰ ਵੀਚਾਰਿ ॥	Sikhi sikhiya gur vīchār
ਨਦਰੀ ਕਰਮਿ ਲਘਾਏ ਪਾਰਿ ॥	Nadri karam laghāye pār
ਕੋਲੂ ਚਰਖਾ ਚਕੀ ਚਕੁ ॥	Kolu charkhā chakki chakk
ਥਲ ਵਾਰੋਲੇ ਬਹੁਤੁ ਅਨੰਤੁ ॥	Thhull varolay bahut anant
ਲਾਟੂ ਮਾਧਾਣੀਆ ਅਨਗਾਹ ॥	Lātū madhāṇīya angāh
ਪੰਖੀ ਭਉਦੀਆ ਲੈਨਿ ਨ ਸਾਹ ॥	Pankhi bhaudīa lain na sāh
ਸੂਐ ਚਾੜਿ ਭਵਾਈਅਹਿ ਜੰਤ ॥	Suai chāṛ bhavāīeh jant
ਨਾਨਕ ਭਉਦਿਆ ਗਣਤ ਨ ਅੰਤ ॥	Nanak bhaudia gaṇat na unt
ਬੰਧਨ ਬੰਧਿ ਭਵਾਏ ਸੋਇ ॥	Bandhan bandh bhavāiey soye

Pauṛi 5

ਪਇਐ ਕਿਰਤਿ ਨਚੈ ਸਭੁ ਕੋਇ ॥	Paiey kirat nachai sabh koey
ਨਚਿ ਨਚਿ ਹਸਹਿ ਚਲਹਿ ਸੇ ਰੋਇ ॥	Nach nach haseh chaleh say roye
ਉਡਿ ਨ ਜਾਹੀ ਸਿਧ ਨ ਹੋਹਿ ॥	Udd na jāhi sidh na hohe
ਨਚਣੁ ਕੁਦਣੁ ਮਨ ਕਾ ਚਾਉ ॥	Nachaṇ kudaṇ mann ka chāo
ਨਾਨਕ ਜਿਨ੍ ਮਨਿ ਭਉ ਤਿਨ੍ਾ ਮਨਿ ਭਾਉ ॥੨॥	Nanak jinn mann bhau tina man bhāo. 2.

Glossary:

ਵਾਇਨਿ	Vāyin	Playing (an instrument)
ਰਾਵਾ	Rāwa	Dust
ਝਾਟੈ	Jhātai	In the hair
ਪੂਰਹਿ ਤਾਲ	Pūreh tāl	Dance to the beat
ਕਰਮਿ	Karam	Lord's grace
ਚੜਾਉ	Charāo	High spirits
ਥਲ ਵਾਰੋਲੇ	Thhull varolay	Whirlwinds in the desert
ਗੁਰ ਵੀਚਾਰਿ	Gur vīchār	Reflecting on the Guru; deep thinking
ਕੋਲੂ	Kolu	The oil press
ਚਰਖਾ	Charkha	Spinning wheel
ਮਾਧਾਣੀਆ	Madhāṇia	Churning staves
ਅਨਗਾਹ	Angāh	Corn threshers
ਸੂਐ	Suai	Stake, wooden pike
ਸਿਧ	Sidh	An adept in yogic achievements

Speaking further on the subject of the street plays the Guru now graphically depicts what transpires during the staging of these. Simply translated this *slok* says that disciples play music and their gurus dance. This raises dust that falls on their heads. People watch and go back amused and with a laugh. For the sake of money are they beating the cadence and throwing themselves on the ground. Posing as *Kānhs* and *Gopīs*, as Rām and Sīta, they sing. The Lord is True, Formless and without fear; and the entire creation is His doing. The Lord's servant blessed with His grace serves Him, and in the bedewed night is their mind filled with elation. Such teaching comes from the Guru's guidance, and we learn that only by the Lord's grace is liberation found. Alluding to the whirling of the actors in the plays the Guru says that in real life we can find many things that whirl. Thus the oilmill, the spinning wheel, the flourmill and the potter's wheel are all continously spinning. The whirlwinds in the deserts are uncountable, the tops, the churning rod, the threshers for foodgrains; all these whirl in the Lord's play. The birds in the sky circle endlessly, without pause. Birds tied to the pike for amusement are made to twirl. There is no count of things in nature and in everyday life that we can find whirling. Bound by our actions, even we are in the circle of rebirths. Those who waste their time in these pointless amusements, and laugh and dance will in the end weep. No one is elevated or is enlightened by such dancing around, which is merely entertainment for the senses. Those who have fear of the Lord in their hearts will have love for Him. Let us now look at it in more detail.

In lines 1 and 2 of this *slok* the Guru refers again to the street plays he had spoken of in the previous *sloks*. He says that in these dramas we see some actors made up as disciples play the musical instruments, while some others dressed up as gurus dance to that music. They move their feet to the rhythm of the music and also sway their heads.

In lines 3 and 4 the Guru says, as these dancers put up their show and are jumping around the dust from beneath their feet rises and falls on their own heads. People watching the show, are amused by it and at the end of it they just go home. That is the extremely limited importance that people really give to these dramas. These are nothing for them but a way of passing some idle time and finding some casual amusement.

In lines 5 and 6 he says these actors go through these gyrations, flinging themselves around and even falling on the ground. And all this strenuous exertion is nothing but merely a device to earn a living. No devotion could possibly be evoked in the minds of the onlookers, because they are only too well aware that all this dancing and jumping around is a purely mercenary activity. People watching it are therfore not impressed and in fact find it funny the way the heads of there actors get smeared with the dust that the stamping of their own feet has raised. Nor are the actors bothered if anyone is moved to devotion or not. Their interest in the proceedings is limited strictly to how much money they can hope to cadge out of the audience, or how much are the organizers paying them. All this elaborate play acting is nothing but a meaningless charade.

In lines 7 and 8 the Guru further describes the scenes from such a play. He says in these plays the actors sing while made up as *gopīs*, the milkmaids of *Vrindāvan* who were such prominent participants in these *Rāsalīlas*, which are supposed to depict the amorous sport of Lord Krishna with the *gopīs* and is viewed in Hinduism as an example of the love of the human for the Divine. In the play-acting of these *līlas* there would be one actor dressed up as *Kānh* or Lord Krishna. Others would be posing as the *gopīs*. Actors, in some other shows would in like manner dress up to represent Sīta and her husband, King Rama. The actors dressed up in this fashion would then sing and play out the stories from the *Purānas*. All this, suggests the Guru, is a hollow and empty show.

In lines 9 and 10 he pauses in this description to tell us that the real devotees sing not in this fashion; rather do they worship the one Lord, who is without fear and is the Formless One; the only Real Truth; the One who has created the entire Universe. The Guru is here continuing this juxtapositioning of the play-acting of these dramas with the real play that the Nature created by the Lord Himself is staging for us everyday. As the Guru has said in the previous *slok*, we should fix our minds on the divine drama, and only then will we be able to evoke in our hearts the proper devotion, and then will we learn to worship the Lord who is staging that grand show for us. The worldly shows with actors seeking to make money for themselves are but a shoddy substitute, evoking at best amusement among the audience.

In line 11 and 12, the Guru says that only those who are blessed by the Lord's glance of grace are lucky enough to serve Him, their life passes in joy. Here again the Guru aims to highlight the contrast between these genuine devotees and the participants in the other type of play-acting of the mercenary actors. These lucky ones serve Him because they have been lucky enough to be bestowed His grace. They serve because their hearts are full of love for Him, and in their minds is the urge to follow the path that leads to Him. And it is not for considerations of money or amusement that they go through the acts of devotion. So their minds are filled with pleasure because their service is from the heart. On the other hand are those who, the Guru says, are merely play-acting and deservedly have the dust thrown on their heads from their own dancing. They are the ones who painfully throw themselves around on the ground, all for the sake of earning a little money.

Gyani Sant Singh Maskin, in his audio-commentary, puts it well when he says that those who serve Him do so because the Lord's grace is upon them. In other words, even meditating on His Name comes only as a result of His blessing. So, let no one feel proud if he is lucky enough to be on the Guru's path. Prof. Talib has rendered line 12 as, "In the dew-drenched cool night are their hearts filled with ecstasy." Macauliffe puts it slightly differently as, "Pleasant is the night for those who long for Him in their hearts." Prof. Teja Singh also uses the same terms except that for the first word he says 'dewy' instead of 'pleasant'. Gyani Maskin however elaborates it a bit and renders it as meaning that these lucky ones rise from sleep in the ambrosial hours of the morning when the night is bedewed. They awaken, he says, not only physically but they also rouse their inner consciousness. Then they meditate on the teachings given to them by the Guru.

In lines 13 and 14 the Guru says that only through deep reflection on the teaching of the Guru does it become clear to the devotee that the passage from this world across the unknown can be safely traversed through the Lord's grace. The two points stressed are, firstly that we have to carefully imbibe the Guru's teaching and contemplate on the message. The second point is that the fearful chasm between this world and the next will then be easily crossed by the Lord's grace. He Himself will pull us across. Thus, the passage is crossed only by His grace, and this knowledge comes from the Guru. The importance of the Guru's teaching has been highlighted here, and this is in tune with the message often repeated that by Lord's grace is the true Guru found, and such a one will help us reach the Lord.

In lines 15 and 16 the Guru returns to the theme of the street plays where the actors are to be seen dancing about. He says if whirling and dancing in the manner of these actors is what we are looking for, then just look around and see how many of God's created things are performing this dance on this earth. He says just see how the *kolu* (oil mill) revolves constantly. An oil mill is the classic example often quoted when the image of a repetitive, circular motion is to be conveyed. The other common example is the *charkhā* (spinning wheel) which in the Guru's time was the most common item to be seen in the village household and was used to spin yarn. It lends itself easily to such imagery because it rotates fast and non-stop as it is worked to spin yarn from cotton. The next examples given are of the *chakki* (flour mill) and the *chakk* (potter's wheel). These rotate and spin constantly as the mills grind cereals and the potter shapes the earth and clay around the spinning axis. Further, the Guru says, there are in the deserts whirlwinds skittering about, rotating hard. All these whirling things continuously spinning somewhere are too numerous to count, says the Guru. In other words, the Guru is telling us that if whirling, dancing figures are what attracts the ignorant to these plays staged by mercenaries, then there are bigger and grander dances being enacted throughout Nature in the mystical play being staged by the Lord all over this earth. Of course only those who by the Lord's grace are enlightened are able to see this play for the divine drama it really is.

In lines 17 and 18 the Guru continues the count of things dancing in Nature's play. The Guru says the *latū* (top) used by chidren as spinning toys are whirling. So are the *madhāṇiya* (churning staves) used for producing butter from milk in households everywhere. The *angāh* (threshing circles) made for crops to be winnowed in rural areas, are also witness to constant rotation as the cattle move around the winnowing circle. Finally, the Guru evokes for us the image of the birds in the sky who circle constantly as they seek prey or food. They do so without tiring and do not even pause for breath says the Guru.

In lines 19 and 20 another example from everyday existence is given. It was the practice at that time to stake parrots and other birds to a stick like a pike, with a cord and get them to fly for the amusement of onlookers. This naturally led to their twirling in a circle around the stick to which the cord was tied. The Guru now sums up and says in line 20 that the examples can be endlessly extended, and that there is no end to the circling and whirling that Nature shows us at all times within God's created world. Though not expressly stated, the thought is implicit in these examples that the human soul itself is swung round a circle of births and deaths. The Guru in the next line, the 21st, now expresses this more explicitly.

In lines 21 and 22 the Guru speaks of the fate of the human. Prof. Talib has nicely rendered the 21st line as, "All bound in bonds of their deeds are whirling along." The Guru is here telling us that this cycle in which the soul is trapped is an outcome of our own past deeds, our own actions in this world, this *karam bhūmi* (field of action). The Lord has placed us here for the precise purpose of testing our mettle. We are required to strive against the evil within us, and if we succeed in overcoming it, we will be giving ourselves a chance to move out of this cycle, to be liberated, subject of course to the Lord's pleasure. Dr. Gopal Singh puts it slightly differently as, "He the Lord binds man to Bondage, within it do we all move, And, as is the Lord's writ, so do we all dance." This rendering seems to somewhat underplay the importance of man's own actions and seems to shift responsibility from our own selves to the Lord, thus giving a more deterministic tinge to this cycle. Since good and proper conduct in accordance with the Guru's prescription is what we are being repeatedly told to observe, the view adopted by most commentators that we are in this cycle because we are bound by our actions, seems the more appealing interpretation.

In lines 23 and 24 the Guru says those who got too engrossed in the play of this world and laughed at the play of the material things will go weeping from here. They are not elevated, *ud na jāhī* he says, nor do they become *sidh* (adepts). The Guru had in the previous lines spoken extensively on the street plays. The reference here is again to these dramas, or *Rās* as it is called popularly. The Rās where stories of Lord Krishna and Lord Rama are enacted are called respectively *Rāsalīla* or *Krishnalīla*, and *Rāmlīla*. The aim of participating in these, or watching these, is to attain spiritual enlightenment. The Guru presents the real picture of these in this *slok* and shows these to be what they really are – just a bunch of humans dressed up as gods, etc. and performing dramas and dances purely as a means of livelihood. These, says the Guru, are mere amusements and some may be able to laugh at what they see but no real spiritual success can be achieved through these. Contrasted with these is the real divine drama the Lord has put in place, which is constantly being enacted, as the Guru told us in the earlier lines of this *slok*. A true involvement in this divine play, with devotion in the heart and knowledge acquired from the true Guru to guide us, is the real way to enlightenment. The ones who are involved in this world's plays may today be able to find amusement and laugh, but they will have to weep when it is time to depart from here. At that time only will they become aware that these amusements did not in any way uplift them spiritually and they really acquired nothing of any lasting value. The phrase "sidh na hoye" has been interpreted as "do not become adepts" by most commentators, including Bhai Vir Singh. He however also offers another view and says these *Rāsalīlas* are supposed to help achieve access to the higher realms of the gods, and then in the final analysis, salvation. He says the phrase "Udd na jaī" thus means you cannot fly up to these realms through this device; nor is the ultimate aim of salvation likely to be fulfilled – which is another way to interpret the phrase "sidh na hoye". Here Bhai Vir Singh takes *sidh* in its sense of 'achieve' or 'fulfil'. Prof. Talib has rendered this line as, "To no destination can they rise nor achieve fulfillment". Dr. Gopal Singh says, "They fly not thereby (into the heavens) nor become the ascesties." Dada Chellaram renders "sidh na hoye" as "do not become perfect". On balance, however, the rendering of this phrase as "do not become adepts" seems more appropriate here.

In the concluding lines, the 25th and 26th, the Guru sums it up to say that all this dancing around may please the mind, the senses but the Lord is reached only by these who through fear of God have acquired great love for Him. Prof. Talib puts it well when he says, "Such dancing and capering is only expression of the mind's passion: Saith Nanak: those that bear fear of God in mind, alone have love for God." Bhai Vir Singh says the reference here is to these actors who staged the *Rāsalīla*. He, therefore, takes these lines to mean that the dancing and prancing by those actors is not really an expression of any real devotion on their part, rather is it for satisfying their own personal purposes. Devotion requires love, respect and awe while these actors impersonating their gods repeatedly will lose any respect for them, and will also lose all fear of them. Guru Nanak here is saying that for love for the Lord to develop in the heart, there has to be fear and respect for Him. Almost all the learned commentators have followed this interpretation of the last line.

In the 5th *pauṛi*, the Guru says:

ਪਉੜੀ ॥	Pauṛi
ਨਾਉ ਤੇਰਾ ਨਿਰੰਕਾਰੁ ਹੈ ਨਾਇ ਲਇਐ ਨਰਕਿ ਨ ਜਾਈਐ ॥	Nau tera nirankār hai naye laiey narak na jaiyai
ਜੀਉ ਪਿੰਡੁ ਸਭੁ ਤਿਸ ਦਾ ਦੇ ਖਾਜੈ ਆਖਿ ਗਵਾਈਐ ॥	Jiu pind sabh tis da de khājai ākh gavāīai
ਜੇ ਲੋੜਹਿ ਚੰਗਾ ਆਪਣਾ ਕਰਿ ਪੁੰਨਹੁ ਨੀਚੁ ਸਦਾਈਐ ॥	Jey loṛeh changa āpṇa kar punhu nīch sadaīai
ਜੇ ਜਰਵਾਣਾ ਪਰਹਰੈ ਜਰੁ ਵੇਸ ਕਰੇਦੀ ਆਈਐ ॥	Jey jarwāṇa parharai jar ves karedi āiyai
ਕੋ ਰਹੈ ਨ ਭਰੀਐ ਪਾਈਐ ॥੫॥	Ko rahai na bhariai paiai. 5.

Glossary:

ਪਿੰਡੁ	Pindd	The body
ਖਾਜੈ ।	Khājai	Food, sustenance
ਕਰਿ ਪੁੰਨਹੁ	Kar punhu	After doing good
ਜਰਵਾਣਾ	Jarwāṇa	Aging process
ਜਰੁ	Jarr	Old age
ਭਰੀਐ	Bhariai	Is filled
ਪਾਈਐ	Pāeeai	The *pāee*, a small measure of volume

The Guru has instructed us, in the sloks above, on how inappropriate and inadequate a form of worship are these shows and dramas depicting the gods. The Guru now, in the 5th *pauṛi*, teaches us about the spiritual aspects of the matter. He is saying that the plays, the dramas, staged may be meant to worship the physical forms of the Lord, but He is the *Nirankār* (Formless One). He is in that form the proper object for our worship. Recitation of His Name is the real way to worship Him, he tells us in this *pauṛi*. The Guru also implies here that the play actors are really seeking monetary reward, while the proper way of living is to honestly earn one's livelihood, and then share from it with those less fortunate; and that too without any sense of pride in giving to others. Think of everything as belonging to the Lord, so that what we give also really belongs to Him, and what is retained is His also. Simply translated this *pauṛi* says that the Name of the Lord is the Formless One and if we recite His Name we do not go to hell. All that exists belongs to Him, so share it but while doing so do not boast of giving lest you lose all the merit from it. If we seek to be gainers for ourselves then we must do pious deeds but remain humble about it. Humans are bound to go from this world, and old age, and then death, will come to all of us. We must not attempt the futility of seeking to evade it. If we find one method of doing so it will just find another route to catch us. When the measure of our allotted life is filled we will have to go from this earth. The Guru is implying that we must take His Name while we have the opportunity, because the opportunity is brief indeed. Do not be diverted by empty amusements such as, for instance, as the Guru earlier pointed out, plays of gods and kings staged by paid actors. Fix your mind instead on the Formless One. Let us now look at this lesson in more detail.

In the first line the Guru says the Lord's Name is the Formless One and if we meditate on His Name we will not go to hell. The context for this is to be found in what has been stated in the previous *sloks*. There we were told staging *Rāsalīlas* and putting on shows and dramas, with humans playing the roles of gods and their incarnations will avail us nothing. The Guru had stated in the previous *slok*, "Nirbhau Nirankār sach nām, ja ka kia sagal jahān", meaning the one without fear is the Formless One, whose Name is the only Truth and who is the Creator of the entire Universe. The same theme is stressed here. Since all that is visible, or has form is liable to destruction and will cease one day to exist, offering worship to such ephemeral things will take us nowhere. So, he says addressing the Lord, "Your Name is the Formless One and by taking that Name we will go not to Hell." The hell spoken of here is the torment of being distanced from the Lord. Wrong living takes us away from Him, and by right living which requires above all the recitation of the Name, we can hope to come nearer to Him. Our actions will determine this. As the Guru said in the concluding *slok* of the *Japji Sahib*, "karmi āpo āpṇi kay nerrey kay dūre", meaning some are near and some are distanced, based on the merits of their own actions. Thus, our own choice of which path to follow can give us the heaven of being with Him, or the hell of being distanced and being thrown into the inexorable cycle of births.

In the 2nd line the Guru says this body, and in fact everything that we have, is a gift from the Lord, and we should share the gifts He has bestowed on us, but we must make sure that when we do so we must never then brag about it, because such boasting is borne of our ego and it loses us all merit. There are small differences among the learned ones in the interpretation of this line, especially about the phrase *De khājai*. Bhai Vir Singh puts it in the sense that since all we have is the Lord's we should share with others before we eat. Having given, we must not say it is we who give, because it all belongs to the Lord and was not ours to give. If we commit the mistake of so boasting then any merit we may have earned from the sharing will be lost. The *Shabdarth* of the *SGPC* also sees it that way. Prof. Sahib Singh however puts it slightly differently. He says that the Lord gives this body and soul and He is giving sustenance to all His creation; and to try and guess just how much is He giving is a useless task. Prof. Talib renders it as, "This life and body all is His. Receive what He grants – to argue further is of no avail." Dr. Gopal Singh says, "When Thou art our body and soul, to ask therefore sustenance is to waste one's breath." Macauliffe puts it as, "… What Thou giveth man eateth: to say aught else were waste of words." Dada Chellaram and Prof. Teja Singh take the line adopted by Bhai Vir Singh and render it as saying that we should share with others but talk not about it. Gyani Maskin has also in his audio-commentary taken a similar view. Both renderings obviously have merit; however, the view taken by Bhai Vir Singh, the *Shabdarth* and Gyani Maskin seems more convincing. Thus, it would imply that all we have, including our own very selves, belongs to the Lord. We must therefore treat everything we own as His property on which others, as the children of the one Lord, also have rights. Give feely therefore of what you have and share the Lord's gifts with all. Do not however make the mistake of presuming that what you are giving is charity, or that it was at all yours to give. If you make the mistake of talking about it, boasting of your philanthropy then all merit is lost.

In the 3rd line the Guru confirms the above interpretation when he says if you seek your own good then do good to others, but do not seek to be lauded for your goodness; stay humble. On the interpretation of this line there are no differences of view among the learned commentators. The Guru's message is here two-fold. Firstly, as he said in the previous line, we need to always share what we have because it, in any case, belongs to the Lord. Secondly, we must not let pride overtake us when we have thus shared. The good that we do for others will avail us only if does not evoke pride and vanity within us, and therefore does not go to feed our *haumai*. As the Guru told as in the *Japji Sahib* and also repeatedly in the SGGS it is *haumai*, our ego, our sense of selfness as being separate from the Lord, that keeps us from reaching Him, from realizing that He is in fact with us at all times. Therefore humility and non-possessiveness, an absence of avarice is often stressed by the Guru, as in this line, as vital to our spiritual well being.

In the 4th line, the Guru says if you think you can evade the ravages of time you will soon realize the error of your assumption. Time is the master of all created beings and it is only the Lord Himself who is *akāl* – beyond the control of Time. Thus, for humans Time will have its way, if not in one manifestation then in another guise. As Bhai Vir Singh says, now is the time to meditate on His Name, and to give to others who are in need. Do not think that inexorable Time will spare you, for you can see that the indications of its advent are apparent in many ways already and there is nothing you can do to stop the inroads of Time. For example, white hair may again be dyed black, but that is deluding yourself and does not defeat Time, because its ravages will come at you in many other ways, such that you will never be able to fight them all. When the measure of your life has been taken by Time you will have to go from this world. Most commentators have taken the more direct meaning of this line. For example, Macauliffe says, "Even if you stave of old age, it shall come to thee in the guise of death." Prof. Talib changes it slightly to say, "Know that old age with its new attire is approaching." Dr. Gopal Singh also follows the view taken by Bhai Vir Singh as we have discussed above and this would seem here the most appealing.

In the concluding line the Guru sums up and says that when the measure of life is full we will have to depart. The wood *Pāee* refers to a small measure used in older times for measuring foodgrains. Weights were not always reliable and so the system was to measure grain by volume, for which three common measures existed, called the *pāee* the *paropa*, and the *topa* in ascending order, the *pāee* being the smallest. In order to make the message clear even to the less educated among his audience the Guru has adopted this commonly used rustic term. He is telling us that our allotted time is little, our span being like the *pāee*, soonest filled. Once the *pāee* is full it has to be emptied if we are to use it again. Similarly, when the *pāee* the allotted span is filled, wewill have to go away from this world.

The message to imbibe is that all the good we can possibly do, all the reciting of His Name we can undertake has to be completed within this short span allotted to us; for soon will our *pāee*. be full and the game will be over. It is because of this very quality of shortness that our life, that our sojourn on this earth is so precious. That is why the Guru has said elsewhere, "Bhaee prāpat mānukh dehuria, Gobind milan ki eh teri baria", meaning you have been given this human form as a precious gift as a special opportunity so that you can strive your very best to try and achieve union with the Lord. The Guru is stressing the point that the opportunity is brief indeed, utilise it fully. Do not be diverted by empty amusements such as, for instance, as the Guru earlier pointed out, plays of gods and kings staged by paid actors. Fix your mind instead on the Formless One.

PAUṚI 6

This *pauṛi* like the previous one also has two *sloks* added, both by Guru Nanak. The first one says:

ਸਲੋਕ ਮ: ੧ ॥	Slok Mahla 1
ਮੁਸਲਮਾਨਾ ਸਿਫਤਿ ਸਰੀਅਤਿ ਪੜਿ ਪੜਿ ਕਰਹਿ ਬੀਚਾਰੁ ॥	Musalmāna sipht sarīyat paṛ paṛ kareh bīchār
ਬੰਦੇ ਸੇ ਜਿ ਪਵਹਿ ਵਿਚਿ ਬੰਦੀ ਵੇਖਣ ਕਉ ਦੀਦਾਰੁ ॥	Banday say jay paveh vich bandi vekhaṇ kau dīdār
ਹਿੰਦੂ ਸਾਲਾਹੀ ਸਾਲਾਹਨਿ ਦਰਸਨਿ ਰੂਪਿ ਅਪਾਰੁ ॥	Hindu sālāhi sālāhan darsan rūp apār
ਤੀਰਥਿ ਨਾਵਹਿ ਅਰਚਾ ਪੂਜਾ ਅਗਰ ਵਾਸੁ ਬਹਕਾਰੁ ॥	Tīrath nāveh archa pūja agar wās bahkār
ਜੋਗੀ ਸੁੰਨਿ ਧਿਆਵਨ੍ਹਿ ਜੇਤੇ ਅਲਖ ਨਾਮੁ ਕਰਤਾਰੁ ॥	Jogi sunn dhiāwan jetay alakh nām kartār
ਸੂਖਮ ਮੂਰਤਿ ਨਾਮੁ ਨਿਰੰਜਨ ਕਾਇਆ ਕਾ ਆਕਾਰੁ ॥	Sūkham mūrat nām niranjan kāia ka akār
ਸਤੀਆ ਮਨਿ ਸੰਤੋਖੁ ਉਪਜੈ ਦੇਣੈ ਕੈ ਵੀਚਾਰਿ ॥	Satīya mann santokh upjai denai kai vīchār
ਦੇ ਦੇ ਮੰਗਹਿ ਸਹਸਾ ਗੂਣਾ ਸੋਭ ਕਰੇ ਸੰਸਾਰੁ ॥	Day Day mangay sahsa gūṇa sobh karay sansār
ਚੋਰਾ ਜਾਰਾ ਤੈ ਕੂੜਿਆਰਾ ਖਾਰਾਬਾ ਵੇਕਾਰ ॥	Chora jara tai kūṛiāra khārāba vekār
ਇਕਿ ਹੋਦਾ ਖਾਇ ਚਲਹਿ ਐਥਾਊ ਤਿਨਾ ਭਿ ਕਾਈ ਕਾਰ ॥	Ik hoda khāye chaleh aithāū tinā bhi kāyi kār
ਜਲਿ ਥਲਿ ਜੀਆ ਪੁਰੀਆ ਲੋਆ ਆਕਾਰਾ ਆਕਾਰ ॥	Jall thhall jīya purīya loā ākāra ākār

ਓਇ ਜਿ ਆਖਹਿ ਸੁ ਤੂੰਹੈ ਜਾਣਹਿ ਤਿਨਾ ਭਿ ਤੇਰੀ ਸਾਰ ॥	Oe ji ākheh su tūnhai jāṇeh tina bhi teri sār
ਨਾਨਕ ਭਗਤਾ ਭੁਖ ਸਾਲਾਹਣੁ ਸਚੁ ਨਾਮੁ ਆਧਾਰੁ ॥	Nanak bhakta bhukh sālahaṇ sach nam ādhār
ਸਦਾ ਅਨੰਦਿ ਰਹਹਿ ਦਿਨੁ ਰਾਤੀ ਗੁਣਵੰਤਿਆ ਪਾ ਛਾਰੁ ॥੧॥	Sada ānand raheh din rāti guṇvantiya pa chhār. 1.

Glossary:

ਸਰੀਅਤਿ	Sarīyat	The Sharia, Muslim religious code
ਬੰਦੀ	Bandee	(Here) in accordance with the Sharia
ਦਰਸਨਿ	Darsan	Philosophy, Hindu religious thought
ਸਾਲਾਹੀ	Sālāhi	Worthy of respect (here, the Lord)
ਅਰਚਾ	Archā	Worship
ਅਗਰ ਵਾਸੁ	Agar wās	Incense
ਬਹਕਾਰੁ	Bahkār	Scent
ਸੁੰਨਿ	Sunn	A state of stillness
ਸੂਖਮ	Sūkham	Fine, beyond the five senses
ਸਤੀਆ	Satīa	Philanthropists
ਸਹਸਾ ਗੂਣਾ	Sahsā guṇa	A thousand times
ਜਾਰਾ	Jāra	Adulterer
ਕੂੜਿਆਰਾ	Kūṛiāra	Purveyors of untruth
ਕਾਈ ਕਾਰ	Kāyi kār	Some service
ਆਕਾਰਾ ਆਕਾਰ	Ākāra ākār	Visible universe
ਸਾਰ	Sār	Power, might support
ਭੁਖ ਸਾਲਾਹਣੁ	bhukh sālāhaṇ	Hunger for prasing the Lord
ਪਾ ਛਾਰੁ	Pa chhār	Dust of the fect

The Guru speaks to us in this *slok* about the various ways that the followers of different belief systems worship the Lord. The theme is to emphasise the essence of such worship, which does not require any formalism but is rather based on true love and devotion to the one Lord, and in which the devotee wants just to laud Him all the time. In this context the Guru in this *slok* says that Muslims read the Sharia and deem necessary conformity to it for reaching the Lord. Hindus laud Him in accordance with the *Shāstras*, and concentrate on bathing at *tīrath*, offerings, and burning of incenses and scents. *Jogis* worship Him as the unknowable but yet in their meditation seek to give Him form. Philanthropists find contentment in thoughts of giving to others, though some of them give but then seek a thousand-fold in return from the Lord and also crave for renown among the people. There are also thieves, adulterers, seekers after pelf and the evil ones. They waste their fortune and their approach to life is totally a waste. In the waters, the lands, the created worlds there are creatures of myriad shapes. He knows what they all want and is their support. In the minds of the true devotees is the hunger to praise Him and they are ever in bliss, and they treat themselves as the dirt of the feet of the virtuous ones.

To better understand the message of this *slok* it is necessary to start by first taking a look at lines 13 and 14, the last two lines of the *slok*. It is the style throughout the Guru's *Bāṇi* that whenever he presents the views about any of the then existing systems of belief he first puts down what those systems prescribe or have to say and then, only at the end will he offer his own message. Thus we will see here in the first twelve lines of the *slok* that he recounts the various views and practices in the other belief systems, also mentioning the evil ones who follow no belief system except self interest, and then in the last two lines he tells us what true devotion should mean. These lines say that the true devotees are those who hunger for somehow reaching the Lord. From this hunger arises their deep attachment and love, which has them singing the praises of the One Lord. Their only sustenance and support during their existence on this Earth is the True Name. Such devotees are forever, day and night, in bliss. In their behaviour is there utter humility and they consider themselves the dust from the feet of those in whom resides the godly virtues. Prof. Talib puts it well when he says, "God's devotees hunger to perform divine laudation; The Name eternal their prop. Day and night in joy they abide; of these bearing noble qualities dust of feet they make themselves." We can now look at the full text of the *slok* in the light of this concluding message. The references to the different categories of persons, both good and bad, has to be examined in the context of what these concluding lines are telling us. The broad message the Guru is conveying to us is that our stress ought to be on acquiring Godly qualities, praising the Lord and staying humble, and at all costs eschewing narrow-minded, bigoted and formalistic observances. Let us look at it in more detail.

In the 1st and 2nd lines the Guru says the Muslims read the Sharia and deem it necessary that anyone wanting to reach the Lord must conform strictly to it and obey its prescriptions. There is some difference of perception in the interpretation of these lines, though not so much in the first line where almost all learned commentators seem to agree, the wording of the line also being clear enough. It says simply that followers of the Muslim religion reflect on the Sharia. Some render the second line, though, to mean that the Muslims deem it essential that a man to be considered a real devotee must bind himself to the Sharia strictly, and that only those within the pale of the Sharia will be able to reach the Lord, while all unbelievers are destined for hell. Prof. Sahib Singh, Bhai Vir Singh and the *Shabdarth* have adopted this interpretation. Some other learned commentators take it as referring not to the Muslim belief but that the phrase "banday say je pavay vich bandi" to mean that the real devotees are those who are immersed in prayer in their effort to see a glimpse of the Lord. Dada Chellaram, Prof. Talib, Dr. Gopal Singh, Macauliffe and Prof. Teja Singh have all rendered this second line in this manner.

Both views have their own merit, but on balance the rendering followed by Bhai Vir Singh, Prof. Sahib and some other learned ones seems more appealing here. This expression is not intended to be a criticism of the Muslim way to God, for it is never the Guru's style to run down another master's message. He seeks always to only put it in perspective. Here, regarding the Muslim path the Guru is simply pointing out the known fact that in their form of worship and in their approach to everyday living they concentrate on the Sharia. As Gyani Maskin says in his audio-commentary the Sharia is a prescription to take us to God. All religious systems, similarly, have their own prescriptions, their own forms of discipline and their own set of rules, with which the followers are supposed to govern their lives. But, says Gyani Maskin, it is important to remember that these are after all only rules, road maps. What is really important is how well are these actually followed, and how sincerely and truly are these practiced. Anyone, in any system, who gets entangled in the mere study of the rules and whose aim then becomes to extol that particular system above all others, is really lost in the wilderness. It is often seen that such persons tend to become bigots and their sole aim then is to concentrate on getting others to follow their system. While doing so they often themselves forget the true practice of their own tenets, and tend to take a narrow exclusionist view, full of hard- hearted cruelty towards those outside their own system. Following the rules is meant to achieve the aim of reaching a state of true devotion for the Lord, which before anything else will teach love and tolerance and the realization that all mankind has the same One Creator. In actual fact some of the followers of many religions, and here in this line the Guru is talking of the Muslim, get so rigidly attached to the strict observance of their own rules that the true aim of their practice, which is to reach the Lord, is forgotten. Prof. Sahib Singh also says that those who interpret the 2nd line as meaning that "the true devotee is he who longs to see the Lord" are missing the point of the entire *slok.* He says that though such a rendering would be in tune with the Sikh approach, but it does not then go with the first line where the reference is to the Muslim approach. He says that in no other *slok* has the Guru used such a method. Bhai Vir Singh has also said that viewed in the light of the last two lines we can see that the moral, the lesson the Guru is seeking to convey is summed up there, and it is not to be sought within each line. In other words, it cannot be said to occur piecemeal within the *slok.* Also, he says the 2nd line is a continuation of the thought in the 1st line and refers to the Muslim injuction to come strictly within the Sharia for reaching the Lord. He refers also to Bhai Gurdas, *Vār* 1, *pauṛi* 10 where he says, "Rozay eid namāz kar karṇi bund kera sansāra", meaning that for some Muslim keeping fasts, celebrating Eid and saying the *namāz* five times, all strict requirements of the Sharia, have become an end by themselves. The implied comment is that the Sharia instead of becoming a vehicle for seeking the Lord has become an end by itself. Though many learned commentators have simply rendered the 2nd line to mean the Lord's servant is he who accepts servitude to see Him, the well-explained interpretation offered by Bhai Vir Singh and by Prof. Sahib Singh definitely seems more convincing here. This line read with the 1st refers thus to the then prevailing Muslim predilection to put all stress only on the rules of conduct and on proselytization and not stressing enough the need for inner focusing of the conscious on the Lord and on virtues like love, devotion and humility.

Having spoken to us of the then prevailing Muslim approach, the Guru now in lines 3 and 4 turns his focus on the Hindu practices of that time. He says they concentrate on visits to *tīraths*, pusificatory baths, offerings in *havans* and *yagyas*, burning of incense, etc. in seeking to praise the Lord. As Bhai Vir Singh says, the Hindus in their *shastras* and *darshans* deem Him to be Infinite and thus Formless but yet they bathe at *tīraths*, worship idols, make offerings in such worship and burn incenses and smear scented essences such as *chandan* (sandalwood). Thus, in practice they seem to treat the Formless One as having Form. Most commentators have interpreted it on these lines.

In lines 5 and 6, the Guru turns his attention to the practices of the *Jogis*. He says they worship Him as *Alakh*, meaning immeasurable, unknowable or unreachable, and so seek to reach Him. But though they deem Him subtle yet in their meditation they seek to give Him a form. Bhai Vir Singh says, "The *Jogis* seek to go into *Sunn* – a state of non-thinking, of void, but since they use their minds for that purpose so what they will visualize will naturally have form, even if they call the Lord 'Formless'. The *Shabdarth* shares the same view. Dr. Gopal Singh also renders it as, "The Yogis who dwell on the void and name the creator unknowable yet to the absolute, the subtle Name, they give the form of a body!" Prof. Talib says, "The Yogis seeking to enter nescience, meditate on the Creator with the name *Alakh* (literally inaccessible), He who is of subtle aspect, whose name is the immaculate – *Niranjan* – Him in embodied form they contemplate." Thus, we can see that there is broad agreement among learned commentators on the interpretation of this line. The formulation by Dr. Gopal Singh as above is though more appealing here. The Guru is here pointing out that reaching the Lord through the device and method followed by the *Jogis* is also fraught with contradictions, and while in theory professing belief in the Formless Lord, yet they visualize Him.

In lines 7th and 8th are addressed another class of the spiritually elevated, that of the compassionate philanthropist. Of course this is not a religious belief system but yet is generally treated as one of the means to reaching Him. The Guru says contentment is there in the mind when the urge to give to those less fortunate arises. However in real fact those who are thus giving think they have earned great merit from their philanthrophy, and therefore often they seek from the Lord in return a thousand-fold what they may have given. Not only do their inner desires stop at this, they also in addition seek name and fame, and want that they should be acclaimed by the world as great philanthropists. Thus are they also not on the right path, because their efforts are not entirely selfless.

In line 9th and 10th the Guru now speaks of those who are not on any religious path at all, but rather are sunk in iniquity. He says there are the thieves, adulterers, the seekers after pelf, the evil depraved ones, the worthless. It is the Hindu belief system that when we come to this world the soul is allotted a certain amount of credit from out of the balance gained from good actions in past lives. So the Guru is here saying that these losers had also come to this world with some *Prālabdh* – credit of past *karma* – but far from adding to it they fritter it all away in these evil ways. Having frittered away their precious capital they go from here, and thus their lives can be said to have hardly been of any use at all. Bhai Vir Singh says the phrase "Tina bhi kāyi kār" in line 10 is to be interpreted to mean that evil actions of these wrongdoers are devoid of any sort of merit at all. Prof. Sahib Singh however renders it as, "All this is the Lord's play and He has given these persons such a way of life." The *Shabdarth* takes it on the lines of Bhai Vir Singh. Prof. Talib also says "what worth is all their doing". Macauliffe says, "Shall they have any business whatever in the next world?", though in the footnote he adds the other interpretation also and says, "had they any other business in this world". Dr. Gopal Singh says "is their life of any avail." Thus we will notice that most commentators have followed Bhai Vir Singh's view. Prof. Sahib Singh's view could of course be extended to mean that useless and fruitless though such lives are yet nothing being outside of the Lord's Will, these evil ones must also be acting in this wrong fashion because the Lord has so decreed. More convincing, however, is the other view because it centres more on something that the Guru elsewhere says; that we carry in this world the free will to do good or evil. The Lord lets us act freely so that we can earn our way to salvation through the temptations and the opportunies of this *karma bhūmi* – this field of action, this world. We have thus the chance to reshape ourselves so as to be fit to be taken into His presence, or we can lose sight of that aim and instead fritter our precious chance away, indulging ourselves in things of this world, enjoying the sensory pleasures and going back into the cycle of deaths and rebirths. If we made the right choice then is our life of some avail indeed.

In lines 11th and 12th the Guru says in the waters, on the lands, in the various worlds and spheres are there countless forms of life. Only the Lord knows what they want, and He is their only support. The Guru has spoken in the previous lines of the various categories of persons existing on this earth, covering most of what his audience could normally have been familiar with. Thus, he counted the Muslims, the Hindus, the *Jogis*, the compassionate philanthropists, and on the other hand also the unfortunate ones who squander their spiritual capital in pointless sensual gratification. Now he tells us that the Lord's created universe is infinite. Within it are an unknown number of spheres, of worlds created and equally large number of diverse forms within the waters and outside on solid earth. He implies that the vast multitude of these creatures makes it impossible to enumerate the diverse ways of their living, and the varied possible ways of seeking the Lord. We cannot know this mystery, but the Lord knows it all, says the Guru. Their diverse and numerous forms are also looked after by the same Power. He sustains them and they depend on Him alone.

In the concluding lines, 13th and 14th, as we saw above the Guru comes to the thrust of the message, that whatever system you follow, the true devotee is he in whose mind there is hunger for being one with the Lord. Such true worshippers hunger to sing praises of Him, or in other words the hunger of these devotees is not satiated except by singing praises of Him. The true Name is the bedrock of their belief. These lucky ones are always in bliss and their lives are marked by such humility that they treat themselves as the dust of those who have high spiritual worth.

We must here understand that such true devotees, the *bhagats*, whose minds are fixed on Him in humility and in a state of bliss, are not the exclusive preserve of any single belief system or any particular region. Such great ones have existed and will continue to be found, not only among the Sikhs, but among Christians, Muslims, and Hindus; or in fact in any class of sincere seekers in any true belief system. The only exception being, of course, those who don't seek Him at all but rather focus only on personal gratification through the pursuit of wealth, power and similar other toys for the senses. The pursuit of any good path, when marked by that hunger for the glimpse of the Divine, and with love and humility in the heart, is beneficial. It is only when this essential ingredient is missing and mere formalism takes its place that there will arise in the mind lack of love for the Lord's creations, and a rigidness of approach where physical acts and formalism overtakes the true pursuit of the path to the Lord. It is a hard reality that the followers of any religious system when they become too stubbornly attached to the form of the prescriptions, and lose sight of the essence of worship, which is love and devotion to the Lord, can create the greatest havoc in the world. As has been often said, more wars and conflicts have been caused by religion than for any other cause. This of course is sad and ironical because religions were created to guide humankind, through the temptations of this material world, to the Divine who is viewed by almost all religions essentially as the embodiment of love, who is said to be the ever merciful, the forgiving father. So where love and peace should have reigned among the followers of these religions, there exists in real fact conflict and the desire to show one's superiority over all others. This has happened because that true religion which engenders in the human breast the hunger for the Lord's glimpse, and which arouses in the heart love and compassion for all – has been forgotten. The Guru has in these lines sought to remind as of what true devotion should mean. He says that in the minds of the devotee is the burning desire to ever laud the Lord, the True One, and ever are they in bliss. They are humble and seek the company of those blessed with Godly qualities.

In the next *slok*, the Guru says:

ਮ: ੧ ॥	M: 1.
ਮਿਟੀ ਮੁਸਲਮਾਨ ਕੀ ਪੇੜੈ ਪਈ ਕੁਮ੍ਹਿਆਰ ॥	Mitti mussalmān kee peṛai paee kumhiār
ਘੜਿ ਭਾਂਡੇ ਇਟਾ ਕੀਆ ਜਲਦੀ ਕਰੇ ਪੁਕਾਰ ॥	Ghaṛ bhānday Itta kīya jaldi karay pukār
ਜਲਿ ਜਲਿ ਰੋਵੈ ਬਪੁੜੀ ਝੜਿ ਝੜਿ ਪਵਹਿ ਅੰਗਿਆਰ ॥	Jal jal rovai bapuṛi jhaṛ jhaṛ paveh angiyār
ਨਾਨਕ ਜਿਨਿ ਕਰਤੈ ਕਾਰਣੁ ਕੀਆ ਸੋ ਜਾਣੈ ਕਰਤਾਰੁ ॥੨॥	Nanak jin kartai kāraṇ kīa so jāṇay kartār. 2.

Glossary:

ਕੀਆ	Kīa	Made
ਜਲਿ ਜਲਿ	Jal Jal	As it burns
ਜਿਨਿ ਕਰਤੈ	Jinn kartai	The Lord who
ਕਾਰਣੁ	Kāraṇ	The cause for this world
ਪੇੜੈ ਪਈ	Peṛai paee	Fell into the hands of
ਬਪੁੜੀ	Bapuṛi	The helpless one

The Guru in this *slok* comments on the inappropriateness of another formalistic belief regarding the ritually proper way to dispose off the body after death. The reference here is to the Muslim belief that burial is the only correct way, and if the body is cremated the soul loses its chance to reach *bahisht*, the Muslim Paradise. In this context the Guru speaks of a situation where the dust of the

Mussulman, who was buried, in due course comes into the hands of the potter, and he makes vessels and bricks from it. When he fires the clay in the kiln it cries as the cinders fall on it. Thus the cremation that was sought to be avoided yet overtakes the body. The Guru is telling us that only the Lord who has made us all knows the real fate we will meet after death. Let us now look at it in more detail.

The first line says the dust of the Muslim fell into the hands of the potter. The reference is to the practice in the Muslim religion to not cremate but rather bury their dead bodies. It is a practice born of the belief that the body will rise on the final day of reckoning, and therefore the burnt body loses the chance of attaining paradise or *bahisht*, as it is called among Muslims. The practice is therefore to inter the bodies in a common graveyard for the community. With the passage of time the bodies would naturally decompose and would gradually merge into the soil. The clay created around the area from this process was found to be especially useful in making pottery. The *kumhārs* – as those who follow the potter's profession are known – would naturally try to dig up such clay for their work. The Guru here says after a Muslim is buried, the clay into which his earthly remains have merged, has fallen into the hands of a potter.

There is an interesting sidenote regarding this line, which had considerable influence on Sikh history. Guru Har Rai, the seventh Nanak, is said to have helped Dāra Shikoh at one time during the struggle for succession to Shah Jahan's throne. This naturally annoyed the ultimate winner, Aurangzeb and so after he was crowned, he summoned the Guru to the court. The Guru decided instead to send his eldest son Rām Rai, who was much liked by the Guru and had been given proper education in the Guru's path. Rām Rai, born in AD 1646 at Kiratpur, was successful in pacifying the Mughal and stayed at the court for some time. During this period Aurangzeb came to learn that there was in *Gurbāṇi* this composition referring to the 'Muslim's clay' falling into the hands of the potter. He summoned the young Rām Rai and asked him why this insulting reference regarding Muslims had been included in the Sikh scriptures. In his anxiety to remain in the Emperor's good books he quickly replied that the actual reference was *mitti beimān ki*, thus changing Mussalman – meaning Muslim – to *beimān* meaning the dishonest or the faithless. The ruler was satisfied all right but when this news reached the Guru, he disowned his son forthwith for daring to alter the Guru's Word. Rām Rai never met his father again and later settled in the Doon Valley with the help of Aurangzeb. He died there at a comparatively young age, in AD 1687. The net result was that the spirit of Guru Nanak then passed to the eighth Nanak Guru Har Krishan who was a younger son of the seventh Nanak.

In the 2nd and 3rd lines the Guru says that the potter fashions from this clay vessels and bricks, and puts these in the potter's kiln for baking. As the heat burns up the clay sparks fly from it, as if the clay were shedding tears. It seems as if the helpless clay is crying out in pain and is seeking succour. Thus, in a way is the clay of the deceased being put apparently through the process of cremation. The very fate, cremation, that was sought to be avoided, is being visited upon the dead body. Macauliffe has evocatively rendered the 3rd line as, "The poor ashes burn and weep, and sparks fly from them." Dr. Gopal Singh also puts it similarly as, "Yea the helpless clay burns and cries out as the fiery coals fall continuously upon it."

In the concluding line the Guru says that only the Creator knows who really has earned merit enough through his actions on this earth to be rewarded or to be punished. Our beliefs such as, for instance, the belief that if we burn the dead body we will lose our chance at heaven, or that it will take us to Hell, have no basis. The example of the clay of the Muslim being put in the potter's fire is meant only to highlight that such happenstance can have no effect on our chances of salvation. Only the merits of our actions will determine our fate. By the body being burnt or being otherwise disposed off, our chance to salvation is neither gained nor lost, because that depends on the merits of our actions, and only the Creator is the judge of our true merit. Only He can determine where we will go and what we will do after death. Prof. Sahib Singh says that the thought we should bear in mind is: "Uttam eh bīchār hai jinn sachay siu chit lāia, jag jīvan dāta pāia", meaning that "the best course is to fix your mind on the True One and you will reach the Creator of the universe". On the subject of the disposal of the dead body he refers to *Rāg Soratth ki Vār*, *Mahla* 4, page 648 of the *SGGS*, where the third Nanak's *slok* quotes the *Mahla* 1 saying, "Ik dajheh ik dabiai ikna kuttay khahe. Ik pāṇi vich ustiyeh ik bhi phir hāsan pāhay. Nanak ev na jāpyi kithai jāye samāhey". This can be translated as "Some bodies are cremated, some buried while yet others become food for dogs. Some are thrown into water, yet others into empty wells: but no one knows where the soul that occupied these bodies would go." It has been said by the Guru in *Rāg Soratth*, *Mahla* 5, page 609 of the *SGGS*, that "Tīn sankiya kar dehi kīni jal, kūkar, bhasmehi", meaning that when the body was created its disposal was prescribed in three ways, these being: throwing in moving water, feeding to animals such as dogs, and burning it. The reference here is additionally to the Zoroastrian way of leaving bodies in the Tower of Silence where carrion birds eat them. But the method of disposal of the dead bodies, says the Guru, has absolutely no bearing on the fate of the soul that had occupied it. Only the Lord who is the cause of all that exists knows that fate. It is axiomatic of course, as the Guru repeatedly tells us that following the right path will help determine the fate of the soul.

The *pauṛi* to which these *sloks* were the prelude runs as follows:

ਪਉੜੀ ॥	Pauṛi
ਬਿਨੁ ਸਤਿਗੁਰ ਕਿਨੈ ਨ ਪਾਇਓ ਬਿਨੁ ਸਤਿਗੁਰ ਕਿਨੈ ਨ ਪਾਇਆ ॥	Bin satgur kinai na pāio bin satgur kinai na pāia
ਸਤਿਗੁਰ ਵਿਚਿ ਆਪੁ ਰਖਿਓਨੁ ਕਰਿ ਪਰਗਟੁ ਆਖਿ ਸੁਣਾਇਆ ॥	Satgur vich āp rakhiyon kar pargat ākh suṇāia
ਤਿਗੁਰ ਮਿਲਿਐ ਸਦਾ ਮੁਕਤੁ ਹੈ ਜਿਨਿ ਵਿਚਹੁ ਮੋਹੁ ਚੁਕਾਇਆ ॥	Satgur miliai sada mukat hai jinn vichoh moh chukāia
ਉਤਮੁ ਏਹੁ ਬੀਚਾਰੁ ਹੈ ਜਿਨਿ ਸਚੇ ਸਿਉ ਚਿਤੁ ਲਾਇਆ ॥	Uttam eh bīchār hai jinn sachay siu chit lāia
ਜਗਜੀਵਨੁ ਦਾਤਾ ਪਾਇਆ ॥੬॥	Jag jīvan dāta pāia. 6.

Glossary:

ਕਿਨੈ	Kinai	Only some
ਪਾਇਓ	Pāio	Obtained, got
ਜਗਜੀਵਨੁ	Jagjīvan	The world's life, the Lord
ਦਾਤਾ	Dāta	Donor

The Guru in this *pauṛi* emphasizes the high importance of the preceptor and says that without the true preceptor no one has reached the Lord. The Lord Himself resides in the true preceptor and through him does He reveal Himself. Liberation will come through meeting the true Guru who will rid us of our attachment to *Maya*. The highest thought is that he who sheds attachments and fixes his mind on the True One will find the Lord. This *pauṛi* again focuses, as did *pauṛi* 4 earlier, on the vital importance of the *Satguru*, the true Guru, the true preceptor. This is a recurring theme in the *SGGS*, and we have of course already discussed it at length in *pauṛi* 4. There we had been told that only by the Lord's grace is a true Guru found, that there is no greater benefactor than the Guru because he speaks to us of the True Lord and through him we lose our sense of separateness from the Lord and thus reach Him. Let us now look at these concepts in more detail.

In the first line the Guru speaks to us in the same vein and says that without a true preceptor no one has ever reached the True Lord. The term *pāio* and *pāia* here have both been used to mean 'obtained'. Some learned ones have taken these to refer to the past and the present, respectively. Grammatically, however, that is not proper and the double use here is meant to stress that such an event has never ever happened. The repetition is meant just to stress the thought. Bhai Vir Singh further elaborates the point and says that *pāio* refers to the distant past and *pāia* to the recent past.

In line 2 the Guru says that the Lord Himself resides in the true Guru and through him does He reveal Himself, speak and inform. Prof. Sahib Singh puts it as, "The Lord resides in the *Satguru* and we hereby openly thus announce." 'We' here means the Guru. Bhai Vir Singh, as also Dada Chellaram, renders it along the same lines. Prof. Talib changes it slightly and puts it as, "The message that in the holy Preceptor has He lodged, this the Preceptor has manifestly proclaimed." Dr. Gopal Singh also says, "In the True Guru lies His essence and, revealing it, he proclaims it to all." Macauliffe translates it as, "God hath put Himself into the true Guru; He hath made manifest and proclaimed this." Thus, there is general agreement among learned ones in interpreting one part of the line as saying that the Lord resides in the Guru. But the learned ones see the second part, "kar pargat ākh suṇāia", meaning it has been revealed and announced, differently. Thus, who has proclaimed or announced it is viewed as either "the Guru is saying it", or "the Lord has said so". Another view is simply that "the Lord manifests, speaks and informs through the medium of the Guru". Both views carry weight; therefore it is better to adopt the latter rendering which to an extent covers both views.

In line 3 the Guru says liberation comes through meeting the Guru who has shed us of attachments. Again there are slightly differing interpretations of the concept "jinn vicho moh chukāia", meaning "who has removed false attachments from within". Prof. Talib renders this line as, "By union with the holy preceptor, who our evil of attachment has annulled, is obtained everlasting liberation". Dr. Gopal Singh puts it similarly. Macauliffe puts it a bit differently as, "Salvation is ever obtained by meeting the true Guru who hath banished worldly love from within

Him." Thus there are two ways the second part of this line has been interpreted. One view is that the preceptor has from within us removed the hindrance caused by the false attachments to the things of this world. Bhai Vir Singh adopts this view. Prof. Sahib Singh and Gyani Maskin have adopted the other view, that the preceptor is one who from within his own self has removed the bonds of attachment. The Guru says that for liberation the bonds of false attachments have to be shed. Obviously the preceptor would have first rid himself of such attachments. Therefore, the interpretation by Prof. Sahib Singh and others, that the preceptor is the one who has shed attachments, seems more appropriate.

In the 4th and 5th lines the Guru says that the highest thought is that he who sheds attachments and fixes his mind on the Guru finds Him. Bhai Vir Singh puts it as, "This thought is the best that if someone on meeting the *Satguru*, uplifts his mind beyond his own self and fixes his mind on the True One he finds that One." Prof. Sahib Singh says, "It is the best of all thoughts that he who fixed his mind on his Guru has reached the Lord." Dada Chellaram holds a similar view. Prof. Talib renders it as, "Noble is this contemplation, One that to the holy Eternal in heart is attached, to the life of the universe, Bestower of boons attained." Most learned commentators take the meaning to be that the mind requires to be fixed on the Lord if one is to find Him. However, some, like Prof. Sahib Singh, render it to say that the mind is to be fixed on the preceptor if one is to find the True Lord. No doubt the thrust of this *pauṛi*, and of the 4th *pauṛi*, is to stress the importance of the Guru, but the term used here is *sachay,* which can be used only for the Lord and not for the Guru. The more appealing interpretation therefore is that only by fixing our minds on the Lord is He to be found. For this the *Satguru*, the true preceptor, is needed to teach us how to rid ourselves of worldly entanglements.

PAURI 7

This *pauṛi* also has two *sloks* adduced to it, one by Guru Nanak and the other by the second Nanak. Both of these are on the subject of *haumai* – the sense of selfness, of being separate and distinct, and not a part of the Lord. This *haumai* in fact is the main hurdle between this soul and its salvation. The day that this is overcome the veil of separation from the Lord will disappear and enlightenment will follow. The first of these *sloks* says:

ਸਲੋਕ ਮ: ੧ ॥	Slok Mahla 1
ਹਉ ਵਿਚਿ ਆਇਆ ਹਉ ਵਿਚਿ ਗਇਆ ॥	Hau vich aiya hau vich gaya.
ਹਉ ਵਿਚਿ ਜੰਮਿਆ ਹਉ ਵਿਚਿ ਮੁਆ ॥	Hau vich jamiya hau vich mūa.
ਹਉ ਵਿਚਿ ਦਿਤਾ ਹਉ ਵਿਚਿ ਲਇਆ ॥	Hau vich dita hau vich laia
ਹਉ ਵਿਚਿ ਖਟਿਆ ਹਉ ਵਿਚਿ ਗਇਆ ॥	Hau vich khattiya hau vich gaya
ਹਉ ਵਿਚਿ ਸਚਿਆਰੁ ਕੂੜਿਆਰੁ ॥	Hau vich sachiyar kūriyāṛ
ਹਉ ਵਿਚਿ ਪਾਪ ਪੁੰਨ ਵੀਚਾਰੁ ॥	Hau vich pāp pun vīchār
ਹਉ ਵਿਚਿ ਨਰਕਿ ਸੁਰਗਿ ਅਵਤਾਰੁ ॥	Hau vich narak surag avtār
ਹਉ ਵਿਚਿ ਹਸੈ ਹਉ ਵਿਚਿ ਰੋਵੈ ॥	Hau vich hasai hau vich rovai
ਹਉ ਵਿਚਿ ਭਰੀਐ ਹਉ ਵਿਚਿ ਧੋਵੈ ॥	Hau vich Bharīai hau vich dhovai
ਹਉ ਵਿਚਿ ਜਾਤੀ ਜਿਨਸੀ ਖੋਵੈ ॥	Hau vich jātī jinsi khovai
ਹਉ ਵਿਚਿ ਮੂਰਖੁ ਹਉ ਵਿਚਿ ਸਿਆਣਾ ॥	Hau vich mūrakh hau vich siāṇa
ਮੋਖ ਮੁਕਤਿ ਕੀ ਸਾਰ ਨ ਜਾਣਾ ॥	Mokh mukat kee sār na jāṇa
ਹਉ ਵਿਚਿ ਮਾਇਆ ਹਉ ਵਿਚਿ ਛਾਇਆ ॥	Hau vich maya hau vich chhaya
ਹਉਮੈ ਕਰਿ ਕਰਿ ਜੰਤ ਉਪਾਇਆ ॥	Haumai kar kar jant upāia

ਹਉਮੈ ਬੂਝੈ ਤਾ ਦਰੁ ਸੂਝੈ ॥	Haumai būjhai ta dar sūjhai
ਗਿਆਨ ਵਿਹੂਣਾ ਕਥਿ ਕਥਿ ਲੂਝੈ ॥	Gyān vihūṇa kathh kathh lūjhai
ਨਾਨਕ ਹੁਕਮੀ ਲਿਖੀਐ ਲੇਖੁ ॥	Nanak hukmi likhiyai lekh
ਜੇਹਾ ਵੇਖਹਿ ਤੇਹਾ ਵੇਖੁ ॥੧॥	Jeha vekheh teha vekh. 1.

Glossary:

ਹਉ	Hau	Sense of selfness, being separate from the Lord; pride, egoisim, ego
ਨਰਕਿ ਸੁਰਗਿ ਅਵਤਾਰੁ	Narak surag *avtār*	Existing in hell or heaven
ਭਰੀਐ	Bharīai	Is soiled (by evil)
ਜਾਤੀ ਜਿਨਸੀ	Jāti Jinsi	Species, caste and kind
ਸਾਰ	Sār	Understanding
ਛਾਇਆ	Chhāiya	Shadow (of *maya*)
ਲੂਝੈ	Lūjhai	Frets, worries, quartets
ਹੁਕਮ	Hukam	By His command
ਲੇਖੁ	Lekh	Writing (of destiny)
ਵੇਖਹਿ	Vekheh	Watches
ਵੇਖੁ	Vekh	Form

Simply translated this *slok* says that man comes under the influence of ego and in ego he goes from this world. He is born and he dies in ego. His giving and taking are all based on ego. His gaining and losing are in ego. In Ego is he true and he is false, his sense of truthfulness and falseness is born from the effect of ego. In ego he experiences hell or heaven. In ego he cries and he laughs. In ego does he get soiled in sin and in ego he washes clean. In ego is he wise or foolish, and in ego does he fail to see the path to salvation. In ego is he under *maya* and its shadow. In ego he takes different births. If he recognizes that he is under the effect of ego then will he be able to sense the Lord's door. The one who cannot do so, just talks and quarrels. If we can realize that the fates of men are under His edict and if we can see ourselves rid of this ego, we shall be liberated from this bondage to ego. The Guru is telling us that it is within us to break the hold of *haumai* on us; and when we succeed we shall see the door to salvation. It is only *haumai* that blinds us to the reality and keeps us off the right path. And what is that path?

Though not mentioned here, it is implicit from the previous *pauṛis*. That path is listening to the *Satguru*, the one without attachments. For a Sikh that *Satguru* is ever present in the message of *Sri Guru Granth Sahib*. Let us now look at these concepts in more detail.

In lines 1st and 2nd the Guru says that the coming of a man is in *hau* (ego), and in ego is his departure. In ego one is born, in ego one dies. The word *hau* is from the Sanskrit root *aham* (I am), a sense of the self as separate from the Lord. Bhai Vir Singh says this sense also has its pure and constructive aspect, but when it asserts itself as an entity separate and distinct then it becomes the *hau*, which is the subject of this *slok*. The *Shabdarth* says that some seek to altogether give up the *hau* so that they could escape its bad effects, but this will mean that they are prevented not only from evil but also the good deeds for which the self is obviously needed. In other words, *hau* is necessary for our existence. But we have to avoid the effects of its evil form. The Guru is saying that as long as the soul is under the influence of this *hau* it will continue to be entangled in the circle of births, and the cycle is repeated as long as the sense of selfness governs the soul. Salvation comes when that false sense of separateness is overcome. Macauliffe renders *hau* as 'Pride', Prof. Teja Singh and Dada Chellaram as 'ego' and Prof. Talib as 'egoism'. All these renderings are correct in their own way. But it is really the sense of selfness, the feeling of separateness from the true Lord that is the root of this *hau* or *haumai*. In everyday human terms, and in our dealings with the world, it will manifest as egoism, pride, vanity, arrogance and similar other characteristics. The root of all these is the same – the sense of selfness, of being separate from the Lord. If we could see that the Lord is all, the only Reality, the question of arrogance or pride in ourselves can just not arise. In this *slok* the Guru is referring to it mainly in its manifestation as pride.

In lines 3 and 4, on the same theme, the Guru says in pride he gives and in pride he takes, in pride he gains and in pride he loses. Prof. Talib puts it as, "in egoism he makes gain, in egoism makes losses". Dr. Gopal Singh says, "in ego one earns, in ego one wastes". A fairly uniform view is thus to be noted, with minor changes in terminology among the learned commentators. The sense, however, clearly remains that man's existence on this earth; his commerce, his losses and his gains, his giving and taking are all governed by this sense of *hau*. Man in his pride deems that he himself is the doer, forgetting the Lord. In this way does he remain bound in the cycle of births unable to pierce through the veil of illusion.

In lines 5 and 6, the Guru says "in pride he is true or false, in pride he has considerations of sin and virtue". Prof. Sahib Singh renders this line to say that as long as man is under the influence of this sense of being separate from the Lord, he is in the eyes of other people sometimes true and sometimes false, and deems all his actions good or bad under the same feeling. Prof. Teja Singh puts it as, "By his ego he is true or false, has considerations of sin and virtue." Dr. Gopal Singh and Macauliffe both take the sense as, "in ego, or pride, one becomes truthful or a liar. In ego or pride one respects, or meditates, on virtue and sin, or good and evil". Dada Chellaram puts the 6th line as, "in ego he thought of sin and virtue". Taking the sense of *hau* as pride, Gyani Maskin takes these lines as saying that we do good deeds and boost our sense of ego. When we do wrong then also we make use of our errors and while owning up add to our ego from the very act of being magnanimous in admitting our wrongs. Thus, when we are virtuous we add pride to our egos and when we sin we again, by owning up, make it an excuse to add to our ego.

In lines 7 and 8 the Guru says our going to hell or heaven, our smiles or sorrows are all governed by this *hau*. Heaven in Sikhism denotes a state where we are blessed with nearness to the Lord, and hell means exile from His presence. The rightness of our actions, of our living, the extent of our implicit obedience to the Guru's message will determine which of these states we will enter. Through all this play, the Guru says our sense of *hau* dominates. Our joys and sorrows are also under that influence. The term *Avatār* here is used in the sense of *utāra* (descent), and not in the usual sense of a divine incarnation. The Guru is saying that governed by this *hau* man comes to this earth or enters heaven or hell. These are not concepts accepted in the conventional sense in Sikhism but the Guru is here making the point that this belief about being punished in hell or rewarded in heaven are all the results of man's *hau*.

In lines 9 and 10, the Guru says that the filling of the self with sins and the washing away of these are again under this sense of *hau*; and he adds that in *hau* does one waste this precious human birth. The term *jāti jinsi* literally means caste and species and some commentators have used it thus. For instance, Dada Chellaram says, "in ego he degradeth his breed and kind". Macauliffe also says, "In pride man loseth his caste and race." Dr. Gopal Singh says it slightly differently as, "In ego do we lose the distinctions of cast and kind." Prof. Talib and Prof. Teja Singh render the phrase in the sense of the human birth. Prof. Sahib Singh renders this to say that because of the sense of separateness the mind gets filled with sins, and sometimes through effort man does manage to wash off these sins. Because of this sense of separateness man sometimes deeming himself of high caste loses all he could have gained from his human existence. Bhai Vir Singh renders it on the lines that when man is proud of his caste he is in *hau*. He also gives an alternate meaning as, "In the pride of his high caste he loses his principal asset which is *Nām*, the Lord's Name." Prof. Talib's and Prof. Teja Singh's rendering here seems more convincing when they say that the *hau* causes man to lose his *jāti jinsi*, this very precious human form.

In lines 11 and 12, the Guru says man's foolishness and his wisdom both are under *hau*, and he knows not the way to salvation. Dada Chellaram puts the 12th line as, "O, he knoweth not the value of deliverance." Prof. Talib renders it as, "Of liberation knowing not the essence". Prof. Teja Singh puts it as, "And loses all consciousness of salvation". Dr. Gopal Singh says, "In ego do we not know the essence of Deliverance". Prof. Sahib Singh renders it to say that in this sense of *hau* one may seem wise to people or as unwise, but as long as man remains bound by *hau* he cannot know the way of getting out of the entanglement of illusion, and finding liberation. In other words, acting under the effect of *hau* we become sometimes wise and at times foolish, but while we are under this influence we will remain entangled and cannot hope to know the way out. Salvation will, implies the Guru, come when these bonds are shed. This happens only when we find the *Satguru* and learn to follow his teachings.

In lines 13 and 14, the Guru says in pride are the *Maya* and its shadow. In pride is our birth and rebirth. Prof. Teja Singh puts it as, "By the ego he is in *Maya* self obscured and goes into lives of different creatures", meaning that he has to take birth in different types of existence. Macauliffe says, "In pride is Mammon and in pride its effect on the heart. In pride are animals created". Dada Chellaram says, "In ego is the *Maya*; in ego its baneful shadow. For the actions in ego is he born and reborn". Prof. Talib says, "From egoism under *Maya* and the shadow of *Maya*. By egoism impelled does creation take birth". He renders the word *chhāya* as meaning the shadow of *Maya*. Gyani Maskin puts it as, "Some men from their ego feel that this existence, this *Maya*, that we see is nothing but a shadow, it is not real." The difference in interpretation among learned ones is apparent here. The 13th line is of course clear enough, that due to the *hau* in man he is under the shadow of *Maya*, meaning illusion. The 14th line appropriately must therefore be referring to the effect of *Maya* on man causing him to remain in the circle of births. It could not possibly be referring to the act of creation by the Lord. What is the subject here is the plight of the individual soul which beguiled by *Maya* remains in the cycle of transmigration, separated from the Lord. This is the view Prof. Sahib Singh has taken, as has Bhai Vir Singh and some of the other learned commentators above, and it seems more appealing. Bhai Vir Singh also nicely explains the difference between *Maya* and its shadow. He says *Maya* is the illusion that causes us to see something that does not even exist. The *chhāya* or shadow is the darkness that prevents us from seeing anything at all, blinding us to the Truth.

In lines 15 and 16, the Guru discloses the remedy to this dire disease. He has already spoken in detail of how all our existence is controlled by the effects of *hau*, our pride and egoism. He now says that when man comes to understand the reality of this *haumai* he will see the Lord's Abode, His Door; and the one who has not acquired that knowledge just talks and quarrels. As Dr. Gopal Singh puts it, "If one spots out the ego within, one Realises the Gate (of Deliverance) but without wisdom one prattles and fights wordy duels in vain." Prof. Talib says, "Should man realize egoism would the Divine Portal to him be revealed. One bereft of enlightenment in disputation indulges in discourse." The essence of the Guru's message here is that the passage to the Lord will remain obscured to us as long as the veil of our *haumai* covers our spiritual eyes. The day realization dawns that all our actions were being governed by our *hau* that the Divine Portal will become visible and accessible. The one who has not yet reached this understanding will only pose as knowledgeable and he will be found indulging in useless disputation. This will only bring anger, tension and burning of the heart and no real purpose will be served by such talk. We must recognize therefore that it is our *haumai* that is obscuring our path, and as soon as this knowledge enters our heart all else will follow.

The concluding lines, 17th and 18th, have been differently interpreted by learned commentators. Prof. Talib has rendered it as, "By Divine ordinance has the writ run. As is thy view of the world, so shalt thou thyself be seen." Prof. Teja Singh has it as,—"Our destiny is recorded by the supreme Will. Oh Lord, as you will, so are created images." Dr. Gopal Singh says, "Through God's Will is the making of our destiny, and as He sees us, so shall we see ourselves." Macauliffe says, "The commander hath thus ordained it, as man regardeth God, so God regardeth him." Macauliffe also gives the alternate renderings as (a) Treat men according to their acts and (b) Treat others as thou would be treated thyself. The *Shabdarth* renders it as, "We write our destiny under the Lord's commands, and as we see ourselves so do we see the Lord's command", meaning that the only mirror we have to see the Lord's will is our *hau*; the cleaner it is the clearer we will see His Will. The *Shabdarth* quotes Bhagat Kabir who, in *Rāg Gauṛi*, page 343 of the *SGGS*, says, "ja kay jīa jaisi budh hoyi, kah Kabir jānega soyi", meaning that, says Kabir, as is a man's level of understanding, or intellect, so will he understand the Lord's mysteries. Gyani Maskin renders the 18th line as, "Whatever he sees is a reflection of his own *haumai*, and he sees not the Lord." Bhai Vir Singh renders it as, "Our *haumai* is created by the Lord and under it we act; our actions shape our destiny which puts us in the cycle of births. So to come out of *haumai* the doors are not closed, only your sight is lacking acuity. As you see so you shall be able to see it, or in other words if you see yourself as one with such *haumai* you will see yourself entangled, but if you see yourself unattached to *haumai* you will see the Divine Portal." He also gives alternate renderings as (a) "As you see pain and joy within you, so see it in others too", (b) "If you want to see your destiny see your actions", and (c) "As you see the world, expect the world to see you similarly". Prof. Sahib Singh renders it as, "Humans become as they see others, and this also is as per the Lord's Will. The actions of the man weave a web around himself and the separate ego is created therefrom, of course all in accordance with the Lord's will." Of all these varying interpretations the one by Bhai Vir Singh, speaks of both the aspects of *haumai*, one as that which enables us to act and thus earn merit, and the second that makes us aware of its entangling qualities and teaches us how to get free of these. It, therefore, is more appealing.

In short, what the Guru is saying to us in these concluding lines is that man's actions determine his fate. This interpretation would be in line with the Guru's message elsewhere too. For instance, in the *Japji Sahib* the Guru said in *pauṛi* 4, "Karmi āvai kapṛa nadri mokh duār", meaning "from our actions come the consequential births, and from His grace alone comes the door to salvation". This *haumai* that we possess is part of what God has ordained for us. It is given to us as a tool to help us control our destiny and by controlling this *haumai* we can find the path to Him. Falling under its control however we get blinded and deluded. As long as it rules us we are born, we die, we gain, we lose, we give, we take, we do good deeds, we indulge in evil, we go to heaven, we go to hell, we laugh and cry, we sin and we cleanse ourselves. We deem ourselves sometimes wise and then we think we are foolish. All through this process we continue to be ruled by our *haumai*. In that state of delusion all these actions only go to further strenghten the hold of *haumai* on us. In this state of delusion we lose track of the path to salvation, the shadow of *Maya* rules us and we either see illusions or, worse, we are blinded altogether and see nothing. The crux, says the Guru, is to understand the nature of this *haumai*, to see that it also is potentially the source from which we could find our passage to the Lord. The Guru will further make this clearer in the next *slok* where he says, "Haumai dīragh rog hai dāroo bhi iss māheh", meaning that *haumai* is a chronic disease but its cure is to be found within it. The moment we see it for what it is, reality dawns and now we see that all that exists, all that happens is by His command alone and not by our volition. Our volition does work, but only to the extent that we can use it to make ourselves worthy and be able, through the Guru's guidance, to see Him. So, the Guru says it is within us to break the hold of *haumai* on us; and when we can succeed in that then we shall see the door to salvation and we will become aware that it was only *haumai* that was blinding us to the reality and keeping us off the right path. And what is that path? Though not mentioned here, it is implicit from the previous *pauṛis*. That path is listening to the *Satguru*, the one without attachments, who will show us the right path which we must then follow and the doors to salvation will open. For a Sikh that *Satguru* is ever present in the message of *Sri Guru Granth Sahib*, and he need not go searching elsewhere for guidance.

In the next *slok*, which is by the second Nanak, the same theme is further elaborated. The Guru says:

ਮਹਲਾ ੨ ॥	Mahla 2
ਹਉਮੈ ਏਹਾ ਜਾਤਿ ਹੈ ਹਉਮੈ ਕਰਮ ਕਮਾਹਿ ॥	Haumai eha jāt hai haumai karam kamāhay
ਹਉਮੈ ਏਈ ਬੰਧਨਾ ਫਿਰਿ ਫਿਰਿ ਜੋਨੀ ਪਾਹਿ ॥	Haumai eyi bandhna phir phir joni pāhay
ਹਉਮੈ ਕਿਥਹੁ ਊਪਜੈ ਕਿਤੁ ਸੰਜਮਿ ਇਹ ਜਾਇ ॥	Haumai kithoh ūpjai kit sanjam eh jāye
ਹਉਮੈ ਏਹੋ ਹੁਕਮੁ ਹੈ ਪਇਐ ਕਿਰਤਿ ਫਿਰਾਹਿ ॥	Haumai eho hukam hai paiai kirat phirāheh
ਹਉਮੈ ਦੀਰਘ ਰੋਗੁ ਹੈ ਦਾਰੂ ਭੀ ਇਸੁ ਮਾਹਿ ॥	Haumai dīragh rog hai dārū bhi iss māheh

ਕਿਰਪਾ ਕਰੇ ਜੇ ਆਪਣੀ ਤਾ ਗੁਰ ਕਾ ਸਬਦੁ ਕਮਾਹਿ॥	Kirpa karay jay āpni ta gur ka sabad kamāheh
ਨਾਨਕੁ ਕਹੈ ਸੁਣਹੁ ਜਨਹੁ ਇਤੁ ਸੰਜਮਿ ਦੁਖ ਜਾਹਿ ॥੨॥	Nanak kahai suṇhu janho itt sanjam dukh jāheh. 2.

Glossary:

ਜਾਤਿ	Jāt	Nature, causing creation or birth
ਕਰਮ	Karam	Action
ਸੰਜਮਿ	Sanjam	Means, discipline
ਕਿਰਤਿ	Kirat	Actions, deeds
ਦੀਰਘ	Dīragh	Deep, long lasting, chronic
ਦਾਰੂ	Dārū	Cure, medicine
ਇਸੁ ਮਾਹਿ	Iss māheh	Is within it

Simply translated, this *slok* says that it is the nature of *haumai* that man does actions under its influence. *Haumai* causes the bonds which lead to the cycle of rebirths. The Guru raises the question as to from where does *haumai* rise and by what discipline is it overcome? He then explains that it comes from the Lord's command and acting under its control we are bound into transmigrations by our actions. *Haumai* is a chronic disease but its cure also lies within it. If the Lord so blesses us we will hear the preceptor's word. Listen people, says Nanak, by this discipline, this method, is it overcome. Let us now look at it in more detail.

In the first line the Guru tells us further about this *haumai* that was discussed in the previous *slok*. He says it is in the very nature of *haumai* that man does actions under its influence. As the *Shabdarth* says, *haumai* is a necessary attribute for a human because we need it to be able to act at all, because without it we would be inert and do nothing. As Prof. Teja Singh says, "It is this ego which gives man his individuality and leads him to action." Most commentators hold the same view except for Macauliffe who says, "It is the nature of pride that it produceth pride." So, the Guru is here telling us that *haumai* gives us our individuality and we indulge in actions governed by this sense of the self. These actions then have the potential of either causing us to be further entangled in *haumai*, or to realize its reality, from which will result salvation.

In the 2nd line the Guru says that as a result of these actions, these entanglements are strengthened and the cycle of transmigration is the result. As Dr. Gopal Singh says, "The bondage of ego is that we are bound to the Round." Thus is the outcome of *haumai* further immersion in the cycle of births, which leads to more actions under *haumai*, and the level of the bondage worsens further. All this happens as long as we do not recognize *haumai* for what it is and let our actions be wholly governed by it.

In line 3 the Guru now poses the vital query and asks from where does this *haumai* arise and how can it be got rid of. Thus far the Guru was narrating how we are being governed by the *hau*, the *haumai*. He had in the previous *slok* implied that awareness of this effect and nature of *haumai* will lead us towards the Lord.

In line 4 the Guru says the *haumai* comes from the Lord's Will and we remain in transmigration because of our accumulated deeds born from *haumai*. The *Shabdarth* explains this to say that our actions are the *karam* here and when these are repeatedly done they form in us a style of living, an ingrained habit, and an approach to existence that it says is called *kirat*, being the accumulated result of our actions. As the Guru says, "paiai kirat phiraheh" – this *kirat* keeps us trapped. Prof. Talib renders this well as he says, "Caught in accumulated deeds man in transmigration is caught." Dr. Gopal Singh says it slightly differently as, "This is the Lord's Will that, in ego, one follows the writ of habit." Most commentators hold a view similar to the *Shabdarth*, and it is quite a convincing rendering.

In the 5th and 6th lines now the Guru provides the answer to the question posed in line 3. He says though *haumai* is a chronic disease, its cure also lies within it. Bhai Vir Singh renders these lines as, "The disease is chronic but not incurable. If the Lord wills it man starts to move on the Lord's path." Prof. Sahib Singh, and in fact most learned ones also interpret it on broadly the same lines. So the remedy, the Guru tells us is not to be obtained from outside, it is inherently available in the problem itself. All that is needed, the Guru tells us, is a subtle change in perspective. The actions that men perform will continue to be performed, but now the underlying cause behind these will be seen to be different. When this shift in perspective is achieved the cure for the disease will become patently clear. This will require that we make sufficient effort and make *haumai* our servant and stop being governed by it. But that will happen only if, and when, He blesses us and we learn to listen to the Guru, through whom the Lord's message comes to us.

In the 7th, the concluding line, the Guru points out that He has explained to us the cure, the remedy in these lines above. He says, listen mankind; by this discipline is the disease of *haumai* cured. The discipline is *Nām Simran*. Focus your mind on Him and take His Name with each breath. Listen to what the Guru tells you and the cure will follow.

In this *pauṛi*, with which these *sloks* were attached, the Guru says:

ਪਉੜੀ ॥	Pauṛi
ਸੇਵ ਕੀਤੀ ਸੰਤੋਖੀਈਂ ਜਿਨ੍ਹੀ ਸਚੋ ਸਚੁ ਧਿਆਇਆ ॥	Sev kīti santokhiyi[n] jini sacho sach dhiāia
ਓਨ੍ਹੀ ਮੰਦੈ ਪੈਰੁ ਨ ਰਖਿਓ ਕਰਿ ਸੁਕ੍ਰਿਤੁ ਧਰਮੁ ਕਮਾਇਆ ॥	Onhi mandai pair na rakhiyo kar sukrit dharma kamāia
ਓਨ੍ਹੀ ਦੁਨੀਆ ਤੋੜੇ ਬੰਧਨਾ ਅੰਨੁ ਪਾਣੀ ਥੋੜਾ ਖਾਇਆ ॥	Onhi duniya toṛay bandhanā ann pāṇi thoṛa khāia
ਤੂੰ ਬਖਸੀਸੀ ਅਗਲਾ ਨਿਤ ਦੇਵਹਿ ਚੜਹਿ ਸਵਾਇਆ ॥	Tū[n] bakhsīsi agla nit deveh chaṛeh sawāia
ਵਡਿਆਈ ਵਡਾ ਪਾਇਆ ॥੭॥	Vaddiāyi vaddā pāia. 7.

Glossary:

ਸੰਤੋਖੀਈਂ	Santokhīyi (n)	The contented ones
ਸਚੋ ਸਚੁ	Sacho sach	Only the True One
ਮੰਦੈ	Mandai	At bad places
ਸੁਕ੍ਰਿਤੁ	Sukrit	Good deeds, honest living
ਧਰਮੁ ਕਮਾਇਆ	Dharam Kamāia	Lived according to the Lord's Will
ਬਖਸੀਸੀ	Bakhsīsi	The Benevolent One
ਅਗਲਾ	Aglā	The Great One, much
ਸਵਾਇਆ	Sawāia	Very much, greatly, more

The Guru in this *pauṛi* tells us of who really deserves to be called a true servant – *sevak* – of the Lord. Simply translated this *pauṛi* says that the truest service is by those who are content in their hearts, and fix their minds on Him. Such ones walk not the evil path and earning an honest living, and doing good deeds they mould their lives according to the Lord's way. They have broken the bonds to the world and they eat but little. The Lord is the great bestower and gives more and more. By lauding the Lord is He to be found. Let us now look at these concepts in greater detail.

In the first line the Guru says the truest service to Him is by those who are content in their hearts and fix their minds on pure truth. It is an unfortunate reality that our approach to our Lord is more often the result of our greed, our hunger for more and more of material things. Our prayers usually carry as an annexure a wish list. This arises from the lack of contentment with what the Lord in His mercy and grace has already provided to us. If we only pause to think we will see that He has given us so much that there could be no words enough to thank Him. This very life we have, every breath we draw is His blessing. Yet it is human nature that guided by our *haumai* we refuse be thankful for, or even to acknowledge what we have and instead like spoilt children we keep asking for more and more. It is an irony that however much we ask for and howsoever much we get, yet are we seeking more. "Sahas khattay lakh ko utth dhāvay, Tripat na āvay maya pāchhay pāvai" says the fifth Nanak in the *Sukhmani Sahib*. It translates as, "When we have earned a thousand, we go seeking a hundred thousand, contentment does not even then come as we chase after illusions." The Guru in the same *astapadi* also says "Bina Santokh nahi ko rājai", meaning without contentment in the heart satiation will not come from these material things. Here the Guru tells us that true service of the Lord requires that there be contentment in the heart and the mind be fixed on the True One, He who is the One and the only, the real Truth.

In the 2nd line the Guru says such true servants of the Lord do not let their steps ever fall on the wrong path. They ever perform good deeds and they order and organise their lives in accordance with *dharma* – the right path laid down by the Lord. This right path is delineated, explained and made clear to us by the *Satguru* through whom the Lord speaks to us. Bhai Vir Singh explains this well in his commentary and says the good deeds done by such true servants of the Lord are performed as part of their obedience to *dharma* and not for any selfish ends or with expectation of any return. Because their good deeds are an end by itself for them, therefore are they truly on the path of *dharma*. He says the term *kamāia* (earned) refers here to their pursuit of *dharma* in this fashion, though *kamāia* is also used to refer to the material things earned through hard labour. The concept here well expresses the basic Sikh dictum of "Nām japna, kirat karni, vand chhakṇa" which translates as, "reciting the Name of the Lord, earning an honest living through hard work, and sharing what we have been granted by the Lord". Bhai Vir Singh's explanation seems here quite appropriate.

Line 3 explains the conduct of these contented true servants of the Lord. The Guru says these fortunate ones have shed all attachment to wordly things and they eat or drink sparingly. The reference is to one of the most common weaknesses that humans are prey to, that for good food and drink. But the allusion is to all types of sensual joys of this world. As Prof. Talib puts it, "Little of the world's substance have they consumed". Minimal pandering to the senses automatically enables maximum focusing on the Lord. It is an ancient tradition in India that spiritual pursuits are always linked with minimising of attachments and with moderation in intake. In Sikhism ritual fasting is not ever approved, so the term used by the Guru here is "aṭe and drank less". Moderated consumption sufficient for comfortable sustenance, but no more than that, is what the Guru is commending here. In other words, leave the lightest footstep possible on the world of matter; make your imprint only on the spiritual world.

In line 4 the Guru says the Lord is the great bestower, giving more and more. As Prof. Teja Singh puts it, "Thou art lavish in thy mercies, of which Thou givest daily ever increasingly." The phrase, "Nit deveh chaṛeh sawāia" is rendered by almost all commentators as, "your bounties keep increasing". Macauliffe has put it more literally as, "Thou givest gifts which increase a quarter fold", 'quarter plus one' being the Punjabi meaning of *sawāia*. Dada Chellaram puts it differently. He says, "And as Thou gave, they rose still higher" using the term *chaṛeh sawāia* to refer to the recipient and not to the gifts. The view of Prof. Teja Singh, followed by many others too, seems more convincing; he holds that the Lord gives bounteously and His blessings are available even more to these contented ones, and these gifts keep ever increasing.

In the concluding line the Guru says by lauding Him they find Him. When we listen to our Guru we will be told that the main device available to us is laudation of the Lord. As the Guru said in *Japji Sahib, pauṛi* 32, "ik dū jībhū lakh hovai, lakh hovai lakhvīs, lakh lakh geṛa ākhiye ek nām jagdīsh", meaning "If we have not one, not two tongues but a hundred thousand, nay twenty folds that, with each should we take the Name of the Lord of the Universe." Through this recitation and singing praises of Him we will one day reach a state where we will begin to gradually acquire a tinge of those same qualities. Our inner selves will get cleansed enough to be worthy of receiving His grace. The Guru here says keep praising Him always, and through this discipline will the devotee one day be able to reach Him. This is also the view adopted by most learned commentators.

PAURI 8

In this, the 8th *pauṛi* there are two *sloks* attached both by Guru Nanak. In the first one the Guru says:

ਸਲੋਕ ਮ: ੧ ॥	Slok Mahla 1
ਪੁਰਖਾਂ ਬਿਰਖਾਂ ਤੀਰਥਾਂ ਤਟਾਂ ਮੇਘਾਂ ਖੇਤਾਂਹ ॥	Purkha[n] Birkha[n] tīrtha[n] tattā[n] megha[n] kheta[n]
ਦੀਪਾਂ ਲੋਆਂ ਮੰਡਲਾਂ ਖੰਡਾਂ ਵਰਭੰਡਾਂਹ ॥	Deepa[n] loā[n] manddlā[n] khanddā[n] varbhanddā[n]
ਅੰਡਜ ਜੇਰਜ ਉਤਭੁਜਾਂ ਖਾਣੀ ਸੇਤਜਾਂਹ ॥	Anddaj jeraj utbhuja[n] khāṇi setjānh
ਸੋ ਮਿਤਿ ਜਾਣੈ ਨਾਨਕਾ ਸਰਾਂ ਮੇਰਾਂ ਜੰਤਾਹ ॥	So mit jānai Nanaka sara[n] Mera[n] jantah
ਨਾਨਕ ਜੰਤ ਉਪਾਇ ਕੈ ਸੰਮਾਲੇ ਸਭਨਾਹ ॥	Nanak jant upai kai samālay sabnāh
ਜਿਨਿ ਕਰਤੈ ਕਰਣਾ ਕੀਆ ਚਿੰਤਾ ਭਿ ਕਰਣੀ ਤਾਹ ॥	Jin Kartai karṇa kīa chinta bhi karṇi tāh
ਸੋ ਕਰਤਾ ਚਿੰਤਾ ਕਰੇ ਜਿਨਿ ਉਪਾਇਆ ਜਗੁ ॥	So karta chinta karay jin upāiya jagg
ਤਿਸੁ ਜੋਹਾਰੀ ਸੁਅਸਤਿ ਤਿਸੁ ਤਿਸੁ ਦੀਬਾਣੁ ਅਭਗੁ ॥	Tis johāri suast tis tis dībāṇ abhagg
ਨਾਨਕ ਸਚੇ ਨਾਮ ਬਿਨੁ ਕਿਆ ਟਿਕਾ ਕਿਆ ਤਗੁ ॥੧॥	Nanak sachay nām bin kya tikka kya tagg. 1.

Glossary:

ਮਿਤਿ	Mit	Estimate
ਤਟਾਂ	Tattā[n]	Shores, banks of rivers

ਮੇਘਾਂ	Meghā[n]	Clouds
ਖਾਣੀ	Khāṇī	Sources (of birth)
ਸਰਾਂ	Sarā[n]	Lakes, bodies of still water
ਕਰਣਾ	Karṇa	Creation
ਸੁਅਸਤਿ	Suast	Salutation
ਤਿਸੁ ਦੀਬਾਣੁ	Tis dībaṇ	His courts
ਅਭਗੁ	Abhagg	Indestructible
ਟਿਕਾ	Tikka	Religious markings on the prehead
ਤਗੁ	Tagg	Holy thread

The Guru speaks here of the vastness of the Lord's doings and His relationship with His creation. He alludes to the meaninglessness of rituals such as the rite of the holy thread, and of the sectarian religious markings, when the mind is not fixed on the True Name. Simply translated this *slok* says that only the Lord knows the estimate of the created humans, trees, *tīraths*, clouds and fields. He only knows the estimate of the islands, worlds, regions, continents, the entire Universe. Of the creatures born of eggs, from placenta and from the ground, and from sweat only He knows the estimate. He knows the estimate of the oceans and the mountains, of all creatures. He has created all and cares for them also. The One who created also worries about them. That Creator who made it all also cares for what He has wrought. Salutations to Him whose courts are eternal. Without devotion to the True Name, he asks, what value are the sectarian marks on the forehead and the sacred thread. Let us now look at it in more detail.

In the 1st and 2nd lines the Guru enumerates the things the Lord has created. He says there are He, the Lord Himself, humans, trees, shores, *tīraths*, clouds, fields, continents, worlds, sectors, and universes. All these are His creation. Only He knows the estimate of how many all these are. *Tīrath* refers to a holy place of pilgrimage in Hinduism. These are more usually to be found on the shores of water bodies. Literally it means a ford, a place where a road crosses a river at a shallow spot. This dates from the olden days when bridges over wide rivers did not exist. Many of these fording spots became the homes of philosophers and religious leaders, and gradually the word *tīrath* acquired in this country a holy connotation. *Khanddā[n], varbhanddā[n]* refers to the sectors of this vast created Universe, and to the Universe – *brahmand* – itself. These lines, and in fact the entire *slok*, is to be read with the fourth line as the key, where the Guru says "so mit jānay Nanaka" – He alone knows the extent, the estimate of these things. The Guru in these lines has enumerated some of those things.

In lines 3 and 4 are further examples given by the Guru of the various things created by the Lord. The Guru says the four sources of birth, the bodies of water, the mountains, are all His creation and only He knows their *mit*. Prof. Teja Singh renders this as, "God Himself knows the extent of animal creation." Dr. Gopal Singh renders *mit* as 'limit' and Prof. Talib as 'the extent of'. Thus, *mit* is generally rendered as measure, extent, limit or as Prof. Sahib Singh says, 'estimate'. The sources of birth were at that time traditionally counted as four. These were *Anddaj* (from the egg), *Jeraj* (from the placenta), *Setaj* (from sweat), and *Utbhuj*– (things that grew from the soil). This covers all fauna and flora, the mammalian, the non-mammalian and the vegetation. The category of *Setaj* covers things like lice and ticks that grew on animal bodies, and which were deemed to have their origin from sweat.

In lines 5 and 6 the Guru adds that having created all these diverse beings and things the Lord also sustains them all. The One who has brought them forth on this Universe also cares for them. The message is to have full faith in the Lord and not needlessly fritter time and energy worrying about the future and about things material. We must surrender and concentrate rather on serving Him. This is not by any means a recipe for non-action, because that is not the Sikh way, which is life affirming and positive. It requires us to involve ourselves fully in the world, work hard and by honest toil make a comfortable living, and also share what we have. While striving and earning we must not however go overboard. We must remember at all times the One who is our Creator and the Creator of all that exists; and He has also the responsibility for sustaining those He created. If we follow this approach in our lives then all our actions will be grounded solidly in this consciousness and our wasteful worry about the outcome will vanish. The actions marked by good intent and righteous thought will become our main focus; the results will become the Lord's responsibility. In this sense it is said here that He sustains all.

In lines 7 and 8, the Guru says that the Creator will care for this creation, I salute Him whose courts are everlasting, eternal. The 7th line is clear enough and is a reiteration of the 6th line. The terms *johāri* and *suast* in the 8th line are forms of salutation. *Johāri* means salutation, obeisance; and *suast* means blessing, benediction. So the Guru is here saying I salute the Lord. Prof. Talib puts these lines as, "To Him I bow, Him I hail whose court is eternal." Dr. Gopal Singh puts it as, "Him I greet and pay obeisance to." Macauliffe and Prof. Teja Singh also have the same rendering. Dada Chellaram slightly alters it as, "For us is to bow in obeisance unto Him. Let us beg for His blessings." The use of the word 'blessings' by some of the learned men, comes from the way in which *suast* was used in those times. This was the typical phrase used by Brahmins to bless those householders who gifted them something. It is a way of invoking blessings and conveying wishes for the well being of the giver. These two terms used thus, carry as we can see a sense of obeisance in addition to saluation. Thus are these used by the Guru for addressing the Lord while giving thanks to Him as the eternal Giver and Creator of all that we can see or even think of. The word *dībāṇ* translates as court and is often used in the *SGGS* to refer to the divine courts of the Lord. Prof. Teja Singh though renders it here as 'administration', while Prof. Sahib Singh renders the phrase "tis dībāṇ abhagg" as "support of that Lord". He translates *dībāṇ* as support and *abhagg* as eternal or indestructible. In the context here, however, the rendering as 'The Divine Court' seems more appealing, as has been followed by most of the learned ones. In fact it needs to be understood as referring to the entire system of the Lord's justice and governance.

In the 9th, the concluding, line the Guru says without the recitation of the True Name what use are religious observances like the forehead markings and the sacred thread. Having enumerated the vastness and the variety of this creation and told us that He cares for it all, the Guru is now saying that our mind needs to be fixed on the Creator, the Sustainer. For this the Guru refers to the two more common Hindu religious observances of that time, the holy thread and the religious markings on the foreheads. The intention is to stress the point that His Name must permeate all our actions, and empty formalism is of no avail. The essence of worship is in surrendering and immersing ourselves totally into Him. For this the prescribed formula is *Nām Simran* – recitation of His Name. It is enjoined upon us to do so continually, at all times, with each breath in our body and with each morsel we ingest. Once that state is reached, any other devices become unnecessary. So, the Guru's approach is that if we must we may follow our observances and rites, but the key requirement is to ensure His Name always permeates these observances. The rites performed without the mind fixed on the Lord are fruitless. When the mind acquires the right focus it will become clear that such rites have become pointless, and we may perform those or not as we may choose. The focus must ever be on the True Name alone and on nothing else.

Pauṛi 8

In the second *slok* with this *pauṛi* the Guru says:

ਮ: ੧ ॥	M: 1
ਲਖ ਨੇਕੀਆ ਚੰਗਿਆਈਆ ਲਖ ਪੁੰਨਾ ਪਰਵਾਣੁ ॥	Lakh nekīya changiāia lakh punnā parwāṇ
ਲਖ ਤਪ ਉਪਰਿ ਤੀਰਥਾਂ ਸਹਜ ਜੋਗ ਬੇਬਾਣ ॥	Lakh tapp uppar tīrtha[n], sehaj jog bebāṇ
ਲਖ ਸੂਰਤਣ ਸੰਗਰਾਮ ਰਣ ਮਹਿ ਛੁਟਹਿ ਪਰਾਣ ॥	Lakh sūrtaṇ sangrām raṇ mai chhuteh parāṇ
ਲਖ ਸੁਰਤੀ ਲਖ ਗਿਆਨ ਧਿਆਨ ਪੜੀਅਹਿ ਪਾਠ ਪੁਰਾਣ ॥	Lakh surti lakh gyān dhyān paṛieh pātth purāṇ
ਜਿਨਿ ਕਰਤੈ ਕਰਣਾ ਕੀਆ ਲਿਖਿਆ ਆਵਣ ਜਾਣੁ ॥	Jin kartai karṇa kīya likhiya āvaṇ jāṇ
ਨਾਨਕ ਮਤੀ ਮਿਥਿਆ ਕਰਮੁ ਸਚਾ ਨੀਸਾਣੁ ॥੨॥	Nanak mati mithhiya karam sachā nīsaṇ. 2.

Glossary:

ਪੁੰਨਾ	Punna	Religious actions, good deeds
ਪਰਵਾਣੁ	Parwāṇ	Accepted
ਬੇਬਾਣ	Bebāṇ	In the wilderness
ਸੁਰਤੀ	surti	Fixing one's mind
ਆਵਣ ਜਾਣੁ	Āwaṇ jāṇ	Rebirths
ਕਰਮੁ	Karam	Benediction, blessing
ਨੀਸਾਣੁ	Nīsāṇ	Mark
ਮਤੀ ਮਿਥਿਆ	Mati mithhiya	One's own wisdom

The Guru is telling us here that we must not let our austerities and good deeds lead us into vanity and pride. In this context he speaks to us of the Lord's grace. Simply translated this *slok* says that (compared to the recitation of His Name) millions of good deeds, beneficent actions, charities however accepted among people these may be, are of no avail. Millions of austerities at *tīraths* and Yoga practices in the wilderness are of no avail. Millions of acts of valour leading to death in the battlefield are of no avail. Millions of recitations of scriptures like the *Shrutis* and *Purānas* are of no avail. This effort is *mati mithhiya* when it is born from one's own wisdom, and is not infused with the Name of the Lord. What matters is the mark of grace from the Creator who made it all and who decides our position in the circle of births.The Guru has in this *slok* adopted the style he has used in th*e pauṛis* in the *Āsa di Vār*, and the lesson is to be found in the concluding lines, that without the Lord's grace, all deeds are unavailing. Let us now look at it in more detail.

In the first line the Guru speaks of numerous virtuous deeds, proper charities and acts of goodness which men traditionally deem to be the way to God. In the previous *slok* we were told of the multifarious forms of creation for all of whom the Creator cares always. We were then told that religious rites without fixing the mind on His Name are pointless. Now the Guru is referring to the various acts that humans perform on the path to God-realization. He speaks of virtuous deeds and good actions. Thus, he speaks in the first line of lakhs, literally one hundred thousand, of virtuous deeds and acts of charity, both of which were considered to be a widely approved activity on the path to God. There may be hundreds of thousands of such acts and the world of humans may accept and even applaud these. Implicit is the thought that without the Lord's grace these are fruitless.

In the 2nd line we are told of another common approach, that of austerities. The Guru says you may perform a hundred thousand austerities at *tīraths* and practices of yoga in the wilderness, yet are these devices of no avail. A *tīrath,* literally a ford, means a holy place of pilgrimage much visited by those seeking salvation. In this country with its numerous streams, paths were found across these at shallow spots, or fords. Many of these were naturally well frequented and a system of giving discourses at these places developed because that is where the audience was. Men of learning then permanently settled these, over a period of time. In some cases, gradually a mythology developed around many of these. A *tīrath* became a term for all holy places even away from streams. Doing austerities and penances is called *tapp*, and some men seeking God go through such disciplines. Performing these austerities at *tīraths* was supposed to bring that much more merit. The Guru is saying that even if you do these a hundred thousand times it will not suffice to help you reach the Lord, unless it is totally imbued with His Name. Similarly, doing yogic practices in wildernesses and jungles away from human distractions, was deemed a way to enlightenment. *Sehaj* yoga, explains the *Shabdarth*, is among *Jogi* sects the *samādhi* in the mystical Tenth Gate. In the Guru's path this is achieved by *Nām Simran, Seva, Sangat* and *Kīrtan*. Here in this line the reference is to the *Jogi's* practice of *Sehaj* yoga, a practice in contrast to another discipline, that of *Hattha* yoga which involves severe and harsh austerities. The Guru says such *Sehaj* yoga in the jungles will also not be any guarantee of a passage to the Lord.

In the 3rd line he says a hundred thousand acts of bravery in battle even to the extent of losing one's life are also insufficient. The reference here is to another accepted practice – that of great valour in furtherance of the right cause. Willingness to die in such a cause was, especially for the Kshatriya clan, deemed to be a passport to heaven. The Guru says without the Lord's grace even this will mean nothing, and will have no fruitful outcome.

In the 4th line the Guru says a hundred thousand recitations of scriptures will be as nothing if the Lord's grace is missing. The term *surati* is rendered by Prof. Sahib Singh and Prof. Talib Singh as 'fixing the mind on', but many learned commentators take it as *Shruti*, one of the class of scriptural literature in the Hindu belief system. Since the Guru is listing various commonly accepted practices on the path to God-realization, and is in this line talking of the scriptures, the latter interpretation seems more appealing. Listed here are, therefore, the *Shrutis*, the *Purānas* and recitation of various religious scriptures and literature, the recitation of which was another very popular method of meditation. All of this may be desirable, and certainly preferable to evil deeds and materal pursuits. But without the Lord's grace, says the Guru here, these will not suffice.

In lines 5 and 6, the Guru comes to the specific lesson of this *slok.* He says the Lord is Himself the arbiter of when we will be in the cycle of births and when He will take us out of it. All the devices mentioned above when they come from a sense of one's self, one's own wisdom are *mithhiya* – as nothing, or in other words not sufficient to reach us to God. In these concluding lines the point of the recitation in the previous lines of all the greatly regarded means of emancipation, or salvation, is finally clarified. The Guru says the essence of all our activity must be to seek His grace, His blessings. Any number of good deeds and religious practices, when tinged with *haumai* are useless as our vehicle to Him. He will not be reached through our efforts and endeavours however lofty or mighy. These efforts are necessary and good, but useful only when with every breath there is the clear realization that the moment of deliverance will come not merely from these, but will come only when the Lord so desires and when He turns His glance of grace on us. When that happens we will get the *nīsān* (mark of approval), the passport out of this world and this cycle of rebirths.

In this, the eighth *pauṛi* to which these *sloks* are attached, the Guru says:

ਪਉੜੀ ॥	Pauṛi
ਸਚਾ ਸਾਹਿਬੁ ਏਕੁ ਤੂੰ ਜਿਨਿ ਸਚੋ ਸਚੁ ਵਰਤਾਇਆ ॥	Sacha sahib ek tū[n] jin sacho sach vartāia
ਜਿਸੁ ਤੂੰ ਦੇਹਿ ਤਿਸੁ ਮਿਲੈ ਸਚੁ ਤਾ ਤਿਨ੍ਹੀ ਸਚੁ ਕਮਾਇਆ ॥	Jis tū deh tis milai sach ta tini sach kamāia
ਸਤਿਗੁਰਿ ਮਿਲਿਐ ਸਚੁ ਪਾਇਆ ਜਿਨ੍ਹ ਕੈ ਹਿਰਦੈ ਸਚੁ ਵਸਾਇਆ ॥	Satguru miliai sach pāiya jis kay hirdai sach vasāia
ਮੂਰਖ ਸਚੁ ਨ ਜਾਣਨ੍ਹੀ ਮਨਮੁਖੀ ਜਨਮੁ ਗਵਾਇਆ ॥	Mūrakh sach na jāṇani manmukhi janam gavāia
ਵਿਚਿ ਦੁਨੀਆ ਕਾਹੇ ਆਇਆ ॥੮॥	Vich dunīya kahay āiya. 8.

Glossary:

ਸਚੋ ਸਚੁ	Sacho sach	The real Truth
ਵਰਤਾਇਆ	Vartāia	Besotwed, distributed
ਕਮਾਇਆ	Kamāia	Have earned
ਵਸਾਇਆ	Vasāiya	Has settled
ਮਨਮੁਖੀ	Manmukhi	Ego-centred ones
ਆਇਆ	Āia	Were born

The Guru tells us here that we find the Lord only when He so wills. Meanwhile, we have to keep ourself ready and clean enough to be able to accept His grace. And for that a true Guru is needed who will lead us on the right path. Simply translated this *slok* says that the Lord is the only Truth who dispenses nothing but the truth. Those on whom the Lord dispenses His grace find the truth and they live a true life. When we find the true preceptor then only do we get access to truth because in the *Satguru* the Lord Himself resides. The ego-centric ones will not find the truth and their lives will be wasted. Why at all did such ones come to this world? Let us now look at it in more detail.

In the first line the Guru says He is the only, the sole Truth who dispenses nothing but the truth. As Prof. Talib puts it, "Thou art the holy Lord who truth solely hast dispensed." Dada Chellaram says, "Only Thou art the one True master, bestowing truth and all truth." Dr. Gopal Singh changes it slightly to, "True, O Lord art thou alone who has manifested thyself in all as Truth." The stress is here on *ek*– (one). The Lord as the Creator, says the Guru, is the 'One' unique by Himself, and as the sole Reality everything that he dispenses or has created is also the truth, being part of Him. Here though the stress is more on the aspect that while all devotees are seeking Him, but among them to some the Lord will dispense that truth. It will come as a *prasād*, a benediction, as and when the Lord so decides.

In the 2nd line the Guru makes this clearer. He says only he to whom the Lord dispenses this grace finds the Truth and only such lucky ones live a true life. As Dr. Gopal Singh puts it, "He whom Thou blessest with Truth, alone practices Truth." This reinforces the point made in the previous *slok* that no amount of efforts if they are born from our *haumai* will bring us near to Him. The knowledge of the reality will come only when He turns His glance of grace on us.

In the 3rd line the Guru says when we find the *Satguru*, the true preceptor, then does this access to the truth follow, because in the *Satguru* the True One Himself resides. For a Sikh this *Satguru* is of course none other than the *SGGS*. The phrase "jinn ke hirdai sach vasāia" is rendered by Bhai Vir Singh, Prof. Sahib Singh and Dr. Gopal Singh to mean that "the Truth permeates our hearts" after we have found the *Satguru*. Prof. Talib, Macauliffe and Dada Chellaram render it slightly differently as, "the Truth is obtained through the *Satguru* in whose heart He has placed the Truth." Since the Guru has earlier also stressed the importance of the *Satguru*, the latter interpretation seems more convincing. Of course it is axiomatic that when by God's grace such a worthy *Satguru* is found by us, he will eventually awaken in our hearts also the same permeating truth.

In lines 4 and 5, the Guru concludes by telling us of the plight of the foolish ones who are ego-centred. He says the fools will know not the truth and in their ego-centrism will have wasted their birth. Why did such ones, he raises the question, at all come to this world? The reference here is to the great value the Guru puts on the human form. As we noted earlier, the fifth Nanak told us in *Rāg Āsa*, page 378 of the *SGGS*, "Bhaī prāpat mānukh dehuriya, Gobind Milan ki eh teri barīya", meaning that the human form is given to you as a gift to give you an opportunity to be one with the Lord. Again, the *SGGS* mentions on page 1366, *slok* of Bhagat Kabir, "Kabir mānukh janam dulambh hai hoye na bārai bār", meaning the human form is priceless; it will not be granted to you again and again. If this rare opporutinity is wasted and we seek not the path our *Satguru* has laid down, because we are overwhelmed by our own ego, our *haumai*, then why did we at all come to this world? Why were we born? The Guru in the last line expresses his sadness that such foolish ones have frittered away this golden opportunity.

PAURI 9

In the previous *pauṛi* the Guru spoke of the real truth coming to us through the *Satguru* and also said that it will happen only when the Lord so wills it. He told us that human actions, howsoever lofty and pure, can never be sufficient to help us reach the Lord. He informed us in other words to suppress our *haumai*, our ego, our sense of self. It was enjoined upon us to recite constantly the Lord's Name, while sincerely following the path laid down by the *Satguru*. In this *pauṛi* now the Guru speaks further of the real truth and of the inadequacy of devices based on our own senses or minds, howsoever clever or high these may be. This *pauṛi* also has two *sloks*, both by Guru Nanak, attached to it. The first one says:

ਸਲੋਕੁ ਮ: ੧ ॥	Slok Mahla 1
ਪੜਿ ਪੜਿ ਗਡੀ ਲਦੀਅਹਿ ਪੜਿ ਪੜਿ ਭਰੀਅਹਿ ਸਾਥ ॥	Paṛ paṛ gaddi ladīai paṛ paṛ bharīeh sāth
ਪੜਿ ਪੜਿ ਬੇੜੀ ਪਾਈਐ ਪੜਿ ਪੜਿ ਗਡੀਅਹਿ ਖਾਤ ॥	Paṛ paṛ beṛi pāīai paṛ paṛ gaddīeh khāt
ਪੜੀਅਹਿ ਜੇਤੇ ਬਰਸ ਬਰਸ ਪੜੀਅਹਿ ਜੇਤੇ ਮਾਸ ॥	Paṛīeh jetay baras baras paṛīeh jetay mās
ਪੜੀਐ ਜੇਤੀ ਆਰਜਾ ਪੜੀਅਹਿ ਜੇਤੇ ਸਾਸ ॥	Paṛīeh jeti ārja paṛīeh jetay sās
ਨਾਨਕ ਲੇਖੈ ਇਕ ਗਲ ਹੋਰੁ ਹਉਮੈ ਝਖਣਾ ਝਾਖ ॥੧॥	Nanak lekhai ik gall hor haumai jhakṇa jhākh. 1.

Glossary:

ਗਡੀ	Gaddi	Carts, vehicles
ਭਰੀਅਹਿ	Bharīeh	Fill up
ਬੇੜੀ	Beṛi	Boat

Pauṛi 9

ਖਾਤ	Khāt	Cellars
ਆਰਜਾ	Ārjā	Span of life; Age
ਸਾਸ	Sās	Breath
ਝਖਣਾ ਝਾਖ	Jhakhṇa Jhākh	Wasting energy, pointlessly
ਸਾਥ	Sāth	Mounds, in laden caravans

The Guru stresses here on the vital importance of focusing on the Name of the Lord with full devotion, and says that all else is of little avail where the search for the Lord is concerned. Simply translated this *slok* says that (without that devotion) we may read cartloads and boatloads of books and fill up our cellars with these. We may study these for all the months and the years of our lives, using every breath we have for this purpose. But one thing only will avail us and that is the devoted recitation of the Lord's Name, all the rest of it is unavailing. As the Guru said in the *Sukhmani Sahib*, *ashtpadi* 3, **"ਸਰਬ ਧਰਮ ਮਹਿ ਸ੍ਰੇਸਟ ਧਰਮੁ॥ ਹਰਿ ਕੋ ਨਾਮ ਜਪਿ ਨਿਰਮਲ ਕਰਮੁ॥"** – "sarab dharma meh srest dharma. Har ko nām jap nirmal karam", meaning that highest of all religions, and the purest of all actions is the recitation of the Lord's Name.

In this *slok* the Guru speaks further on the futility of actions when these are unredeemed by *Nām Simran*, and which arise from a sense of *haumai*. The specific reference is to a practice very common at that time, which was to participate in philosophical/religious disputation based on knowledge of the holy books. Since the printed word was not yet invented, these *shāstras* (holy books) were all hand-written on scrolls. These manuscripts were naturally bulky and were also precious because copies were hard to make. The scholars therefore carried these with them when they travelled from their seminaries. The more the number of these the greater the stature of the scholar was deemed to be. The really great ones thus had cartloads or boatloads of these books depending on which mode of travel they were using. It was also a practice to challenge scholars to debates with the owner having the right to the loser's library, thus increasing his own stock greatly. A big cartload was also therefore the mark of a scholar who was so learned that he must have bested many another on the finer points of religious and philosophical interpretations. The Guru is here referring to this practice. Let us now look at it in more detail.

In line 1 he says we may read and read, so much that our books fill up whole carts. Prof. Sahib Singh renders the word *sāth* as 'mounds' or 'heaps'. The

Shabdarth renders it as 'caravans'. Bhai Vir Singh explains it as meaning 'accompanying' or 'group of people joining one'. He says it is from the Sanskrit *sārath* (herd of animals of the same kind). So he says, *sāth* would mean loaded oxen, or camels or other pack animals. This seems a convincing rendering. So the term here is used to denote caravans carrying heaps of books packed on animal backs. The Guru is evoking for us the image of the scholar who has cartloads of books and is going with a caravan containing many animals loaded with his books alone.

In line 2 the Guru stresses the same point. He says we may fill up boatloads of books we have read, or we may fill up whole cellars with these. The term **'ਖਾਤ'** (*khāt*), refers to the underground silos used for storing foodgrains. If these *khāts* were not to be filled up with foodgrains for which these were traditionally used, but, says the Guru, were instead to be the storehouse for the books of the learned scholars.

The 3rd and 4th lines now refer to the amount of time the great scholars may devote to the reading of these accumulated books. The Guru says we may read them throughout the years that we have and for all the months in those years. On the same theme, in line 4 he says we may read them in fact for the entire allotted span of our lives, using for the purpose each breath that we take.

In the concluding line, the 5th, the Guru concludes in his usual style by driving home the exact point of his message. All these feats of learning and great scholarliness, he says, are of no avail when it comes to reaching the Lord. For that only one thing is needed, and that, as he has repeatedly told us, is *Nām Simraṇ* – reciting wholeheartedly the Name of the Lord; singing his praises. That one single activity is the only key to success. All these other mighty feats of the intellect and of learning will only go to strengthen the *haumai* within us. Learning to control that *haumai*, can come only from singing His praises, from *Nām Simran*. All else in born of ego and will lead only to wasted effort and frustration. The term *Jhakhṇa Jhākh* is used to describe an activity that entailed much effort but produced little by way of fruitful results. All our effort to show how bright and learned we are is nothing, according to the Guru, but *Jhakhṇa Jhākh*. Only singing His praises will extinguish our *haumai* and take us on the path that leads to the Lord.

In the second *slok* with this *pauṛi*, the Guru elaborates this point further. He says:

ਮ: ੧ ॥	M: 1
ਲਿਖਿ ਲਿਖਿ ਪੜਿਆ ॥	Likh likh paṛia
ਤੇਤਾ ਕੜਿਆ ॥	Teta kaṛia
ਬਹੁ ਤੀਰਥ ਭਵਿਆ ॥	Bahu tīrath bhavia
ਤੇਤੋ ਲਵਿਆ ॥	Teto lavia
ਬਹੁ ਭੇਖ ਕੀਆ ਦੇਹੀ ਦੁਖੁ ਦੀਆ ॥	Bahu bhekh kīa dehi dukh dīa
ਸਹੁ ਵੇ ਜੀਆ ਅਪਣਾ ਕੀਆ ॥	Sahu ve jīya apṇa kīa
ਅੰਨੁ ਨ ਖਾਇਆ ਸਾਦੁ ਗਵਾਇਆ ॥	Unn na khāiya sād gavāia
ਬਹੁ ਦੁਖੁ ਪਾਇਆ ਦੂਜਾ ਭਾਇਆ ॥	Bahu dukh pāiya dūja bhāia
ਬਸਤ੍ਰ ਨ ਪਹਿਰੈ ॥	Bastra na pahrai
ਅਹਿਨਿਸਿ ਕਹਰੈ ॥	Ahnis kahrai
ਮੋਨਿ ਵਿਗੂਤਾ ॥	Maun vigūta
ਕਿਉ ਜਾਗੈ ਗੁਰ ਬਿਨੁ ਸੂਤਾ ॥	Kio jāgay gur bin sūta
ਪਗ ਉਪੇਤਾਣਾ ॥	Pagg upetāṇa
ਅਪਣਾ ਕੀਆ ਕਮਾਣਾ ॥	Apṇa kīya kamāṇa
ਅਲੁ ਮਲੁ ਖਾਈ ਸਿਰਿ ਛਾਈ ਪਾਈ ॥	Ull mull khāi sirr chhāi pāi
ਮੂਰਖਿ ਅੰਧੈ ਪਤਿ ਗਵਾਈ ॥	Mūrakh andhai pat gavāi
ਵਿਣੁ ਨਾਵੈ ਕਿਛੁ ਥਾਇ ਨ ਪਾਈ ॥	Viṇ nāvai kichh thāye na pāi
ਰਹੈ ਬੇਬਾਣੀ ਮੜੀ ਮਸਾਣੀ ॥	Rahai bebāṇi maṛi masāṇi
ਅੰਧੁ ਨ ਜਾਣੈ ਫਿਰਿ ਪਛੁਤਾਣੀ ॥	Andh na jānai phir pachhtāṇi
ਸਤਿਗੁਰੁ ਭੇਟੇ ਸੋ ਸੁਖੁ ਪਾਏ ॥	Satguru bhettay so sukh pāye
ਹਰਿ ਕਾ ਨਾਮੁ ਮੰਨਿ ਵਸਾਏ ॥	Har ka nām mann vasāye
ਨਾਨਕ ਨਦਰਿ ਕਰੇ ਸੋ ਪਾਏ ॥	Nanak nadar karay so pāye
ਆਸ ਅੰਦੇਸੇ ਤੇ ਨਿਹਕੇਵਲੁ ਹਉਮੈ ਸਬਦਿ ਜਲਾਏ ॥੨॥	Ās andesay tay nihkewal haumai sabad jalāye. 2.

Simply translated, this *slok* says that the more the book learning the greater the sense of ego. The more frequent the visits to *tīraths*, the greater the pride about it. The more the guises donned the more the body is troubled. Such a one will suffer the effects of his actions. If one starves the body, all one loses is the satisfaction of satisfying a bodily need. Such a one forgets the Lord and is engrossed in other things. Not wearing clothes is only more trouble for the body. Vows of silence are a waste and without the Guru you will not rise. If you go barefoot you will suffer the results. Eating dirt and with ashes on the head the blind fool only loses respect. Without the Lord's Name you cannot reach anywhere. Spending time in graveyards and wildernesses are those blind to reality and they will repent. He who finds the true preceptor will find peace and the Lord's Name will enter his heart. Only he finds Him on whom the Lord's glance of grace is there. Such a one becomes free from doubts and desires and his *haumai* is eradicated from the root. In the previous *slok* the Guru spoke of the *ik gal*, the one thing that mattered – singing His praises. He contrasted it with what men of learning instead do; read big tomes and attain merely greater vanity, more pride in their own learnedness. Here he speaks further of what the effect of similar other activity is on us. Let us now look at it in more detail.

In lines 1 and 2 he says the more book learning is acquired the hotter burns the fire of our *haumai* inside us. The word *kaṛia* is rendered as 'burnt' or 'seared' by the *Shabdarth* as also by Dr. Gopal Singh and Dada Chellaram. Bhai Vir Singh translates it as 'burning, fuming'. Prof. Sahib Singh renders it as 'becomes arrogant'. Prof. Teja Singh also translates it similarly as 'haughty'. Prof. Talib says 'more by anxiety is he overcome' – a meaning closer to burning, etc. Macauliffe calls it 'tormented'. The meaning as 'burning', 'tormented', anxious', etc. may literally be correct, but in the context here the view taken by Prof. Sahib Singh seems more appropriate. We have to keep in mind what the Guru is telling us. He has said that such activities are born of *haumai* and lead to further strengthening of that *haumai* – the ego. The greater the number of volumes read, the greater the pride, the arrogance, which is how Prof. Sahib Singh has rendered this phrase.

In lines 3 and 4 the Guru says the more the *tīraths* visited the more the verbosity. *Lavia* means chattering. The more the frequency of these religious pilgrimages the greater the pride acquired, the more the urge to tell others about one's achievement, to prate, to brag.

In lines 5 and 6, the Guru says the more guises you don, the more you trouble your body; you suffer for your own actions, he says. The reference is to the various practices where marks and signs are put on the body or where it is placed in various uncomfortable postures. For example, some sects of sadhus seek to mortify the spirit by inflicting various types of pain on the body, such as piercing some part, standing for long periods on one leg and so on. The Guru says all these do nothing for you except to put your body in pain. If you stubbornly insist on trying to impress people through such actions then it will go only to bolster your *haumai*. Thus, the body suffers pain and discomfort and the soul is tarnished by *haumai*. Then, says the Guru, all we can say is that go ahead and be ready to suffer the effects of your actions.

In lines 7 and 8, the Guru says if you give up food you are uselessly depriving yourself. Such a one forgets the Lord and his mind is occupied in these other activities. Losing sight of the Lord in this fashion will bring much sorrow. The reference here is to the practice of prolonged fasting as a way of mortifying the self. It brings no merit in the Lord's courts, the Guru is telling us, but is only depriving you of the pleasure of fulfilling a bodily need which arises in accordance with the Lord's Will. The body created by Him is meant to be fed and looked after so that it can be our vehicle for *Nām Simran*. Starving it is a pointless torture. This activity is born of ego and thus will only take us away from the 'One'. It will only bring trouble – to the body from starvation and to the soul from the *haumai* it generates.

In lines 9 and 10, the Guru says going without clothes also brings trouble only. This is in the context of the practice followed by some sects who go around naked. The Guru says you will only suffer from the cold and the heat and inflict pain day and night on the body. Such things only bring pride and are not going to help you kill your *haumai* and reach Him.

In lines 11 and 12, the Guru says observing vows of silence one wastes oneself, how will such a one sunk in ignorance rise without the Guru's help. This has reference to another practice – that of taking vows of silence as a form of worship. Such persons will not utter a sound and will communicate only by sign or the written word. The point the Guru is stressing is that such persons will also be caught in the trap of pride. They cannot awaken from this pit of ignorance, except when they are lucky enough to find a *Satguru*, a true preceptor.

In the 13th and 14th lines the Guru says some go barefoot. So what is the outcome? Their feet will hurt and they will suffer. This is self-inflicted punishment, to no useful purpose. The proper course rather is the singing of the Lord's praises and thus gradually extinguishing the *haumai* within.

In lines 15 and 16 the Guru refers to the sects who smear ashes on their heads and eat dirt. This is meant as a form of self-abnegation, thus seeking to weaken the ego, and is deemed by them the proper way to worship. The Guru says such activity does nothing for you except that you lose respect in the eyes of others. Prof. Talib renders it as, "by eating filth he brings ignominy on his head". Most learned ones have similarly rendered it. The Guru's view expressed repeatedly in the *SGGS* is that these are all outward actions and manifestations of formalism, while the Lord is to be reached only through cleansing of the inner self, for which *Nām Simran* is the proper course.

In line 17, the Guru now makes the point quite clear. He speaks to us of the one device that will work. He says all those indulging in various forms of physical activity involving punishing of the body or those relying on the strength of their intellect, their knowledge and their learning are in fact going astray. He says without the Lord's Name they will not find their destination.

In lines 18 and 19 the Guru refers to another set of people. These are the ones who go and spend nights in graveyards or in lonely wilderness. There are some sects whose form of worship requires the performance of rituals in the wilderness, in haunted houses and other scary places like graveyards. Such ones, says the Guru, are blind to the reality and will repent their foolishness one day.

In lines 20 and 21 and the next, concluding, ones the Guru sums up the argument. Having listed the various practices which go only to strengthen the *haumai* within us, he now says that peace of mind will come only to the one who finds the *Satguru* and in whose heart the true Name resides. Through the Guru alone is this path to be found, and true devotion means having the Name reside in one's heart. This will not happen through odd practies of the esoteric kind; it will happen only by listening to the Guru's message.

In the concluding lines, the 22nd and 23rd, the Guru says only he finds the *Satguru* on whom the Lord's Benediction descends. Such a fortunate one becomes free from doubts or fears, hopes and desires and burns his *haumai* from the root. Our *haumai* keeps us tied to this world. In this state our minds are full of things we crave. We want more and more of material things, because after all it is a harsh reality that power and possessions are for most humans in this world, the most keenly sought rewards. Many of us also carry in our hearts serious doubts as to what is the correct way of approaching the Lord; and even whether He exists at all. We are told here by the Guru that once we find the *Satguru* all such desires and hopes will disappear, and all such doubts and fears will vanish. The path to the Lord will be clear to us.

In the *pauṛi* that goes to which these *sloks* were attached, the Guru speaks to us of the true devotees, the *bhagats* who have found the Lord in their hearts. He says:

ਪਉੜੀ ॥	Pauṛi
ਭਗਤ ਤੇਰੈ ਮਨਿ ਭਾਵਦੇ ਦਰਿ ਸੋਹਨਿ ਕੀਰਤਿ ਗਾਵਦੇ ॥	Bhagat terai mann bhavday darr Sohan kīrat gāvday
ਨਾਨਕ ਕਰਮਾ ਬਾਹਰੇ ਦਰਿ ਢੋਅ ਨ ਲਹਨੀ ਧਾਵਦੇ ॥	Nanak karma bahray darr ddhoe na lahni dhāvday
ਇਕਿ ਮੂਲੁ ਨ ਬੁਝਨਿ੍ ਆਪਣਾ ਅਣਹੋਦਾ ਆਪੁ ਗਣਾਇਦੇ ॥	Ik mūl na bujhaṇ āpṇa anhoda āp gaṇāiday
ਹਉ ਢਾਢੀ ਕਾ ਨੀਚ ਜਾਤਿ ਹੋਰਿ ਉਤਮ ਜਾਤਿ ਸਦਾਇਦੇ ॥	Hau ddhāddhī ka nīch jāt hor uttam jāt sadāiday
ਤਿਨ੍ ਮੰਗਾ ਜਿ ਤੁਝੈ ਧਿਆਇਦੇ ॥੯॥	Tinn manga je tujhai dhiāiday. 9.

Glossary:

ਦਰਿ	Darr	At the (Lord's) door
ਕੀਰਤਿ	Kīrat	Praises, laudation
ਕਰਮਾ ਬਾਹਰੇ	Karma bāhray	Luckless ones
ਮੂਲੁ	Mūl	Root
ਅਣਹੋਦਾ	Aṇhoda	Lacking
ਗਣਾਇਦੇ	Gaṇāiday	Deem themselves
ਢਾਢੀ	Ddhaddhi	Bard, singer of praises
ਜਾਤਿ	Jāt	Caste, class

Simply translated this *pauṛi* says that the Lord's devotees are pleasing to Him as they sing His praises at His door, from the core of their hearts. There are others, not blessed by Him who will find not the Divine door and keep wandering. Some do not recognize the reality within them and yet boast of their non-existing merits. The Guru says he deems himself of low caste and a professional singer of praises while others call themselves of high caste, but he seeks the company only of those whose minds are fixed on the Lord in adoration. Standing at the

Lord's door implies here a state of surrender to Him and ordering one's life in accordance with His *Hukam*. Let us now look at the lesson here in more detail.

In line 1 the Guru says that the Lord's *bhagats* are pleasing to His heart as they sing His praises at His door. The word *darr* literally means portal, gate or threshold. Since the Lord is not confined to any one abode, the *darr* here has to be taken as signifying proximity, being 'near Him'. This happy state comes about when the mind is fixed on Him and we are in a state of total acceptance detached from things that are *Maya*. As the Guru has repeatedly told us no activity, no religious rites, no observances are pleasing to the Lord except when the mind is wholly fixed on Him. So, says the Guru, "the *bhagats* singing your praises are close to you in their spirits and are effulgent as a result". Such true devotees are pleasing to the Lord.

In the 2nd line the Guru speaks of the other kind, the ones not fortune enough to be able to sing His praises. The Guru says they do not find sanctuary at His door, and they keep wandering. The wandering here is obviously referring to the cycle of rebirths, of transmigration into which the unredeemed soul is trapped. *Dhāvdey* means rushing about which is how Prof. Talib puts it. Prof. Teja Singh puts it as, "find no refuge at thy gate and wander away from it". Dada Chellaram and Dr. Gopal Singh also render it as 'wander'. Macauliffe puts it well as, "Those who are outside thy favour find no entrance and wander in many births." Bhai Vir Singh says in his commentary that some also translate it to say "since such ones leaving *Nām Simraṇ* aside remain rushing about in outside activities they find no shelter." He also however deems the correct meaning as, "they remain unredeemed, unliberated from rebirths".

In the 3rd line the Guru says some do not recognise their own reality, but boast even then about their non-existing merits. The term *mūl* means 'root', so the meaning of the term *mūl na bujhaṇ* literally is 'recognise not their roots'. Since the 'root' of all souls is the Lord Himself, the only Reality, the line should be rendered as "he does not recognise the Divine spark within himself". *Aṇhoda* means not having within, lacking and *Āp gaṇāiday* meaning "want themselves counted", or in other words brag about themselves. Taken together the correct meaning would be that he is boasting about what he does not have. In this context *mūl* would refer not only to the Divine within man but also to the inner, real worth of the person. Prof. Sahib Singh has well combined the two shades of meaning and rendered this line as, "he has not achieved the divine qualities – which come from the Lord – and even though lacking these they claim to be great".

In the concluding lines, the 4th and 5th, the Guru says, "I am low of caste, a professional singer of praises; others call themselves of high caste. I want the company of those whose minds are fixed on you." He is obviously referring here to the Lord. *Nīch jāt* clearly means low caste, and has been so rendered by the learned ones. The word *Ddhāddhi ka* needs explanation. A *ddhādi* in the Punjab is a term used for village minstrels, who compose and sing poems of praise to the affluent and the mighty. As such the profession does not enjoy a very high social standing. Also, usually *ddhaddhīs* usually came from castes deemed lower in the social structure at that time. Prof. Talib renders this line as, "God's minstrel am I, low of caste … others of high caste are called." Bhai Vir Singh puts it as, "What am I, a mere *ddhāddhi* who sings your praise, and the caste system dubs me of low status. Others call themselves of high caste. But all I ask is that please reward me with the company of those who love you, meditate on you." Prof. Sahib Singh puts the last line slightly differently as, "I seek your Name from those who sing your praises." Most commentators however put it as, "I seek the company of those who meditate on you", which seems a more fitting interpretation.

The Guru true to his style of conveying his divine message without an iota of arrogance has couched this lesson also in that true spirit of humility. He is saying, "I am a mere *Ddhāddi* and as such I boast not of high social standing. Others claim to have high pedigree, but let them be, because the ones whom I seek are those who meditate on the Lord."

PAUṚI 10

Bhai Vir Singh tells us that according to the *Purātan Janam Sākhi* the fifteen *pauṛis* from here till the last, numbers 10 through 24, were spoken to one Duni Chand Dhuppar of Lahore. Prof. Sahib Singh though, in his commentary, has convincingly argued that the entire *Vār* is an integral unit and there is nothing to suggest that the various parts are addressed to different individuals. In this *pauṛi* the Guru speaks to us about shunning material possessions and fixing the mind on the Lord. There are two *sloks* attached to the *pauṛi*, both by Guru Nanak. In the first of these *sloks* the Guru tells us that whatever exists in this material world, is false. He says:

ਸਲੋਕ ਮਃ ੧ ॥	Slok Mahla 1
ਕੂੜੁ ਰਾਜਾ ਕੂੜੁ ਪਰਜਾ ਕੂੜੁ ਸਭੁ ਸੰਸਾਰੁ ॥	Kūṛ rāja kūṛ parja kūṛ sabh sansār
ਕੂੜੁ ਮੰਡਪ ਕੂੜੁ ਮਾੜੀ ਕੂੜੁ ਬੈਸਣਹਾਰੁ ॥	Kūṛ mandap kūṛ māṛi kūṛ baisaṇ hār
ਕੂੜੁ ਸੁਇਨਾ ਕੂੜੁ ਰੁਪਾ ਕੂੜੁ ਪੈਨ੍ਹਣਹਾਰੁ ॥	Kūṛ suina kūṛ rūpa kūṛ painaṇhār.
ਕੂੜੁ ਕਾਇਆ ਕੂੜੁ ਕਪੜੁ ਕੂੜੁ ਰੂਪੁ ਅਪਾਰੁ ॥	Kūṛ kāiya kūṛ kappaṛ kūṛ rūp apār
ਕੂੜੁ ਮੀਆ ਕੂੜੁ ਬੀਬੀ ਖਪਿ ਹੋਏ ਖਾਰੁ ॥	Kūṛ mīya kūṛ bībi khapp hoye khār
ਕੂੜਿ ਕੂੜੈ ਨੇਹੁ ਲਗਾ ਵਿਸਰਿਆ ਕਰਤਾਰੁ ॥	Kūṛ kūṛai neh lagga visiriya kartār
ਕਿਸੁ ਨਾਲਿ ਕੀਚੈ ਦੋਸਤੀ ਸਭੁ ਜਗੁ ਚਲਣਹਾਰੁ ॥	Kis nāl kīchai dostī sabh jagg chalaṇhār
ਕੂੜੁ ਮਿਠਾ ਕੂੜੁ ਮਾਖਿਉ ਕੂੜੁ ਡੋਬੇ ਪੂਰੁ ॥	Kūṛ mittha kūṛ mākhiyo kūṛ ddobay pūr
ਨਾਨਕੁ ਵਖਾਣੈ ਬੇਨਤੀ ਤੁਧੁ ਬਾਝੁ ਕੂੜੋ ਕੂੜੁ ॥੧॥	Nanak vakhāṇai benti tudh bājh kūṛo kūṛ. 1.

Glossary:

ਕੂੜ	Kūṛ	Falsehood, illusion
ਮਾੜੀ	Māṛi	Palace
ਕਾਇਆ	Kāiya	Body
ਪੂਰ	Pūr	A group of persons in a boat, boatload
ਵਖਾਣੈ	Vakhāṇai	States, says

Simply translated this *slok* says that the kings, their subjects, the entire world is false, because it is ephemeral and will soon be no more. False are the impressive abodes and mansions and false those who reside in these. False is the attire, the adornments and false the body and its beauty. False are the husband, the wife and their relationship when it is attached to *kūṛ* and they have forgotten the Lord. With whom can there be attachment when the entire world is ephemeral. False are the worldly things, sweet outwardly like sugar and honey, which have led to the sinking of whole boatloads of mankind. The Guru, in prayer says that without Him all else is only *kūṛ*. Let us now look at these concepts in more detail.

The meaning of the first eight lines of this *slok* would be more clearly understood if we examine first the 9th, the concluding line where the Guru says, "I prayerfully state that other than Thee all else is false." The term *kūṛ* comes from the Sanskrit *kūt* or Prākrit *kūd*, meaning untrue, false, illusionary, etc. So here *kūṛ* is used in the sense of false, that which is illusionary; which of course covers all material things of this world. Let us be clear though that they are not unreal; in fact since the Lord resides inside each atom, but when we see not that Reality within this creation, but start treating the world as real by itself, forgetting that Divine Presence which animates it then indeed it is nothing but *kūṛ*. This is what the Guru is saying, that without Him all that exists is an empty shell. Now let us see what the simple, literal rendering is.

In lines 1 and 2 the Guru says false is the king, false his subjects, false the entire world. False are the ornate abodes, the impressive mansions and false those residing in these. We have to appreciate that these are not mere illusions. It is not as if they do not really exist. But the reality and existence that they have is only when we see and realize that the Lord resides in these. When He is there the dramatis personae will be seen to perform their appointed roles – doing good or doing evil, growing, falling, building, destroying, earning their way to salvation and sometimes lapsing into perdition. Only He is the Truth because only He is eternal. All other things are there today but will be gone tomorrow. The king occupies a throne in pride but he forgets that others reigned from it yesterday and some others will occupy it in the future. The palaces, the grand mansions are similarly only apparently ours. We are transient owners and ephemeral occupants. Hence are these not reality but are *kūṛ*.

In lines 3 and 4, the Guru says false is the attire, false the ornaments, false the body that wears these, false the beauty. As Prof. Talib puts it, "Evanescent is the human frame, the raiment and the unique beauty over which this is thrown." All these seemingly attractive things are *kūṛ* (false) for the very reason that these are evanescent. Only the Lord is eternal and hence not false.

In lines 5 and 6 the Guru says false are the husband the wife and their relationship which ends in ignominy because false is their attachment to this falsehood and they have forgotten the Lord. This relationship sunk in self-indulgence and oblivious of the Lord is, like Prof. Talib says, "Evanescent with the evanescent has formed relationship".

In line 7, the Guru says with whom should one form attachments when the whole world is false, is evanescent. Prof. Sahib Singh renders this line along with line 6 as, "The one beguiled by this illusion has fallen in love with the illusion, and in the process has forgotten his Creator. He has forgotten that this entire world is evanescent and therefore getting too deeply involved with anything in it is in the ultimate reckoning fruitless." Bhai Vir Singh's interpretation is similar, and in fact there is fair unanimity on the rendering of this line.

In line 8 the Guru says these false things of the world are sweet like sugar and like honey, leading us astray and figuratively, causing whole boatloads of mankind to sink. The word *pūr* means a load, and is commonly used to describe a load of a similar kind of things or beings. Thus, a boatload of humans would be called a *pūr* as would a herd of cattle of the same kind. Here we are being told of the myriads of humans through the ages who have sunk to perdition enmeshed in this beguilement. This beguilement tastes to us as sweet as honey, which is why so many are drawn this way, away from the true path; and are oblivious to the Lord.

In the last line, the 9th, the Guru says to the Lord that it is his plea that without the Lord all is illusion. The term *kūṛo kūṛ* is used to reiterate the utter falsehood of the *kūṛ* that we are beguiled by. In other words, he seeks the Lord's grace to keep him free from the meshes of this evil thing. It is also a way of telling us to realize the one Truth and operate in this world of illusion in full consciousness of this underlying Reality. Let all our actions, all our thoughs be informed by the realization that without the Lord the world is false, being ephemral.

In the second *slok* with this, the 10th, *pauṛi* the Guru tells us how to realise this Truth that he spoke of in the previous *slok.* He says:

ਮਹਲਾ ੧ ॥	Mahla 1
ਸਚੁ ਤਾ ਪਰੁ ਜਾਣੀਐ ਜਾ ਰਿਦੈ ਸਚਾ ਹੋਇ ॥	Sach ta parr jāṇiai ja ridai sacha hoye
ਕੂੜ ਕੀ ਮਲੁ ਉਤਰੈ ਤਨੁ ਕਰੇ ਹਛਾ ਧੋਇ ॥	Kūṛ ki mull utrai tann karay hachha dhoye
ਸਚੁ ਤਾ ਪਰੁ ਜਾਣੀਐ ਜਾ ਸਚਿ ਧਰੇ ਪਿਆਰੁ ॥	Sach tā parr jāṇiai ja sach dharay pyār
ਨਾਉ ਸੁਣਿ ਮਨੁ ਰਹਸੀਐ ਤਾ ਪਾਏ ਮੋਖ ਦੁਆਰੁ ॥	Nau suṇ mann rahsiai ta pāye mokh duār
ਸਚੁ ਤਾ ਪਰੁ ਜਾਣੀਐ ਜਾ ਜੁਗਤਿ ਜਾਣੈ ਜੀਉ ॥	Sach tā parr jāṇiai ja jugat jāṇai jīo
ਧਰਤਿ ਕਾਇਆ ਸਾਧਿ ਕੈ ਵਿਚਿ ਦੇਇ ਕਰਤਾ ਬੀਉ ॥	Dharat kāiya sādh kai vich day karta bīo
ਸਚੁ ਤਾ ਪਰੁ ਜਾਣੀਐ ਜਾ ਸਿਖ ਸਚੀ ਲੇਇ ॥	Sach ta parr jāṇīai ja sikh sachi lay
ਦਇਆ ਜਾਣੈ ਜੀਅ ਕੀ ਕਿਛੁ ਪੁੰਨੁ ਦਾਨੁ ਕਰੇਇ ॥	Daya jāṇai jee ki kichh punn daaān karay
ਸਚੁ ਤਾਂ ਪਰੁ ਜਾਣੀਐ ਜਾ ਆਤਮ ਤੀਰਥਿ ਕਰੇ ਨਿਵਾਸੁ ॥	Sach tā parr jāṇiai ja ātam tīrath karay niwās
ਸਤਿਗੁਰੂ ਨੋ ਪੁਛਿ ਕੈ ਬਹਿ ਰਹੈ ਕਰੇ ਨਿਵਾਸੁ ॥	Satguru no pucch kai baih rahai karey niwās
ਸਚੁ ਸਭਨਾ ਹੋਇ ਦਾਰੂ ਪਾਪ ਕਢੈ ਧੋਇ ॥	Sach sabhna hoye dāru pāp kaddhai dhoye
ਨਾਨਕੁ ਵਖਾਣੈ ਬੇਨਤੀ ਜਿਨ ਸਚੁ ਪਲੈ ਹੋਇ ॥੨॥	Nanak vakhāṇai benti jin sach pallai hoye. 2.

Glossary:

ਤਾ ਪਰੁ	Tā parr	Only if, only then
ਸਚੁ	Sach	Truth, here opposite of *kūṛ*, reality
ਰਹਸੀਐ	Rehsīai	Is in bliss
ਮੋਖ ਦੁਆਰੁ	Mokh duār	Door to salvation
ਬੀਉ	Bīo	Seed
ਧਰਤਿ ਕਾਇਆ	Dharat kāia	The body as the field
ਕੂੜ ਕੀ ਮਲੁ	Kūṛ kī mull	Grime of falsehood

Simply translated this *slok* says that truth is realised when the Lord resides in the heart, which removes the grime of falsehood from the mind. Truth is realised if in the heart is love for truth and the mind experiences bliss on hearing His Name; such ones find salvation. Truth is realised when the right way of living is found and having cultivated this body as a field is sown therein the seed of the Lord's Name. Truth is realised when the right instruction is taken, and with compassion in the heart charity is given and wealth is shared with the less fortunate. Truth will be realised when one stays in the *tīrath* within our inner self, and with the true preceptor's guidance says steadfastly in that *tīrath*. This *tīrath* within comes into existence when the soul within has achieved the state of bliss from focusing on the Lord's Name. The Truth is the cure for all ills; the Guru pays obeisance to those who have acquired and achieved truth in their hearts. Let us now see it in more detail.

In lines 1 and 2 the Guru says truth is known when the True One resides in the heart, which removes the grime of falsehood from the mind. Having concluded the previous *slok* with *Tudh bājh kūṛo kūṛ*, meaning "Without you, O Lord, all is false and illusionary." The Guru now elaborates and narrates what is that *sach* and how will it come to us. He says you will know what truth is when the True One resides in your heart. In other words, the realization of truth and the knowledge of the True One in the heart are events that occur simultaneously. When we have recognized that the world's reality is underpinned by the Lord permeating it, then the mind turns away from the toys of this material world and reality dawns; the mind comes to rest on the one Reality. That realization washes away immediately the miasma of materialism coating our souls, the mind shines with the truth, and with it the body also takes on lustre.

In lines 3 and 4 the Guru says truth will be known when you have love for the truth in your heart. When that happens, the mind starts losing interest in the false; it is no longer entranced by the baubles of this world. As it detaches from the material it turns to the Truth, the Lord. Such a person feels the glow of joy in his heart on hearing the Name of the Lord. This sense of elation is a sign that the mind is now on the right path and it will soon lead to the door of salvation. When the falsehood interests you not and the Name of the Lord uplifts your spirits you are well on the way to achieving liberation from the bonds of this world.

In lines 5 and 6 the Guru further elaborates the message. He says true is such a one who has learnt the right way of living, and having cultivated this body plants the seed of God's Name therein. Prof. Talib puts it as, "Preparing the soil of his body, the Creator in it should he sow." The right way of living has already been explained by the Guru. It requires of you to fix your mind on the Lord, singing his praises; and living in this world fully involved, but always seeing the Lord as the real spirit behind the material. When this frame of mind has been achieved you can say the right way of living has been learnt. In this way is the soil that is this body prepared for planting of the seed that will fructify in God-realization. There are in this world many good men who feel that they are living morally correct lives and not indulging in any evil, and so they need do nothing further. Here the Guru tells us that though such a course of action is necessary, is even mandatory, but it is not sufficient, by itself, for reaching our goal. It is very necessary to be good and pure because that way the field that is this body is readied to receive the Lord's Name. But mere preparation of the field is a fruitless exercise if the seed is not to be planted in it at the right time. Therefore, it is essential to go one step further; we have to plant the seed by learning to sincerely and strictly follow the Guru's path, singing always the Lord's praises. Then only will the preparation of the body be of any real meaning, and that meaning is given by planting the Lord's Name in our hearts. As the Guru says in *Rāg Sūhi, Mahla* 1, page 728 of the *SGGS*, "Bhānda dhoye bais dhūp devo tau dūdhaih ko jāvo", meaning that we have to purify the vessel (body and mind) before we use it for milking. Similarly, without the preparation of a field the planting is impossible, but to prepare ourself and then not plant the seed of His Name would be wasteful and a tragedy. The Guru says, till the field that is your inner self, and then plant within the seed of His Name.

In lines 7 and 8 the Guru says that true is such a one who receives the true instruction. He will have compassion in his heart and will want to give alms and charity to those less fortunate. Many learned commentators have rendered line 7 as, "if we receive the true instruction". The reference here obviously is to the earlier *sloks* regarding finding the *Satguru*, the true preceptor. When we are lucky enough to find him he will give us the correct guidance and he will put us on the path towards the Lord. The Guru here, in lines 5 to 8, uses again an example from the everyday lives of his audience. He talks of a field of agricultural land, which is ploughed, freed from weeds, levelled and watered to make it ready for the crop. The field here is our own selves and its preparation lies in training the mind and the body to follow the path that the Guru has prescribed. When our inner self is ready, the Guru says plant the seed, which here is the Lord's Name. And the crop that we will reap, the fruit that we will get is union with the Lord. This state is bound to be marked by compassion and charity.

In lines 9 and 10 the Guru says such a one is true who resides in the *tīrath* within himself, who takes guidance from his Guru and then steadfastly stays in that *tīrath*. The reference here is to the practice of holy pilgrimages to the *tīraths*, especially the sixty-eight deemed the holiest. Many devotees then would at some stage in their lives shift residence to one of these *tīraths* and then stay there till the end of their lives. The Guru, however, has another perspective on this practice in keeping with his constant message of not counting outside activity as important, but rather emphasizing the need for seeking Him through heart, from the core of one's being. He has elsewhere also spoken to us of the *tīrath* within us, which comes into existence when the soul through reciting the Lord's Name has achieved the state of bliss. For instance he says in the *Japji Sahib, pauṛi* 21, "Antargat tīrath mull nāo" – wash your sins at the *tīrath* within. Here he is telling us that merely visiting such *tīraths* is not to be considered a sign of holiness. He is also describing the way we can judge and see whether a man is true. He says such a true devotee seeks the *tīrath* within. This will not happen on our own strength but through the *Satguru*, and so, says the Guru, such a man seeks guidance from his Guru and he then follows the correct path. His permanent abode becomes that internal *tīrath* where no grime can touch him and free from sins he abides on the Lord's path.

In the concluding lines, 11th and 12th, the Guru says that truth is the panacea; it washes away all ills of the soul. As the Guru says in the *Sukhmani Sahib, astapadi* 9/5, "sarab rog ka aukhadh nām", meaning the Name of the Lord is the panacea for all ills and sins. The Guru says he offers salutations to those who follow this correct path and have acquired this state of spiritual growth. The inner self having found abode in the inner *tīrath*, truth is all that prevails for them now and the sins accumulated through the long attachment to *Maya* are now cleansed from the fabric of our souls; and no new sins can attach to us within that *tīrath*.

At the end of *pauṛi* 9 the Guru says, "Tinn manga jay tudhay dhiāiday" – I seek those whose minds are fixed on you. Here in the same vein he says in the 12th line, "I pray to those, offer them obeisance who have acquired that truth in their hearts."

Now in the 10th *pauṛi* the Guru says:

ਪਉੜੀ ॥	Pauṛi
ਦਾਨੁ ਮਹਿੰਡਾ ਤਲੀ ਖਾਕੁ ਜੇ ਮਿਲੈ ਤ ਮਸਤਕਿ ਲਾਈਐ ॥	Dān mahinda tali khāk jay milai ta mastak lāīai
ਕੂੜਾ ਲਾਲਚੁ ਛਡੀਐ ਹੋਇ ਇਕ ਮਨਿ ਅਲਖੁ ਧਿਆਈਐ ॥	Kūṛa lālach chhaddīai hoye ik mann alakh dhiāīai
ਫਲੁ ਤੇਵੇਹੋ ਪਾਈਐ ਜੇਵੇਹੀ ਕਾਰ ਕਮਾਈਐ ॥	Phal teveho pāīai jevehi kār kamāīai
ਜੇ ਹੋਵੈ ਪੂਰਬਿ ਲਿਖਿਆ ਤਾ ਧੂੜਿ ਤਿਨ੍ਹਾ ਦੀ ਪਾਈਐ ॥	Je hovai pūrab likhiya ta dhūṛ tina dī pāīai
ਮਤਿ ਥੋੜੀ ਸੇਵ ਗਵਾਈਐ ॥੧੦॥	Mat thoṛi sev gavāīai. 10.

Glossary:

ਦਾਨੁ	Dān	Gift, blessing, alms
ਮਹਿੰਡਾ	Mahindda	For me, to me
ਤਲੀ ਖਾਕੁ	Tali khāk	Dust from the soles of feet
ਅਲਖੁ	Alakh	Not visible, beyond measure

ਪੂਰਬਿ	Pūrab	From the past
ਮਤਿ	Matt	Intelligence

The Guru here further lauds such right living souls, and says he seeks the dust from the feet of such men of God. This symbolically refers to being able to acquire the quality of total humility and learning from those who are truly holy. Simply translated this *pauṛi* says that if we find the dust of the feet of the true devotees we should apply it to the forehead, in other words bow in total humility to these men of God and learn from them. We should forgo covetousness for the false worldly attachments, and single-mindedly fix the mind on the Lord. The fruit we reap will depend on the seeds we plant. If our previous merit is strong then only will this dust of the feet of the men of God become available to us. We must not waste our service in acts of scant discrimination. Let us now look at the lesson here in more detail.

In the first line the Guru says the gift he seeks is the dust of the soles of the feet of the true ones, which if he gets he will apply to the forehead. This applying of the dust to the forehead is not to be understood as the ritual of physically applying it; rather, the Guru is exhorting us to reach such a state of humility and acceptance that we can truly acquire Godly qualities from the company of such holy men of God. This is in tune with the Guru's noted humility we see expressed elsewhere too. He speaks not as a master but as a humble servant of the Lord, not only in this hymn but throughout the *SGGS*. The ones, he says, who are worthy of worship are those in whose heart the Lord resides and who have thus become the true ones themselves.

In line 2 he says covetousness for the false world we must forsake and focusing our minds we should concentrate on the *Alakh* (Immeasurable One). Continuing with the lesson imparted in the first line, where he sought the dust of the feet of the true ones, the Guru is saying that seeking things other than the dust is nothing but greed. He says forsake this covetousness for things that are false. Instead, focus the mind on the *Alakh* – that which cannot be seen, which is not measurable by any of the senses, the *Nirankār*, the Formless One. This term *Alakh* has been variously rendered by learned ones as 'Inaccessible', 'Unseen', 'Unknowable' and 'Unfathomable'. It clearly refers to the 'Lord' Himself.

In line 3 the Guru says the fruit we reap shall be relatable to the seed we planted, through our actions. It is a sad but hard reality that men spend their lives in actions that are governed by their egos. Their actions are concentrated on acquiring power and pelf but when it comes to the results, they expect nothing but the best for themselves. They go through the motions of some charity or some religious observances and vainly expect this will exempt them from having to face the evil consequences that their ego-centred lives are bound to bring upon them. The Guru is here pointing out the harsh truth, that the seed we planted with our actions will produce very strictly the fruit we deserve from it. As the Guru says later in the *Āsa di Vār*, page 474, *SGGS*, "Bijay bikh mangai amrit vekho eh niāo", meaning look at man, he has sown poisonous weeds and expects nectar to come from the fruit.

In line 4 the Guru says if we have sufficiently good fortune allotted to us by the Lord then only will we find the dust of the feet of the achieved souls. The term *Pūrab likhiya* refers to the thought in the Indian belief systems that our actions go towards creating good or bad *karma*. Out of this bank balance of earned merit we are allotted some *pralabdh* when we are sent to this world. If our past actions are sufficiently good, only then will our allotted *karma* be good enough to allow us the good fortune of earning the dust of the feet of the men of God, or the 'saints' as Macauliffe puts it.

In the 5th and concluding line the Guru says waste not your service with scant discrimination. There are different renderings of this line. Dada Chellaram says, "Ye lose all service if ye are of small understanding." Prof. Teja Singh uses similar terminology. Dr. Gopal Singh says, "But, through (the ego) our little minds, we lose even the merit of service". Macauliffe says, "Ruin not thyself with scant service". Prof. Talib says, "One with small discrimination makes waste of service". The *Shabdarth* renders it as, "because our intellect is limited and our views narrow and bigoted, the service we perform gets wasted". Prof. Sahib Singh elaborates slightly to say that when we ignore the learning that the *gurmukh* give us and instead of depending on their guidance we decide to rely on our own limited intellect then our striving towards the Lord bears little fruit. Bhai Vir singh has taken a similar view but further explains that some learned ones also view it as, (a) through service we can get rid ourselves of the smallness of our intellect, and (b) thinking our intellect petty we should not ignore the service even if it is little, because whatever service we can perform is all to the good. The sense of this line becomes clearer if we see it in continuation of the first four lines. The Guru has told us to set aside our petty covetousness and seek instead the dust of the feet of the Lord's true devotees. The rendering by Prof. Sahib Singh fits in more closely with this aspect. Our own efforts and intellects are of necessity limited, we need to seek guidance from the *Satguru* and emulate the men of God whose loftiness above us is such that we should deem ourselves lucky to be allowed to symbolically apply to our foreheads, as we discussed above, the dust from their feet. If we follow the roadmap they lay down, our efforts will bear fruit and our journey from this world to the Divine would be a success. If we bother not for them and rely on our own limited capacities then the same amount of striving will produce nothing but wasted effort.

PAURI 11

In this *pauri* the Guru speaks to us of the situation in the present times, which is called the *Kaliyuga*; and on how to reach the Lord in these circumstances. There are three *sloks* attached with this *pauri*, all by Guru Nanak. The first *slok* goes thus:

ਸਲੋਕੁ ਮ: ੧ ॥	Slok Mahla 1
ਸਚਿ ਕਾਲੁ ਕੂੜੁ ਵਰਤਿਆ ਕਲਿ ਕਾਲਖ ਬੇਤਾਲ ॥	Sach kāl kūṛ vartia kal kālakh betāl
ਬੀਉ ਬੀਜਿ ਪਤਿ ਲੈ ਗਏ ਅਬ ਕਿਉ ਉਗਵੈ ਦਾਲਿ ॥	Biu bīj patt lai gaye ab kiu ugvai dāl
ਜੇ ਇਕੁ ਹੋਇ ਤ ਉਗਵੈ ਰੁਤੀ ਹੂ ਰੁਤਿ ਹੋਇ ॥	Je ik hoye ta ugvai rutī hū rutt hoye
ਨਾਨਕ ਪਾਹੈ ਬਾਹਰਾ ਕੋਰੈ ਰੰਗੁ ਨ ਸੋਇ ॥	Nanak pāhai bahrā korai rung na soye
ਭੈ ਵਿਚਿ ਖੁੰਬਿ ਚੜਾਈਐ ਸਰਮੁ ਪਾਹੁ ਤਨਿ ਹੋਇ ॥	Bhai vich khumb chaṛāiyai saram pah[u] tann hoye
ਨਾਨਕ ਭਗਤੀ ਜੇ ਰਪੈ ਕੂੜੈ ਸੋਇ ਨ ਕੋਇ ॥੧॥	Nanak bhagti je rapai kūṛai soye na koye. 1.

Glossary:

ਕਾਲੁ	Kal	Kaliyug
ਕਾਲਖ	Kālakh	Darkness, grime of wrong deeds
ਦਾਲਿ	Dāl	A split lentil, not whole
ਬੀਉ	Bīo	Seed

ਪਾਹੁ	Pāhu	Chemical treatment, for cloth prior to dyeing
ਕੋਰੈ	Korai	The virgin cloth
ਸਰਮੁ	Saram	Honest toil
ਸੋਇ	Soye	Clue, news

Simply translated this first *slok* of the 11th *pauṛi* says that there is a famine of truth, falsehood is everywhere and men have become like demons. In former ages men sowed *dharam* and earned the fruit but now it yields not fruit because the seed is split and not whole. If it were whole it would grow, provided the seasons were also favourable. Our selves are like raw cloth that cannot take the dye until it is chemically prepared. For making our inner selves ready for the Lord, honest effort should be the preparartion, and fear and awe of the Lord, the treatment. If we thus dye ourselves in the Name then falsehood will not come near us. Let us now look at the *slok* in more detail.

In line 1 the Guru says there is a dearth of truth; falsehood prevails and men have become like demons with the darkness of this age. The implicit reference is to the *Dharam* of each of the four *yugas*. It is believed in the Indian belief system that the cycle of time moves in a cycle of four *Yugas* of duration totalling 4.32 million years, and each *Yuga* has its distinctive spirit. Thus the *Satyuga* had *satya* as its ethos, humans were pure and pious and no special observances were needed on the path to the Lord. In the *Treta Yuga* a fourth of this purity was lost and reliance was on *yagya* (specialized holy rites). This was followed by the *Dwāpar Yuga* when half of purity was gone, and prayers and worship became the necessary path. Finally, *Kaliyuga* dawned, about 3200 years ago according to the *Purānas*, when *dharma* became only one-fourth and the lure of *Maya* overwhelmed mankind. This is in spiritual terms a dark age and under its influence the souls of men are darkened by the evil that prevails. Men are but distorted caricatures of what they were in purer *Yugas*. The word *betāl* means literally "out of tune, or out of step". It is also used to describe someone undead, whose body has died and the soul is gone but the shell remains animated. Thus it can mean ghoul, demon or poltergeist. It is in the latter sense that most commentators have rendered it. Dr. Gopal Singh renders it as, "Kali dances a wild dance", using *betāl* in the sense of 'out of tune'. The rendering as evil spirit or demon seems more appropriate here.

In the 2nd and 3rd lines the Guru gives an analogy from farming and says in previous *Yugas* humans planted *dharma* and earned merit but in *Kaliyuga* it cannot yield fruit because it is like the split seed. The seed can fructify only if it is whole and the season is also right. Neither situation obtains in this *yuga*. The reference here is to the lentil seed commonly eaten that can also be planted fruitfully. It is, however, for common consumption in the household usually milled and split into two, when it is called *dāl*. In this form it is no longer viable as seed. So, says the Guru, "kiu ugvai dāl" – how will the split seed sprout. It has to be whole – *ik hoye* – and also the season has to be right: "ruti hū rutt hoye". No crop will bear fruit if it is not planted according to its growing season. The same thought occurs on page 1129 of the *SGGS*, in *Rāg Bhairon*, *Mahla* 3 where the Guru says, "Kalyug mah bahu karam kamāhay. Na rut na karam thāye pāhay. Kaljug mah ram nām hai sār", meaning many actions does he attempt in the *Kaliyuga* but the season is not right so it yields to no fruit. Only the Name of the Lord will suffice in the *Kaliyuga*. The analogy of the split seed, the *dāl* used here is to describe the situation where we humans are forever torn within our hearts between the wish to seek the Lord and the overpowering lure of the material glitter around us. This duality of thought is our bane and we reach not the Lord. Thus we become like the *dāl*, unfit for fruitful results. Thus the season is bad and unsuitable, but worse still, our inner self is split between the urge to reach the Lord and the lure for the material, and such split seed can produce nothing.

In lines 4 and 5 the Guru uses another analogy to describe our plight, that of the process of weaving and dyeing of new cloth. He tells us that just as the raw cloth cannot take on the dye until it has been chemically treated, in the same way the fear and awe of the Lord should be the chemical treatment for us so that our inner selves become fit to become dyed, meaning totally imbued with His Name. But for that chemical treatment to be effective there has to be on our parts sincere and honest effort to train and control ourselves. When cloth is freshly woven it is rough and raw and cannot straightaway be put through the dyeing process. For that it is chemically treated and only then can the dye take effect. The Guru is saying that the minds of men are in the same fashion rough and raw and cannot successfully take on the dye of the Lord's Name, of His worship, of Love for Him. Further, says the Guru, we must have in our hearts the *bhai* (fear or awe) of that Lord. This *bhai* is that holy and pure fear that removes from our hearts other fears, the fears of wordly powers, the fears of losing worldly possessions. With the fear of the Lord in our hearts will we be dyed in the colours of His love. Before that, and with it, must we also give ourselves the chemical treatment of *saram*. This word has on the one hand the Persian meaning of 'shame, modesty'. It can also be used in the Sanskrit meaning of 'effort, toil, and hard work'. Bhai Vir Singh, Prof. Talib, Macauliffe, Dr. Gopal Singh and Dada Chellaram have used it in the sense of modesty. The *Shabdarth*, Prof. Teja Singh and Prof. Sahib Singh render it as hard work. This dichotomy in interpretation may be seen wherever this term occurs in the *Gurbāṇi*. In the context here the interpretation as 'hard work' seems more appropriate. It is part of the Guru's message that we have to strive to train ourselves, to kill our lazy and wrong tendencies and overcome our greed for the many enticing things of this world. While 'modesty' is not entirely illogical to use here but the concept of working hard, of striving to curb and train ourselves seems more appropriate.

In the concluding, the 6th, line the Guru says if we have dyed ourselves in this fashion in the love of the Lord, then falsehood will not come near us. This line sums up the message of this *slok*, that if we properly train ourselves by working hard to overcome our wrong tendencies, and if we imbibe within us the fear of the Lord then will we gain the fruit. We will become pure, in spite of the ethos of the times being uncongenial, and the falsehood that prevails will have no power over us. The word *soye* is rendered by Bhai Vir Singh as 'the touch of', and so the line becomes "the filth will not touch such *bhagats*". Earlier the Guru had spoken of the darkness engendered by the spirit of this age that prevents men from achieving union with the Lord. Here he says that darkness will not be able to stain the purity of the person who has dyed himself in the colours of the Lord.

In the second *slok*, the Guru says:

ਮ: ੧ ॥	M: 1
ਲਬ ਪਾਪ ਦੁਇ ਰਾਜਾ ਮਹਤਾ ਕੂੜ ਹੋਆ ਸਿਕਦਾਰੁ ॥	Labb pāp doye raja mehta kūṛ hoa sikdār
ਕਾਮ ਨੇਬੁ ਸਦਿ ਪੁਛੀਐ ਬਹਿ ਬਹਿ ਕਰੇ ਵੀਚਾਰੁ ॥	Kām neb sad puchhīai beh beh karay bīchār

ਅੰਧੀ ਰਯਤਿ ਗਿਆਨ ਵਿਹੂਣੀ ਭਾਹਿ ਭਰੇ ਮੁਰਦਾਰੁ ॥	Andhi rayyat gyān vihūṇi bhāh bharay murdār
ਗਿਆਨੀ ਨਚਹਿ ਵਾਜੇ ਵਾਵਹਿ ਰੂਪ ਕਰਹਿ ਸੀਗਾਰ ॥	Gyani nachay vājay vāveh rūp kareh sīgār
ਊਚੇ ਕੂਕਹਿ ਵਾਦਾ ਗਾਵਹਿ ਜੋਧਾ ਕਾ ਵੀਚਾਰੁ ॥	Ūchai kūkeh vāda gāvai jodha ka vīchār
ਮੂਰਖ ਪੰਡਿਤ ਹਿਕਮਤਿ ਹੁਜਤਿ ਸੰਜੈ ਕਰਹਿ ਪਿਆਰੁ ॥	Mūrakh pandit hikmat hujjat sanjai kareh pyār
ਧਰਮੀ ਧਰਮ ਕਰਹਿ ਗਾਵਾਵਹਿ ਮੰਗਹਿ ਮੋਖ ਦੁਆਰ ॥	Dharmi dharam kareh gavāvaih mangaih mokh duār
ਜਤੀ ਸਦਾਵਹਿ ਜੁਗਤਿ ਨ ਜਾਣਹਿ ਛਡਿ ਬਹਹਿ ਘਰ ਬਾਰ ॥	Jati sadāveh jugat na jāṇeh chhadd bahai gharbār
ਸਭ ਕੋ ਪੂਰਾ ਆਪੇ ਹੋਵੈ ਘਟਿ ਨ ਕੋਈ ਆਖੈ ॥	Sabh ko pūra āpay hovai ghatt na koyi ākhai
ਪਤਿ ਪਰਵਾਣਾ ਪਿਛੈ ਪਾਈਐ ਤਾ ਨਾਨਕ ਤੋਲਿਆ ਜਾਪੈ ॥੨॥	Pat parwāṇa pichhai pāiai ta Nanak toleya jāpai. 2.

Glossary:

ਲਬ	Labb	Gluttony, avarice
ਮਹਤਾ	Mehta	Chief
ਨੇਬੁ	Neb	Second in command, advisor
ਰਯਤਿ	Rayyat	The subjects, populace
ਵਿਹੂਣੀ	Vihūṇi	Lacking
ਭਾਹਿ ਭਰੇ	Bhāh bharay	Carry out the will
ਵਾਵਹਿ	Vāveh	Play (the instruments)
ਹੁਜਤਿ	Hujjat	Demur, objection
ਸੰਜੈ	Sanjai	Accumulate
ਜਤੀ	Jati	One who has controlled his senses
ਪਤਿ	Pat	Respect, esteem
ਪਰਵਾਣਾ	Parwāṇa	Measure, weight

Guru Nanak describes here the condtitions prevailing at that time. He speaks of how low the rulers had sunk and how corrupt the polity had become. Simply translated this *slok* says that avarice rules and evil is its minister, falsehood is the chief under them. Lust is the advisor whom they all consult. The people bereft of true knowledge blindly and unresistingly serve these evil ones. The learned ones sing and dance and don various guises. Loudly they sing of valorous warriors. The *Pandits*, the learned ones, indulge in tricky semantics, disputatious and arguments only to amass wealth. The religious ones follow *dharma* but then lose it all by asking in return for salvation. The ones doing austerities know not the way and forget their householders' duties. Yet do all of them think they are perfect and admit no fault in themselves. The real worth will only be known in the Divine Court when we are measured at the Lord's touchstone, and only such actions will be accepted as were honorable in the Lord's judgement. Let us now look at it in more detail.

In lines 1 to 3, the Guru says that the role of a ruler and his minister in these times is being performed by avarice and other wrong actions, and falsehood is the chief under them. Lust is the advisor with whom they hold consultations. The populace is blinded and listlessly and unresisting they serve these evil rulers. Bad indeed must have been the social conditions for the Guru to use such strong words. Pandering to the senses and to the lower instincts was the prevailing ethos. There was rampant greed, avarice and the sins that inevitably follow from trying to achieve such low ends. Thus did falsehood prevail among the people. These governing passions are born of, and all controlled by lust. So the Guru here describes lust as the advisor who is constantly consulted. Thus, the Guru is telling us that all the baser passions prevailed fully at that time. What was more unfortunate was that the populace, like zombies, ignorant and unresisting followed these wrong directions. The overwhelming presence of greed with its attendants lust, falsehood and sin was completely dominating the public psyche.

The Guru in lines 4 and 5 now describes what was the condition of the religious leaders of this misguided population. He says the *gyānīs* (learned preachers) sing and dance and don various disguises. Loudly they chant the tales of valorous warriors. The learned ones whose function in society is to teach had forgotten how to guide the people on the path to the Lord, or even towards a spirtual life. Instead all they did was to enact plays depicting great warriors. They wore costumes and adorned themselves seeking to pose as great heroes. The Guru says that in accompaniment to music they danced and loudly sang these tales. The allusion is to the *rāsalīlas* about which the Guru had told us earlier also in the second *slok* of the 5th *pauṛi*. The Guru implicitly means that these plays and dramas are no substitute for true devotion to the Lord, which requires a humble mind focused on the Lord, singing His praises. Yet, says the Guru, at that time the learned ones wasted their time and energy in such empty theatrical displays instead of performing their proper function of teaching the populace the right path, the right way to live and the way to achieve God-realization.

In line 6 the Guru speaks of another category, the *pandit*. He says foolish *pandits* revel in argumentation and their minds are fixed on amassing material goods. The term "sanjai karay pyār" is rendered thus by most commentators though Dr. Gopal Singh puts it as "… cherish their set codes". Amassing of wealth though seems as a more appropriate rendering. The *pandits*, traditional spiritual teachers and educators had strayed grievously and more occupied with proving their own views as right and in misleading people into superstitious ways to line their own pockets; and above all were focused on earning and amassing wealth.

In line 7 another class, the religious men, is now referred to. Says the Guru, these good men follow *dharma* but then lose it all by putting a price on their devotion, when they ask for the door to salvation. When devotion is tainted with a demand it assumes the character of a trade, of commerce. What we are really doing in such a case is that we are saying that, Lord here is some service and prayer for you; now give us in return what we want. Most such prayers will seek worldly goods and avoidance of unpleasant events. When this happens these prayers have become commercial currency. A prayer to the Lord will be meaningful when a devotee is speaking to his master because it gives him joy to do so, when the prayer is an end in itself. It is a different matter that very often the Lord will bestow even material goods on those whose hearts are good and who are truly devoted, because as the Guru says in *Rāg Soratth*, *Mahla* 3, page 638 of the *SGGS*, "achint kamm karay prabh tinn ke jin har ka nām piara" – on His own, unasked, does the Lord give success to those who love the Name of God. But asking for something in return, even for salvation, taints the prayer with the mark of commerce. This is how Bhai Vir Singh. Prof. Sahib Singh, Gyani Maskin ji, Prof. Talib and the *Shabdarth* have construed it. It has also been rendered by Dada Chellaram as, "The religious ones perform religious duties, but in self praise; and they ask for salvation!" Prof. Teja Singh also says, "…waste their merit by seeking cheap popularity still they want salvation as their reward." This however is less convincing and the meaning as taken by Prof. Sahib Singh *et al.* seems more appealing.

In line 8 the Guru says some claim to be *jati* but know not the way and just leave their home and hearth. The sense here again is that the *jati*, the ones of deep austerity who have learnt to control their senses could have been another source of leadership for the ignorant. These also unfortunately have forgotten the true way. They think that just leaving their homes and taking to austerities in inhospitable surroundings is an end by itself, forgetting that the way to the Lord is not through such antics. It will require instead that we abase our ego, fix our minds on Him and with every breath sing His praises. So such ones are just trying to copy the true *jatīs*, and instead of learning to control their selves they just leave, escaping the householders duties, and deem that sufficient to give them the status of *jati*. The real *jati* in Sikhism would be the one who while being a householder is yet useful to society and productively adds to the general well being helping those who are less fortunate, and learns to discipline his inner self on the way of the Lord. The *jati* quitting home is of no use to any one. So, says the Guru, they know not the true way.

In line 9 the Guru says that even though trapped into these misdirected actions yet do all of them deem themselves perfect and admit to no lack. Vanity and an intense sense of the ego are a hallmark of these misguided ones. Lacking all merit yet is everyone convinced that he is perfect in his actions. The *gyāni*, the *pandit*, the *dharmi*, the *jati*, the common man, each one thinks that whatever he is doing is right and there are no flaws in his approach to life and to the Lord. How sadly ironical it is that even today, half a millennium later, we continue to face exactly the same situation. How similar is the situation today to what the Guru is describing.

In the concluding, the 10th line the Guru now gives us a word of caution. He says no matter what illusion people may harbour, the real worth will get known only in the Divine Court where our true value will get measured at the Lord's touchstone. The lack or otherwise of true merit in our actions will get certified only if these lead to honour before the Lord, if these actions are acceptable to Him. The Lord will determine our true worth. Thus, any illusions about our spiritual attainments, any claims of being perfect, will get thoroughly exposed in that Divine forum. If the Lord gives us honour then only would our actions have been worthwhile.

In the third *slok*, with the eleventh *pauṛi* the Guru says:

ਮ: ੧ ॥	M: 1
ਵਦੀ ਸੁ ਵਜਗਿ ਨਾਨਕਾ ਸਚਾ ਵੇਖੈ ਸੋਇ ॥	Vadi su vajag Nanka sacha vekhai soye.
ਸਭਨੀ ਛਾਲਾ ਮਾਰੀਆ ਕਰਤਾ ਕਰੇ ਸੁ ਹੋਇ ॥	Sabhnī chhāla mārīya[n] karta karay so hoye
ਅਗੈ ਜਾਤਿ ਨ ਜੋਰੁ ਹੈ ਅਗੈ ਜੀਉ ਨਵੇ ॥	Aggai jāt na jor hai aggai jīo navay
ਜਿਨ ਕੀ ਲੇਖੈ ਪਤਿ ਪਵੈ ਚੰਗੇ ਸੇਈ ਕੇਇ ॥੩॥	Jin kī lekhai pat pavai changay seyi kaye. 3.

Glossary:

ਵਦੀ	Vadi	What is ordained, His will
ਵਜਗਿ	Vajag	Will happen
ਸਚਾ	Sacha	The true one, the Lord
ਛਾਲਾ	Chhāla	Leaps; best efforts
ਜਾਤਿ	Jāt	Caste
ਜੋਰ	Jor	Force
ਅਗੈ ਜੀਉ ਨਵੇ	Aggai jīo navey	New order of beings
ਸੇਈ ਕੇਇ	Sayi kay	Those few ones
ਲੇਖੈ	Lekhai	At the time of judgement

The Guru speaks to us here about the inevitability of the Lord's Will prevailing always and the importance of acceptance. Simply translated this *slok* says that what the Lord has ordained shall come to pass because the Lord Himself watches over His creation. Humans make mighty efforts but ultimately the Will of the Lord shall prevail. The power or high caste we may hold here are of no avail in the hereafter where a newer type of beings exist and a different set of criteria applies. Only those shall be considered pure there whose devotion the Lord counts worthy. Let us now look at it in more detail.

In the 1st line the Guru says that what the Lord has ordained will come to pass, because the True Lord Himself watches over all creation and has decided what each one needs. There are differing interpretations of this. Some learned ones take "vadi" as "badi", evil, which is how the *Mahan Kosh* of Bhai Sahib Bhai Kahan Singh also renders it. Thus, Dada Chellaram says, "Man's evil must come out ringing", or as Macauliffe says, "Man's evil becometh known, O Nanak; the True One seeth all." Dr. Gopal Singh has another view and he renders it as, "The world knows what a deed shows (but) He the Lord sees (within) all." Prof. Teja Singh takes *vadi* to mean 'happens' and renders it as, "The True one is looking on; to Him everything rings as it happens." The *Shabdarth* of the *SGPC* explains *vadi* as being from the *shāhpuri* dialect meaning 'that which has actually happened'. Bhai Vir Singh puts it as, "When the person was performing an act he knew what was in his heart, the reality of it will become apparent because the Lord sees all." Prof. Sahib Singh considers *vadi* as 'ordained', 'the inevitable' and interprets the line, as "whatever the Lord has ordained will inevitably come to pass. This is because the Lord watches over all His beings and sustains each." This is the sense also in which Gyani Maskin takes it in his audio-commentary. The various interpretations have their merit but the rendering by Prof. Sahib Singh seems here more convincing. This will become clearer when we consider the next line.

In line 2 the Guru says everyone put in their best endeavour, but ultimately what the Lord had ordained is what will come to pass. The Guru is here stressing the omnipotence of the Lord, and says He is the arbiter of all that happens. Most commentators are agreed on this rendering. Bhai Vir Singh, however continuing in the same vein as in the above line, interprets the concept as, "Whatever was intended by man will appear in the outcome because the Lord sees inside us. Every one does his best in this field of action but it is the intention inside that will determine the outcome and whatever the Lord decides based on that will be right." Bhai Sahib, the great mystic and scholar, explains in the footnotes in his *Panj granthi* that some learned ones also take *vadi* as meaning 1) the dark half of the Lunar month, 2) that which the Lord has determined, 3) actions undertaken by men, and 4) the ringing tocsin of Time. In the context here the more appealing view still is, as we had discussed above, that *vadi* refers to what the Lord has determined. As Bhai Vir Singh further says the word *vadna* means 'to determine'. The two interpretations possible here are whether this *vadna* – this determining – is that by man, or is the reference here to the *vadi* by the 'Lord'. The latter seems a more convincing view.

In line 3 the Guru says high caste is of no relevance in the next world where there is a new order of beings. The term *jīo navay* has been rendered by Prof. Teja Singh as, "the souls have to bow (before the Lord)", taking *navay* in the sense of lowering or bowing. Most learned ones have however rendered it as "a new order of beings" or "new species of creation" or "new order of life". Dr. Gopal Singh slightly changes it as, "for a new man is born into the world of God". The message behind this lesson is obviously to rid us of the most popular misconception of that time, when high caste was deemed a certificate or a passport to the Lord. The Guru consistently seeks to remove this error and has often stated that caste is immaterial; what matters is man's devotion to the Lord. In that context the Guru says here that any illusions about caste had better be shed because all these are mere labels meaninglessly applied to humans in this world. Once the soul crosses over from this world, there will be seen a whole new type of creation, and a new set of criteria will apply. The high worldly position or the so-called high caste will have no relevance to that system.

In line 4, the Guru tells us what assets will be of any value in that sphere. He says only those are honored there whose actions were good and pleasing to the Lord. Thus, the only currency that may buy us the Lord's blessing is our good actions, our righteous way of living. As Prof. Talib puts it, "Only those, whose devotion in God's reckoning is entered, shall be considered pure." Thus, neither power, nor high postion, nor caste has any relevance before the Lord. Only the account of our good deeds will determine whether we will receive honour.

In this, the 11th *pauṛi*, the Guru says:

ਪਉੜੀ ॥	Pauṛi
ਧੁਰਿ ਕਰਮੁ ਜਿਨਾ ਕਉ ਤੁਧੁ ਪਾਇਆ ਤਾ ਤਿਨੀ ਖਸਮ ਧਿਆਇਆ ॥	Dhur karam jina kau tudh pāia ta tini khasam dhiāia
ਏਨਾ ਜੰਤਾ ਕੈ ਵਸਿ ਕਿਛੁ ਨਾਹੀ ਤੁਧੁ ਵੇਕੀ ਜਗਤ ਉਪਾਇਆ ॥	Ena janta kai vass kichh nāhi tudh veki jagat upāia
ਇਕਨਾ ਨੋ ਤੂੰ ਮੇਲਿ ਲੈਹਿ ਇਕਿ ਆਪਹੁ ਤੁਧੁ ਖੁਆਇਆ ॥	Ikna nau tu(n) meil laih ik āpoh tudh khuwāia
ਗੁਰ ਕਿਰਪਾ ਤੇ ਜਾਣਿਆ ਜਿਥੈ ਤੁਧੁ ਆਪ ਬੁਝਾਇਆ ॥	Gur kirpa tay jāṇiya jithhai tudh āp bujhāia
ਸਹਿਜੇ ਹੀ ਸਚਿ ਸਮਾਇਆ ॥੧੧॥	Sehjay hee sach samāia. 11..

Glossary:

ਧੁਰਿ	Dhur	The source, from the beginning
ਕਰਮ	Karam	Benediction
ਵੇਕੀ	Veki	Many types, variegated
ਖੁਆਇਆ	Khuāiya	Lead astray
ਸਹਿਜ	Sehjay	With ease
ਸਮਾਇਆ	Samāiya	Is absorbed in

Simply translated this *pauṛi* says that only those whom the Lord has blessed with his glance of grace will meditate on Him. Mortals have no power in their hands to determine the final outcome of events. The Lord has created a universe of great variety, and he Himself brings some closer to Himself and distances some others. Those to whom the Lord has granted enlightenment, obtain His grace through the Guru and easily merge into the Lord. Let us now look at the lesson in more detail.

In line one the Guru says only those meditate on Him whom He has so blessed. The term *dhur* means 'source' or here, 'from earliest time'. In other words, only those destined to do so will meditate on Him, implying that it is a sign of the Lord's grace if someone is on the path to Him. The concept the Guru is stressing is that man's efforts, necessary as they are, cannot by themselves produce any substantive results in the spiritual arena. It is only the Lord's grace that can take us to Him. So our spiritual bent of mind, our good deeds, and our devotion should not make us vain, but must be seen as a blessing for which we must ever thank the Lord. Never let pride overtake you if you are on the path of true devotion; know that it is a gift bestowed on us by the Lord.

In lines 2 and 3 the Guru stresses the same thought and says that on our own we mortals do not have the power to even meditate on Him. The Lord has created a multihued world with beings of all kinds, some of whom He brings closer to Himself and others He distances. Bhai Vir Singh says that the 3rd line was in earlier days also rendered as, "Some who are *Gurmukh* He joins to Himself, and others who are *Manmukh* are sent into the cycle (of rebirth)." Another rendering, he says, is also sometimes taken as, "Some have through their own actions alienated themselves from Him." The more accepted rendering however is that we do not have control over our union with Him. He has created highly diverse beings of which some He grants the grace of union with Him while others he sends away from Him. The underlying thought of course is that our good actions are essential and will be weighed to determine our worth in His court, but the last word on our disposal will be His; the judgement is entirely in His hands.

In the concluding lines, the 4th and 5th, the Guru says whomsoever He has granted enlightenment has through the Guru obtained the Grace and has *sehjay* – easily - merged into the Lord. The stress here again is on the need for a Satguru, a true preceptor through whom the Lord speaks to us, and through whom we will learn how to follow the path that will lead to Him. In Sikhism that Satguru is ever available, it is the *SGGS*. Other belief systems may of course differently prescribe. But this knowledge will also come to us only when He Himself imparts it to us. When that lucky moment arrives then our endeavours become irrelevant and effortlessly will such a lucky one merge into the Lord. The message is that it is only in the Lord's hands to grant us His presence. This happens when He turns His glance of Grace on us. Of their own will, through merely their own efforts, men cannot reach anywhere. Above all is the need for the Lord's Grace, but still vital are the efforts of the human to tread the proper path, and the need for prayer. In humility and through self- discipline will our inner selves be made ready. For this to happen we all need a true preceptor to prepare us spiritually to receive the Lord. However our reaching the Lord is entirely in the Lord's Hands.

PAURI 12

With this *pauri* are attached four *sloks*, two each by Guru Nanak and the Second Nanak. The theme broadly is that the Lord pervades everything, and no man is higher or lower than another. In the first *slok* the Guru says:

ਸਲੋਕ ਮ: ੧	Slok M: 1
ਦੁਖ ਦਾਰੂ ਸੁਖ ਰੋਗ ਭਇਆ ਜਾ ਸੁਖੁ ਤਾਮਿ ਨ ਹੋਈ ॥	Dukh dārū such rog bhaia ja sukh tām na hoyi
ਤੂੰ ਕਰਤਾ ਕਰਣਾ ਮੈ ਨਾਹੀ ਜਾ ਹਉ ਕਰੀ ਨ ਹੋਈ ॥੧॥	Tu[n] karta karṇa mai nāhi ja hau kari na hoyi. 1.
ਬਲਿਹਾਰੀ ਕੁਦਰਤਿ ਵਸਿਆ ॥	Balihāri kudrat vasya
ਤੇਰਾ ਅੰਤੁ ਨ ਜਾਈ ਲਖਿਆ ॥੧॥ ਰਹਾਉ ॥	Tera unt na jāyi lakhiya. 1. Rahāo.
ਜਾਤਿ ਮਹਿ ਜੋਤਿ ਜੋਤਿ ਮਹਿ ਜਾਤਾ ਅਕਲ ਕਲਾ ਭਰਪੂਰਿ ਰਹਿਆ	Jāt maih jott jott maih jātā akal kala bharpūr rahiya.
ਤੂੰ ਸਚਾ ਸਾਹਿਬ ਸਿਫਤਿ ਸੁਆਲਿਉ ਜਿਨਿ ਕੀਤੀ ਸੋ ਪਾਰਿ ਪਇਆ ॥	Tu[n] sachā sahib sipht suāliyo jin kīti so pār paiya
ਕਹੁ ਨਾਨਕ ਕਰਤੇ ਕੀਆ ਬਾਤਾ ਜੋ ਕਿਛੁ ਕਰਣਾ ਸੁ ਕਰਿ ਰਹਿਆ ॥੨॥	Kahu Nanak kartay kīya bāta jo kichh karṇa so karr rahiya. 2.

Glossary:

ਤਾਮਿ	Tām	Then
ਕਰਣਾ	Karṇa	The doer
ਜਾਤਿ	Jāt	Creation, beings
ਜੋਤਿ	Jott	The Lord's light

Pauṛi 12

ਜਾਤਾ	Jāta	Can be seen
ਅਕਲ	Akal	Complete
ਕਲਾ	Kala	Portion
ਸੁਆਲਿਉ	Suālio	Beautiful

Simply translated this *slok* says that worldly pleasure is a disease because it causes us to forget the Lord, and pain is then the cure. The Lord is the Doer, and I (human beings) can control nothing and whatever happens is because of His *Hukam*, His ordinance. The Guru says he is a sacrifice to that Lord who resides in all Nature, and is thus Immanent, and whose limits are immeasurable. The Lord is manifest in all that exists and all beings are part of Him. The Lord is the only Reality, His qualities are splendid and those who laud Him find salvation. Praise the Lord who in His will does that which is required to be done. Let us now look at it in more detail.

In line one the Guru says the pleasures of the world are a disease where there is no devotion for the Lord and then pain becomes the medicine. This line has been varyingly interpreted. The Guru is presenting here the irony of that commonly experienced reality, that pain becomes the medicine and pleasure a disease. He says where there is overindulgence in pleasures; devotion to the Lord is absent. We all see that when a man is sunk in pleasure he will rarely remember the Lord, but the moment tragedy strikes, thoughts turn promptly enough to God, and we are moved to undertake acts of piety and to worship. All those exertions revert soon enough to ease and indulgence the moment the troubles go away. The phrase "tām na hoyi" means– 'then is not'. What is not? This has led to different interpretations because the *slok* itself does not mention it. Some say it means the 'desire for devotion' is missing. Others say it refers to the Lord, that when pleasure is, the Lord is not. Some even put is as meaning that "where, spiritual peace is there trouble is not". Some view *tām* as coming from *tamha* (avarice, greed). Some render this phrase as, "the malady of rebirths is cured by the medicine of *Nām Simran*." Prof. Sahib Singh renders it as, "here man gets spiritual peace troubles go away". The more convincing, and the more commonly used interpretation, however, is that when pleasures overtake us devotion to God vanishes. Bhai Vir Singh uses it in this sense as does Prof. Talib, Macauliffe, Dada Chellaram and Prof. Teja Singh.

In the 2nd line the Guru says the Lord is the Creator, the Doer; I am nothing and whatever happens is not by my effort but because of Him. The omnipotence of the Lord is the theme here. The Guru says all that happens in this world is not by man's volition. Even when he strives hard the results that ensue are often not as he wished. The final outcome of our efforts is solely in the hands of Him who is both the Creator – *karta* – and the Doer – *karṇā*.

In lines 3 and 4, the Guru says he is a sacrifice to the Lord who is manifest in the entire universe, whose limits we cannot delineate. The term *lakhiya* is rendered as 'understood', 'seen', 'is unknowable', 'is inscrutable'; but the sense sought to be conveyed is clearly of a God who is totally beyond the human capacity to measure Him in any way.

Bhai Vir Singh nicely explains these four lines. He says amazing are the Lord's ways. When we think something will give us *sukh* (joy), and we accumulate such things we find it gives not pleasure but manifests as a disease of our inner selves. When the Lord sends us *dukh* (pain and troubles), we react with panic and revulsion, but it turns out to be the remedy for the disease we had acquired from our pursuit of pleasure. So the *sukh* that will give us real spiritual *sukh* can come only from the Lord who is the *karta*, the *karṇā* – the giver of such *sukh*. For whenever I myself try to get such *sukh* it does not come. So the short point is that we must not take worldly pleasures to be our aim in life because these will only damage out inner selves. Nor must we cry out when pain or trouble comes because it will bring the spiritual cure for our diseased inner self. We must stop running after empty illusions and seek the true and lasting joy – *sukh* – from the Lord alone.

In line 5 the Guru says the Lord is manifest in His creation and all beings are in Him. He permeates every bit that exists. The term *kala* is rendered by Dada Chellaram as 'Powers', by Prof. Teja Singh as 'Art', which is a Sanskrit meaning of the word, by Dr. Gopal Singh as 'Attributes', by Macauliffe as 'Animate', and by Prof. Talib as 'Might'. The *Shabdarth* renders it as 'Art' and translates *Akal kala* as meaning the 'art that is artless' – or 'comes without effort'; which says the *Shabdarth* is the highest art. Prof. Sahib Singh and Bhai Vir Singh, however, seem to have a more appealing interpretation. They say that *kala* means portion, and thus *Akal* means entire, unbroken. So they interpret this line as saying that the Lord is manifest in all His beings and to that extent He can be perceived as being in distinct parts throughout the created world. However, he is also *Akal*, entire and complete. So even while being part of each being and thus divided yet is He fully manifest as One and Unique in the entire universe.

In line 6 the Guru says praise the Lord who is the only Reality. His qualities are splendid and whosoever has worshipped Him has found salvation. The term *pār paiya* means 'crossed over'. This comes from the concept of the world as an ocean of sorrow that we have to cross, which can only be done with the Lord's grace. The other thought in this line is of *sipht suālio* – beautiful is thy praise. The Lord has all splendid attributes, and there is no way anyone can overstate these qualities. The singing of praises of the Lord is the prescribed path to salvation in Sikhism. So the Guru is saying splendid and beautiful are the qualities – *sipht* – of the Lord; and now using *sipht* in its other sense as 'praising', he adds that whosover has sung these praises has 'gone across', 'crossed over' this ocean that separated us from Him.

In line 7 the Guru says praise the Lord for He in His own will does what is required to be done. Bhai Vir Singh renders it as, "Talk of the Lord, sing His praises but don't start probing into His acts; for He does what He has to do." Most learned ones have rendered it on these lines. The Guru is stressing the omnipotence of the Lord, as the sole authority determining the course of the entire created universe. Also is he telling us again to sing His praises and implicitly instructs as to surrender to Him unquestioningly, to accept His will, for what He wishes to happen will come about and there is no way we can alter it by demurring or raising questions.

In the second *slok*, which is by the second Nanak, the Guru speaks of the real religion, which is beyond and above all belief systems. He says:

ਮ: ੨	M: 2
ਜੋਗ ਸਬਦੰ ਗਿਆਨ ਸਬਦੰ ਬੇਦ ਸਬਦੰ ਬ੍ਰਾਹਮਣਹ॥	Jogg sabad[ng] gyān sabad[ng] beid sabad[ng] brāhmṇaih
ਖਤਰੀ ਸਬਦੰ ਸੂਰ ਸਬਦੰ ਸੂਦ੍ਰ ਸਬਦੰ ਪਰਾ ਕ੍ਰਿਤਹ॥	Khatri sabad[ng] sūr sabad[ng] sūdra sabad[ng] pra kritaih
ਸਰਬ ਸਬਦੰ ਏਕ ਸਬਦੰ ਜੇ ਕੋ ਜਾਣੈ ਭੇਉ॥	Sarab sabda[ng] ek sabda[ng] je ko janai bheo
ਨਾਨਕ ਤਾ ਕਾ ਦਾਸੁ ਹੈ ਸੋਈ ਨਿਰੰਜਨ ਦੇਉ॥੩॥	Nanak ta ka dās hai soyi niranjan deo. 3.

Glossary:

ਸਬਦੰ	Sabad[ng]	The Guru's word, lesson, ordinance, *dharma*
ਬ੍ਰਾਹਮਣਹ	Brāhmṇaih	Of Brahmins
ਪਰਾ ਕ੍ਰਿਤਹ	Pra kritaih	Service of others
ਭੇਉ	Bheo	Secret
ਦੇਉ	Deo	The Lord

Simply translated this *slok* says that the *dharma* prescribed in Yoga is to know about the Lord, the *dharma* of Brahmins is to study the *Vedas*, the Kshatriya's *dharma* is valour and the Sudra's *dharma* is providing service to all. There is however only one real *dharma* (and that is the 'Name'), if someone knows the Truth. The Guru says that he would be a slave to the one who has this knowledge, that the Lord is Immaculate. Let us now look at it in more detail.

In the first line Guru says the *dharma* on the path of Yoga is to obtain knowledge of the Lord. The *dharma* of Brahmins is to ponder on the *Vedas*. The reference in this entire *slok* and the next line is to the pernicious *varna* system that did so much damage to society and to this country. Under this system society was divided into four sections, the Brahmins, Kshatriyas, Vaishyas and Sudras. Initially it may have been intended as a division of labour, based on aptitude or merit, with the intellectual and the teacher called a Brahmin, the warrior and soldier a Kshatriya, the tradesman and commercial workers as Vaishyas, and the manual labour as Sudras. Soon, however, it got stratified into a system based on birth. So a Brahmin's son however dull, remained a Brahmin and the son of the Kshatriya however physically weak and cowardly, was bound to remain a warrior. Worst of all however was the effect on the members of the lowest caste, the Sudras. Being born into that caste bound all its members to an eternity of servitude. So evil did this situation become that a Sudra's touch or even his shadow was deemed impure by a Brahmin. The most intelligent or valorous of Sudras were not allowed to move out of their menial existence. This on the one hand led to great resentment building among the underclass and on the other hand it deprived the country of the benefits that could have been available if this sizeable chunk of society were part of a cohesive society. It effectively restricted the defense of the country to a small percentage of its population. No wonder then that there were a series of defeats over centuries for India. Many men of wisdom saw the unfairness of this and revolted against this inequity. Thus, we have in the Middle Ages saints and religious teachers emerging from the deprived classes, like Bhagat Kabir, Bhagat Ravidās, Bhagat Nāmdev, and many others.

Guru Nanak's campaign against this evil was strong and wholehearted. He strongly advocated the equality of men as children of the same Creator and refused to honour class and caste distinctions. This movement culminated with the tenth Nanak creating the complete man, the *Khalsa*, in whom the intellect had to be like the Brahmin, valour like the Kshatriya, who had to be earn his own living by honest work like a Vaishya, and who did not shirk from offering service to all like a Sudra.

This *slok* points to that continuing movement. The second Nanak is telling us in this first line that it is said that the *dharma* of the Brahmin is the study and knowledge of the *Vedas*, the scriptures; and the *dharma* of the Yogis is the pursuit of divine knowledge. The Yogis meditate in long *samādhis* – a state of trance – and they practice austerities to acquire the knowledge of the Divine. The Brahmins devote their lives to studying the *Vedas* that are supposed to be the repository of all knowledge. They are supposed to study, understand and teach to others these scriptures.

In the 2nd line the Guru refers to the Kshatriya – or Khatri as they are commonly called in Punjabi – and says it is required that they acquire the warrior's qualities and show valour. The Vaishya caste is not specifically mentioned but the allusion is implicit. The Guru adds that the *dharma* (duty) of the Sūdra is deemed to be providing service to all the other castes and performing the manual tasks. Bhai Vir Singh says that some take the phrase *Pra kritaih* in this line as referring to the Vaishya, taking the word as *Prākrit* (good business) such as trade and agriculture. However, he says the more likely meaning is as 'service to others'. This is more appealing because the Guru has used the phrase in juxtaposition with Sudra.

In lines 3 and 4, the Guru concludes that the reality is that there is only one real *dharma* and that is the 'Name'. If someone recognises this truth, the Guru says, he would be a slave to such a one, for this knowledge raises that human to the status of the Divine. In other words, the Guru is telling us that the restrictions of various castes to various limited tasks is wrong, and for all of them the true path is the same, that of *Nām Simran*.

In the same vein the 2nd Nanak in the next *slok* speaks of the universality of the true religion. He says:

ਮ: ੨	M: 2
ਏਕ ਕ੍ਰਿਸਨੰ ਸਰਬ ਦੇਵਾ ਦੇਵ ਦੇਵਾ ਤ ਆਤਮਾ ॥	Ek krisna[ng] sarab deva dev deva ta ātma
ਆਤਮਾ ਬਾਸੁਦੇਵਸਿ ਜੇ ਕੋ ਜਾਣੈ ਭੇਉ ॥	Ātma bāsdevas je ko jāṇai bheo
ਨਾਨਕ ਤਾ ਕਾ ਦਾਸੁ ਹੈ ਸੋਈ ਨਿਰੰਜਨ ਦੇਉ ॥੪॥	Nanak ta ka dās hai soyi niranjan deo. 4.

Glossary:

ਏਕ ਕ੍ਰਿਸਨੰ	Ek Krisna(ng)	One Lord
ਦੇਵ	Dev	Gods and godlings
ਬਾਸੁਦੇਵਸਿ	Bāsdevas	The Lord
ਨਿਰੰਜਨ	Niranjan	Untainted

Simply translated this brief *slok* says that the Lord is the soul of all gods and godlings, and of other beings too. The Lord is the One Reality if we understand the reality. The Guru is willing to be the slave of him who recognizes this truth. Let us now look at it in more detail.

In the first line the Guru says the one Lord is the soul of all the gods. The word *Krishna* also refers to Lord Krishna, who is viewed as an incarnation of Lord Vishnu, and who came in the *Dwāpar Yuga*, the revealer of the *Bhagvad Gīta*. Bhai Vir Singh and Prof. Sahib Singh say that it refers here to the universal spirit for which also the term is used. As Bhai Sahib says in the footnotes of his *Panj granthi*, the *tippi* on the word makes it in grammatical terms gender neutral, and so it refers to the Lord. The term *sarab Deva Dev Deva* is rendered by Bhai Vir Singh as 'gods and asuras', or non-gods, taking *devādev* as the composite of *Dev + Adev*. Prof. Sahib Singh renders it as 'gods', and the 'gods of the gods' meaning the trinity of Brahma, Vishnu, and Mahesh. Dr. Gopal Singh puts it as, "Krishna may be the god of gods, but higher still is the self, yea, the soul." Prof. Talib says, "The supreme Lord is the God of all gods and beings other than gods, and their inspiring self." This is quite close to Bhai Vir Singh's interpretation, and is more appealing. The Guru is, in short, telling us that there is but One Lord who is the God of all, gods or others, meaning all created beings high or low.

In the 2nd line, the Guru says this reality is universal and immanent, if someone understands this fact. Dr. Gopal Singh renders it as, "But the soul too derives its power from the over soul." Dada Chellaram says, "That soul is *Vāsudeva* – the Prime Father." Prof. Talib interprets it as, "This self is all pervasive, should one realize this secret." The word *Vasudeva* is used also for Lord Krishna, as son of Vasudev. The other meaning of the word is the Universal Spirit, the *Brahm*, the one Lord, and is so used even in the *Purānas*. Here the Guru is saying is that the soul within us, our real self is but a reflection of the universal self, the Lord who pervades all that exists.

In the 3rd line the Guru says if someone were to be awaken to this realization then he would willingly be the slave of such a one. This line was also the concluding line of the previous *slok*. The Guru is telling us that the one who realizes that the soul within is but a temporarily separated part of the One Lord is deserving of the highest respect. Such knowledge is called self-realization and is the forerunner to union with the Divine and the termination of the cycle of transmigrations.

In the next *slok* Guru Nanak tells us about the vital importance of the Guru. He says:

ਮ: ੧	M: 1
ਕੁੰਭੇ ਬਧਾ ਜਲੁ ਰਹੈ ਜਲ ਬਿਨੁ ਕੁੰਭੁ ਨ ਹੋਇ ॥	Kumbhay badha jal rahai jal bin kumbh na hoye
ਗਿਆਨ ਕਾ ਬਧਾ ਮਨੁ ਰਹੈ ਗੁਰ ਬਿਨੁ ਗਿਆਨ ਨ ਹੋਇ ॥੫॥	Gyān ka badha mann rahai gur bin gyān na hoye. 5.

Glossary:

ਕੁੰਭ	Kumbh	Water pot
ਬਧਾ	Badha	Bound
ਜਲ	Jal	Water

In this brief *slok* the Guru says the relation between mind and knowledge is as between water and its container. The mind cannot be stopped from wandering without true knowledge, and true knowledge cannot come without the Guru. In olden times the potters made water pots from clay on their spinning wheels. After shaping them they were baked in a kiln until they became firm, and then the pot was used in the household for holding drinking water. While the clay is being formed the potter will make liberal use of water to soften the clay for moulding. So most commentators have interpreted the first line to say that if the pot were not there, there would not be any place to store drinking water but if there were no water, the pot itself could not be shaped.

Using the same analogy these learned commentators interpret the second line to say that the mind cannot be contained productively without knowledge. It is of course not the worldly education that is being mentioned, nor mere reading of even the scriptures. Regarding that the Guru had earlier told us in the second *slok* to the 9th *pauṛi* that, "likh likh paṛiya teta kaṛiya", meaning the more he has studied the more his arrogance increases and he stews in the sense of his own erudition. Here the reference is to the knowledge of the Divine. The mind has an irresistible tendency to splinter itself into myriad thoughts, chasing odd fancies and flitting purposelessly. Only one container can hold it in place – the knowledge of the Lord. That knowledge is the constraint that will keep the mind bound into purposeful avenues. In this context does the Guru say, "The mind can be held only by knowledge." But this knowledge will come only through the Guru. The *Shabdarth* at this point renders 'Guru' as the 'mind', thus rendering the line as "without the mind the knowledge cannot be acquired." Bhai Vir Singh renders it as, "The mind is settled when true knowledge is acquired, but without the Guru that divine knowledge cannot be obtained." This is quite appealing for indeed the mind cannot be contained and stopped from wandering without the true knowledge and that knowledge cannot come except through the true Guru. This essentiality of the Guru has been stressed often in the *SGGS*.

This, the 12th *pauṛi*, to which there *sloks* are attached, says:

ਪਉੜੀ ॥	Pauṛi
ਪੜਿਆ ਹੋਵੈ ਗੁਨਹਗਾਰੁ ਤਾ ਓਮੀ ਸਾਧੁ ਨ ਮਾਰੀਐ ॥	Paṛia hovai gunahgār ta omi sādh na māriai.
ਜੇਹਾ ਘਾਲੇ ਘਾਲਣਾ ਤੇਵੇਹੋ ਨਾਉ ਪਚਾਰੀਐ ॥	Jeha ghālay ghālṇa teveho nau pachāriai.

Pauṛi 12

ਐਸੀ ਕਲਾ ਨ ਖੇਡੀਐ ਜਿਤੁ ਦਰਗਹ ਗਇਆ ਹਾਰੀਐ ॥	Aisi kala na khedīyai jit dargah gaiya hārīyai
ਪੜਿਆ ਅਤੈ ਓਮੀਆ ਵੀਚਾਰੁ ਅਗੈ ਵੀਚਾਰੀਐ ॥	Paṛiya atay omīya vīchar aggai vīchārīyai
ਮੁਹਿ ਚਲੈ ਸੁ ਅਗੈ ਮਾਰੀਐ ॥੧੨॥	Muh challai su aggai māriai [12]

Glossary:

ਪੜਿਆ	Paṛia	Educated person
ਗੁਨਹਗਾਰ	Gunahgār	Sinner
ਓਮੀ	Omi	Illiterate
ਸਾਧੁ	Sādh	Gentle person
ਘਾਲੇ ਘਾਲਣਾ	Ghāllay ghālṇa	Earns, works for
ਪਚਾਰੀਐ	Pachārīai	Is known
ਕਲਾ	Kala	Game
ਮੁਹਿ ਚਲੈ	Muh challai	Works at his own will

Simply translated this *pauṛi* says that being well read is no protection if one is sinful, while the illiterate man is not punished in the Lord's court if he is good. As the actions are, so shall be the reputation. Play not the game such that you are the loser before the Lord. Both the learned and the illiterate will be judged solely on the merit of their actions. Those who follow their own willful minds will suffer in the hereafter. Let us now look at the lesson in more detail.

In line 1, the Guru says a literate man if sinful will yet face punishment while the good man is not punished merely because he is illiterate. The allusion here is to the sense of pride, of arrogance that is engendered in most of us from having studied a lot, from being learned. Most such scholars start assuming an air of moral superiority and feel that they have earned immunity for any of their wrong doings. The Guru says the level of your scholarliness is not the measure of your worth in the Lord's eyes. If such a scholar sins then in the Divine Court not his learning but his sins will be the determinant of whether he is to face punishment. As against that, if someone is illiterate that will not be held against him if his actions are good and pure. The word *Omi sādh* describes a pious but illiterate person. *Omi* is from the Arabic root *umm* and means illiterate. Gyani Maskin says that it refers euphemistically to someone who has no learning except enough to say *Om*. The equivalent among Sikhs is the phrase that he is just *Satnām* only, meaning that he is not very learned and just knows enough to say *Satnām*. The lack of knowledge of such a simple but pious person will be no bar, says the Guru, in the Divine Court provided his conduct has otherwise earned him merit.

In line 2 the Guru says as are your actions so shall be your renown or reputation. As Prof. Teja Singh puts it, "A man is known by the work he does." *Ghālay ghālṇa* means actions, *ghālay* literally means 'strives for' and *ghālṇa* means 'results, action'. The Guru says even in this world your renown is determined by the sort of deeds you strive to perform. Obviously then the Lord who sees inside of us will know not only the deeds but also the intentions behind those deeds. In His court therefore the renown or honour, or punishment, will even more exactly fit the deed.

In line 3 the Guru stresses further this point and instructs us not to play the game in such a way that we are losers before the Lord when we face judgement. *Kala* here means 'game' though its more usual meaning is 'art' or 'skill'. The Guru seems to be suggesting that clever and artful men usually arrange their lives so as to try and obtain the maximum material possessions. The really smart ones do it so cunningly that they also seem to wear a guise of goodness, fooling the people about their real intentions and actions. Such artfulness will often fool people in this world, but in the Lord's court their subterfuges will be exposed and the reality will emerge painfully bare. So, says the Guru, stop such cleverness and play not games that will declare you ultimately a loser in His court. Dr. Gopal Singh renders it well as, "Why play then such a play through which one loses in the True Court".

In line 4 the Guru now directly restates the idea behind the above three lines and says that the literate and the illiterate will be judged only on the merit of their goodness. As the Guru told us also in the *Japji Sahib* in *pauṛi* 34, page 7of the *SGGS*, "karmi karmi hoye vīchār, sacha āp sacha darbār", meaning "by our actions are we judged. True is the court of the True One". *Vīchar* means thought, consideration. Here, though, it is used in the sense of judgement, which ensues from the consideration of our merit on the Lord's touchstone.

In line 5 the Guru says he who follows His own mind's will, shall suffer in the hereafter. As the Guru said earlier in the *slok* with the 1st *pauṛi,* "**ਨਾਨਕ ਗੁਰੂ ਨ ਚੇਤਨੀ ਮਨਿ ਆਪਣੈ ਸੁਚੇਤ॥**" – "Nanak guru na chetni mann āpṇay suchet", meaning a person who heeds not the Guru and instead is led solely by the passions of his own mind. Such a one is called *Manmukh* or ego-directed, as opposed to *Gurmukh* – the one heeding his Guru. The one who follows his own mind usually does it from arrogance, from a feeling that he is superior and needs no guidance. The one who heeds the Guru will do so because he realizes that he has yet much to learn. This humility brings with it an open mind, a receptiveness which allows such a fortunate one to learn from the Guru the path of *Nām Simran*, of self-discipline, of controlling the mind that will lead, when the Lord so decides, to union with Him. But the one who is guided by his willfulness, his arrogance will be distanced from Him and will keep suffering transmigration and its eternal pain. Depending on the deeds these births may also start occurring into lower and worse life forms, for the Guru has also told us in the *Japji Sahib* in *pauṛi* 4, page 2 of the *SGGS*, "karmi āvai kapṛa nadri mokh duār" – "our deeds determine the forms into which we are born, but only by His Grace will salvation come".

PAUṚI 13

In this *pauṛi* the Guru has attached two *sloks*, both by Guru Nanak. In the first one the Guru talks of the nature of each *Yuga*, the divisions of time in the Hindu belief system. He says:

ਸਲੋਕ ਮ: ੧	Slok M: 1
ਨਾਨਕ ਮੇਰੁ ਸਰੀਰ ਕਾ ਇਕੁ ਰਥੁ ਇਕੁ ਰਥਵਾਹੁ ॥	Nanak mer sarīr ka ik rath ik rathwāh
ਜੁਗੁ ਜੁਗੁ ਫੇਰਿ ਵਟਾਈਅਹਿ ਗਿਆਨੀ ਬੁਝਹਿ ਤਾਹਿ ॥	Jugg jugg pher vattāiai gyāni bujheh tāh
ਸਤਜੁਗਿ ਰਥੁ ਸੰਤੋਖ ਕਾ ਧਰਮੁ ਅਗੈ ਰਥਵਾਹੁ ॥	Satjug rath santokh ka dharam aggai rathwāh
ਤ੍ਰੇਤੈ ਰਥੁ ਜਤੈ ਕਾ ਜੋਰੁ ਅਗੈ ਰਥਵਾਹੁ ॥	Tretai rath jatai ka jor aggai rathwāh
ਦੁਆਪਰਿ ਰਥੁ ਤਪੈ ਕਾ ਸਤੁ ਅਗੈ ਰਥਵਾਹੁ ॥	Dwapar rath tapai ka sat aggai rathwāh
ਕਲਜੁਗਿ ਰਥੁ ਅਗਨਿ ਕਾ ਕੂੜੁ ਅਗੈ ਰਥਵਾਹੁ ॥੧॥	Kaljug rath agan ka kūṛ aggai rathwāh. 1.

Glossary:

ਮੇਰੁ	Mer	The prime among a group, here the human form
ਰਥ	Rath	Chariot, here the body
ਰਥਵਾਹ	Rathwāh	Charioteer
ਜੁਗ	Jugg	A *yuga*, one of the four *Satya*, *Treta*, *Dwāpar* and *Kali*
ਜੋਰ	Jor	Power, strength
ਵਟਾਈਅਹਿ	Vattāiai	Keep changing

Simply translated this *slok* says that this prime among all forms, the human form rides a chariot and it has one charioteer. The main trait of the human form and its ruling passion, or controlling influence changes with each Age and the wise ones know this. In *Satyuga* Contentment was the chariot and Righteousness the charioteer. In the *Treta*, Continence was the chariot and Inner strength the charioteer. In the *Dwāpar*, the chariot was Austerities and Purity the charioteer. In the *Kaliyuga*, the present *Yuga*, *Agni* (Fire) is the chariot and Falsehood the charioteer. Let us now look at this concept in more detail.

In line 1, the Guru says that this prime among forms, the human is like a chariot and it has a charioteer. The word *Mer* is used to describe anything that is the prime, the best among a category. Thus, among mountains the best is deemed the Meru, also called Sumeru Mountain which is the loftiest, the biggest and is deemed to be the abode of the gods in the Hindu pantheon. Similarly, among the 108 beads that constitute the rosary in Hinduism, the prime bead is called *Mer*. Among the various forms granted by the Lord to living things, the *Mer* is deemed to be this human form. Incidentally all religious belief systems hold that the human form is the highest of all created things. Even modern science says the human form is the culmination of the evolutionary process. The belief in Hinduism is that we reach this stage after going through a whole range of different forms of life, which are believed to number 84 lakhs, or 8.4 million. It is at the end of this tortous journey that the soul reaches the human shape. It is thus especially precious and the supreme among all forms, and hence is called *Mer* by the Guru.

Bhai Vir Singh says in his *Panj granthi* that this likening of the human body to a chariot has also been done in the *Kathopnishad*. However there the concept is that the body is the chariot and the soul inside is the rider. The intellect is the charioteer and the mind provides the reins. The five senses are the horses driving this chariot on the road of the material things. When the soul remains under their influence it suffers and can not reach the goal of God-realization, and he says that the Guru here is altering this to say that the inner urges of the human can not let go of the attraction for the material, and that has been so in all the four *Yugas*. The methods mentioned in the *Kathopnishad* will not therefore work, and the only effective device is *Nām Simran*. In Budhism too, he says, the body has been viewed as the chariot. Bhai Sahib says that in this *slok* the journey of the human through this mortal world is compared to a chariot ride and the body has been called the chariot, and the bond created by the inner desires is the charioteer. The soul rides this vehicle. Just as a ride to be successful needs a sound chariot and a good charioteer, similarly in this spiritual journey it is essential that the actions by the body be good and pure, and the desires inside free from taint of *Maya*. This explains the thought well, except that, says Bhai Sahib, the phrase used here is, "Mer sarīr ka ik rath, ik rathwāh", meaning the *Mer* (human form) has a chariot and a charioteer. Thus the body is spoken of as possessing a chariot, and, unlike in the *Kathopnishad*, is not itself called the chariot.

What is the chariot the Guru has mentioned here? Gyani Sant Singh Maskin in his audio-commentary has explained it well. He says in this journey at all times, and in all ages, there has to be a main method, or a guiding principle, adopted by the devotees for reaching the Lord, and there has to a governing principle controlling the lifestyles. These change from time to time. Thus, at one time pursuit of righteousness prevails, and at another time the method of austerities is more common. The prevailing spirit of the times then determines which *Yuga* we could be said to be living in. Prof. Teja Singh calls this the 'governing ideal'. We will discuss this further as we examine each of the further lines.

In line 2 the Guru says that the chariot and the charioteer change as the Wheel of Time turns and the Ages, or *Yugas* as they are called in Hinduism, follow one after the other. With each *Yuga* the guiding principle and the governing ideals undergo a change. The chariot changes and so does the charioteer. This reality is well understood by the wise ones. Prof. Sahib Singh and Gyani Maskin have taken these lines to refer not to the mythical *Yugas* that lasted millions of years. Rather, they say, that these here are meant to only indicate that the governing spirit of the times and the nature of the people and the guiding principle that the majority chooses to follow. Thus, when contentment and righteouness dominate that Age, that time is called *Satyuga*. Even in such an Age there could well be humans existing whose nature is not of the *Satyuga* but fits more properly with the latter and lesser *Yugas*. Thus, for example, though in the *Kaliyuga* the dominant influence is supposed to be *Agni* (passion) and the prevailing spirit that of *Kūr* (falsehood), there could yet be individuals who would possess contented minds and show righteous behaviour more characteristic of the *Satyuga*. However, when overwhelming majorities think in a particular way then that way becomes the governing genius of the times, the Zeitgeist.

In line 3 the Guru says in the Satyug *santokh* (contentment) was the chariot and *dharam* (righteousness) was the charioteer. Learned men have also rendered the term *dharam* as, 'Religion', 'Piety' or 'Law or Duty'. The term 'Righteousness', however, would seem closest to the concept here. Prof. Teja Singh has rendered the term *santokh* as 'temperateness', which also is not too far from the generally accepted meaning as contentment. Thus, it can be said that *Satyuga* was the time when the majority of human beings possessed a contented nature and the prevailing spirit was righteousness. The guiding principle therefore was 'contentment', and so men sought to reach the Lord through this path and they followed their *dharma* as a matter of accepted routine. *Dharma* was the governing ideal of the times.

In line 4 the Guru says that in the *Yuga* that followed, the *Treta*, the method followed, the guiding principle was continence and the governing ideal was power. Thus, continence became the chariot and strength was the charioteer that drove it. Men as a whole were disciplined and their minds were under control. Power or strength, however, was now the guiding spirit.

In line 5 the Guru speaks of the next *Yuga*, the *Dwāpar*. During this Age pursuit of 'austerities' was the method, the guiding principle, which was followed by most men. Contentment and continence were no longer deemed to be important. People instead started observing elaborate rites of austerity. The governing ideal now was the urge to live a life of *satt* – a pure life. Some learned commentators have also rendered *satt* as truth or righteousness. Dr. Gopal Singh calls it 'compassion'. Prof. Sahib Singh and Gyani Maskin have, however, both rendered it as pure living and high morality, and in the context here this seems a more appealing interpretation.

In the 6th line the Guru comes to the present times, the *Kaliyuga*. Now the vehicle men ride is of *agni* – (Fire), and the governing spirit is *kūṛ* (falsehood). The fire spoken of here is that of greed, avarice and acquisitiveness. Men forever seek more and more and are never satisfied. The fire inside is insatiable and burns ever brighter. Falsehood prevails. Cheating, lying and trying to make foul seem fair by putting on false facades have become the norm. Prof. Sahib Singh and Gyani Maskin say that it is not because of any *Kaliyuga* that this deterioration in the quality of human nature has occurred; rather it is because of this change in the nature of humans do we call this Age a *Kaliyuga*.

Thus, the nature of the times changed as men started to live under different guiding principles. It does not however follow that the way to salvation changed with the change of the *Yuga*. Even in the best times, the *Satyuga*, men still were in the cycle of transmigrations, as they continued to be even in the succeeding *Yugas*. The effect of the guiding spirit, the governing principle – Power or Righteousness – did not obviate the need for *Nām Simran*. Nor did the formulaic austerities followed in the *Dwāpar Yuga* lead to any change in that requirement. There has always been, in all ages, the underlying urge to power and possessions and the joys of the material word. Only those who could shed these false attachments and turn their minds to the Lord obtained salvations. If in those less corrupted times it was difficult to overcome the attraction to falsehood, then imagine just how much tougher it is for the denizen of the present *Yuga* when the dominating spirit is the passion for material things, and when falsehood rules over all. In such times the path to the Lord is that much harder to follow, or even to find. Yet is the path throughout all these ages the same. Only through *Nām Simran* will enlightenment come.

In the next *slok* the Guru speaks about the four *Vedas*. He says:

ਮ: ੧	M: 1
ਸਾਮ ਕਹੈ ਸੇਤੰਬਰੁ ਸੁਆਮੀ ਸਚ ਮਹਿ ਆਛੈ ਸਾਚਿ ਰਹੇ ॥	Sām kahai setambar swāmi sach maih āchhai sāch rahay
ਸਭੁ ਕੋ ਸਚਿ ਸਮਾਵੈ ॥	Sabh ko sach samāvai
ਰਿਗੁ ਕਹੈ ਰਹਿਆ ਭਰਪੂਰਿ ॥	Rig kahai rahiya bharpūr
ਰਾਮ ਨਾਮੁ ਦੇਵਾ ਮਹਿ ਸੂਰੁ ॥	Rām nām deva maih sūr
ਨਾਇ ਲਇਐ ਪਰਾਛਤ ਜਾਹਿ ॥	Nāye laiai parāchhat jāhay
ਨਾਨਕ ਤਉ ਮੋਖੰਤਰੁ ਪਾਹਿ ॥	Nanak tau mokhantar pāhay
ਜੁਜ ਮਹਿ ਜੋਰ ਛਲੀ ਚੰਦ੍ਰਾਵਲਿ ਕਾਨ੍ ਕ੍ਰਿਸਨੁ ਜਾਦਮੁ ਭਇਆ ॥	Juj maih jor chhali chandrāwal kanh krishan jādam bhaia
ਪਾਰਜਾਤੁ ਗੋਪੀ ਲੈ ਆਇਆ ਬਿੰਦ੍ਰਾਬਨ ਮਹਿ ਰੰਗੁ ਕੀਆ ॥	Pārjāt gopi lai āiya bindrāban maih rung kīya.
ਕਲਿ ਮਹਿ ਬੇਦੁ ਅਥਰਬਣੁ ਹੂਆ ਨਾਉ ਖੁਦਾਈ ਅਲਹੁ ਭਇਆ ॥	Kal maih beid atharbaṇ hūa nau khudāyi alhu bhaia
ਨੀਲ ਬਸਤ੍ਰ ਲੇ ਕਪੜੇ ਪਹਿਰੇ ਤੁਰਕ ਪਠਾਣੀ ਅਮਲੁ ਕੀਆ ॥	Nīl bastra lay kapṛay pahray turk patthāṇi amal kīya.
ਚਾਰੇ ਵੇਦ ਹੋਏ ਸਚਿਆਰ ॥	Chāray ved hoye sachiār
ਪੜਹਿ ਗੁਣਹਿ ਤਿਨ੍ ਚਾਰ ਵੀਚਾਰ ॥	Paṛhe guṇhe tin chār vīchar

ਭਾਉ ਭਗਤਿ ਕਰਿ ਨੀਚੁ ਸਦਾਏ ॥	Bhau bhagat kar nīch sadāye
ਤਉ ਨਾਨਕ ਮੋਖੰਤਰੁ ਪਾਏ ॥੨॥	Tau Nanak mokhantar pāye. 2.

Glossary:

ਸਾਮ	Sām	The *Sāma Veda*
ਸੇਤੰਬਰ	Setambar	Clad in white
ਮੋਖੰਤਰ	Mokhantar	The door to salvation
ਜੁਜ	Juj	The *Yajur Veda*
ਚੰਦ੍ਰਾਵਲਿ	Chandrāwal	A *gopi* (milkmaid), abducted by Lord Krishna
ਪਾਰਜਾਤ	Pārjāt	A divine tree
ਬਿੰਦ੍ਰਾਬਨ	Bindrāban	Vrindavan, where Lord Krishna spent his childhood and early youth
ਅਥਰਬਣ	Atharbaṇ	The *Atharva Veda*

The Guru tells us in this *slok*, that the *Sāma Veda* says that the Lord was white vestured. Men lived in truth and in truth were they absorbed. The *Rig Veda* says that the Lord is all pervading, and He was called Rama who was among the *Devtas* as the Sun is among lights. The *Yajur Veda* says His name became Krishna Jadam, and forcibly and trickily did he take Chandrāwal. He brought the *Pārjāt* for his *gopi* and he made sport in Bindraaban. In *Kaliyuga* the *Atharva Veda* applied and His name became *Allah* and *Khuda*. He wore blue clothing and the way of the Turks and the Pathans prevailed. All the four *Vedas* are true and studying them brings high thinking. He only obtains salvation that worships God with devotion and stays humble. Let us now look at it in more detail.

Just as the Guru had in the previous *slok* described the changing spirit of the times in each *Yuga*' and its correlation with the nature of the populace, he in this *slok*' describes the situation with regard to the *Vedas*. This is neither a critique nor criticism of the *Vedas*, because the Guru has never at any time condemned another's belief system. His advice has always been that whatever path you follow, do it with God's Name in your heart. Humility, self control, charity and *Nām Simran*' – reciting His Name – must be the guiding principles of behaviour and thinking in your life.

To better appreciate and more easily understand the message here we need to take a look first at the summing up, which has been done by the Guru in the last two, the concluding lines, which prescribe, "Love God, worship Him but assume not arrogance, call yourself lowly and humble. Then will you find the door to salvation." The Guru says worship the One Lord with love in your heart. But do not let pride at your piety enter your heart or seek to be acclaimed for it. Deem yourself lowly, let humility rule your mind. That is the path to salvation. The paths described in this *slok* for the various *Yugas* are good in their own way and will bring some benefit to the soul but the path that will lead to cessation of the cycle of births for us is *Nām Simran*. With this background we can now look at each line.

In the first two lines the Guru says according to the *Sāma Veda*, the Lord was white vestured. Men lived in Truth and in Truth they were absorbed. There are different interpretations of these lines. Macauliffe and Prof. Talib render *setambar* as the *Hamsa Avtār*, the 'swan incarnation'. Prof. Sahib Singh renders it as, "*Sām* Veda says that in the *Satyuga* the *swāmi* (master) of the world was known as *setambar* who ever resides in Truth." Bhai Vir Singh in his *Panj granthi* says that it is a lesson given to Shwetaketu, the son of a great *rishi* named Udalak and quotes from the *Chandogya Upanishad* to say that *swetambar* and *shwetketu* both mean 'white-clad'. So he takes the term *setambar swāmi* as referring to *Shwetaketu's* father who is giving this lesson to his son.

The *Shabdarth* however says that *Sāma Veda* tells us that the *swāmi* (Lord) was deemed white in the *Satyuga*. In the *Mahabharata* in 'Vaṇ Parva', Lord Krishna is also quoted as saying so. In the *Gāyatri* also the colour of *Sāma Veda* is said is said to be white. In this light the rendering according to the *Shabdarth* becomes, "In *Satyuga* the colour of the Lord was white and men lived pure and true lives." The rendering of *setambar* as the *Hamsa Avatār* does not quite appeal because in the *Purānas* it is deemed a relatively minor *Avatār* of Lord Vishnu. The myth is that it was assumed for the specific purpose of instructing Brahma's son, Sanat Kumar in the finer points of theology. There were many *Avatārs* of Lord Vishnu in the ages before *Treta Yuga*, which are counted among *Das Avatārs* – ten major incarnations. These include the *Matsya Avatār,* the *Kurma Avatār,* the *Varaha Avatār,* the *Narsimha Avatār, and the Parshuram Avatār*. So why would the Guru refer to a minor *Avatār* for illustrating his point. It seems more likely therefore that the use of *setambar* is for *svetambar*, meaning white-clad, which as we noted above is said to have been used for the Lord in *Satyuga*. It also very aptly reflects the nature of the Age that was marked by purity and righteousness.

In the 3rd and 4th line the Guru says the *Rig Veda* calls Him all pervading. Gyani Maskin explains that the 'One pervading' would be rendered in Punjabi as *Ramia hoya*, from which also comes the word Raam, or Rama, a commonly used name for God in India. The Guru is saying that according to the *Rig Veda*, in the *Treta Yuga*, the Lord's Name was renowned as 'Rama'. 'Rama', says the Gurus was in that age among the *Devtas* like the Sun is among all lights, outshining and resplendent.

In lines 5 and 6 the Guru says that men took His Name and all sins were removed, so tells the *Rig Veda*. The theme of taking the Lord's Name as a vehicle for enlightenment is again brought in here. Since Rama was deemed God in that age, so taking His Name became like taking the Lord's Name. Those who took His Name found salvation. The Guru of course does not support the view of any *Avatār* or super *Devta* becoming the proper subject of worship or the granter of emancipication. As we noted above, he will in the last lines make clear the proper way of worship and emancipication, which is *Nām Simran* or reciting the Name of the formless One.

In lines 7 and 8 the Guru speaks of the *Yajur Veda*, which he links, to the *Dwāpar Yuga*. He says that the Name of the Lord became prevalent as *Jadam,* or *Yādav*. The Guru says in this age of the *Yajur Veda*, He was called 'Kānh', 'Krishan', 'Yādav', who abducted Chandrāwal, and brought *Pārjāt* for his *gopi*, with whom he made sport in Bindrāban. The references here are to stories about Lord Krishna's younger years when he resided in Vrindāvan with Nanda and Yashoda, his adoptive parents. He is said to have had dalliance with a number of milkmaids, the most clebrated being Radha. Another such maid, or *gopi* as they were called, was Chandrāwal, a cousin of Radha and married to one Goverdhan. It is said that she was abducted by Krishna through a clever device of dressing as a woman and taking her from her home. The reference here is to that event. *Pārjāt* is the name of a divine tree which was supposed to be a special attraction in the garden of Lord Indra, and is one of five such divine trees called *Mandār, Pārjāt, Santān, Kalp vriksha* and *Harichandan*. The *Pārjāt* is also counted as one among the fourteen jewels wrested from the Primal Ocean in the churning by the *Devtas* and the *Asuras*. His queen Satyabhama being insistent, Lord Krishna brought that tree down to earth leading to many interesting events that ensued. His beloved wife Satyabhama is here referred to as a *gopi* – because the *gopis* are in mythology deemed to be especially dear to Lord Krishna, and adored him while in return they were also deeply loved by him. All there stories about the sport of the *Krishna Avatār* are famously narrated in the *Bhāgwat Purāṇa*, and being a well recognised part of folklore, these have been mentioned here by the Guru, to make it easier for his audience to understand his mystic message.

In lines 9 and 10 the Guru speaks of the present *Yuga* where he says that the *Atharva Veda* is prominent and the name of the Lord has become renowned as *Allah* and *Khuda*. The reference here obviously is to the ascendancy of the Muslim faith. In this age, says the Guru in line 10, men took to wearing blue clothes, the colour preferred by the Muslims, and shaped their actions according to the way of the Turk and the Pathaan, the two races which converted largely to Islam and which were ruling over India at the time of the Guru.

Guru is not seeking here to create a relation between the *Vedas* and the *Yugas*. The stress rather is on explaining the prevalent mores and the lifestyles of the people over different periods of time. The Guru had used the same device qua the *Yugas* in the precious *sloks*. Now he uses the *Vedas* to the same effect. How people change their lifestyles and modes of worship is related here to the *Vedas*, with references also to the *Yugas*.

In lines 11 and 12 the Guru says the four *Vedas* are true and studying and pondering on them brings high thinking. The term *chār vīchār* means beautiful thoughts, high thinking which is how Prof. Sahib Singh and Bhai Vir Singh have rendered it. Some learned commentators have rendered it as, "Get knowledge of *karma*-lore". Prof. Teja Singh holds the same view. Macauliffe puts it as, "found therein four different doctrines". Prof. Talib says, "realize what is appropriate action from what is inappropriate". Dr. Gopal Singh and the *Shabdarth* share a similar view. Dada Chellaram follows Macauliffe's view. The rendering by Prof. Sahib Singh and Bhai Vir Singh seems more appealing. The sense essentially is that the *Vedas* contain their own truths, and are thus deserving of respect. Their study will give knowledge and lead to elevation of the mind.

In lines 13 and 14, the concluding ones, the Guru sums up the argument. In various ages and times changing modes of worship and changing ideals have prevailed. However, the true path to the Lord is ever the same and that path has here unambiguously been delineated. The Guru says worship the Lord, raise in your heart love and awe for Him. Be a thoroughly devoted servant of the Lord, but do not boast about it or wish to be honored for it. Consider yourself lowly, have humility rule over your heart. Then only, says the Guru, will you see the door to salvation. *Bhakti* is essential, and while we are in that state of devotion, what should be our internal state? We should have *Bhāo* for the Lord – love, adoration and awe, all mixed together. When we are in that state inside of us, then only will our acts of devotion be acceptable to the Lord, and then will we be on the path to salvation. The important requirement is that we must not let pride overtake us. So the Guru puts in a warning – he says do *Bhāo Bhagti* but seek not to be called holy. Stay humble and never claim high status. Then only will the path of salvation open. The evil of pride and arrogance is what we are being warned against.

In this, the 13th *pauṛi*, the Guru lauds the *Satguru* who leads us to the Lord. He says:

ਪਉੜੀ ॥	Pauṛi
ਸਤਿਗੁਰ ਵਿਟਹੁ ਵਾਰਿਆ ਜਿਤੁ ਮਿਲਿਐ ਖਸਮੁ ਸਮਾਲਿਆ ॥	Satgur vittoh vāria jit miliai khasam samālia
ਜਿਨਿ ਕਰਿ ਉਪਦੇਸ ਗਿਆਨ ਅੰਜਨੁ ਦੀਆ ਇਨ੍ਹੀ ਨੇਤ੍ਰੀ ਜਗਤੁ ਨਿਹਾਲਿਆ ॥	Jinn kar updes gyān anjan dīa inhi netri jagat nihālia
ਖਸਮੁ ਛੋਡਿ ਦੂਜੈ ਲਗੇ ਡੁਬੇ ਸੇ ਵਣਜਾਰਿਆ ॥	Khasam chhod dojai laggay dubbay say vaṇjāria
ਸਤਿਗੁਰੂ ਹੈ ਬੋਹਿਥਾ ਵਿਰਲੈ ਕਿਨੈ ਵੀਚਾਰਿਆ ॥	Satguru hai bohetha virlai kinai vīchāria
ਕਰਿ ਕਿਰਪਾ ਪਾਰਿ ਉਤਾਰਿਆ ॥੧੩॥	Kar kirpa pār utāria [13]

Glossary:

ਵਿਟਹੁ	Vitoh	From
ਸਮਾਲਿਆ	Samālia	Remembered
ਅੰਜਨ	Anjan	Taint, here used for the collyrium applied to the eye
ਨਿਹਾਲਿਆ	Nihālia	Seen
ਵਣਜਾਰਿਆ	Vaṇjāria	Traders
ਬੋਹਿਥਾ	Bohetha	Ship, boat

Simply translated, in this *pauṛi* the Guru says that he is a sacrifice to the *Satguru* meeting whom the mind thinks of the Lord. He through his teaching has bestowed the gift of knowledge to see with these eyes the reality of the world. Those merchants [human beings in this world] who turn not to the Lord but choose to fix their minds on other things will suffer total ruin. The *Satguru* is the ship that can take us across the ocean from this world to the Lord, but only the rare ones recognize this. Let us now look at it in more detail.

In the first line the Guru says that I am sacrifice to the *Satguru* in meeting whom my mind remembers the Lord. The stress in this *pauṛi*, as it was in many of the earlier compositions too, is on the true preceptor – the *Satguru*. The preceptor is the one who imparts to us the right learning and who brings to us the word of the Lord. From him is to be learnt the proper way to approach Him. The *Satguru* is the one who lays out and then explains to us the roadmap to salvation, which for a Sikh is none other than the *SGGS*.

In the second line the Guru says this *Satguru* has given to us the special spiritual collyrium for our eyes that removes our ignorance and enables us to look at the reality that underlies this world. The term *Anjan* means a taint, but is also commonly used in India to describe a sort of medicinal paste that used to be applied to the eyes to keep them healthy and which was supposed also to improve the eyesight. The Guru says that through his teaching the *Satguru* has imparted that *Anjan* which has opened the spiritual eyes within. After that enlightenment the way we look at the world changes. The material objects we see remain the same outwardly, unchanged physically, but now to the newly enlightened eye the reality inside these starts becoming apparent. This happens because of the *Gyān Anjan* we got from the Guru.

In line 3 the Guru refers to those who did not turn to the Lord but were attracted by ephemeral phenomenon, and fixed their minds elsewhere. The Guru says such traders will suffer total loss and will be ruined. He teaches us that the only wealth we must strive to earn is that of the Name of the Lord, because only this will go with us to the Lord's presence. All souls are sent to this world endowed with a certain capital depending on and emerging from merit previously accumulated; and what will be allotted is determined entirely by the Lord's Will. We all also get for our sojourn here an allotted quota of years. It is then left open to us by the Lord to utilize this capital of our past merits and our allotted years in any way and for whatever purpose we may choose. Some fortunate ones choose the Lord, and are then blessed with finding a *Satguru* through whom the passage to salvation is delineated and also smoothened. On this road however there are many glittering things – power, money, and gratification of the senses, which can easily allure us away from the right path. Most of us lose track of this path that leads to the Lord and instead start chasing after these baubles. Our invaluable capital is then wasted collecting these alluring but valueless trinkets. The Guru says do not be allured by these. If you enter into this false commerce this trade will result in a total loss for you. As Bhagat Kabir says on page 1366 of the *SGGS*, "Kabir mānus janam dulambh hai hoye na bārai bār", meaning the human form is a rare gift, is priceless and we may not get again. Yet there are many sadly wasting this rare opportunity in mere self-indulgence. They are losers, says the Guru, because they forgot the Lord and chased after other things. Some learned ones have taken *dūjai laggay* as referring to those who are attached not to the One Lord but to the other lesser gods of which there is a large number in the Hindu pantheon. However, in the context here the interpretation as "attached to things other than the Lord" seems more appealing here.

In lines 4 and 5 the Guru says the *Satguru* is a ship to take us across to the Lord, but few are there who recognise this. Only when He gives us the blessing will we get to the other shore. The analogy of the passage through this world with the crossing of an ocean has often been used in the *SGGS*. This world is also called *bhav sāgar* – the ocean of dread. So that we may not sink and be lost we need a boat, a ship to keep us afloat. That ship, says the Guru, is the *Satguru* who teaches us the Lord's Name. For a Sikh such a *Satguru* is easily found and is ever present in the *SGGS*. Among the others too, many lucky ones will perhaps find a *Satguru*, but many will just wander. So alluring are the toys that *Maya* dangles before us that there are few indeed who even recognise the need for a *Satguru*, a true preceptor. Most of us think we are very wise and in full control of our fate, and thus need no one to guide us. The rare ones who have the good fortune to attain the necessary humility and recognise such a need will seek out the *Satguru* who will then impart to their eyes the *Anjan* of spiritual knowledge. *Anjan* is collyrium, a paste, which in India is applied to the eye to keep the eyes healthy. Here the Guru is using the analogy to say that the *Anjan* of spiritual knowledge will do the same for our souls. This will open the eye to the sight behind the apparent.

PAURI 14

With this *pauṛi* are attached two *sloks*, both by Guru Nanak. In the first one he says:

ਸਲੋਕ ਮ: ੧	Slok M: 1
ਸਿੰਮਲ ਰੁਖੁ ਸਰਾਇਰਾ ਅਤਿ ਦੀਰਘ ਅਤਿ ਮੁਚੁ ॥	Simal rukh sarāira att dīragh att much
ਓਇ ਜੇ ਆਵਹਿ ਆਸ ਕਰ ਜਾਹਿ ਨਿਰਾਸੇ ਕਿਤੁ ॥	Oye je āvaih ās kar jāhe nirāsay kitt
ਫਲ ਫਿਕੇ ਫੁਲ ਬਕਬਕੇ ਕੰਮਿ ਨ ਆਵਹਿ ਪਤ ॥	Phal phikkay phul bakbakay kam na āvaih patt
ਮਿਠਤੁ ਨੀਵੀ ਨਾਨਕਾ ਗੁਣ ਚੰਗਿਆਈਆ ਤਤੁ ॥	Mitthat nīvi Nanaka guṇ changiāia tatt
ਸਭ ਕੋ ਨਿਵੈ ਆਪ ਕਉ ਪਰ ਕਉ ਨਿਵੈ ਨ ਕੋਇ ॥	Sabh ko nivai āp kau par kau nivai na koye
ਧਰ ਤਾਰਾਜੂ ਤੋਲੀਐ ਨਿਵੈ ਸੁ ਗਉਰਾ ਹੋਇ ॥	Dharr tarājū toliyai nivai so gaura hoye
ਅਪਰਾਧੀ ਦੂਣਾ ਨਿਵੈ ਜੋ ਹੰਤਾ ਮਿਰਗਾਹਿ ॥	Aprādhi dūna nivai jo hanta mirgāhay
ਸੀਸਿ ਨਿਵਾਇਐ ਕਿਆ ਥੀਐ ਜਾ ਰਿਦੈ ਕੁਸੁਧੇ ਜਾਹਿ ॥੧॥	Sīs nivāiai kiya thīyai ja, ridai kusudhay jāhay. 1.

Glossary:

ਸਿੰਮਲ	Simal	Silk-cotton tree
ਸਰਾਇਰਾ	Sarāira	Straight
ਦੀਰਘ	Dīragh	Long lasting, also tall

ਮੁਚੁ	Much	Robust, thick
ਨਿਰਾਸੇ	Nirāsay	Disappointed
ਬਕਬਕੇ	Bakbakay	Insipid, tasteless
ਮਿਠਤ	Mitthat	Sweetness
ਗਉਰਾ	Gaura	Heavy
ਹੰਤਾ	Hanta	Killer
ਕੁਸੁਧੇ	Kusudhay	Impure, nasty, unclean

The Guru in this *slok* speaks to us of the virtue of humility and the insignificance of outward grandeur. Simply translated this *slok* says that the *simal* (silk-cotton) tree is tall, straight and durable. Why then do those who come to it in hope go back disappointed? Because its fruit is tasteless, the flower insipid and the leaves are of no use. Sweetness and humility are on the other hand the essence of genuinely good qualities. We often see that people only pretend to lower themselves for their own advantage. Genuine lowering of the self will be to our own advantage. If we look at the balance the lower side is always the heavier. The bad ones bow even lower, like a hunter when he sets out to kill deer. Like that hunter the ones with evil in their hearts will manifest great outward humility. What use is it to bow the body if the heart is filled with ill and impure thought? Let us now look at it in more detail.

In the first three lines the Guru gives the example of the *simal* (silk-cotton) tree. The Guru says the *simal* is very impressive because it is tall and straight, very high and thick. Why, then, do those, the birds, who come to it in hope, go back disappointed? Because, he explains, its fruit is tasteless, the flower insipid and the leaves are of no use at all. The woolly texture of its flowers makes these inedible. Its leaves can also not be put to any practical use, and in fact are harmful for the fertility of the ground underneath on which these happen to fall. This huge, beautiful profusely vegetating tree is grand to look at, but in fact it is non-productive, yields nothing of practical use to anyone and thus brings no joy to any man, bird or animal.

In line 4 the Guru says sweetness and humility are in contrast of great use. The term *mitthat* in also used for a berry tree – the *ber* – which is small, twisted and unimpressive to look at but produces such juicy and sweet fruit that it is of great attraction to birds and humans alike. The point the Guru is making is that grandeur, size and showiness are of little importance if they do no good to anyone. Rather, humility and sweetness is what is important, regardless of outer appearance.

In line 5 the Guru then puts in a word of caution, that mere bowing as a sign of humility is no guarantee of good intention. Most learned ones have rendered this line to say that the Guru is saying that all really bow for their own purposes and no one bows for the good of another. However, Bhai Vir Singh explains it slightly differently and says that *mitthat*, humility and sweetness, may seem like lowering oneself but this lowering is the crux of all goodness. Such lowering is in fact bringing honour to one's own self. No one is therefore bowing for the benefit of another. He is lowering himself, because there is solidity inside – and the heavy side of the scales always is the lower, as we will see in the next line. So the bowing is to earn honour for himself. This is an elegant and very appealing construction and explains the concept without changing the essence of the thought.

In line 6 the above thought is reinforced. The Guru says that when we put two things on the balancing scales, it is the heavier, the weightier side, which lowers itself. Bhai Vir Singh's interpretation as we saw above centres round this point. His argument was that the one lowering himself is doing so to earn honour, and the proof of this can be seen on the balance where the heavier thing lowers itself. The word *Gaura* means not only heavy but also momentous or weighty. Thus, the one willing to lower himself will prove the more important.

In the concluding lines, 7th and 8th, the Guru says the criminal bows twice as low when he sets out to kill a deer. So what use is it to lower the body if the mind is impure? All lowering is not from solidity or humility, the Guru says here. He implies that the real lowering of the self is when the mind is humble and pure. Mere bending of the body is pointless. The reference here is to the practice of hunters with bows and arrows stalking deer. They would hide behind every cover bending as low as necessary, but in their heart was murder as they sought to slay the unsuspecting animal. Using this analogy the Guru says if the bowing and lowering is for ulterior purpose then it is obviously not desirable; such lowering does not make one important. The purpose behind any show of humility is therefore what matters. There are enough apparently humble ones putting on an act to deceive the world of men to achieve some ulterior ends.

Some learned ones also render *simal* as referring to those self-proclaimed Gurus who put on a grand appearance, and exhibit great pomp and show, but have not any real knowledge to impart. The seekers who come to these Gurus are then the *jāye nirāsay* – the ones going back disappointed.

In the next *slok* the Guru says:

ਮ: ੧	M: 1
ਪੜਿ ਪੁਸਤਕ ਸੰਧਿਆ ਬਾਦੰ॥	Paṛ pustak sandhya bād(ng)
ਸਿਲ ਪੂਜਸਿ ਬਗੁਲ ਸਮਾਧੰ॥	Sil pūjas bagul samādh(ng)
ਮੁਖ ਝੂਠ ਬਿਭੂਖਣ ਸਾਰੰ॥	Mukh jhūth bibūkhaṇ sār(ng)
ਤ੍ਰੈਪਾਲ ਤਿਹਾਲ ਬਿਚਾਰੰ॥	Traipāl tihāl bichār(ng)
ਗਲਿ ਮਾਲਾ ਤਿਲਕੁ ਲਿਲਾਟੰ॥	Gall māla tilak lilāt(ng)
ਦੁਇ ਧੋਤੀ ਬਸਤ੍ਰ ਕਪਾਟੰ॥	Duey dhoti bastr kapāt(ng)
ਜੇ ਜਾਣਸਿ ਬ੍ਰਹਮੰ ਕਰਮੰ॥	Je jāṇas brahma(ng) karam(ng)
ਸਭਿ ਫੋਕਟ ਨਿਸਚਉ ਕਰਮੰ॥	Sabh phokat nischau karam(ng)
ਕਹੁ ਨਾਨਕ ਨਿਹਚਉ ਧਿਆਵੈ॥	Kahu Nanak nihchau dhiāvai,
ਵਿਣੁ ਸਤਿਗੁਰ ਵਾਟ ਨ ਪਾਵੈ॥੨॥	Viṇ satguru vāt na pāvai. 2.

Glossary:

ਪੁਸਤਕ	Pustak	Books; here, scriptures
ਬਾਦੰ	Bād[ng]	Argument
ਸਿਲ	Sil	Stone, idol
ਬਗੁਲ	Bagul	Like a heron
ਬਿਭੂਖਣ	Bibhūkhaṇ	Ornaments
ਸਾਰੰ	Sār[ng]	Beautiful
ਤ੍ਰੈਪਾਲ	Traipāl	Three-leaved, the *Gayatri mantra*
ਲਿਲਾਟ	Lilāt(ng)	On the forehead
ਕਪਾਟ	Kapātan(ng)	On the head, a curtain
ਵਾਟ	Vāt	The way

Simply translated this *slok* says that the hypocritical priests read books, perform the *sandhya* rituals, in the morning and evening. They engage in contentious discussion, and sit heron-like in false *samādhi* (meditation). In their mouth is untruth but they spout words pretty as jewels. They recite the three-lined *Gāyatri mantra* thrice a day. They wear a *māla* (necklace of beads) around the neck and sport ritual religious marks on the forehead. They wear the prescribed two *dhotis* and tie the cloth around the head. If they truly knew the Lord's way they would realize that all this formalism is meaningless. We must fix our minds on the Lord and meditate on Him, and this path is not to be found without the *Satguru*, the true preceptor. Let us now look at it in more detail.

In lines 1 and 2 the Guru says you read books, perform your *sandhya* rites, argue, worship stones and sit in *samādhi* like a heron. Addressing the *pandit* pretending to be holy, the Guru speaks of what the reality is. He says the *pandit* reads the books, the *Vedas* and scriptural literature. He performs the devotional rites prescribed for the twilight hours (*sandhya*) and then is disputatious on points of theology. He offers worship to stones and strikes the pose as if he is in a *samādhi*. This devotional pose is supposed to lead to union with the Lord, but here it is just a mere pretense, just a pose, similar to the pose a heron assumes when it stands on one leg motionless in water waiting for a fish or a water creature to swim within range so that he can then pounce. The *samādhi* posture usually involves cross-legged sitting, or standing upright on one leg. The dichotomy between the *pandit's* pose and his real aim is here alluded to. He is really seeking new followers, or seeking wealth from the existing ones. Just like the heron his pious pose is a sham and he is in reality seeking prey.

In lines 3 and 4 the Guru says in the *pandit's* mouth are lies but he spouts words as beautiful as jewels. He reads the *Gāyatri mantra* thrice a day. Brahmins are required to read the *traipal* (three-lined) holy *Gāyatri mantra* thrice every day. The reality of such poseurs is, says the Guru, that in their hearts there is no spirituality and all that they do is a pretense, for which they put on all the accoutrements of a true worshipper, a holy man. Their entire lives are personified by falsehood. So, says the Guru, what these *pandits* are uttering is a lie. The phrase *bibhūkhan sār[ng]* literally means beautiful jewellery. Dr. Gopal Singh renders it as "their bodies are decked with piety". Most commentators however take it as saying that the *pandit* utters falsehoods from his mouth but try to show as if these were like excellent jewels. Bhai Vir Singh says some learned ones also construe the 4th line as, "the sustainer of the three worlds considers your condition also", taking *traipāl* as the one tending to the three worlds, and *tihāl* as your condition. The more convincing rendering however is on the lines that the hypocritical *pandit* spouts falsehoods with such skill that he tries to make this false jewellery seem like real. He goes through the rituals of reading the *Gāyatri mantra* thrice a day.

In lines 5 and 6 the Guru says this *pandit* wears necklaces and ritual markings on the forehead. He wears two *dhotis* – (wrap-around muslin cloth for the lower extremities) – as prescribed, and ties a cloth around the head. These lines describe the *pandit* as wearing all the properly prescribed items of the *pandit's* dress. He wears the mandatory beads around the neck, and applies the prescribed markings on his forehead. A double *dhoti* and cloth for the head were the other essential components of the dress for a Brahmin. These items completed the guise for the *pandit* to appear as truly a preceptor, but in reality merely served to hide his hypocrisy. Bhai Vir Singh renders *kapāt(ng)* as a curtain cloth that the *pandit* stretches for privacy when he sits for worship. However, most learned commentators have interpreted it as meaning 'headcloth', which is one of the prescribed items of attire, and it seems a more appealing rendering.

In lines 7 and 8 the Guru says if this *pandit* knew what constitutes truly godly activity, he would know that all this ritualism is pointless. As Prof. Talib puts it, "One that knows the way of godly actions, regards all such as mere husks." Bhai Vir Singh has also used a similar interpretation in his *Panj granthi*. Dr. Gopal Singh renders the 7th line as, "If only they knew the nature of God", which is how the *Shabdarth* also puts it. Learned ones have put somewhat varying constructions on it, but the rendering as by Prof. Talib above seems more convincing.

In lines 9 and 10 the Guru concludes the presentation of this message with, "The real need is to fix your mind on the Lord. And this path will not be reached without the *Satguru*." This is how Bhai Vir Singh, Prof. Sahib Singh and Gyani Makin all render it, when they say, "The real need is that with firm faith should one meditate on Him. But this path is not to be found without the *Satguru* to guide you." This is quite close to the view taken by some of the other learned commentators also, and is quite convincing.

In this, the 14th *pauṛi*, the Guru says:

ਪਉੜੀ ॥	Pauṛi
ਕਪੜੁ ਰੂਪੁ ਸੁਹਾਵਣਾ ਛਡਿ ਦੁਨੀਆ ਅੰਦਰਿ ਜਾਵਣਾ ॥	Kappaṛ rūp suhāvṇa chhad dunīa andar jāvṇa

ਮੰਦਾ ਚੰਗਾ ਆਪਣਾ ਆਪੇ ਹੀ ਕੀਤਾ ਪਾਵਣਾ ॥	Manda changa āpṇa āpay hee kīta pāvṇa
ਹੁਕਮ ਕੀਏ ਮਨਿ ਭਾਵਦੇ ਰਾਹਿ ਭੀੜੈ ਅਗੈ ਜਾਵਣਾ ॥	Hukam kīye mann bhāvday rāh bhīṛai aggai jāvṇa
ਨੰਗਾ ਦੋਜਕਿ ਚਾਲਿਆ ਤਾ ਦਿਸੈ ਖਰਾ ਡਰਾਵਣਾ॥	Nanga dojak chāliya ta disai kharā darāvṇa
ਕਰਿ ਅਉਗਣ ਪਛੋਤਾਵਣਾ॥੧੪॥	Karr augaṇ pachhutāvṇa. [14]

Glossary:

ਕਪੜੁ	Kappaṛ	The body
ਸੁਹਾਵਣਾ	Suhāvṇa	Pleasant, beautiful
ਮਨਿ ਭਾਵਦੇ	Mann Bhāvday	From one's own will
ਭੀੜੈ	Bhīṛai	Narrow
ਦੋਜਕਿ	Dojak	*Dozakh* – the Muslim hell

The Guru speaks to us in this *pauṛi* of the need for high thinking and good deeds, and living with a detached mind. Bhai Vir Singh has opined that this *pauṛi* seems to relate to some rich and powerful man departing this world, probably a Muslim, because the term *dojak* has been employed. The message of course is universally applicable to all humans. Simply translated this *pauṛi* says that this pleasing human form shall be left behind. The good and the evil that we do will visit befitting consequences upon us. We may in this world lord it over others but the road beyond that we have to travel is narrow and difficult. When denuded of all pretenses one goes to hell and sees one's dreadful visage then one will regret the evil deeds committed here. Let us now look at it in more detail.

In line 1 the Guru says this body is very pleasing but this shall have to stay behind in this world. *Kappaṛ* literally means apparel, so some learned ones have rendered this line to say that the pleasing raiments, or attire that we are so enjoying here, shall have to be left behind when we go from this world. Macauliffe puts it as, "Raiment and pleasing beauty …." Bhai Vir Singh says *kappaṛ* here refers to all worldly wealth, and *rūp* refers to the human form. Dr. Gopal Singh on the other hand says, "Beauteous is the form (of life), but one leaves it." The point the Guru is making is obvious; that we ought not to get too deeply attached to this body and its adornments, because it is mortal and our journey to the next world will be without all of this. Too many of us get narcissistically attached to our bodies, pandering to all the sensuous pleasures to keep the body happy. They spend great energy and time adorning it with clothes and jewels. But this vehicle for the soul is but a short-term companion. On the same theme earlier also we were told in the 2nd *slok*, 4th *pauṛi,* "Lakh takiya ke mundṛey lakh takiya ke hār, jitt tann paiyai Nanka so tann hosi chhār", meaning the body that we are adorning will soon be dust. This is not a directive to ignore or neglect the well being of the body, which is a very precious gift from the Lord, the vehicle for the soul to exisit in this mortal world and to perform the right actions in this *karma bhūmi* (arena) so as to earn our passage to the Lord. The Guru is only saying be aware of its mortality and keep your level of attachment to it accordingly adjusted.

In line 2 the Guru says the good and the evil that we do will visit precise consequences upon us. So, the body that will not go with us should not be the focus of our attention. Instead we need to focus on the deeds that the body performs. It is the effect of these deeds, good or bad, pure or evil, that goes with us to the next world. In the Lord's court, as the Guru has told us repeatedly, the judgement will be determined purely by the merits of our actions. We, the soul that will appear before the Lord's court, will carry with us only one defense, the only support, and that is our good deeds. So, keep the body healthy and functional but don't bother for it beyond that, do not pander to it. Focus instead on performing good actions in accordance with the path laid down for you by your preceptor – which for a Sikh is the *SGGS*.

In line 3 the Guru says you were lording it over others but now you will have to travel a narrow and difficult road. The word *Bhīṛai* means 'narrow' but is also used for 'difficulty'. Here both these senses of the word apply. The Guru says all your high position in this world and your command over others may have given you great latitude to work your will upon others. However, once this sojourn is over, the passage beyond is narrow and difficult. You will no longer have that position which allowed you to order others. The ease and pleasures and freedom of worldly rulership will vanish abruptly, and a narrow and difficult road will be there to be traversed – which will require us to shrink our egos down. The narrowness of the passage to the Lord is a theme found in other belief systems too. The *Bible* tells us, in Mark 10:25, "It is easier for a camel to go through the eye of a needle than for a rich man to enter the kingdom of heaven." The allusion is to the pride and inflated ego of the rich man, which will prevent him from reaching the Lord.

In lines 4 and 5 the Guru concludes by telling us that "when one goes to hell naked and sees his dreadful visage, then he regrets the evil deeds he committed." The term *Nanga* means bare, nude. The allusion is to the evil that men do in this world, hidden from the public eye. They think it is known to none and so they are safe and will escape the consequences. But when we start to traverse the passage to the next world, all such guises and covers are removed and our real selves are stripped bare and naked. Then will be uncovered before the Lord's eye all our sins. *Dojak*, or *Dozakh*, is the hell spoken of in the Muslim belief system, where evil ones face eternal torture. A similar concept is *Narak* in Hinduism. However, a Lord who physically tortures His own creation is quite out of tune with the Sikh belief system, which postulates a kindly, compassionate, loving and just God. The *Dojak* referred here in this context for a Sikh means distancing from the Lord, and the continuing torment of being trapped in the circle of rebirths. As the Guru said in the *Japji Sahib*, "karmi āpo āpṇi kay neṛai kay dūr", meaning according to the merits of one's actions is our position – some near and some distant from the Lord. So here the Guru says, having committed evil deeds the man knows he is bound for exile away from his Lord and into the cycle of transmigration, maybe even into a very low life form – for *karmi āvai kappṛa* – 'through our action is our next birth determined' – as the Guru says in the *Japji Sahib*, *pauṛi* 4. So, the Guru is saying that the one who was evil is now travelling the narrow road out of this world to the Lord, all his secrets laid bare and the hell of exile, away from the Lord, staring him in the face.

The term *darāvṇa* means scary. It is also used for a 'scarecrow'. The rendering of this phrase has been done both ways. Dada Chellaram says, "To hell they are dragged naked, seeing which they stand aghast, struck with terror." Dr. Gopal Singh uses similar terminology. Prof. Teja Singh says, "When he goes stripped to hell, it will then look horrible indeed." Prof. Sahib Singh however puts it as, "His own visage seems dreadful to himself." Bhai Vir Singh says similarly, "He appears horrible." Prof. Talib also shares the same view. Gyani Maskin in his audio-commentary says the appearance of the evil man is dreadful at that time like a 'scarecrow', which is also one meaning of the word *darāvṇa*. The more appealing interpretation seems to be that the man is now stripped bare of pretences and his real form is horrible to behold – which he himself also becomes aware of at that time. So, says the Guru, in the last line, the ones guilty of evil actions will in the final reckoning repent and will deeply regret the sins they committed.

PAURI 15

In this *pauri* there are attached four *sloks*, all by Guru Nanak. These, especially the first one, are said to relate to the Guru's *janeu* (sacred thread investiture ceremony). In the first *slok* the Guru says:

ਸਲੋਕ ਮ: ੧	Slok M: 1
ਦਇਆ ਕਪਾਹ ਸੰਤੋਖੁ ਸੂਤੁ ਜਤੁ ਗੰਢੀ ਸਤੁ ਵਟੁ ॥	Daya kapāh santokh sūte jat ganddhi sat vatt
ਏਹੁ ਜਨੇਊ ਜੀਅ ਕਾ ਹਈ ਤ ਪਾਡੇ ਘਤੁ ॥	Eh janeu jīa ka hayi ta pādday ghat
ਨਾ ਏਹੁ ਤੁਟੈ ਨਾ ਮਲੁ ਲਗੈ ਨਾ ਏਹੁ ਜਲੈ ਨ ਜਾਇ ॥	Na eh tuttai na mull laggai na eh jalai na jāye
ਧੰਨੁ ਸੁ ਮਾਣਸ ਨਾਨਕਾ ਜੋ ਗਲਿ ਚਲੇ ਪਾਇ ॥	Dhann so māṇas Nanaka jo gull chalay pāye
ਚਉਕੜਿ ਮੁਲਿ ਅਣਾਇਆ ਬਹਿ ਚਉਕੈ ਪਾਇਆ ॥	Chaukaṛ mull aṇāia baih chaukai pāia
ਸਿਖਾ ਕੰਨਿ ਚੜਾਈਆ ਗੁਰੁ ਬ੍ਰਾਹਮਣੁ ਥਿਆ ॥	Sikha kann chaṛāīya guru Brahmin thīya
ਓਹੁ ਮੁਆ ਓਹੁ ਝੜਿ ਪਇਆ ਵੇਤਗਾ ਗਇਆ ॥੧॥	Oh mua oh jhaṛ paia vetagga gaia. 1.

Glossary:

ਦਇਆ	Daya	Compassion
ਜਤ	Jat	Continence
ਗੰਢੀ	Ganddhi	Knots
ਸਤ	Sat	Pure conduct
ਜਨੇਊ	Janeu	Sacred cotton

		thread, customarily worn by higher Hindu castes
ਹਈ	Hayi	If you have
ਨਾ ਜਾਇ	Na jāye	Doesn't go
ਚਲੇ ਪਾਇ	Chalay pāye	Those who have worn it
ਚਉਕੜਿ	Chaukaṛ	Four cowries
ਅਣਾਇਆ	Aṇāia	Summoned

Simply translated this *slok* says that the sacred thread for the self should be made from the cotton of compassion, with contentment as the yarn, continence the knot and purity, the twist in the thread. If such a thread exists, the Guru says he will wear it. Such a thread will neither break, nor be soiled nor burnt, nor is it lost or wasted, and blessed are those who wear such a *janeu*. The *janeu* was a thread made by twisting virgin cotton and then installed ritually to the accompaniment of prescribed *mantras* by the Brahmin who was the spiritual guide of that household. It is donned at prescribed ages according to the *varna* and is to be worn all life. This is supposed to be a vital initiatory rite for the three upper castes, the Sudra being debarred from wearing it. The Guru highlighting the formalistic nature of this act says that the thread that we don in this world can be bought for four cowries and be donned easily sitting in the kitchen. When the wearer dies such a *janeu* falls off, so the man has to go to the beyond without the thread. Let us now look at it in more detail.

The reference in these lines is to the process of forming the *janeu*. It was made from virgin cotton; the yarn was spun, knotted and twisted to give it a loose rope-like shape. In lines 1 and 2 the Guru says the sacred thread that we need to wear is the one that is made from the cotton of compassion with contentment as yarn. The knotting of the thread should come from personal continence and the purity of thought and conduct should provide the twist that completes the making of the thread. The Guru asks the Brahmin priest that if he has such a thread he will gladly wear it. Guru Nanak's ever- repeated message has been to forget ritual observances of religion and to replace these with a true spiritual approach to the effort. The practice of investing the highter castes with a sacred cotton thread, called the *janeu*, is an ancient part of the Hindu rituals. Brahmins, Kshatriyas and Vaishyas, but not the Sudras, are at a certain age put through a ritual where a Brahmin priest puts this sacred thread around their bodies in a special ceremony.

The *Mahan Kosh* tells us that this age is 8 years for a Brahmin, 11 years for a Kshatriya and 12 years for a Vaishya. The clothes to be worn for the occasion also vary according to the *varna* (caste). This formally donned holy thread is then supposed to stay with them till death. For a Brahmin this ceremony is especially important because it is deemed to be his second birth. That is why the Brahmin is called *Dwij* (twice born). As a member of a Kshatriya family, Guru Nanak would also have been put through this ritual. It is said that when the *pandit* priest was about to put the thread over his body he stopped him, refusing to wear the thread; and instead through this hymn posed to the *pandit* the question which is the subject matter of this *slok*. In the process he gave to all of us the vital message that true spirituality will arise from the heart, by improving our thinking and our conduct, and not through such formulism. Whatever the timing of its composition, the *slok* contains an eternal verity and is another example of the Guru rebelling against the meaningless rituals that had overtaken the practice of religion.

In line 3 the Guru says that such a sacred thread woven from spiritual ingredients will neither break, nor be soiled, nor burnt nor is it lost or wasted. The sacred thread woven from cotton and worn by the higher castes was obviously subject to all these eventualities. Being made of common cotton it could easily break. It would also be soiled by daily wear, and fire could destroy it, or like all other material possessions it could be lost. Not so the spiritual sacred thread, the Guru here suggests. He says that thread is beyond the dangers of such damage. It is of the spirit and is permanent.

In line 4 the Guru says blessed are those men who wear such a *janeu*. Bhai Vir Singh explains that the phrase "Jo gall chalay pāye" – go wearing it around the body – here is to be related to the last line where the Guru says *Vetaggā gaya* or went away without this thread. So the meaning here is that the men who have donned such a thread of the spirit will find that it will accompany them to the next world. Such an investiture is thus permanent and not susceptible to the ravages of time.

In line 5 and 6 the Guru reverts to the worldly sacred thread. He says you can buy it for four cowries and don it easily sitting in the kitchen. Then the Brahmin priest whispers some words into your ears and becomes your Guru. The practice for the investiture ceremony was that the kitchen area was purified and an area within it was marked out where the candidate was seated. The *pandit* would then read the prescribed *mantras*, and would then whisper the *Gāyatri mantra* into the ear and put the thread around the bare upper body. The words whispered would be in Sanskrit and probably not even be understood by the recipient. So really speaking this exercise by the pandit would hardly have elevated the recipient spiritually, yet after the ceremony is the *pandit* deemed to be the Guru. A Guru's function is to put the student on the path to God, to elevate him with education and spiritual guidance. A few whispered words do not perform that function, yet is the *pandit* called the Guru. Then the thread itself, says the Guru, can be bought for a mere four cowries from the market. The cowrie was a coin of extremely low value. Macauliffe calls it a *damṛi*. So, says the Guru, a cheaply bought, easily installed piece of cotton and some whispered words cannot create a Guru. The real Guru, when found, will create the real sacred thread for the soul, made from the godly qualities like compassion, contentment, continence and purity of life and thought.

In the concluding line the Guru says when the wearer dies, the *janeu* falls off. So, such a man will have gone to the beyond without his sacred thread. As opposed to this, the spiritual thread is permanent and goes into the next world with us, as the Guru explained in line 4 above.

In the next *slok* the Guru speaks of some of the other manifestations of outward religiosity. He says:

ਮ: ੧	M: 1
ਲਖ ਚੋਰੀਆ ਲਖ ਜਾਰੀਆ ਲਖ ਕੂੜੀਆ ਲਖ ਗਾਲਿ॥	Lakh chorīa lakh jārīa lakh kūṛīa lakh gāl
ਲਖ ਠਗੀਆ ਪਹਿਨਾਮੀਆ ਰਾਤਿ ਦਿਨਸੁ ਜੀਅ ਨਾਲਿ॥	Lakh thaggīya pahnāmīa rāt dinas jīa nāl.
ਤਗੁ ਕਪਾਹਹੁ ਕਤੀਐ ਬਾਮ੍ਹਣੁ ਵਟੇ ਆਇ॥	Tagg kapahu katīai bāhmaṇ vattay āye.
ਕੁਹਿ ਬਕਰਾ ਰਿੰਨਿ੍ ਖਾਇਆ ਸਭੁ ਕੋ ਆਖੈ ਪਾਇ॥	Kuh bakra rinn khāia sabh ko ākhai pāye
ਹੋਇ ਪੁਰਾਣਾ ਸੁਟੀਐ ਭੀ ਫਿਰਿ ਪਾਈਐ ਹੋਰੁ॥	Hoye puranā sutiai bhee phir pāiai hor
ਨਾਨਕ ਤਗੁ ਨ ਤੁਟਈ ਜੇ ਤਗਿ ਹੋਵੈ ਜੋਰੁ॥੨॥	Nanak tagg na tuttyi jay tagg hovai jor. 2.

Glossary:

ਕੂੜੀਆ	Kūṛīa	Falsehood
ਪਹਿਨਾਮੀਆ	Pahnāmīa(n)	Deceptions, cheating
ਜਾਰੀਆ	Jārīa	Adultery
ਕੁਹਿ	Kuh	To butcher

Simply translated this *slok* says that myriad of thefts, adulteries, falsehoods and foul words are uttered by the ones wearing the sacred thread. Myriad deceptions and hidden acts of evil leave their taint day and night. The Brahmin comes, says the Guru, and makes the thread by twisting new cotton. A goat is slaughtered and eaten and thus the *janeu* ceremony is said to be completed. When the thread becomes old it is shed and a new one replaces it. If the thread had real power it would not thus wear out. Let us now look at it in more detail.

In line 1 the Guru says, still on the subject of the *janeu*, and the *pandit* that the sacred thread has not made the wearer pure or spiritually enlightened. In fact the one wearing such thread may also be indulging in myriads of thefts, adulteries, falsehoods and foul words. The Guru is depicting a hard reality that weakness of the flesh is an inevitable and ineluctable companion of one born on this earth. The effects of these transgressions can never be expected to go away merely because a cotton thread has ceremoniously been put around the body. Their evil impact can be shed only through an effort of the spirit. So the mere act of wearing it cannot endow us with some magic formula to take away the evil of all these repeated transgressions. That magic will be seen only when the mind is trained under the true preceptor's guidance to follow the path to the Lord.

In line 2 the Guru adds that myriad deceptions and hidden acts of evil taint human lives day and night. *Pahnāmīa[n]* is from the Persian root *Pinh*, meaning hidden. So, apart from the overt cheating there are so many hidden bad acts the effects of which stick to the soul every day. Continuously does the soul thus acquire the grime of this world; the grime that will get washed only by the recitation of the Lord's Name. As the Guru told us in the *Japji Sahib* in *pauṛi* 20, page 4 of the *SGGS*, "bharīai mat pāpa ke sung, o dhopay navay ke rung" – when the intellect is begrimed it can only be cleansed by the power of the Lord's Name.

In lines 3 and 4 the Guru, describing the ceremony, says the Brahmin comes and twists the cotton into the thread. Then to celebrate the occasion a goat is slaughtered and cooked. It was customary for the invited guests; usually family and kin, to semi-formally announce after the feast that the investiture ceremony of the *janeu* had been completed. What is the fate of that thread after all this elaborate ritual?

The Guru answers this in lines 5 and 6, and says when the thread has become old it is shed and is simply replaced with a new one. But, says the Guru, if the thread really had some power inherent in it, it would not break thus. In other words, this worldly *janeu* is a powerless piece of thread made of cotton. As the Guru told us in the previous *slok* the real thread we need is the sacred thread of the soul, of the spirit; and that one is made not from cotton but from the godly qualities of compassion, contentment, purity and discipline. That spiritual thread will break not, nor will it ever need to be replaced. That is the thread we need to wear, that is the one that contains within itself real power.

In the third *slok* with this *pauṛi*, again on the subject of the *janeu*, the Guru says:

ਮ: ੧	M: 1
ਨਾਇ ਮੰਨਿਐ ਪਤਿ ਊਪਜੈ ਸਾਲਾਹੀ ਸਚੁ ਸੂਤੁ ॥	Nāye maniai pat ūpjai sālāhi sach sūte
ਦਰਗਹ ਅਮਦਰਿ ਪਾਈਐ ਤਗੁ ਨ ਤੂਟਸਿ ਪੂਤ ॥੩॥	Dargah andar pāiai tagg na tūttas pūte. 3.

Glossary:

ਪਤਿ	Pat	Honour, esteem
ਸਾਲਾਹੀ	Sālāhī	Praising God
ਸਚੁ	Sach	True, eternal
ਪੂਤ	Pūte	Pure

In this brief *slok* the Guru says by accepting God's will, honour will come and through His laudation is the true thread produced. This thread never breaks and we can wear it even when we appear before Him for judgement. In other words, this is the sacred thread that will render us protection in our moment of trial. This is the thread that has power inherent in it.

With this the Guru completes the discussion on the sacred thread and the ones who wear it. He has told us that a hundred thousand evils are the everyday part of human existence on this world. Thieving, adultery, cheating, bad deeds both open and covert, foul utterances taint our inner selves. The formulistic wearing of a piece of cotton is not going to remove these blemishes. Nor is that cotton thread a lasting campanion and it certainly will not go with us at the time of our appearance in the Lord's court for judgement. The sacred thread of godly qualities is pure and, unbroken, will be our protection when we appear in the Lord's court.

In the next *slok* the Guru says:

ਮ: ੧	M: 1
ਤਗੁ ਨ ਇੰਦ੍ਰੀ ਤਗੁ ਨ ਨਾਰੀ ॥	Tagg na indri tagg na nāri
ਭਲਕੇ ਥੁਕ ਪਵੈ ਨਿਤ ਦਾੜੀ ॥	Bhalkay thukk pavai nit dāṛi
ਤਗੁ ਨ ਪੈਰੀ ਤਗੁ ਨ ਹਥੀ ॥	Tagg na pairi tagg na hathi
ਤਗੁ ਨ ਜਿਹਵਾ ਤਗੁ ਨ ਅਖੀ ॥	Tagg na jihva tagg na akhi
ਵੇਤਗਾ ਆਪੇ ਵਤੈ ॥	Vetagga āpay vatai
ਵਟਿ ਧਾਗੇ ਅਵਰਾ ਘਤੈ ॥	Vatt dhāggay avra ghatai
ਲੈ ਭਾੜਿ ਕਰੇ ਵੀਆਹੁ ॥	Lai bhāṛ karay viyāh
ਕਢਿ ਕਾਗਲੁ ਦਸੇ ਰਾਹੁ ॥	Kaddh kāgal dasay rāh
ਸੁਣਿ ਵੇਖਹੁ ਲੋਕਾ ਏਹੁ ਵਿਡਾਣੁ ॥	Suṇ vekho loka eh vidāṇ
ਮਨਿ ਅੰਧਾ ਨਾਉ ਸੁਜਾਣੁ ॥੪॥	Mann andha nāo sujāṇ. 4.

Glossary:

ਇੰਦ੍ਰੀ	Indri	Organs
ਨਾਰੀ	Nāri	Woman; here sex organs
ਭਲਕੇ	Bhalkay	Every morning, daily
ਦਾੜੀ	Dāṛi	Beard
ਜਿਹਵਾ	Jihva	Tongue
ਵਤੈ	Vatai	Roams, goes
ਭਾੜਿ	Bhāṛ	Wages
ਕਾਗਲ	Kāgal	Paper, horoscope
ਵਿਡਾਣੁ	Vidāṇ	Wonders
ਸੁਜਾਣ	Sujāṇ	Wise

The Guru now speaks about the one, who performs this investiture ceremony, the Brahmin, who, he says has no restraints on his own self. Simply translated this *slok* says that there is no sacred thread on the sense organs, or on the women. Daily are their beards spat on [they face disgrace]. The feet, the hands, the tongue, the eyes wear no thread of restraint; they follow the wrong path. Such a one without the restraints of any thread makes threads he puts on the bodies of others. The *pandit* takes money to solemnize weddings and produces books for giving guidance to others. The Guru says, "O people look at this wonder. The spiritually blind are being treated as wise ones". Let us now look at it in more detail.

In the first line the Guru says there is no thread on the sense or on women. The word *Nāri* is also taken by some learned ones as *Naṛi*, meaning the sex organs. So they render the lines as, "There is no thread to restrain you senses and your lust". The other rendering is there is no thread on the senses, nor are women – who constitute half of mankind – invested with the thread. Dr. Gopal Singh, Macauliffe, Dada Chellaram take it as 'woman'. Prof. Teja Singh puts it as, "There is no string to bind the male and the female organs." Prof. Talib on the other hand says, "The Brahmin throws not the sacred thread over his own passions, and lusts for woman." Prof. Sahib Singh also takes the meaning as 'organs', and holds a similar view that the Brahmin has not put the thread of restraint on his own senses and lusts which is why he is daily disgraced. Gyani Maskin uses the meaning of *Nari* as 'woman', though he refers to the other view also. Bhai Vir Singh uses *Nari* for the mystic lines of spiritual energy inside us, such as *Iṛa* and *Pingla*.

In the midst of all these varying interpretations the one by Prof. Sahib Singh that has been broadly followed by many other learned ones also, seems more appealing. The thrust of this *slok* is to point out the incongruency of the *pandit*-Brahmin, himself lacking any lofty qualities and yet seeking to become the Guru of the initiate merely through a ritual of investing him with a sacred thread. The purpose of the thread is to bring discipline and control over the mind and the senses. So the Guru is telling the Brahmin that you have not put your own senses under check, you lust after women like any ordinary person with uncontrolled appetites.

In line 2 the Guru says daily do they spit on your beard. This is the traditional way of describing disgrace. Before the shaved face became the norm among

Hindus, the beard was worn as a mark of honour and virility. For someone to touch another's beard was an insult. The height of disgrace of course was the act of spitting on a beard. So, says the Guru to the priest-brahmin, because of your own lack of control and lustful conduct you are facing disgrace everyday.

In lines 3 and 4 the Guru refers to the parts of the body to make the same point. He says your feet have no thread to keep them from straying down the wrong path, nor your hands any thread to stop them from taking what is not yours. Your tongue has no thread to stop you from speaking evil nor your eyes any sacred thread to stop them from seeing evil. This is really by way of restressing the point made in line 1, that the senses of the *pandit* are uncontrolled.

In lines 5 and 6 the Guru says the one without the restraints of any thread is going around making the thread, which then he puts around the bodies of others. The term *vatai* is from the *Lahndi* dialect, meaning 'to go', 'to move around'. So, says the Guru, the threadless one moves without any restraint on himself, but considers himself qualified to make sacred threads and put these on others, and on top of that claiming to have become their Guru.

In lines 7 and 8 the Guru refers to some more of the undesirable characteristics of this poseur seeking to become a spiritual guide. He says you take money to solemnise marriages and produce books to give guidance to others. The Brahmin was the officiating functionary at weddings in the families of his *yajmāns* – the clients for whom he was the family priest. As the third Nanak says in *Rāga Āsa patti*, page 435, *SGGS*, "**ਸਾਈ ਪੁਤਰੀ ਜਜਮਾਨ ਕੀ ਸਾ ਤੇਰੀ ਏਤੁ ਧਾਨਿ ਖਾਧੈ ਤੇਰਾ ਜਨਮੁ ਗਇਆ॥**" – "sāyi putri jajmān ki sa teri et dhān khādhay tera janam gaia", meaning that "the daughters of your *yajmān* are like your own daughters, so by accepting money to preside over their wedding ceremonies you have lost all merit". It is as if the *pandit* had commercialised his own daughter's wedding. The mercenary character of the relationships, and of the *pandit*-Brahmin himself is stressed here. These Brahmins also read the*kāgal,* the almanacs and astrological charts used by them for suggesting the ways to overcome the supposed hinderances caused by planetary influences, usually after charging money.

In lines 9 and 10 the Guru sums up and says, "Oh people look at this wonder, the one spiritually blind are called wise ones." The point the Guru has made is that the real sacred thread is the spiritual one, which the *Satguru* puts around us. This ensures that we acquire self-discipline, that we live our lives according to the roadmap that leads us to the Lord.

The rituals of thread investiture have been the focus here, but the Guru has taken, one by one, many of these empty rituals, of the main religions and sects in India at that time, the Hindus, the Muslims, the *Jogis*, to say that these are meaningless unless redeemed by an infusion of the knowledge of the True Lord. The activity that elevates the spirit within is good, the empty formalistic rituals are pointless.

So, here the Guru speaks of the sad and ironical situation of the *pandit*-Brahmin who controls not his own senses, his lust, one who does not stop his eyes from covetously eyeing beautiful things, the ears from hearing ill of others, the tongue from speaking lies and being rough, the hands from grabbing what is not rightfully his, the feet from straying along forbidden paths. Such a one, if he prepares these sacred threads and puts them around his clients, how much spiritual benefit will that bring? None, even though he may whisper the *mantra* into his *yajmān*'s ear and claim that the Brahmin is now his Guru, *yajmān* meaning the householder for whom the Brahmin was the family priest. Such a Guru is no *Satguru* and will not be able to guide us to salvation. Such a one is blind in the spirit though he may claim great wisdom for himself.

In this, the 15th *pauṛi* to which these *sloks* were attached, the Guru speaks to us of who can be a true devotee. He says:

ਪਉੜੀ ॥	Pauṛi
ਸਾਹਿਬੁ ਹੋਇ ਦਇਆਲੁ ਕਿਰਪਾ ਕਰੇ ਤਾ ਸਾਈ ਕਾਰ ਕਰਾਇਸੀ ॥	Sāhib hoye dayāl kirpa karay ta sāyi kār karāisi
ਸੋ ਸੇਵਕੁ ਸੇਵਾ ਕਰੇ ਜਿਸ ਨੋ ਹੁਕਮੁ ਮਨਾਇਸੀ ॥	So sevak seva karey jisno hukam manāisi
ਹੁਕਮਿ ਮੰਨਿਐ ਹੋਵੈ ਪਰਵਾਣੁ ਤਾ ਖਸਮੈ ਕਾ ਮਹਲੁ ਪਾਇਸੀ ॥	Hukam maniyai hovai parvāṇ ta khasmai ka mahal pāisi
ਖਸਮੈ ਭਾਵੈ ਸੋ ਕਰੇ ਮਨਹੁ ਚਿੰਦਿਆ ਸੋ ਫਲੁ ਪਾਇਸੀ ॥	Khasmai bhāvay so karay manhu chindiya so phal pāisi
ਤਾ ਦਰਗਹ ਪੈਧਾ ਜਾਇਸੀ ॥੧੫॥	Ta dargah paidha jāisi [15]

Glossary:

ਸਾਈ ਕਾਰ	Sāyi kār	That action
ਹੁਕਮਿ ਮੰਨਿਐ	Hukam maniyai	If we accept the command

ਪਰਵਾਣ	Parvāṇ	Accepted
ਮਨਹੁ ਚਿੰਦਿਆ	Manhu chindiya	Wished for result
ਪੈਧਾ	Paidha	Clad in honour

Simply translated this *pauṛi* says that when the Lord blesses us with His compassionate glance of grace then only do we act in accordance with His wishes. Those only are His true servants whom He teaches to obey His command. If we live in obedience to His *Hukam* and mould ourselves to His Will, then will we be accepted and allowed to reside in His abode. The ones who act in accordance with the Lord's Will obtain their heart's desire and will go to Him clad in honour. Let us now look at it in more detail.

In line 1 the Guru says when the Lord is compassionate and decides to turn His glance of grace then only do we act in accordance with His wishes. In other words, no one can even find that approved path on his own strength. The man on the right path, living his life in accordance with the way of the Lord, as laid out for us by the *Satguru*, should be seen not as an achiever but as a recipient of the Lord's glance of grace. Even the good and God-fearing way of living is but a gift from Him.

In line 2 the Guru says only those are truly His servants whom He teaches to obey His command. The oft-repeated dictum of serving the Lord is explained here. What service can we offer someone who is is Omnipotent and the Master of all material things that we may own? The Guru says that the only service we humans can render to the Lord is by living in obedience to Him. As the Guru says in *Rāg Gauṛi*, *Mahla* 5, page 187 of the *SGGS*, "ਮੀਤੁ ਕਰੈ ਸੋਈ ਹਮ ਮਾਨਾ॥ ਮੀਤ ਕੇ ਕਰਤਬ ਕੁਸਲ ਸਮਾਨਾ॥" – "mīt karai soyi hum māna. Mīt ke kartab kusal samāna", meaning that whatever my dear one [the Lord] does is acceptable to me, His actions bring me peace. Living in accordance with His Will, accepting with equanimity whatever He has in store for us is the essence of service to Him. Such a mode of living, this ability to accept readily His gifts even when they momentarily appear onerous, is also a gift, not to be attained except through His grace.

In line 3 the Guru clarifies further and says if we live in obedience to His *Hukam* – His Will – and readily mould ourselves to whatever He may choose to bestow on us, then we can hope he accept us and reside in His abode.

Khasmay ka mahal literally translates as 'house of the master'. If we accept someone as our Lord, then to be allowed to reside in his house is the highest honour. The key to this honour is the willing acceptance of His command. Surrender to Him; accept whatever He has in store for us. And of course this blessed state will come only from heeding the *Satguru*, living according to the way prescribed by him; and above all reciting His Name with every breath, and always singing the Lord's praises.

In lines 4 and 5 the Guru concludes by saying the one who acts in accordance with the Lord's Will shall obtain his heart's desire and go to His portal clad in honour. The rewards of acting righteously and surrendering to the Lord's Will are spelt out here. Firstly, says the Guru, you will gain access to the Lord's abode. In other words, your life will come in tune with His purpose, and immediately peace and serenity will start to prevail in your life on this Earth, in this mortal existence. The Lord also grants the *manhu chindiya phal* – innermost yearnings – of such an obedient servant. By living the right kind of life we will also get the good things that we crave in this world, and gradually any evil desires within us will begin to be extinguished. As the Guru also told us in *Rāga Soratth*, *Mahla* 3, page 638 of the *SGGS*, "Achint kamm karay prabh tinn ke jin ko Har ka nām pyāra" – those who love the Lord's Name will find their needs met without effort. Secondly, and more importantly, says the Guru, such a servant will go from this world into the Divine Presence clad in honour. In the previous *pauṛi* he had told us of the fate awaiting those who follow an ego-centred, evil course. They will go to hell denuded of cover; as he said, "Nanga dojak chāliya ta disay khara drāvṇa" – "horrible he appears when stripped naked he goes to hell". Here the opposite is said – he will be clad in robes of honour when he travels from this world, when the time comes for his appearance in the Lord's court.

PAUṚI 16

This *pauṛi* has two *sloks* attached to it, both by Guru Nanak. Both of these touch upon the degradation that had set in among the Hindu society in those days, battered as it was by repeated attacks by Muslim invaders and prolonged alien rule hostile to their religion. The previous *pauṛi* and the *slok*s aṭtached with it had the false *pandit* as the subject, and so, in a way the Brahmin caste, the foremost in the hierarchy among the four Hindu castes, was addressed. Here the Guru talks now about the next caste group in the ancient hierarchy, the Kshatriyas. In the first *slok* he says:

ਸਲੋਕ ਮ: ੧	Slok M̤: 1
ਗਊ ਬਿਰਾਹਮਣ ਕਉ ਕਰੁ ਲਾਵਹੁ ਗੋਬਰਿ ਤਰਣੁ ਨ ਜਾਈ ॥	Gaū Birāhmaṇ ko kar lavoh gobar taraṇ na jāyī
ਧੋਤੀ ਟਿਕਾ ਤੈ ਜਪਮਾਲੀ ਧਾਨੁ ਮਲੇਛਾਂ ਖਾਈ ॥	Dhoti tikka tai japmāli dhān malechha[n] khāyi
ਅੰਤਰਿ ਪੂਜਾ ਪੜਹਿ ਕਤੇਬਾ ਸੰਜਮੁ ਤੁਰਕਾ ਭਾਈ ॥	Antar pūja paṛeh kateba sanjam turka bhāi
ਛੋਡੀਲੇ ਪਾਖੰਡਾ ॥	Chhodīlay pākhanda
ਨਾਮਿ ਲਇਐ ਜਾਹਿ ਤਰੰਦਾ ॥੧॥	Nām laiyai jahe taranda. 1.

Glossary:

ਕਰੁ	Karr	Tax, toll
ਗੋਬਰਿ	Gobar	Cow dung
ਜਪਮਾਲੀ	Japmāli	The necklace of beads, the rosary
ਧਾਨੁ	Dhān	Food grains

ਮਲੇਛਾਂ	Malechha[n]	Outcast
ਸੰਜਮੁ	Sanjam	Practice, usage, way of living

Simply translated this *slok* says that you tax the Brahmin and his cow and yet hope to be purified by the same cow dung. You don the *dhoti* – the wrap-around cloth for the lower extremities – and you apply the *tikka* – the caste mark on the forehead. You wear the rosary. In your homes you perform Hindu religious services but outside you kowtow to the Muslim masters. Discard this *pākhand* (hypocrisy), take the name of the Lord and you will find salvation. Let us now look at it in more detail.

Macauliffe narrates in his translation of the *SGGS* that this composition resulted from an event that was actually witnessed by Guru Nanak. He says that it so happened that at Lahore some householder presented a cow to a Brahmin, who decided to take it back to Sultanpur with him. However, when he came to the river ferry point, on the way the toll-keeper would not let him pass because he did not have the money to pay the due toll. This forced the Brahmin to camp there with his cow. Sometime later the keeper came and took the dung from the same cow and applied it to his cooking area, this being the prescribed method among Hindus for purifying it. Mardana, the inseparable Muslim companion of the Guru, went near the keeper but was shooed away lest he defiled the place. The Guru witnessed this farce and is said to have addressed these words to the keeper. There is of course a universal truth and a spiritual message behind the composition, that outward formalism is a blind alley and the Lord is to be found only by fixing the mind on Him. This composition also well delineates the plight of the higher Hindu castes as they struggled to reconcile their beliefs with the requirements of making a living under the Muslim rulers. It is a fact that the Kshatriya and the Vaishya castes formed the bulk of the staff that ran the day- to- day administration for the rulers. They were compelled to follow the Muslim rules for dress and observe the other necessary interactions to keep the rulers happy, but in their homes they still practiced the rites of Hinduism. They perforce had to execute the policies and the dictates of the Muslim rulers, which were often harsh on the non-Muslim population. So the Guru is highlighting the hypocrisy inherent in this situation, by referring to the general situation of these employees oppressing their own religious compatriots and yet following the practices of the same religion.

In the 1st line the Guru says on the one hand you tax the Brahmin and his cow and on the other hand you think the cow dung from the same cow will purify you. You hold the cow sacred, and believe that the Brahmin is the preceptor of the Hindu society, yet you have no compunction in demanding the toll from such a one even when he does not have the capacity to pay it. It is hypocrisy indeed to expect that in such a situation the cow dung will purify your cooking place. What purity does this outward application bring when you have troubled the same Brahmin and taxed the same cow?

In the 2nd line the Guru describes another hypocrisy that was much prevalent. He says you don the *dhoti*, which is a wrap-around cloth prescribed for the lower extremities among the caste Hindus, you apply the *tikka* – the caste mark for the forehead – and you wear the *japmāli* or the rosary. By these observances you seek to establish your credentials as a pure Hindu. But when it comes to your sustenance you obtain it from those whom you call *Malechhas* (impure). This term was a pejorative used to describe any person outside the Hindu caste structure, and was an appellation commonly used for the Muslim. It denotes someone outside the pale, not a part of the Hindu structure and thus the most impure. The Guru is here stressing the bitter irony, and the hypocrisy, of those seeking to appear to be sincere and pure practitioners of their religion earning a living from those very persons whom they style as the most impure.

In the 3rd line the same point is more directly made. The Guru says in your homes you perform Hindu religious services and rites but outside you kowtow to your Muslim masters. Dr. Gopal Singh puts it as, "Within, they worship (their idols); (outside), they read the *Quran* and observe the code of the Turks." Prof. Talib says, "In your home the Hindu service you perform, but outside read books of Muslims, and adopt their ways." This dichotomy between the public and private lives of these men must have been not so easy for them to reconcile but they had thus found their modus vivendi with the alien ruler. The Guru is trying to waken their self-respect, and in the next lines speaks to them to shed this false pretence and be true to themselves.

In lines 4 and 5 the Guru concludes with a direct exhortation. He says discard this *pākhand* (hypocrisy), take the Name of the Lord and earn salvation. Mere formalistic observances cannot be a substitute for true worship. The Guru has of course already told us that true service requires that you fix your mind on the Lord. You need worry about nothing else thereafter, for salvation will follow.

The next *slok* speaks further about this situation. The Guru says:

ਮ: ੧	M: 1
ਮਾਣਸ ਖਾਣੇ ਕਰਹਿ ਨਿਵਾਜ ॥	Māṇas khāṇay karay niwāj
ਛੁਰੀ ਵਗਾਇਨਿ ਤਿਨ ਗਲਿ ਤਾਗ ॥	Chhuri vagāyin tinn gull tāg
ਤਿਨ ਘਰਿ ਬ੍ਰਾਹਮਣ ਪੂਰਹਿ ਨਾਦ ॥	Tinn ghar Brahmiṇ pūray nād
ਉਨ੍ਹਾ ਭਿ ਆਵਹਿ ਓਈ ਸਾਦ ॥	Una bhi āvaih oyi sād
ਕੂੜੀ ਰਾਸਿ ਕੂੜਾ ਵਾਪਾਰੁ ॥	Kūṛi rās kūṛa vāpār
ਕੂੜੁ ਬੋਲਿ ਕਰਹਿ ਆਹਾਰੁ ॥	Kūṛ bol kareh āhār
ਸਰਮ ਧਰਮ ਕਾ ਡੇਰਾ ਦੂਰਿ ॥	Saram dharam ka dera dūre
ਨਾਨਕ ਕੂੜੁ ਰਹਿਆ ਭਰਪੂਰਿ ॥	Nanak kūṛ rahiya bharpūr
ਮਥੈ ਟਿਕਾ ਤੇੜਿ ਧੋਤੀ ਕਖਾਈ ॥	Mathai tikka teṛ dhoti kakhāyi
ਹਥਿ ਛੁਰੀ ਜਗਤ ਕਾਸਾਈ ॥	Hath chhuri jagat kāsāyi
ਨੀਲ ਵਸਤ੍ਰ ਪਹਿਰਿ ਹੋਵਹਿ ਪਰਵਾਣੁ ॥	Nīl vastar paher hoveh parvāṇ
ਮਲੇਛ ਧਾਨੁ ਲੇ ਪੂਜਹਿ ਪੁਰਾਣੁ ॥	Malechh dhan le pūjai purāṇ
ਅਭਾਖਿਆ ਕਾ ਕੁਠਾ ਬਕਰਾ ਖਾਣਾ॥	Abhākhiya ka kuttha bakrā khāṇa
ਚਉਕੇ ਉਪਰਿ ਕਿਸੈ ਨ ਜਾਣਾ ॥	Chaukay uppar kisai na jāṇa
ਦੇਕੈ ਚਉਕਾ ਕਢੀ ਕਾਰ	Dekai chaukā kaddhi kār
ਉਪਰਿ ਆਇ ਬੈਠੇ ਕੂੜਿਆਰ ॥	Uppar āye baitthay kūṛiyār
ਮਤੁ ਭਿਟੈ ਵੇ ਮਤੁ ਭਿਟੈ ॥	Mat bhittai vay mat bhittai
ਇਹੁ ਅੰਨੁ ਅਸਾਡਾ ਫਿਟੈ ॥	Eh unn asādda phittai
ਤਨਿ ਫਿਟੈ ਫੇੜ ਕਰੇਨਿ ॥	Tann phittai pheṛ karein
ਮਨਿ ਜੂਠੈ ਚੁਲੀ ਭਰੇਨਿ ॥	Mann jūtthai chuli bharein
ਕਹੁ ਨਾਨਕ ਸਚੁ ਧਿਆਈਐ ॥	Kahu Nanak sach dhiyāiai
ਸੁਚਿ ਹੋਵੈ ਤਾ ਸਚੁ ਪਾਈਐ ॥੨॥	Such hovai ta sach pāiai. 2.

Glossary:

ਮਾਣਸ ਖਾਣੇ	Māṇas khāṇay	Cannibals, man-eaters
ਨਿਵਾਜ	Niwaj	The *Namāz*, Muslim prayers
ਤਾਗ	Tāg	The sacred thread
ਪੂਰਹਿ ਨਾਦ	Pūreh nād	Blows the conch

ਸਰਮ	Saram	Modesty, shame
ਕਖਾਈ	Kakhāyi	A specially tied *dhoti*, also saffron coloured
ਅਭਾਖਿਆ	Abhākhiya	Using alien language
ਕਾਸਾਈ	Kāsāyi	Butcher
ਕੁਠਾ	Kutthā	The *halāl* (kosher) meat, from animal killed ritually by Muslims
ਭਿਟੈ	Bhittai	Made impure
ਸੁਚਿ	Such	Purity

The compromises that the Hindu subjects had to make with their Turkish rulers were clearly degrading, but too many nevertheless did so. In such circumstances the observance of the rituals in the safe secrecy of their own homes could hardly have qualified as worship. The Guru here exhorts them to stand up, leave behind this hypocrisy and follow the path of true worship, which is reciting the Name of the Lord. Simply translated this *slok* says that the man-eaters perform the *Namāz*, referring to the ruling Muslim class. He further adds that those wearing the sacred thread wield the knife, referring here to the administrative support staff of the Muslims, who were mainly from the upper Hindu castes. In the homes of those very wielders of knives the Brahmins go and perform the prescribed rituals. They also get the same taste, meaning they will equally face the blame. False is the entire play, false the trade; and the food eaten comes from falsehood. Modesty and righteousness have vanished and falsehood prevails. They wear the caste marks and the prescribed *kakhāyi dhoti*, but are butchers of humans. They wear blue clothes to appease the rulers and earn their bread from the same ones they call *Malecchas*. They eat the goat killed as per Muslim rites and then say do not enter my kitchen lest it be tainted, forgetting that those sitting in the purified square are themselves *kūriyār* (false). They cry out to say do not touch our food lest it be tainted but with defiled bodies they perform foul deeds and with defiled minds they rinse their mouths. Fix your mind on the True One, says the Guru, and only then will purity come. Let us now look at it in more detail.

In lines 1 and 2 the Guru says the man-eaters perform the *Namāz* and the wearers of the sacred thread wield the knife. The reference is to the ruling Muslim elite who had turned oppressors. They levied heavy taxes, did not provide a fair system of government and corruption prevailed. Prof. Sahib Singh in fact takes *māṇas khāṇay* as not meaning man-eaters but as meaning the venal ones taking huge bribes and impoverishing the people. The employees of these oppressive rulers were largely Hindus, many from the Kshatriya and Vaishya castes – the ones who had not long ago been themselves the rulers. The oppressiveness of the system was in reality inflicted on the unfortunate populace not directly by the Muslim rulers but through this class of officials. Therefore, the Guru refers to them as the wielders of the knife.

In lines 3 and 4 the Guru says that while these Kshatriyas and Vaishyas do these sinful things, the Brahmins yet go and perform all the prescribed rituals in their homes. *Pūreh nād* means 'make the sound', and it refers to the blowing of the conch shell after the completion of the rituals. He adds, "they also get the same taste". The reference is to the food served at these rituals; though implicitly the Guru is saying that the Brahmin will equally share the blame for wrongdoing. The livelihood of these householders being based on a falsehood and wrong doing, the food cooked in their houses would also be expected to carry the effect of its shameful origin. So, the Brahmin eating this holy feast is not earning any holy merit, rather will the effect on him be the same bad one as it will be for those who earned such tainted living. On this very theme the parable of Malik Bhago and Bhai Lalo is well known. Guru Nanak refused to eat the feast at the house of the rich Malik because the food served had been earned from oppression and by foul means, while the poor Bhai Lalo earned an honest living from the sweat of his brow. It is said that to prove his point for the Malik's satisfaction he squeezed the bread taken from his feast and lo, blood oozed from it. Bhai Lalo's bread had milk dripping from it when squeezed. The parable was meant to teach us that by sharing in such ill-earned wealth we will also share in the evil. Thus is the Brahmin here said to be becoming a partner in the Kshatriya's wrongdoing.

In lines 5 and 6 the Guru says that "false is the entire play, false the trade and the food being eaten is ill begotten". Bhai Vir Singh interprets these lines to say that for the Hindus to so supinely accept slavery under the Turks was wrong, and since this basic wrong had been committed then all actions that ensued also had to be wrong. Such was the degradation then that even daily sustenance was earned through lies; because a slave cannot survive unless he is willing to dissimulate in his dealings with the master. Some learned ones also render these lines as referring to the trader class, because the Brahmins and the Kshatriyas had in the previous lines been addressed and this would complete the enumeration of all the three higher castes of Hindus who were the employees of the Muslims, the Turks. These interpreters say the lines mean that the traders are, so to say, trading in lies. Their entire commerce is built on falsehood and this is how they earn their living. Both interpretations have their merit, but Bhai Vir Singh's view seems more appealing. The general atmosphere of lying and dissimulation that prevailed has been well evoked here by the Guru.

In lines 7 and 8 the Guru says modesty and righteousness have vanished and falsehood prevails everywhere. The right way of living for the Hindus had gone as soon as the mastery of the Turks was accepted. So, *dharma* did not prevail anymore. Even shame at this degradation and disgrace was absent. Brazenfaced, they indulged in this shameful conduct. It is of course natural that when *dharma* is removed from the lives of men only falsehood will prevail.

In the 9th and 10th lines the Guru further addresses these high caste slaves of the alien ruler and says, "You wear the religious caste marks on the forehead, and below you wear the *kakhāyi dhoti.*" The term *kakhāyi* has been rendered by Bhai Vir Singh as referring to a specially tied *dhoti*. This required one end of it, after wrapping, to be taken between the legs and tucked in at the back. This was the prescribed way of wearing the *dhoti* for a householder. Some prescribed even three, or sometimes five, folds being so taken and tucked in. However, Prof. Sahib Singh renders *kakhāyi dhoti* as a light saffron-coloured wrap-around, probably from the root *kakh*, meaning straw. This was the colour usually worn by the Brahmins. Gyani Maskin has another view and renders it as a necklace made from straw. The more appealing view is that the reference is to the specially tied *dhoti* because this would go with the reference to special caste marks in the previous line. The Guru says in line 10, that though they wear such religiously appropriate garb, yet are no better than butchers for the populace, wielding the knife of iniquity, and wreaking violence on the hapless populace at the behest of the Turk rulers.

In lines 11 and 12, the Guru further describes this category of persons. He says they wear blue clothes to appease the rulers and earn their bread. The wearing of blue cloth was usually considered lowly but to please the rulers and be accepted these clothes were gladly worn. The dichotomy between public conduct and private religious observances revealed the rampant hypocrisy that marked the conduct of those who could have stood up to alleviate the rigours that the alien rule imposed on the common public. The source of livelihood was the same *malecch* who was deemed so impure, yet after all this they still performed their religious rites unconcerned. Bhai Vir Singh renders *malecch dhān* to say that this food is itself *malecch*, and yet after partaking of it these persons go home and recite the *Purāṇas* in worship. Most other commentators however render it to mean that these persons earn their *dhān* (food grain), their livelihood, from serving the same *malechhas* and then having tainted themselves by eating this food they go and perform worship. This seems a more appealing view.

In lines 13 and 14 the Guru says, "You eat the goat killed as per Muslim rites and then say do not enter my kitchen lest it get tainted". The term *abhākhiya* literally means 'non-language', or 'alien language'. The word for Sanskrit came to be *bhākhiya*, says Bhai Vir Singh, so the language that was alien or came from outside was *abhākhiya*. This here would refer to Arabic in which the Muslim scriptures are written. The specific reference is to the *kalima* being uttered while slitting the throat of the goat, this being the kosher way for Muslims. Such meat is called *halāl*, or kosher, and it is mandatory for Muslims to eat only such meat. Here the Guru is referring to this being the only meat available and the Hindu employees of the Turks naturally also having to eat the same. Yet they performed the olden ritual of purifying the kitchen, or cooking area, and would not let anyone enter it for fear that it will become tainted and impure.

In lines 15 and 16 the Guru explains this further. He says they mark off the square and purify it, forgetting that those sitting inside that sacred square are themselves *kūriyār* or false. The Guru has in the previous lines given a number of examples of the dichotomy existing between public posture and private practice. For the sake of earning a livelihood these persons were willing to live a life full of pretence. It was falsehood personified. Thus is the Guru calling them *kūṛiyār*, the false ones.

In lines 17 to 20 the Guru says that they cry out 'do not touch lest our food be tainted,' but with defiled bodies do they perform foul deeds, and with defiled minds rinse their mouth. This bogus religiosity that bars anyone touching their food or even entering the kitchen area, lest they defile the food, is shown up here by the Guru. He says what impurity should such persons be afraid of whose lives are a living lie. When the mouth is impure and defiled what does it any taint on the food or water taken in through that mouth matter? The word *chuli* refers to a bit of water taken in the cupped palm of the hand, which was commonly then used for rinsing out the mouth after eating. No *chuli*, implies the Guru, can cleanse a mouth that has been defiled by false living.

As usual it is at the end of each *slok* that the Guru delivers the crux of the message. So, here in the concluding lines, the 21st and 22nd, the Guru says fix your mind on *sach* – the True One – and then only will *such* (purity) come. As Dr. Gopal Singh puts it, "Dwell, O man, on the (Lord's) truth, for only if one be pure (of heart) one attains the Truth." Prof. Sahib Singh renders it as, "Meditate on God because only then will purity come." Gyani Maskin puts it well when he says that "Truth and purity are inextricably intertwined. When the mind is fixed on the Lord only then will true purity come, and that in turn will lead to God-realization." So, says the Guru, forget about these ritual purificatory actions, which are in this case any way false. Forget all these games, he says, and meditate instead on the Lord alone and all purification will automatically follow.

We now come to the 16th *pauṛi* to which these *sloks* were attached. The subject here is the Almighty, that ineffable Lord of all creation. The *pauṛi* goes as follows:

ਪਉੜੀ ॥	Pauṛi
ਚਿਤੈ ਅੰਦਰਿ ਸਭੁ ਕੋ ਵੇਖਿ ਨਦਰੀ ਹੇਠਿ ਚਲਾਇਦਾ ॥	Chitai andar sabh ko vekh nadri hetth chalāida
ਆਪੇ ਦੇ ਵਡਿਆਈਆ ਆਪੇ ਹੀ ਕਰਮ ਕਰਾਇਦਾ ॥	Āpay day vaddiāia āpay hee karam karāida
ਵਡੋ ਵਡਾ ਵਡ ਮੇਦਨੀ ਸਿਰੇ ਸਿਰਿ ਧੰਧੈ ਲਾਇਦਾ ॥	Vaddo vadda vadd medni siray sirr dhandai lāeda
ਨਦਰਿ ਉਪਠੀ ਜੇ ਕਰੇ ਸੁਲਤਾਨਾ ਘਾਹੁ ਕਰਾਇਦਾ ॥	Nadar upatthi jay karay sultāna ghah karāida
ਦਰਿ ਮੰਗਨਿ ਭਿਖ ਨ ਪਾਇਦਾ ॥੧੬॥	Darr mangan bhikh na pāida. 16

Glossary:

ਚਿਤੈ	Chitai	In the mind
ਕਰਮ	Karam	Deeds, actions
ਵਡ ਮੇਦਨੀ	Vadd	Medni Large creation, big world
ਘਾਹੁ	Ghāh[u]	Grass, straw
ਉਪਠੀ	Upatthi	Adverse

Simply translated this *pauṛi* says that the Lord has all of His creation ever in His mind and we all perform our tasks under His eye. The Lord decides whom to exalt, He guides the actions of all created entities. The Lord is the greatest of all and great is His creation in which He has set tasks for each one. If He were to turn His glance of grace away, the greatest of emperors can be reduced to the lowest level and even turned into beggars who are refused alms and are turned away from every door. Let us now look at the message in more detail.

In line 1 the Guru says the Lord has each and every one of us in His mind and we all perform our tasks under His eye. The universe is infinite, the worlds therein equally so. Created beings on these worlds are also unimaginably vast in their numbers. So, does the Lord find it difficult to keep track of this vast complexity? No, says the Guru. The Creator is greater than, and beyond all of His creation and has the capacity to watch at all times each and every part of His creation; even while He simultaneously permeates every part of it. Let no one therefore think that he can act and escape being found out in his wrongdoing. The Lord has His eye on each one of us and everyone is in His mind. Thus is each created being performing his appointed task. Not just the humans on this tiny Earth but all created things, and all created powers, in the entire, unimaginably vast universe.

In the 2nd line the Guru says the Lord Himself decides who will be exalted, and He Himself guides the actions of the created entities. The stars, the planets, the oceans on the Earth and all created things act in accordance with the destiny He has laid down for each. None is free to break away and follow his own course. The Lord guides each movement. To some will come glory and honour, but only when, and if, He so ordains. This is not to say that men are helpless puppets dancing on a string. To the humankind there is indeed some freedom granted, and that is for us human beings to do good deeds or to do bad ones. The consequences for each deed will ineluctably ensue; but this much freedom He does give us on this Earth, this *karmabhūmi*, our testing ground. Here are human souls allowed to strive and improve their *Karma* and make themselves fit for His grace.

In line 3 the Guru says that the Lord is the greatest of the great, and great is His creation in which He has set tasks for each one. This is a restatement of the message outlined in the previous lines. The vastness of these Earths or of the entire creation does not hamper Him in any way from setting tasks for each component or each being of His creation. For He is the greatest of all, existing within each component of His creation, yet beyond and above all that exists.

In lines 4 and 5 the Guru says if He were to turn His glance of grace away, the greatest of emperors can get reduced to the status of a grass-cutter. He adds that even worse, such ones may get turned into beggars who do not even get alms and are turned away from door after door. The greatness of the individual, or in other words any earthly honours that we may feel like boasting about are nothing but a favour that was granted by the Lord in His grace, and were this glance of grace to be withdrawn, or it were to become adverse, all honours and the trappings of power and glory can vanish overnight. The phrase *ghāh[u] karāida* is rendered by most commentators as 'turns into a blade of grass', implying that material weightiness of the *sultān* can evaporate fast, leaving him light as a blade of grass. Bhai Vir Singh however explains that in the *lehnda*, the western, dialect it means 'cutting grass.' In this rendering the meaning becomes 'turns into a grass-cutter'. This seems a more appealing interpretation because the Emperor's position being the highest is contrasted with one of the lowest possible professions, that of a grass-cutter. The last line, the fifth, reinforces this view. The Guru says, not merely reduce him to a grass-cutter but, worse, may turn him into a beggar who goes from door to door and is not even offered alms.

Thus, in this *pauṛi* the Guru has highlighted once again the greatness of the Lord, of His creation and the fact that in His greatness He is able to oversee, guide and direct every component of this vast and mysterious creation. The point is finally driven home by telling us that it is only His glance of grace that keeps us in our earthly glory. Were this to turn adverse, the glory can vanish like a whiff of smoke leaving us lowly as dirt.

PAURI 17

This *pauri* has attached with it two *sloks*, both by Guru Nanak. The Guru continues with his commentary on the pointlessness of formalistic rituals. The first *slok* says:

ਸਲੋਕ ਮਃ ੧	Slok M: 1
ਜੇ ਮੋਹਾਕਾ ਘਰੁ ਮੁਹੈ ਘਰੁ ਮੁਹਿ ਪਿਤਰੀ ਦੇਇ ॥	Jay muhāka ghar muhai ghar muh pitri dey
ਅਗੈ ਵਸਤੁ ਸਿਞਾਣੀਐ ਪਿਤਰੀ ਚੋਰ ਕਰੇਇ ॥	Aggai vasat sijhāṇiai pitri chor karay
ਵਢੀਅਹਿ ਹਥ ਦਲਾਲ ਕੇ ਮੁਸਫੀ ਏਹ ਕਰੇ ॥	Vaddhiai hath dalāl kay musafi eh karay
ਨਾਨਕ ਅਗੈ ਸੋ ਮਿਲੈ ਜਿ ਖਟੇ ਘਾਲੇ ਦੇਇ ॥	Nanak aggai so milai je khattay ghālay day

Glossary:

ਮੋਹਾਕਾ	Muhāka	Thief, robber
ਘਰੁ ਮੁਹਿ	Ghar muh	Looting the house
ਅਗੈ	Aggai	In the next world
ਪਿਤਰੀ	Pitri	Ancestors
ਵਢੀਅਹਿ	Vaddhiai	To cut, lop off

The Guru here touches upon another common ritual that was much prevalent then and still is popular. It was customary to perform specific rituals called the *shrādh* in honour of the departed ancestors. The male members of the family would perform certain ceremonies and then offer costly gifts to the Brahmins who presided over and actually conducted these ceremonies.

Simply translated this *slok* says that were the robber to steal from a house and with that money offer oblations, the stolen goods would be recognized in the next world and the ancestors would have become partners in the crime. The judge would order the hands of the agent to be cut off by way of punishment. In the next world you will get rewarded only for what you have earned through your own effort. Let us look at it in more detail.

The Guru says in lines 1 and 2, that were the robber to steal from a house and with this wealth he were to offer oblations, the stolen goods will be recognized in the next world and the ancestors will also have been forced to become partners in the crime. The reference is to the propitiatory offerings made to the manes at the *shrādh* ceremony for the benefit of the departed souls of the ancestors. The Guru gives us a two-fold message here. Firstly, he is saying that if you must perform such rites, at least make sure that the offerings come from honestly earned money. Secondly, and more importantly, he means to tell us that it is not these rites that will matter, but the honest and upright living that is important. If your life is pure, your prayers from the heart will reach the next world and the spirits of your ancestors will reap the benefit. The offering of money and material things for such a purpose is of no avail. To bring home the uselessness of such rituals, and to drive home the real lesson, he says the offerings being made could well be stolen property, or in other words anything dishonestly gained. This of course could be true for most of the things men possess in this world of falsehood. Such offerings may pass muster in the eyes of the people around. But, says the Guru, the theft will not stay hidden from the divine eyes in the next world where we are aiming to send these goods. There, all truth is laid bare, and all dissimulation is dissolved. The real nature of our offering will immediately become known. Then the possessors of these stolen goods, our ancestors, would have been turned by our actions into thieves. Receivers of stolen property are as guilty as the thief even in the eyes of the law in this world. In the hereafter the unsuspecting ancestors would be turned into criminals in this way by those very well wishers who sought to lighten their spiritual burden.

In line 3 the Guru says there the judge will order the hands of the agent to be cut off. The reference is to the *pandit* (priest) who presides over and conducts the ceremony where the offering is made. By so doing he becomes the agent through whom the stolen goods have passed to the ancestors. In those times the Muslim system of jurisprudence required that the hands of thieves be cut off. The agent, the one who deals in these goods being equally guilty, the same punishment must also be visited upon him. So the hands of the Brahmin would be ordered to be cut by the *musafi* (judge). The *pandit* – priest is being enjoined upon here to not be a party to these empty rituals for dishonest men.

In line 4 the Guru says in the next world you will get rewarded only for what you have earned through your own toil. Let your offerings come from your honest earnings. Most learned commentators have interpreted it in this manner. Dr. Gopal Singh puts it well when he says, "That alone is received whole in the Yond that one gives out of one's honest bread." Prof. Talib also says similarly, "In the hereafter is received reward for what man from his own earning offers." The message is two-fold and is clear; firstly, give only from what you have honestly earned, and secondly, do not think that material offering can bring spiritual upliftment. If you want to help your departed ancestors pray from the heart and waste no time in empty rituals.

Bhai Vir Singh says in his commentary that some have interpreted line 2 also to mean that the ancestors of the victims of the theft will recognize the goods and the ancestors of the thief will then also be called thieves. This refers to the common juridical practice of treating the receiver of stolen goods as equally guilty. The other rendering as we have discussed above seems more appealing and is also the more generally accepted.

In the next *slok* the Guru touches upon another superstition, that of impurity attributed to the menses. He says:

ਮ: ੧	M: 1
ਜਿਉ ਜੋਰੁ ਸਿਰਨਾਵਣੀ ਆਵੈ ਵਾਰੋ ਵਾਰ ॥	Jiu joru sirrnāvṇi āvai vāro vār
ਜੂਠੇ ਜੂਠਾ ਮੁਖਿ ਵਸੈ ਨਿਤ ਨਿਤ ਹੋਇ ਖੁਆਰੁ ॥	Jūthay jūtha mukh vasai nit nit hoye khuār
ਸੂਚੇ ਏਹਿ ਨ ਆਖੀਅਹਿ ਬਹਨਿ ਜਿ ਪਿੰਡਾ ਧੋਇ ॥	Sūchay eh na ākhiyeh bahan je pinda dhoye
ਸੂਚੇ ਸੇਈ ਨਾਨਕਾ ਜਿਨ ਮਨਿ ਵਸਿਆ ਸੋਇ ॥੨॥	Sūchay seyi Nanaka jinn mann vasiya soye. 2.

Glossary:

ਜੋਰੂ	Joru	Woman, housewife
ਸਿਰਨਾਵਣੀ	Sirrnāvṇi	Menstrual cycle
ਜੂਠੇ	Jūtthay	False
ਸੂਚੇ	Sūchay	Pure
ਸੇਈ	Seyi	Those persons

The Guru here tells us now of what true purity should mean. He uses the then popular misconception, that there is impurity in a menstruating woman, to make his point. Simply translated this *slok* says that like the menstrual blood flowing regularly, falsehood habitually flows from the mouth of an untruthful man, and this is always degrading him. Cleanliness cannot come from washing or bathing; only those are truly pure in whose heart the Lord's Name resides. Let us now look at it in more detail.

Lines 1 and 2 refer to the very natural phenomenon of the menstrual blood flowing. So does falsehood flow habitually from the mouth of a lying man always degrading him, says the Guru. Macauliffe renders it as, "As a woman hath her recurring courses, so falsehood dwelleth in the mouth of the false one, and he is ever despised." It was a widely prevalent practice in those times to treat the menstruating woman as unclean. It was the custom that once the flow started the woman would not be allowed to enter the kitchen, because, being unclean, she could not cook for others also. This association of a purely natural phenomenon with uncleanliness was illogical but unfortunately still persists in some sections of society. The Guru is referring to this belief not to endorse it, but to say that the way you treat as unclean, for no reason, a woman in the midst of her seasonal course you should in fact for good reason treat the false man. From the mouth of such a one there flows an equally regular flow of something truly repulsive – falsehood. This will bring him ignominy in the Lord's eyes, and deserves contempt here too. Some learned ones render the first line to say that the menstruating woman is unclean. This does not however fit in with the Guru's vision expressed throughout the *SGGS*. The Guru spoke against treating natural events as making someone impure; thus, for instance, elsewhere he speaks against the *sūtak* custom, which deemed a woman unclean after childbirth. A natural flow regularly occurring cannot be deemed to make anyone unclean. The use of these examples is meant only to stress the fact that the falsehood in the mouth of the false one will spew forth inevitably, and as regularly as the menstrual cycle. And such a one will for his falsehood suffer disgrace forever.

Lines 3 and 4 conclude the message with, “cleanliness comes not from bathing, only those are pure in whose heart the Lord’s name resides”. It has been the tradition in this country to take ritual baths at places called *tīraths*, or in rivers or lakes labelled especially holy. Such baths were deemed to wash away all accrued sins of the devotee. Such persons after the bath would feel themselves especially pure and would avoid contact with persons of certain castes and categories. Even otherwise the bath, essential of course for cleansing the body, came to be considered, even in the home, a cleanser of the soul also. The Guru here says such cleansing is superficial. The real cleansing we need is of the soul, our inner selves. This can come only from the ‘Name’. Sing the Lord’s praises, fix your minds on Him; and when He starts to reside in our hearts only then does real cleanliness come to us.

The reference to this periodical phenomenon of menstruation and cleansing is also intended to remind us that the human mind and soul are also undergoing continuous and repeated pollution from our contact with the things of this world. We need to do *Nām Simran* with equal regularity to keep cleansing this taint.

So, here in this brief *slok* the Guru has restated the meaning of real cleansing which has to be of the soul. The body’s cleansing can only be superficial, such as the menstruating woman who at the end of the flow of blood will wash and cleanse herself. This will have no bearing on her inner self, her soul. The false man on the other hand spouting falsehood with the same regularity as a woman’s periods is dirtied in the soul and no bodily wash is now going to suffice for him in whatever *tīraths* it may be. His cleansing, as for all of us, will come only from the bath of the soul which comes only from *Nām Simran*.

In the *Pauṛi* with which these *sloks* are attached, the Guru tells us of the false attachments to worldly goods from which all of us suffer. He says:

ਪਉੜੀ ॥	Pauṛi
ਤੁਰੇ ਪਲਾਣੇ ਪਉਣ ਵੇਗ ਹਰ ਰੰਗੀ ਹਰਮ ਸਵਾਰਿਆ ॥	Turay palānay pauṇ veig har rangi haram sawāria
ਕੋਠੇ ਮੰਡਪ ਮਾੜੀਆ ਲਾਇ ਬੈਠੇ ਕਰਿ ਪਾਸਾਰਿਆ ॥	Kotthay manddap māṛīya lāye baitthay kar pāsāria

ਚੀਜ ਕਰਨਿ ਮਨਿ ਭਾਵਦੇ ਹਰਿ ਬੁਝਨਿ ਨਾਹੀ ਹਾਰਿਆ ॥	Chīj karan mann bhāvday har bujhaṇ nāhi hāria
ਕਰਿ ਫੁਰਮਾਇਸਿ ਖਾਇਆ ਵੇਖਿ ਮਹਲਤਿ ਮਰਣੁ ਵਿਸਾਰਿਆ ॥	Kar phurmāyis khāiya vekh mahlat maraṇvisāria
ਜਰੁ ਆਈ ਜੋਬਨਿ ਹਾਰਿਆ ॥੧੭॥	Jarr āyi joban hāria [17]

Glossary:

ਤੁਰੇ	Turay	Horses, steeds
ਪਲਾਣੇ	Palāṇay	Well-saddled
ਵੇਗ	Veig	Pace, speed
ਹਰਮ	Haram	The palace where women stayed
ਮੰਡਪ	Manddap	Pavilions
ਚੀਜ	Chīj	Wonders
ਫੁਰਮਾਇਸਿ	Phurmāyis	Order, demand
ਜਰੁ	Jarr	Old age
ਜੋਬਨਿ	Joban	Youth

Simply translated this *pauṛi* says that they have fast steeds fleet as the wind, beautifully saddled; and harems colourfully bedecked. They have impressive chambers, mansions and pavilions and are absorbed in showing these off. They indulge in revelry to their heart's content but have forgotten the Lord, and will in the end be losers. These lovers of things material eat what they wish, forgetting death, and then one day old age overtakes them and youth is lost. Let us now look at it in more detail.

In the first line the Guru refers to the rich ones who have great material wealth. They have fast-paced steeds, fleet as the wind beautifully saddled; and harems colourfully bedecked. He refers to some other of the beguiling things in the lines that follow. At the time when the Guru gave us this message these were some of the things and possessions that denoted high status and great wealth. Horses, especially of the Arab breed, fast and sleek, were greatly valued. The saddle fittings of these animals were another way to flaunt the wealth of the owner. Costly, beautifully carved and expensively inlaid saddles were thus fitted on these horses. The larger the number in the stables the greater the wealth of the owner deemed to be. The other prized possession in those times was the harem, which term is used to indicate not only the living quarters of the consorts of the ruler, but was also the number of women, wives and concubines both, in these quarters. The larger the number and the more beautiful the occupants, the greater was the repute of the ruler. For the same reason these palaces were made ornate and grand. It is a different matter that the position of the occupants of the harem was not much better than that of merely a costly possession, something to be boasted about. Thus, the fast-paced, well-accoutered horses, beautiful harems were prized possessions and the Guru here says some wealthy ones may have all these.

In line 2 the Guru adds they have impressive chambers, mansions and pavilions and are absorbed in showing these off. Apart from the possession listed in the first line, some of the other more coveted things are here enumerated. High mansions, beautiful pavilions, etc. were the signs of wealth that materialistically inclined men liked to flaunt, and in fact still do! *Kotthay* means literally 'buildings', and is used here for the mansions built by these rulers, the higher they were the greater the pomp! *Manddap* is used for a temporarily erected pavilion usually covered with canvas or cloth. These were built for temporary use of the rulers when they went hunting or entertained guests far away from their homes, usually in jungles owned by them. *Māṛīya* is used together with *Kotthay* to describe any sort of residential buildings. The Guru says these men caught in the material world have all of these and flaunt their lavish lifestyles living in these.

In line 3 the Guru describes now the personal behaviour of these men. He says they indulge in revelry to their heart's content but have forgotten the Lord, and in the end will be losers. Great material possessions have been described in the first two lines and here the Guru says they enjoy all these to their heart's content. Life for them is all play and gratification of the senses. But totally lost in material pursuits they have forgotten that there is a Lord from whom all this has come, and he watches every action. Having forgotten this vital fact they are truly lost. The purpose, for which the Lord bestowed on us this invaluable human form, and allowed us this sojourn on this *karma bhūmi*, is nothing but to reach the Lord from whom this soul has been temporarily separated. For that purpose we have to seek guidance from the *SGGS*, or from whichever Guru we follow if Sikhism is not our chosen path. In accordance with this instruction we have to then mould our existence. Only then is the path to Him likely to become clear to us. If we forget the existence of the Lord then obviously we will never even have the opportunity to set off on that divine path to God-realization. The very purpose of this invaluable gift of the human form would have been defeated. This is why the Guru is here saying that these misguided lovers of material pleasures are losers. Elsewhere in the *SGGS*, in *Rāg Bhairav*, page 1158, Bhagat Kabir says, "chalay juāri doye hath jhāṛ" – "the gambler goes empty-handed from this world having lost everything". The great wealth in the form of this human form is gambled away on mere baubles and pauperized do such unlucky ones go away from this world.

In lines 4 and 5 the Guru says these lovers of the material eat what they wish, or in other words indulge their every whim, forgetting death till old age overtakes their youth. Always remembering death is an excellent device to keep our excesses under check; when death is forgotten the pleasures of the moment consume us totally and guide us down the path away from the Lord. One may even forget that the Lord exists. Here the Guru talks of the ones who in this world have only to demand and their lackeys will rush to fulfil their wishes.. Their living is thus not earned by honest toil, but they command everything by force. *Vekh Mahlat* is to say they 'look at their wealth'; but what the Guru is telling us is that they are so engrossed in admiring the extent of their own wealth and possessions that they have *maraṇ visāriya* (forgotten death). Then one day, old age comes inexorably in, overtaking the youth that encouraged them to such excesses. The body starts to fail and soon the pleasures of the senses will become a faint memory, long gone. In the battle between youth and old age the latter is always the victor, such is the *Hukam* of the Lord. This old age will be followed inevitably by death, again as per His *Hukam*. If we frittered away our allotted span in seeking material baubles and pandering to the senses then is the game indeed lost.

PAURI 18

There are three *sloks* attached with this *pauṛi*, all by Guru Nanak. These touch upon the commonly held superstition of *Sūtak*, or ritual impurity attributed to certain periods in life. The Guru, as usual, seeks to debunk such illogical beliefs. In the first *slok* he says:

ਸਲੋਕ ਮ: ੧	Slok M: 1
ਜੇਕਰਿ ਸੂਤਕੁ ਮੰਨੀਐ ਸਭ ਤੈ ਸੂਤਕੁ ਹੋਇ ॥	Jekar sūtak mannīai sabh tai sūtak hoye
ਗੋਹੇ ਅਤੈ ਲਕੜੀ ਅੰਦਰਿ ਕੀੜਾ ਹੋਇ ॥	Gohay atay lakṛi andar kīra hoye
ਜੇਤੇ ਦਾਣੇ ਅੰਨ ਕੇ ਜੀਆ ਬਾਝੁ ਨ ਕੋਇ ॥	Jetay dāṇay unn ke jiya bājh na koye
ਪਹਿਲਾ ਪਾਣੀ ਜੀਉ ਹੈ ਜਿਤੁ ਹਰਿਆ ਸਭੁ ਕੋਇ ॥	Pahla pāṇi jiu hai jit haria sabh koye
ਸੂਤਕੁ ਕਿਉ ਕਰਿ ਰਖੀਐ ਸੂਤਕੁ ਪਵੈ ਰਸੋਇ ॥	Sūtak kiu kar rakhīai sūtak pavai rasoye
ਨਾਨਕ ਸੂਤਕੁ ਏਵ ਨ ਉਤਰੈ ਗਿਆਨੁ ਉਤਾਰੇ ਧੋਇ ॥੧॥	Nanak sūtak ev na utrai gyān utāray dhoye. 1.

Glossary:

ਸੂਤਕੁ	Sūtak	(Ritual) impurity
ਸਭੁ ਤੈ	Sabh tai	Everywhere
ਗੋਹੇ	Gohay	In the cow dung
ਕੀੜਾ	Kīṛa	Germs, bacteria, insects
ਬਾਝੁ	Bājh	Without
ਰਸੋਇ	Rasoye	Kitchen

The irrational belief in *sūtak* was another pernicious social problem permeating Hindu society in the Guru's time. It was believed that when a woman had been delivered of a child she was unclean for a certain number of days thereafter. This impurity was called *sūtak* and the woman was not allowed in the kitchen for that period. Similarly, when a death occurred an impurity called *pātak* was said to have set in, and the kitchen was closed for some days. Both types are generically called *sūtak*. The Guru all his life crusaded against such meaningless and often demeaning beliefs.

Simply translated this *slok* says that if you believe in *sūtak* then know that it is all pervasive, because even the firewood and the cow dung cakes with which the cooking fire is lit are full of living organisms. Every grain of food you eat has living things inside. The water itself, before the food grain, is full of living things and then this water nurtures all growth. How will you maintain this *sūtak* when it is ingrained deeply in your very kitchen from where your entire intake comes? These worldly types of so-called *sūtak* are mere superstition, but there is indeed a *sūtak* inside us which could harm our soul and against which we need to protect ourselves. The imaginary impurities arising out of births and death do not need to be washed away by ritual purifications and baths. The evil actions that we indulge in do create a *sūtak* which will make our souls, our real selves, unclean. The real *sūtak* from within will be removed only through divine knowledge. Let us now look at it in more detail.

In lines 1 and 2 here the Guru says if you believe in *sūtak*, then know that this *sūtak* is all pervasive, because even the firewood and the cow dung cakes with which the cooking fires are lit have living organisms inside them. It was usual in those days to use for fuel either firewood, or cakes prepared from a mixture of straw and cow dung, for preparing food in the kitchens. Thus, says the Guru, death and birth at this invisible level is going on ceaselessly right inside your kitchens. Insects, and even tinier organisms, are born and they die also, even if we cannot always see it happening with our eyes. So with each such birth and death *sūtak* must set in. The very kitchen where you cook your food is then impure, always under *sūtak*.

In line 3 the Guru says every grain of food you eat has living things inside. Thus, apart from the *sūtak* caused by the cow dung and the firewood, there is the additional *sūtak* arising from the births and deaths within the food grain being cooked and which we will consume.

Line 4 is rendered by learned ones in two different ways. Prof. Sahib Singh puts it as, "Firstly the water itself is a living entity because it is the support of every life." Dr. Gopal Singh, Prof. Teja Singh and Prof. Talib also follow this interpretation. The other view is as Dada Chellaram puts it, "In the first place, the very water wherewith all becomes fresh and green is full of creatures." Macauliffe has a similar view. Bhai Vir Singh renders it as, "(Before food grain) the water itself is full of living things, and then this water is the basis of life for all things." He cites from *Rāga Āsa,* Bhagat Namdev, page 854 of the *SGGS*, "Byalīs lakh jīa jal meh hotay", meaning there are over four million living things in the water. Since in this *pauṛi* the Guru is referring to life contained, unseen, within the things we use, the view taken by Bhai Vir Singh seems more appealing. The Guru is saying that food grains apart even the water used in the cooking, the essential ingredient for all growth, is full of living things itself.

In line 5 the Guru now directly restates the above thoughts. He says how will you maintain the requirements of your *sūtak* in real life when it is so inextricably linked with your every activity, and is ever present in your very kitchen from where your entire intake comes? It is impossible therefore to observe such *sūtak*; it is therefore meaningless to believe that there is *sūtak* inside your home at births and deaths, which are after all perfectly natural phenomenons.

In the 6th line here the Guru concludes with an explicit exhortation stressing the message that was implicit in the *slok*. He says the real *sūtak* from inside us will be removed only through divine knowledge.

The Guru, in the next *slok* speaks of the *sūtak* that occurs at the spiritual level inside the mind, and will have to be washed clean by seeking the knowledge of the Lord.

He says:

ਮ: ੧	M: 1
ਮਨ ਕਾ ਸੂਤਕੁ ਲੋਭੁ ਹੈ ਜਿਹਵਾ ਸੂਤਕੁ ਕੂੜੁ ॥	Mann ka sūtak lobh hai jihwa sūtak kūṛ
ਅਖੀ ਸੂਤਕੁ ਵੇਖਣਾ ਪਰ ਤ੍ਰਿਅ ਪਰ ਧਨ ਰੂਪੁ ॥	Akhi sūtak vekhṇa parr trīa parr dhan rūp

ਕੰਨੀ ਸੂਤਕੁ ਕੰਨਿ ਪੈ ਲਾਇਤਬਾਰੀ ਖਾਹਿ ॥	Kanni sūtak kann pai lāyatbāri khāhay
ਨਾਨਕ ਹੰਸਾ ਆਦਮੀ ਬਧੇ ਜਮਪੁਰਿ ਜਾਹਿ ॥੨॥	Nanak hansa ādmī badhay jampur jāhay. 2.

Glossary:

ਕੂੜੁ	Kūṛ	Lies, falsehood
ਤ੍ਰਿਅ	Trīa	Woman
ਲਾਇਤਬਾਰੀ	Lāyatbāri	Slander
ਹੰਸਾ	Hansa	Swan-like
ਜਮਪੁਰਿ	Jampur	City of Yama, hell

Simply translated this *slok* says that the *sūtak* of the mind is greed and avarice, and of the tongue speaking falsehood. The *sūtak* of the eye is covetously looking at the other man's woman. The *sūtak* of the ear is listening to, and talking, slander. The men who may seem pure as swans but covertly, or even in their minds indulge in these impurities will go to the city of Yama in chains. Let us now look at it in more detail.

In the 1st line the Guru tells us of what should really be counted as *sūtak*. He says the *sūtak* of the mind is greed and avarice; and of the tongue telling lies and speaking falsehood. Man is truly under the interdiction of a *sūtak*, when he is indulging in these evils; and not when there has been a death or a birth in the family. *Sūtak* does occur when the mind is avaricious and covets what belongs to others. Then indeed is the mind impure and then truly such a mind needs to be shunned. Similarly, impurity comes when the tongue utters falsehood.

In line 2 the Guru says that impurity comes when the eye covetously looks at the *parr trīa* (woman other than your wife), or at *parr dhan* (wealth that rightfully belongs to another). When you see that the woman who is not your wife is beautiful, or that a man has much wealth, and your eye uncontrollably strays to these and hunger fills your mind then are you indeed impure, in a state of *sūtak*.

In line 3 the Guru says the impurity comes when the ear listens to slander. The word *lāyatbāri* comes from the Arabic *la etabari*, meaning disbelief or undependability. Most commentators render it here as 'listening to slander'. Bhai

Vir Singh however explains that the phrase *lāyatbāri khāye* is more correctly rendered as 'creating or carrying slander'. Dr. Gopal Singh also puts it as, "the ear's impurity is to hear and carry tales". Since the Guru is talking here of the impurity pertaining to the ear, the view taken by Bhai Vir Singh would perhaps not entirely cover the phrase as used in the *slok*. The more appealing view here would seem to be the one taken by Dr. Gopal Singh and Bhai Vir Singh, covering as it does both aspects of the bad habit of slander mongering; believing it and carrying it.

In line 4 the Guru says the men who indulge in these impurities, however pure – *hansa* – meaning swanlike, the swan being the epitome of grace and purity – they may look will go in chains to the city of Lord Yama. Learned commentators have rendered *hansa* varyingly. Dr. Gopal Singh renders it as, 'the purest of men'. Macauliffe says, "… even the pretended saint who practiseth such things, shall go bound to hell". Prof. Teja Singh puts it as, 'the soul'. Prof. Talib sees it as 'selves'. Dada Chellaram sees the word as 'violence', probably from *hinsa* in Sanskrit. He renders it as, "… to hell repair all these men of violence". Prof. Sahib Singh's rendering is that, "such men may seem beautiful as swans even then they will go bound to hell". Bhai Vir Singh puts it as, "men who may bathe enough to become clean like swans but if they suffer these impurities of the mind they will go to hell". Bhai sahib also explains that there are a number of other possible meanings of *hansa*, such as Swan, Brahma, Vishnu, Shiva, the Guru, the *Hansa avatār*, the soul, sun, sadhu, a content ruler; and it is also rendered as *Kāmdev* (the god of Love), or as enmity. Since the reference here by the Guru is to the various bad qualities, Bhai Vir Singh suggests that *hansa* is used satirically here. All these various interpretations have some relevance, but Prof. Sahib Singh's view seems more appealing here, that men who seem pure as swans would yet go to Yama's court in chains, or in other words suffer the consequences for these sins of the mind.

Having given us some examples of the real *sūtak*, the Guru has further to say on the same subject in the next *slok,* which runs as:

ਮ: ੧	M: 1
ਸਭੋ ਸੂਤਕੁ ਭਰਮੁ ਹੈ ਦੂਜੈ ਲਗੈ ਜਾਇ ॥	Sabho sūtak bharam hai dūjai laggai jāye
ਜੰਮਣੁ ਮਰਣਾ ਹੁਕਮੁ ਹੈ ਭਾਣੈ ਆਵੈ ਜਾਇ ॥	Jammaṇ marṇa hukam hai bhāṇai āvai jāye

ਖਾਣਾ ਪੀਣਾ ਪਵਿਤ੍ਰੁ ਹੈ ਦਿਤੋਨੁ ਰਿਜਕੁ ਸੰਬਾਹਿ ॥	Khana pīṇa pavitar hai ditonu rijak sambāhay
ਨਾਨਕ ਜਿਨ੍ਹੀ ਗੁਰਮੁਖਿ ਬੁਝਿਆ ਤਿਨ੍ਹਾ ਸੂਤਕੁ ਨਾਹਿ ॥੩॥	Nanak jinnhi Gurmukh bujhiya tinha sūtak nāhay. 3.

Glossary:

ਸਭੋ	Sabho	Entire, purely
ਦੂਜੈ ਲਗੈ ਜਾਇ	Dūjai laggai jāye	Is enticed by *Maya*, goes to others than God
ਦਿਤੋਨੁ	Ditonu	Has given
ਸੰਬਾਹਿ	Sambāh	Collected, gathered

Simply translated this *slok* says that this *sūtak* is but a superstition and it shows that we have attachments to things other than the Lord. Death and birth are part of the divine ordinance and occur at His will. The Lord has blessed His creation with all types of food to sustain us and therefore these cannot be subject to any illusory impurity. Those who have realized this through the Guru will not believe in such notions of impurity and superstitions. Let us now look at it in more detail.

In line 1 the Guru says all this *sūtak* is but a *bharam* (false belief, superstition) and if we are under such an impression then it only goes to show that our faith is weak and that we have attachment to things other than the Lord. This line has been rendered variously. Prof. Sahib Singh renders it to say, "*Sūtak* is purely a superstition and it catches those who are beguiled by *Maya* and are away from God." Macauliffe, Dada Chellaram and Prof. Talib also see it this way. Dr. Gopal Singh has a slightly different view. He says, "The impurity of impurities is that one loves the other", the other here meaning some powers or entities other than God. Bhai Vir Singh in his *Panj granthi* sees it yet another way and says, "The belief that *sūtak* will also attach to others in the family is all illusion." He seems to suggest that while the new mother may be deemed under *sūtak* but how can it be considered to attach also to others in the family. He however says that some give another rendering, which is, "All *sūtak* is an illusion which leads men to losing focus on the one Lord and getting attached to others." Prof. Talib has also adopted the latter view as we saw above, and Prof. Sahib Singh's interpretation is also very close to it. This seems clearly a more appealing interpretation capturing as it does the essence of the message and consistent as it is with the rest of the composition, which stresses on us to focus on the Lord to the exclusion of anything else.

In line 2 the Guru says death and birth are part of the divine ordinance and occur at His will. Something that occurs in accordance with His purpose cannot ever be deemed impure. The One that is Purity personified cannot be passing on impurity to His creation. The natural order is ever pure, ever correct. Things that happen within it are therefore to be accepted as proper and necessary. Births occur because He ordains it, and then we pass from this world when He so wills. Where then is the room for impurity in this process? The Guru says do not delude yourself and label the natural order of things as impure.

In line 3 the Guru seeks to remove our doubts on another wrongly held belief, that there is impurity attached to any particular type of food. He says the Lord has blessed His creation with all types of food as a means to our sustenance, and therefore these cannot be subject to any illusory impurity. What is required is for the inner self to be pure and fixed on the Lord; there need be no fussing about the food being kosher or not kosher, as long as it provides healthy sustenance. *Sambāh* is from the Sanskrit and means 'to gather' or 'to take'. Here, says Bhai Vir Singh, it is used in the singular and is to be translated 'provides'. A similar usage is to be found in *Rāga Gūjri*, *Mahla* 5, page 10 of the *SGGS*, where the Guru says, "sirr sirr rijak sambāhay thākur", meaning the Lord provides sustenance to each being.

In line 4 the Guru concludes with, "Those who have realized this through the Guru will not believe in such notions of impurity." Dr. Gopal Singh renders it as, "To them impurity sticks not." Learned commentators have used slightly differing terminology but the broad sense is quite clear, that the one who recognizes and fully accepts the natural order of things moves in accordance with the Will of the Lord, and is then freed from these superstitious delusions.

The 18th *pauṛi* speaks of the importance of the Guru to help rid ourselves of the taints of this world and achieve God-realization. The Guru says:

ਪਉੜੀ ॥	Pauṛi
ਸਤਿਗੁਰੁ ਵਡਾ ਕਰਿ ਸਾਲਾਹੀਐ ਜਿਸ ਵਿਚਿ ਵਡੀਆ ਵਡਿਆਈਆ ॥	Satguru vadda kar sālāhīai jis vich vaddia vaddiāia

ਸਹਿ ਮੇਲੇ ਤਾ ਨਦਰੀ ਆਈਆ ॥	Seh melay ta nadri āīa
ਜਾ ਤਿਸੁ ਭਾਣਾ ਤਾ ਮਨਿ ਵਸਾਈਆ ॥	Ja tis bhāṇa ta mann vasāia
ਕਰਿ ਹੁਕਮੁ ਮਸਤਕਿ ਹਥੁ ਧਰਿ ਵਿਚਹੁ ਮਾਰਿ ਕਢੀਆ ਬੁਰਿਆਈਆ ॥	Kar hukam mastak hath dhar vichoh mār kaddhīya buriāia
ਸਹਿ ਤੁਠੈ ਨਉ ਨਿਧਿ ਪਾਈਆ ॥੧੮॥	Seh tutthai nau nidh pāia [18]

Glossary:

ਸਾਲਾਹੀਐ	Salāhīai	Praise
ਸਹਿ	Seh	The Lord
ਨਦਰੀ ਆਈਆ	Nadri āīa	Are seen
ਤੁਠੈ	Tutthai	If is pleased
ਨਉ ਨਿਧਿ	Nau Nidh	Nine treasures, here material wealth

Simply translated this *pauṛi* says that we must praise the true Guru in whom there is all greatness. These good qualities become visible when the Lord puts us in touch with the true Guru. When it pleases the Lord then do our minds get imbued with these good qualities. Our evils are driven out when He lays His hands on our foreheads, and by the Lord's pleasure do we obtain the nine treasures. Let us now look at it in more detail.

In the 1st line the Guru says to praise *Satguru* – the true preceptor – in whom there is all greatness. The repeated and constant stress by the Guru on the importance of the true Guru, the right preceptor, emerges here again. Since the preceptor is going to put on the path to the Lord, he is vital for us. As the Guru said in the *Sukhmani Sahib, Rāg Gauṛi Mahla* 5, page 286, "**ਸਤਿ ਪੁਰਖ ਜਿਨਿ ਜਾਨਿਆ ਸਤਿਗੁਰ ਤਿਸ ਕਾ ਨਾਉ॥ ਤਿਸ ਕੇ ਸੰਗਿ ਸਿਖ ਉਧਰੈ ਨਾਨਕ ਹਰਿ ਗੁਨ ਗਾਉ**]" – "sat purakh jin jānia satgur tis ka nāo. Tis ke sung sikh udhrai Nanak har gunn gāo", meaning that the one who has realized God is the *Satguru* and the Sikh will attain salvation through him by singing the Lord's praises. For the Sikh that *Satguru* today is, of course, the *SGGS*. For a true Guru to be able to guide us on the divine path obviously his qualities have to be lofty. So the Guru says here that the preceptor is the possessor of great goodness.

In line 2 the Guru says these good qualities became visible when the Lord put us in touch with the true Guru. Prof. Talib renders this as, "By the union divinely ordained are these made visible." Most learned commentators have similar interpretations of this idea, implying that the high qualities referred to are those of the preceptor. Dr. Gopal Singh's view, however, is that the qualities spoken of here are those of the Lord, and not of the preceptor. He puts it as, "When the Lord takes us to the Guru, then alone do we see His virtues." The view that the lofty qualities alluded to are those of the Guru is, however, more appealing, since the focus here is on the preceptor who is found by God's grace and who will take us on the right path.

In line 3 the Guru says when it pleases the Lord then do our minds get imbued with these good qualities. This is meant again to stress the necessity of the true preceptor, but above all it stresses that the single-most important and essential ingredient is the Lord's glance of grace. Only when He is pleased to bestow His grace do these good qualities come to us.

In lines 4 and 5 the Guru says our evils are driven out when he lays his hands on our foreheads, and by the Lord's pleasure do we obtain the nine treasures. We have nothing but evils within us. These will be expelled and our inner selves purified when the Guru places his hand on our forehead. *Mastak hath dhar* is an idiom commonly used in India to convey that someone has been taken under the aegis. When the Guru takes us under his tutelage he gives us the right instruction, he teaches us the right way to live, which is to ever sing praises of the Lord. When he thus symbolically puts his hand on our forehead, the evils within are driven out. This however requires that the Lord's favour be on us. Then only, says the Guru, the nine treasures of this world come to us. This phrase refers to the treasures of Earth, or in other words all the good things that exist. The 'Nine Treasures' is an ancient myth and these were supposed to belong to *Kuber*, believed in Hinduism to be the ruler of the race of semi-divine beings called the *Yaksha*, and also the the god of wealth, with his abode in the northern quarters, and residence on the sides of the Kailash Mountain. Here the phrase is meant to describe all earthly treasures we could crave for. The meaning truly is that in having our evils driven out with the Guru's intercession and the Lord's grace, we have gained the equivalent of the fabled nine treasures.

PAUṚI 19

In this *pauṛi* and the two *sloks* attached with it, the Guru speaks to us on the practice of purificatory rituals, which had become associated with eating. In keeping with his debunking of all meaningless superstitions and empty ritualism, Guru Nanak speaks on the common superstitions about the process of food preparation and eating. In the first *slok* he says:

ਸਲੋਕ ਮ: ੧	Slok M: 1
ਪਹਿਲਾ ਸੁਚਾ ਆਪਿ ਹੋਇ ਸੁਚੈ ਬੈਠਾ ਆਇ ॥	Pahla sucha āp hoye suchai baittha āye
ਸੁਚੈ ਅਗੈ ਰਖਿਓਨੁ ਕੋਇ ਨ ਭਿਟਿਓ ਜਾਇ ॥	Suchai aggai rakhiyon koye na bhittio jāye
ਸੁਚਾ ਹੋਇ ਕੈ ਜੇਵਿਆ ਲਗਾ ਪੜਣਿ ਸਲੋਕੁ ॥	Sucha hoye ke jeviya lagga paṛan slok
ਕੁਹਥੀ ਜਾਈ ਸਟਿਆ ਕਿਸੁ ਏਹੁ ਲਗਾ ਦੋਖੁ ॥	Kuhthī jayī sattiya kis eh lagga dokh
ਅੰਨੁ ਦੇਵਤਾ ਪਾਣੀ ਦੇਵਤਾ ਬੈਸੰਤਰੁ ਦੇਵਤਾ ਲੂਣੁ ਪੰਜਵਾ ਪਾਇਆ ਘਿਰਤੁ ॥	Unn devta pāṇi devta baisantar lūne panjwa pāiya ghirat
ਤਾ ਹੋਆ ਪਾਕੁ ਪਵਿਤੁ ॥	Ta hoa pāk pavit
ਪਾਪੀ ਸਿਉ ਤਨੁ ਗਡਿਆ ਥੁਕਾ ਪਈਆ ਤਿਤੁ ॥	Pāpi siu tann gaddia thukka paīa tit
ਜਿਤੁ ਮੁਖਿ ਨਾਮੁ ਨ ਊਚਰਹਿ ਬਿਨ ਨਾਵੈ ਰਸ ਖਾਹਿ ॥	Jit mukh nām na ūchreh bin nāvai ras khāhay
ਨਾਨਕ ਏਵੈ ਜਾਣੀਐ ਤਿਤੁ ਮੁਖਿ ਥੁਕਾ ਪਾਹਿ ॥੧॥	Nanak avai jāṇiyai tit mukh thukka pāhay. 1

Glossary:

ਸੁਚੈ	Suchai	In the pure kitchen
ਭਿਟਿਓ	Bhittiyo	Tainted, made impure
ਜੇਵਿਆ	Jeviya	Eaten
ਕੁਹਥੀ ਜਾਈ	Kuhthi jāyi	In a bad or dirty place
ਪਾਕੁ	Pāk	Pure, also cooked
ਗਡਿਆ	Gaddia	Mixed
ਰਸ ਖਾਹਿ	Ras khāhay	Eat tasty things

Simply translated this *slok* says that (the Brahmin) first purifies himself and then sits in the ritually cleansed area. The food placed before him is also to be pure, and no one must have touched it. After all the purification he recites the holy *sloks* over it before eating. The food, the water, the fire, the salt, all deemed to be gods in Hinduism, are added and thereafter *ghee* (clarified butter) is also put in; and then it all is supposed to have become holy and pure. This thoroughly pure food then enters the body that is itself impure. The food then becomes impure as if it had been spat upon. The mouth that utters not the Name of the Lord but eats the pure food will be figuratively spat upon, or disgraced, in the court of the Lord. Let us now look at it in more detail.

In lines 1 and 2 the Guru describes how a person, probably a Brahmin considering the rituals described, obsessed more with bodily cleanliness but in his arrogance unmindful of the Lord, goes about the ritual of eating. He says the Brahmin washes up, purifies his body and then sits in the kitchen area which also he has ritually cleansed. Then the food, which is placed before him also has to be pure and ritually prepared. No part of it should have been tasted by anyone before then. Only such food, pure and untouched, could be served to the Brahmin and that also within the sanctified square of the eating area.

In lines 3 and 4 the Guru says this food that has been partaken, after all this lengthy rigmarole, then reaches a dirty place. So, who incurs the sin for this lapse in purity? The Guru has in conclusion in lines 8 and 9 clarified the sense of this concept. He says all the purificatory rites for eating are of no avail if the body into which this pure food goes belongs to the sinful man who does not recite the Name of the Lord. He is referring to the fact that the food goes into the stomach, is digested and then egested into the latrine; the fate of this extra pure food is no different from the food eaten by another person who did not go through this drill of purification. So, suggests the Guru, if spiritual merit was sought to be gained through ensuring all that purity, then surely the demerit of casting it into a dirty and unclean place must also befall this person. On whom is the odium of this, asks the Guru. As Prof. Talib very nicely puts it, "Subsequently this food turned into offal, in a foul spot is thrown – to whom does the sin of desecration attach?"

In lines 5 and 6 the Guru says the food, water, fire, salt and, the fifth, *ghee* (clairified butter) – all considered holy – were added and with these the food was sanctified. In Hinduism food grains, fire and water are treated as deities. Salt and specially *ghee* added to food were considered efficacious as purificatory ingredients. So, says the Guru, all these divine and holy things had been brought together to ensure that the food became really pure. He then tells us in the next line the pointlessness of this charade, unredeemed by the recitation of the Lord's Name.

In line 7 the Guru says all this highly purified matter then entered the body which itself was impure and sinful. It then became as impure as if it had been spat upon. The point of the lesson is that purity of the food cannot ever be sufficient enough to purify the body into which it is ingested. If that body is impure, or in other words sinful, the level of purity of the food is irrelevant. If the soul within is not pure then the purest of food will be of no avail. In fact it will itself become impure, fit only for being spat upon, meaning disgraced. Conversely, if the person has a pure mind the lack of purificatory rituals about the food would not matter.

In lines 8 and 9 the Guru says the mouth that utters not the Name but enjoys the eating of such food will be disgraced, or so to say, spat upon. In these concluding lines the Guru brings us to the crux of the message. He says all the purificatory rites for eating are of no avail if the body into which this pure food goes belongs to the sinful man. Such food will go through the normal process of digestion and will then be egested as waste, leaving the soul no purer. Instead, if your mind is immersed in the Lord then does the body become pure. For such ones the Guru has said in *Rāg Soratth*, *Mahla* 4, page 648 of the *SGGS*, **"ਤਿਨ ਕਾ ਖਾਧਾ ਪੈਧਾ ਮਾਇਆ ਸਭ ਪਵਿਤੁ ਹੈ ਜੋ ਨਾਮਿ ਹਰਿ ਰਾਤੇ॥"** - "tin ka khādha paidha māia sabh pavit hai jo nām har rātay", meaning that those imbued with the Name are pure whatever they may eat or wear. Without the Name eating all the tasty food will bring only disgrace. As Macauliffe puts it, "The mouth which uttereth not the Name and eateth even delicacies without the Name, consider, O Nanak as if spat upon." The essence is therefore the purity of the inner self and for that food is irrelevant and only the Name of the Lord is efficacious.

In the second *slok* the Guru touches upon the status of women in society at that time. He says:

ਮ: ੧	M: 1
ਭੰਡਿ ਜੰਮੀਐ ਭੰਡਿ ਨਿੰਮੀਐ ਭੰਡਿ ਮੰਗਣੁ ਵੀਆਹੁ ॥	Bhandd jammīyai bhandd nimmīai bhandd mangaṇ viyāh(u)
ਭੰਡਹੁ ਹੋਵੈ ਦੋਸਤੀ ਭੰਡਹੁ ਚਲੈ ਰਾਹੁ ॥	Bhanddoh hovai dosti bhanddoh challai rāh[u]
ਭੰਡੁ ਮੁਆ ਭੰਡੁ ਭਾਲੀਐ ਭੰਡਿ ਹੋਵੈ ਬੰਧਾਨੁ ॥	Bhandd mua bhandd bhālīyai bhandd hovai bandhān
ਸੋ ਕਿਉ ਮੰਦਾ ਆਖੀਐ ਜਿਤੁ ਜੰਮਹਿ ਰਾਜਾਨ ॥	So kiu manda ākhīyai jit jammai rājān
ਭੰਡਹੁ ਹੀ ਭੰਡੁ ਉਪਜੈ ਭੰਡੈ ਬਾਝੁ ਨ ਕੋਇ ॥	Bhanddoh hee bhandd ūpjai bhanddai bājh na koye
ਨਾਨਕ ਭੰਡੈ ਬਾਹਰਾ ਏਕੋ ਸਚਾ ਸੋਇ ॥	Nanak bhanddai bāhra eko sacha soye
ਜਿਤੁ ਮੁਖਿ ਸਦਾ ਸਾਲਾਹੀਐ ਭਾਗਾ ਰਤੀ ਚਾਰਿ ॥	Jit much sada sālāhīyai bhāga rati chār
ਨਾਨਕ ਤੇ ਮੁਖ ਉਜਲੇ ਤਿਤੁ ਸਚੈ ਦਰਬਾਰਿ ॥੨॥	Nanak tay mukh ūjlay tit sachai darbār. 2.

Glossary:

ਭੰਡਿ	Bhandd	Woman
ਜੰਮੀਐ	Jammīai	Are born
ਮੰਗਣੁ	Mangaṇ	Is betrothed
ਨਿੰਮੀਐ	Nimmīai	Is built
ਬੰਧਾਨੁ	Bandhān	Relationship
ਭਾਗਾ	Bhāga	By fortune

Simply translated this *slok* says that we are born from *bhandd*– (woman); in her body we grow; with her are we betrothed and to woman are we married. With woman we conduct relationships and through her proceed the way of the human species. If woman dies we seek another; through woman are bonds of society established. We should not then run down the woman from whom are born all of us, even the highest kings. From woman are born women and there is none outside this requirement, except the True One Himself, the Lord. The mouth that is lucky enough to praise the Lord will be resplendent in His Court. Let us now look at it in more detail.

Bhai Vir Singh in his commentary has discussed at length the term *bhand*, one meaning of which is 'ridiculing' or 'jesting'. In Hinduism the term was used for woman as well as for Shudra. but Bhai sahib says that according to one scholar it is from the Sanskrit root *bhedra*, meaning 'to be lucky', and it has here been used for woman in an ironical sense, in the same way it was used for Shudra, the lowest among the Hindu castes, when at that time their position was truly bad in Hindu society! *Bhandd* could also be from *bhāndda* or vessel, an appellation used for women even in the *Bible*, says Bhai Vir Singh. Thus, in 1 Thessalonians 4:4, the *Bible* says, "That every one of you should know how to possess this vessel in sanctification and honour"; and again in 1 Peter 3:7 it says, "Likewise, ye husbands, dwell with them according to knowledge, giving honour unto the wife, as unto the weaker vessel ...." This is the sense in which Macauliffe has rendered it in his commentary and he says the Greeks also used the word in the same sense. Some learned ones have also said that it is here meant not to describe woman but in the sense of the 'lowly and contemptible', meaning those who take not the name of the Lord. They interpret the entire *slok* in that context. However, most commentators take this as referring to woman, which seems the more logical in the context, because we know women were not accorded their due status and the Guru is therefore speaking against this injustice.

In line 1 and 2 the Guru says that we are born from woman, in her body we grow; with her are we (in due course) betrothed and to her are we married. The inextricable bonds between the life of a man and the life of a woman in the form of mother or wife, is delineated here by the Guru to show how important her role is in the lives of mankind. In line 2 the Guru says, "With woman do we conduct relationships and through her proceeds the way of the human species." As Prof. Talib puts it, "With women is man's companionship. From woman originate new generations." Woman as the lifelong companion for man is also stressed in the Christian belief system. The *Bible*, in Genesis 2:20, says, "... but for Adam there was not found an helpmeet for him". Then, in Genesis 2:21 and 2.22 it says, "And the Lord God caused a deep sleep to fall upon Adam, and he slept: and he took one of his ribs, and closed up the flesh instead thereof; and the rib, which the Lord God had taken from man, made he a woman, and brought her unto the man." The relationship is undeniably vital, and is so recognized by all religions. It is a necessary requirement for the propagation and continuation of the human race.

In line 3 the Guru says if woman dies we seek another, through woman are the bonds of society established. This is how most learned ones have rendered it. However, *Bandhān* is rendered by Prof. Talib as 'restraint' and so he interprets this line as, "With woman's help is man kept in restraint." Macauliffe also says, "... to a vessel he is bound". Since, however, the message is about the importance of woman to society the rendering adopted by most of the learned ones and by the *Shabdarth* that, "through woman are the social bonds maintained" seems more appropriate. Thus, the Guru is telling us that it is the woman who keeps the social, the familial and even the racial bonds healthy, making clear her vital role in human existence.

In line 4 the Guru says we should not run down those from whom are born even kings. In the first three lines the Guru had recounted the vital essentiality of womankind to the continuation of the human race, to the health of the social fabric and to the maintenance of the immediate relationship cycle among humans. He now says apart from all this, remember also that it is from woman that great men enter this world. The word used is *rājān*, kings literally, but obviously the allusion is to all men who could be considered high or great. The most powerful men, the greatest rulers, the most brilliant minds, all exist on this earth only because women exist. So, says the Guru, if you are extolling the greatness of all these then how can can you in good conscience denigrate the woman who brought them into this world.

In lines 5 and 6 the Guru says that from women are born men and women and there is none outside of this requirement. The only one not beholden to women for existence is the Lord Himself. The Lord is *Ajoni*, *Akāl*, *swayambhav- or, saibha[ng]* – not born, beyond time and self-created. He alone is not born of woman, and there is none else, says the Guru.

In the concluding lines, the 7th and 8th, the Guru says the mouth that by good luck utters the praises of the Lord will be resplendent in the court of the Lord. The term *bhāga rati chār* is rendered in different ways by learned ones. Gyani Maskin says it is 'four *rattīs* of good luck', and refers to the common Punjabi saying about four *ratīs* of good luck. The *rati'* is a small seed used also as a weight for precious metals. So the phrase means 'with a bit of luck'. Thus, the rendering of this line would be that we sing the Lord's praises if we are lucky. Bhai Vir Singh feels that the word *rati* here is from the word *ratan*, meaning gems, and the phrase needs to be seen as "the begemmed necklace of good luck". The word *chār* means four but is also used for beautiful or good. So, one way of rendering this, says Bhai Vir Singh, would be as the four gems which are *Dharma*, *Artha*, *Kām*, and *Moksha*, all of which are bestowed on the one lauding God. Prof. Sahib Singh sees it as, "Those who sing the Lord's praises have the gem of good luck on their forehead." Dr. Gopal Singh says, "That fortunate and gracious pearl-like mouth that utters the Lord's praise is luminescent." Prof. Talib says, "The tongue by which the Lord is praised is fortunate and rendered beautiful." Macauliffe puts it as, "The mouth which ever praiseth Him is fortunate and beautiful." The *Shabdarth* renders it as "glowing and beautiful because of good luck". The term *bhāga rati* is also seen by some as 'endowed with luck', using *rati* as from the root *ratia* meaning thoroughly imbued with, and by some as *bhāg*, meaning luck, and *rati* meaning gems or pearls. Thus, we see a number of interpretations centring on *rati* as either 'imbued with', or as 'jewels'. Also, *chār* has two meanings, as 'four' and as 'beautiful'. Either rendering has merit, but the more generally used and the more appealing rendering is in the sense that Bhai Vir Singh *et al.* have taken it. According to them, it is "the mouth that ever praises the Lord has the jewel of good fortune marked on his forehead". Such a one will go to the Lord with his face resplendent.

In the *pauṛi* with which these *sloks* were attached, the Guru says:

ਪਉੜੀ ॥	Pauṛi
ਸਭੁ ਕੋ ਆਖੈ ਆਪਣਾ ਜਿਸੁ ਨਾਹੀ ਸੋ ਚੁਣਿ ਕਢੀਐ॥	Sabh ko ākhay āpṇa jis nāhi so chuṇ kaddhiai
ਕੀਤਾ ਆਪੋ ਆਪਣਾ ਆਪੇ ਹੀ ਲੇਖਾ ਸੰਢੀਐ ॥	Kīta āpo āpṇa āpay hee lekha sanddhiai
ਜਾ ਰਹਣਾ ਨਾਹੀ ਐਤੁ ਜਗਿ ਤਾ ਕਾਇਤੁ ਗਾਰਬਿ ਹੰਢੀਐ ॥	Ja rehṇa nahi ait jagg ta kāyat gārab handdhiai
ਮੰਦਾ ਕਿਸੈ ਨ ਆਖੀਐ ਪੜਿ ਅਖਰੁ ਏਹੋ ਬੁਝੀਐ ॥	Manda kisai na ākhiyai par akhar eho bujhīai
ਮੂਰਖੈ ਨਾਲਿ ਨ ਲੁਝੀਐ ॥੧੯॥	Mūrkhai nāl na lujhīai [19]

Glossary:

ਆਖੈ ਆਪਣਾ	Ākhai āpṇa	Claims as own
ਸੰਢੀਐ	Sanddhiai	Settle, render
ਕਾਇਤੁ	Kāyat	How
ਗਾਰਬਿ	Gārab	In arrogance, proudly
ਹੰਢੀਐ	Handdhīai	Waste, use up
ਲੁਝੀਐ	Lujhīai	Be embroiled

Simply translated this *pauṛi* says that all people claim the Lord as exclusively belonging to them. All of us will ultimately have to render our account before the Lord, strictly on the merits of our actions. When our sojourn on this world is ephemeral and transient then why should we presume to go about in arrogance? We must not denigrate anybody and also never waste energy in wrangling with a fool. Let us now look at it in more detail.

Lines 1 and 2 of this *pauṛi* have been rendered differently by learned ones. One view is that the reference is to the acquisitive aspects of man's nature where he craves to claim ownership of everything. The other view is that the subject of the lesson is the Lord Himself whom religions claim as exclusively their own. Gyani Maskin in his audio- commentary takes this to refer to the human tendency to claim material things of the world as belonging to them, and puts it as, "Everyone is immersed in love of things, and claims everything as his own." That is also the rendering adopted by Prof. Sahib Singh. The *Shabdarth* of the *SGPC* has another take and says that this is meant by the Guru as a further argument in favour of treating women with honour. It says that men and women equally claim God as their own, and the both are, as the 2nd line says, responsible for their own conduct before the Lord; so how could we call women as being lesser. Bhai Vir Singh instead renders these lines as referring to the competition among various religions to lay exclusive claim to the Lord and says, "All claim God as their own." He goes on to explain that in a way such a claim is correct also because every person on this earth does belong to Him. But merely claiming this relationship is not enough, he says. What needs to be seen is how much we have moulded our actions while claiming Him to be ours, because ultimately each one of us is answerable in His court for our own actions. All these renderings certainly have their own logic but the more appealing view is the one adopted by Bhai Vir Singh that the reference here is not to worldly things, but to the tendency of people to claim the Lord as exclusively belonging to them.

The phrase *chuṇ kaddhiai* in the first line has been generally rendered as 'show us', implying that there really is no such a one. Some learned ones however have also rendered the line as, "the ones who own up not to God are removed or put away". Macauliffe and Dada Chellaram for instance have taken this view. Most learned ones, however, render it on the lines of 'show me such a one'. The phrase *lekha sanddhiai* means to settle, or render an account, but *sanddhiya* has, according to Bhai Vir Singh, thirty different meanings of which one is settling a fine or paying up. Prof. Talib renders it as 'reckoning'. What we are being told is that the answerability to the Lord is strictly on the merits of our actions. Regardless of who or what we are the accounts will have to be settled. So it also implicitly includes the sense taken by the *Shabdarth*, that none should presume to treat one sex as superior to the other.

In line 3 the Guru says when we are not permanent residents of this world then why do we presume to go about in arrogance. The term *handdhiai* means to wear away, to use up and also to practise, to conduct ourselves. Our sojourn here is very short in duration. We came from the Lord and will soon enough go back to Him for further reckoning. Yet in this brief time we are foolish enough to acquire attachments, start claiming ownerships and swell in pride at how much we own. Such attachments are foolishness. So, says the Guru, remember you are soon going away from this transit house and do not go about strutting in false pride.

In the concluding lines, the 4th and 5th, the Guru says learn never to call anybody bad and never waste energy in wrangling with a fool. Bhai Vir Singh sees this as an injunction to not denigrate another's belief system and that from education we should learn that in seeking to extol our own belief system we should not argue with fools. Prof. Sahib Singh sees it as a general guidance to not denigrate others or quarrel with fools. The *Shabdarth* still seeing it as a continuing presentation in favour of respecting women sees it as the Guru saying that even if the woman is not educated and you are, do not denigrate her, and never quarrel with a fool. Many commentators follow the simple and direct rendering, as for instance, Dr. Gopal Singh who says, "Call no one bad: this is the essence of knowledge, and argue not with a fool." Though the more dirct interpretation also has merit, the view taken by Bhai Vir Singh seems here more appealing, that is to say that just to extol our own view we must not enter into contention.

PAURI 20

There are two *sloks* attached with this *pauṛi*, both by Guru Nanak. The first one is on the subject of a sharp tongue, and the need to speak softly. The Guru says:

ਸਲੋਕ ਮਹਲਾ	Slok Mahla 1
ਨਾਨਕ ਫਿਕੈ ਬੋਲਿਐ ਤਨੁ ਮਨੁ ਫਿਕਾ ਹੋਇ ॥	Nanak phikkai boliai tann mann phikka hoye
ਫਿਕੋ ਫਿਕਾ ਸਦੀਐ ਫਿਕੇ ਫਿਕੀ ਸੋਇ ॥	Phikko phikka sadiai phikkay phikki soye
ਫਿਕਾ ਦਰਗਹ ਸਟੀਐ ਮੁਹਿ ਥੁਕਾ ਫਿਕੇ ਪਾਇ ॥	Phikka dargah sattiai muh thukka phikkay pāye
ਫਿਕਾ ਮੂਰਖੁ ਆਖੀਐ ਪਾਣਾ ਲਹੈ ਸਜਾਇ ॥੧॥	Phikka mūrakh ākhīyai pāṇa lahai sajāye. 1.

Glossary:

ਫਿਕੈ ਬੋਲਿਐ	Phikkai boliai	If we utter abrasive, unpleasant words
ਸੋਇ	Soye	Repute
ਪਾਣਾ	Pāṇa	Footwear

The word *phikka* used here literally means insipid or tasteless. It is however extensively used idiomatically to depict the lack of warmth in personal interactions, or for unpleasant and graceless behaviour. Thus, an unhelpful, dry and rude person is said to be *phikka*. Words that are unpleasing to the hearer are said to be *phikka*. It is in this sense that the Guru has employed this term here.

Simply translated this *slok* says that if we speak hurtful words, our own minds and bodies are also hurt. The abrasive one will be called as such by the world and his repute for hurtfulness will always precede him. The hurtful one is rejected in the Divine Court and his face is spat upon, which means he will face disgrace. The hurtful one is a fool who with shoes will be beaten; in other words, he will face disgrace. Let us now look at it in more detail.

In the 1st line the Guru says if we speak hurting words, our own minds and bodies are also hurt. Bhai Vir Singh says the allusion is to the religious discourses where harsh criticism would often be exchanged between the disputants and hurtful language would be uttered. Most commentators have translated it in a more literal fashion as being an injunction against rude and hurtful verbal interactions. The point is that words spoken to hurt others do not leave our own selves unaffected. If we are abrasive in speaking, our mind loses its peace and the body its grace. The essence of the message is that the same Lord resides in each of us, and if we realize this basic truth how can we even think of hurting another.

In lines 2 and 3 the Guru says the abrasive one will be called as such by the world and his repute for hurtfulness will travel with him. The hurtful one is rejected in the Divine Court and his face is spat upon; in other words, he will be treated with contempt. Thus, not only will he have earned ill repute among his fellows, he will pay for his hurtfulness even before the Lord. The point is that words can injure someone as severely as any weapon, even more. What gets hurt is the heart, the inner self. For this aggression, as for any other bad action, the perpetrator will pay when the final reckoning is taken before the Lord. The wages of this sin will be rejection and in the Lord's court even worse – ignominy. To spit on someone is the highest form of disgrace in earthly terms. This is the sort of disgrace the abrasive one will suffer for the hurt he causes others.

In the last line, the 4th, the Guru says call the hurtful one a fool who with shoes will be beaten. Prof. Talib renders it as, "The foul of tongue is reputed foolish, and in ignominy is chastised." The word *pāṇa* means footwear, and *sajāi* means punishment. So literally, this line translates as 'with shoes is he punished'. Shoe beating, like spitting on a person, is an idiomatic way to describe a particularly ignominious form of chastisement.

The man who speaks rough and harsh words is very likely in real life to be a man without love or compassion in his heart. He is also likely to be arrogant. Such a one will be far removed from godliness. So the ill repute and the punishment mentioned in this *sloka*, that will come due to his rough words and foul language really implies that lack of love and gentleness in his heart will earn him these just desserts.

In the second *slok* with this *pauṛi*, the Guru speaks to us of the need for real and true worship, shunning ostentatious displays of religiosity. He says:

ਮ: ੧	M: 1
ਅੰਦਰਹੁ ਝੂਠੇ ਪੈਜ ਬਾਹਰਿ ਦੁਨੀਆ ਅੰਦਰਿ ਫੈਲੁ ॥	Androh jhootthay paij bāhar dunia andar phail
ਅਠਸਠਿ ਤੀਰਥ ਜੇ ਨਾਵਹਿ ਉਤਰੈ ਨਾਹੀ ਮੈਲੁ ॥	Atthsatth tīrath jay nāveh utrai nāhi maill
ਜਿਨ੍ ਪਟੁ ਅੰਦਰਿ ਬਾਹਰਿ ਗੁਦੜੁ ਤੇ ਭਲੇ ਸੰਸਾਰਿ ॥	Jinn patt andar bāhar guduṛ tay bhalay sansār
ਤਿਨ੍ ਨੇਹੁ ਲਗਾ ਰਬ ਸੇਤੀ ਦੇਖਨੇ ਵੀਚਾਰਿ ॥	Tinn neh lagga rabb seti dekhnay vīchār
ਰੰਗਿ ਹਸਹਿ ਰੰਗਿ ਰੋਵਹਿ ਚੁਪ ਭੀ ਕਰਿ ਜਾਹਿ ॥	Rangg haseh rangg roveh chupp bhi kar jāhay
ਪਰਵਾਹ ਨਾਹੀ ਕਿਸੈ ਕੇਰੀ ਬਾਝੁ ਸਚੇ ਨਾਹ ॥	Parvāh nāhi kisai keri bājh sachay nāh
ਦਰਿ ਵਾਟ ਉਪਰਿ ਖਰਚੁ ਮੰਗਾ ਜਬੈ ਦੇਇ ਤਾ ਖਾਹਿ ॥	Darr vātt uppar kharach manga jabai day ta khāhay
ਦੀਬਾਨੁ ਏਕੋ ਕਲਮ ਏਕਾ ਹਮਾ ਤੁਮ੍ਾ ਮੇਲੁ ॥	Dībān eka kalam eka huma tuma meil
ਦਰਿ ਲਏ ਲੇਖਾ ਪੀੜਿ ਛੁਟੈ ਨਾਨਕਾ ਜਿਉ ਤੇਲੁ ॥੨॥	Darr laye lekha pīṛ cchuttai Nanaka jiu teil. 2.

Glossary:

ਪੈਜ	Paij	Pose (of respect)
ਫੈਲੁ	Phail	Extent, spread, show
ਗੁਦੜੁ	Guduṛ	Rough quilt
ਦੇਖਨੇ	Dekhnay	Desire to see
ਰੰਗਿ	Rangg	Rapt, pleasure
ਬਾਝੁ	Bājh	Without
ਨਾਹ	Nāh	Lord, master, husband
ਦੀਬਾਨੁ	Dībān	Court
ਪੀੜਿ	Pīṛ	Squeeze

Simply translated this *slok* says that those who are false from inside but keep up a pose for the world will not be able to shed their grime even if they wash at the sixty-eight *tīraths*. Those who are outwardly rough and shabby but are soft and silk smooth inside, desire for the Lord's glimpse. Such ones are not bothered by society's conventions and at their pleasure do they laugh or weep, or even lapse into complete silence. They care not for anything but the True Name. They sit at the Lord's door and ask only from Him, eating whatever He provides. There is only One Court, One pen writing everyone's fate and all of us will finally gather in that Court. Before the Lord will our accounts be scrutinized minutely, as thoroughly as oil is extracted from the oilseed. Let us now look at it in more detail.

In lines 1 and 2 the Guru says those who maintain the pose of being very pure for the world, but are false inside will not be able to shed their grime even if they wash at all the sixty-eight *tīraths*. In Hinduism the ritual purificatory bath carries great importance. Then, beyond that if the bath is at one of the sixty-eight especially holy places then its merit is much enhanced. Even such supposedly surefire devices, says the Guru, will not cleanse the sins of such false poseurs. The object of opprobrium here are the ones who are all falsehood inside, mean no good to anyone and live egocentric lives – the life of a *Manmukh*. However, they maintain a pose of being virtuous showing the world a false face of purity, thus often securing worldly success. Their cheating ways are however not hidden from the Lord. The grime of evil they acquire will be such that no amount of cleansing rituals will remove the taint.

In lines 3 and 4 the Guru speaks of the other type of humans, the sort who are smooth and soft like silk inside even if outwardly they are unsophisticated and appear rough and crude, or as the Guru says, their exterior may be rough like unspun cotton and coarse like rags. Such ones have that most vital of all qualities – love for the Lord in their hearts and in their minds the desire to behold Him. They may not present to the world a smooth or sophisticated exterior, and they may lack social skills and smoothness of the tongue. But their kind heart and love for the Lord more than makes up for it. They may have little worldly success, but they are the ones most acceptable to the Lord.

In lines 5 and 6 the Guru describes further the qualities of these noble, if roughhewn, ones. He says they are so rapt in the love of the Lord that their laughter, their weeping or their lapsing into silence come from that deep adoration.

They care not for the conventions of society and are focused only on the True Name. The point here is to contrast their behaviour with the worldly ones who will laugh when it benefits them, and cry only because it suits their purpose. In contrast, these men of God in His love laugh or weep innocently and only from thoughts of the Lord. Gyani Maskin explains it well in his audio-commentary when he says most laughter arises from seeing the shortcomings, troubles or the downfall of others. But the true man of God, the real devotee cries or laughs when he sees his own shortcomings, and may cry when he is highly moved by his love for the Lord. His silence is also for introspection and not meant to hurt anybody. In expressing these emotions they are not concerned if their behaviour may seem odd, or how the onlookers may react. They are not bothered by the opinions of men. Their only concern is their relationship with the Lord and with their own inner selves.

In line 7 the Guru says they sit at the Lord's door, and ask only from Him, eating whatever He provides. This is meant to describe a state of inner contentment which comes naturally to a person truly devoted to the Lord. Such contented ones do not go seeking help from humans because their faith in the Lord is total. The Lord's door is the only one they knock at. From Him alone do they ask. And in full acceptance and contentment they eat what the Lord has in His grace chosen to bestow. Bhai Vir Singh has in his *Panj granthi* rendered this a bit differently. He puts it as, "I sit at the door of these ones who are beloved of the Lord and seek alms from them, when they give me the gift of the Lord's Name I will imbibe it." Prof. Talib says, "Sitting at the Lord's doorstep provision I beg." Prof. Sahib Singh says, "They seek the food of His Name from the Lord and eat when He gives." Dr. Gopal Singh, Prof. Teja Singh and Dada Chellaram share a similar view. Thus, Bhai Vir Singh implies that the Guru is saying he waits at the door of these beloved of the Lord. Prof. Talib sees it as the Guru saying that he waits at the Lord's door. The third view is the one followed by Prof. Sahib Singh and others who see it as a reference to these beloved of the Lord who sit at the door of the Lord alone seeking His Name, and then happily accept whatever He gives. The various renderings have their own merit, but the latter one seems here more appealing.

In line 8 the Guru says there is only one Court, one Pen and all of us will gather in that Court. The reference is to the fact that the entire world is His creation and each part thereof; each person is in the final reckoning answerable to Him. These men of God immersed in Him know this reality, that there is one Divine Court where all of us will have to appear for judgement. Earthly powers therefore do not matter. There is but one Pen that writes down the fates of all as the Guru says in the *Japji Sahib, pauṛi* 16, "jee jāt ranga(n) kay nām sabhna likhiya vuṛi kalām", meaning that the Lord has written from the beginning their fates. So, seeking betterment from earthly powers is pointless. In that court for the final judgement will all gather, whether big or small, good or evil. There is only one authority whose decisions, therefore, we need to bother about.

In line 9 the Guru concludes by saying that at the Lord's door will account be taken like oil is extracted from oilseeds. Many learned ones interpret this line as, "The evil ones, the sinners will there be crushed as oilseed is crushed in the mill." Bhai Vir Singh however puts it as, "When He takes account it will be like oil being extracted from seed." This seems the more appealing construction, being more in consonance with the concept of a loving, forgiving Lord. The connotation of the sinner being crushed is too reminiscent of the Hell described in many religious belief systems. However, this is not so in Sikhism. The Lord is kind, loving and benevolent and just; a doting father who wants His children to improve and is happy when good men do good deeds and saddened by evil. The only hell for a believer in Sikhism is to be distanced from the Lord and being thrust back into the cycle of births. These births can even be regressive into cruder human lives or even into an animal existence, depending on the merits of our deeds. But the image of the Lord as a torturer fails altogether to fit into the Sikh view. That is where Bhai Vir Singh's interpretation fits in well. The rendering of our accounts in His court is rigorous but totally fair. No fact about us, none of our actions in this world will there remain hidden. All truth will come pouring out in His court, like oil comes pouring out from the oil mill. It is the rigour of the examination that is referred to here. In this context and on the same lines, Guru Nanak has said in *Rāg Māru*, *Mahla* 1, on page 1028 of the *SGGS*, "lekha lījai til jiu pīṛi", meaning the rendering of the account will be as strict as sesame seeds being crushed.

In this, the 20th, *pauṛi* the Guru says:

ਪਉੜੀ ॥	Pauṛi.
ਆਪੇ ਹੀ ਕਰਣਾ ਕੀਓ ਕਲ ਆਪੇ ਹੀ ਤੈ ਧਾਰੀਐ ॥	Āpay hee karṇa kiu kal āpay hee tai dhārīai

ਦੇਖਹਿ ਕੀਤਾ ਆਪਣਾ ਧਰਿ ਕਚੀ ਪਕੀ ਸਾਰੀਐ॥	Dekhay kīta āpṇa dhar kachi pakki sārīai
ਜੋ ਆਇਆ ਸੋ ਚਲਸੀ ਸਭੁ ਕੋਈ ਆਈ ਵਾਰੀਐ ॥	Jo aiya so chalsi sabh ko āyi vārīai
ਜਿਸ ਕੇ ਜੀਅ ਪਰਾਣ ਹਹਿ ਕਿਉ ਸਾਹਿਬੁ ਮਨਹੁ ਵਿਸਾਰੀਐ ॥	Jiskay jīa parāṇ haih kiu sāhib manoh visārīai
ਆਪਣ ਹਥੀ ਆਪਣਾ ਆਪੇ ਹੀ ਕਾਜੁ ਸਵਾਰੀਐ ॥੨੦॥	Āpaṇ hathi āpṇa āpay hee kāj sawārīai [20]

Glossary:

ਕਰਣਾ	Karṇa	Forms, creation
ਕਲ	Kal	Power
ਧਰਿ	Dhar Kept	(good or bad ones)
ਕਚੀ ਪਕੀ	Kachi pakki	All kinds, good or bad

Simply translated this *pauṛi* says that the Lord has created everything and His Power sustains the universe. He watches over His creation, the created beings are like pieces in a board game, some good some bad. When our turn comes we will all have to go, just like the pieces in a board game. We must never forget the Lord because our very existence is in His hands. We have been accorded this gift of the human form and this is our chance to follow His path and realize Him. In our own hands lies the performance of this task. This is to be understood always to mean that our efforts are important but that these must be imbued with prayer to the Lord. Ultimately, of course, our fate will be determined by the Lord's Will. The task of approaching the Creator is not for some other person to perform on our behalf. It has to do be done *āpaṇ hathhi* (by ourselves), fixing our minds on Him, disciplining our inner selves and making all effort to control our *haumai*. Let us now look at it in more detail.

In line 1, the Guru says the Lord has created everything and by His power is it sustained. The word *kall* means might or power. He alone is the Creator, so all that we see is there by His Will alone. He is also manifest in every part of it, or in other words His *kal* (power) infuses every part of creation, and thus is it sustained. Some learned ones have rendered this in a slightly different manner, but this is the view adopted by most of them, and it is an appealing interpretation.

In the 2nd line the Guru says the Lord watches over His creation. The word *sārīai* comes from *sāri* meaning 'pieces used in a game' such as the pieces used in chess; or in the ancient Indian game of *chaupaṛ*, where the pieces were specifically called *narad* and were moved around a cross-shaped board made of cloth. These could during the game be taken and removed from the game but could then be brought back during the course of further play. The Guru is comparing the created beings to these *narads* in the *chaupaṛ*. The same also would apply to the pieces on a chessboard which once taken are returned to the board when a new game is set up. The Guru is saying the human beings are like the *sāri* in that they die and then come back in another birth. The same concept was stated by him also in *Rāg Āsa*, *Mahla* 1, page 26 *patti*, *SGGS*, where the Guru says, "babbay bāji khelaṇ lagga chaupaṛ kītay chār juga. Jīa jant sabh sāri kītay pāsa dhālaṇ āp lagga", meaning that He has created the four *Yugas* as the *chaupaṛ* cloth on which the game is played by Him with the created beings as the *sāri* (pieces used in the game). The Guru says here that these *narads* are *kachi pakki*, meaning that some have attained the right stage of spiritual growth while others still lag behind. Literally, it means 'ripe and unripe', and the Guru is terming the ego-driven ones as *kachi* and the good ones as *pakki*. The allusion is also to the abrasive ones spoken of in the *sloks*. The unripe ones are obviously sour, unpleasant and tart – just like the man who speaks *phikka*. The Lord has placed us all on this earth as *narads* and watches over both the *kachi* (the imperfect), and the *pakki* (the perfect or the good ones). Both types are equally subject to His law.

In line 3 the Guru says when our turn comes we will all have to go. The analogy of the *chaupaṛ* game is continued. When its turn comes the piece will have to go regardless of whether it is *kachi* or *pakki*. The game will go on with some pieces leaving the board altogether. The game of life on this created world is played by that single player, the Lord, and He alone will determine when it is the turn of which piece to leave the scene.

In line 4 the Guru says why forget the Lord in whose hands is our very existence. The *narad* is moved inexorably, when the Lord has so determined. In other words, human beings will reside on this earth at the Lord's pleasure. Our very existence is in His hands to take away as and when He so desires. He must be a very foolish person who can forget this momentous reality and become engrossed in the ephemeral pleasures around us, and let his ego rule him so completely that he forgets death, and forgets too, the existence of the Lord and the fact that He can take away in a trice all these baubles, nay, our very existence away. Remember Him always, therefore, says the Guru.

In the last line the Guru says, in your own hands lies the success of the task for which we have been granted this human birth. What is this task the Guru refers to? It is nothing else but to attain reunion with the Lord, from whom this soul was separated, and is kept away by the actions of this body in this world. For this we need to break through this veil of illusion into which we have trapped ourselves. For this we will need to seek instruction from the *Satguru*, follow the discipline the enlightened ones have prescribed, and work to purify our inner selves to the level we may become worthy of receiving His grace. For achieving this end the most vital practice is *Nām Simran* – lauding the Lord, taking His Name with each breath. This is not a task to be delegated to another. Unfortunately, today, in the world of religion and spirituality, commerce has so intruded that even worship is sought to be done for money, through surrogates. Thus, we have the rich paying handsome sums to have religious rites performed for them. Among Hindus there is the performance of *yagyas* and *havans* (religious rites); and among Sikhs performing *akhand pātths* (an uninterrupted reading of the *SGGS* usually taking 48 hours and done by a relay of *granthīs* taking turns). People will pay professionals to recite the Name and read the *Gurbāṇi* on their behalf. What a travesty this is of the method prescribed by the Guru! It is like asking someone to eat on your behalf when you are hungry. The task of approaching the Creator is not some other persons to perform on our behalf. It has to do be done by ourselves, fixing our minds on Him and disciplining our inner selves, making all efforts to kill our *haumai*. The task is ours alone, and so the Guru says, perform it *āpaṇ hathhi* (with your own hands).

PAUṚI 21

This *pauṛi* and the two attached *sloks*, both by the second Nanak, touch on the relationship between man and his Lord. In the first of these the Guru says:

ਸਲੋਕ ਮਹਲਾ: ੨	Slok Mahla: 2
ਏਹ ਕਿਨੇਹੀ ਆਸਕੀ ਦੂਜੈ ਲਗੈ ਜਾਇ ॥	Eh kanehi āski dūjai laggai jāye
ਨਾਨਕ ਆਸਕੁ ਕਾਂਢੀਐ ਸਦ ਹੀ ਰਹੈ ਸਮਾਇ ॥	Nanak āsak kānddhīai sad hee rahai samāye
ਚੰਗੈ ਚੰਗਾ ਕਰਿ ਮੰਨੇ ਮੰਦੈ ਮੰਦਾ ਹੋਇ॥	Changay changa kar mannay mandai manda hoye
ਆਸਕੁ ਏਹੁ ਨ ਆਖੀਐ ਜਿ ਲੇਖੈ ਵਰਤੈ ਸੋਇ ॥੧॥	Āsak eh na ākhiyai je lekhai vartai soye. 1.

Glossary:

ਦੂਜੈ	Dūjai	Another (not the Lord)
ਕਾਂਢੀਐ	Kānddhīai	Is said
ਮੰਦੈ	Mandai	Bad
ਲੇਖੈ	Lekhai	Accounts

Simply translated this *slok* says what sort of love is it that goes seeking another. The true lover is one who is totally immersed at all times. If a devotee starts to label some things or events as bad and some as good then his devotion is not true. The one who approaches his love like an accountant counting profits is no true lover, for true love is undemanding and seeks not return favours. Let us now look at it in more detail.

In line 1 the Guru says what sort of love is this that goes seeking someone other than the Lord. Love, or devotion, to the Lord has to be focused and fixed on Him alone. If the focus is distracted and you have love in your hearts for not the Lord alone but also for other, lesser, powers or for things material, the attractions of this world, then your love is not pure. It is then flawed and cannot be called true love at all. So the Guru asks, what sort of love is it that gets diverted and is attracted to persons or things other than the Lord.

In line 2 the Guru says the true lover is one who is totally immersed in the Lord at all times. Such a devotee has no other allurements diverting him. At all times is his mind fixed on the Lord alone, his true love.

In line 3 the Guru says that if someone starts labeling whatever the Lord bestows as good or bad, then he is no true devotee. The allusion is to the need for total acceptance of the Lord's Will. True love is always blind to any flaws in the beloved. The Lord is of course a beloved without a flaw, and perfect in every way. But yet do many of us, imperfect in our devotion, question His actions. Because whatever He does is as per His own higher plan. There are times when we fail to understand and start raising questions on what happens to us. We are only too happy to accept what suits us, but will complain about what, in our ego-centered blindness, we did not want. By our own flawed standards will we assign approval to the Lord's actions. This is not love, says the Guru, as he elaborates in the next line.

In line 4 he says the one who approaches his love like an accountant is no true lover. In our foolish way in our dealings with Him we start assigning values to His actions. We start saying the Lord has done a particular thing which was good for me, but some other things he did were bad. Then we go a further step down and fall into the trap of trying to propitiate Him through offerings and *pūjas*. We will often see people saying they will recite such and such *Bāṇi* such and such number of times if the Lord does such and such thing for them. Once the love enters into this account-keeping, faith gets shaky. We have in other words stopped loving the Lord and have instead entered into a commercial transaction at the spiritual level with Him. This is not love, says the Guru, and it will not take us to Him. For that to happen we must follow the dictum, **"ਸੇਵਾ ਕਰਤ ਹੋਇ ਨਿਹਕਾਮੀ॥ ਤਿਸ ਕਉ ਹੋਤ ਪਰਾਪਤਿ ਸੁਆਮੀ॥"** – "seva karat hoye nehkāmi. Tis ko hote prāpat swāmi", meaning that our service must be without expectation of return; then only will we reach the Lord. Our love has to be unquestioning;

we must accept whatever comes from Him and must always keep our mind fixed on him.

In the next *slok* the Guru tells us more on the subject of the flawed devotee. He says:

ਮ: ੨	M: 2
ਸਲਾਮੁ ਜਬਾਬੁ ਦੋਵੈ ਕਰੇ ਮੁੰਢਹੁ ਘੁਥਾ ਜਾਹਿ ॥	Salām jabāb dovai karay munddho ghuthha jāhay
ਨਾਨਕ ਦੋਵੈ ਕੂੜੀਆਰ ਥਾਇ ਨ ਕਾਈ ਪਾਇ ॥੨॥	Nanak dovai kūṛiyar thāye na kāyi pāye. 2.

Glossary:

ਸਲਾਮੁ	Salām	Salutations
ਜਬਾਬੁ	Jabāb	Objections, demurring
ਮੁੰਢਹੁ	Munddho	From the root

In this brief *slok* the Guru says the devotee who on the one hand bends his head in acceptance but then also raises questions, will be cut off from the root. We remember the Lord because our inner self knows He is the root from which we have sprung. It is because of Him that we exist in the midst of this vast and mysterious creation. To remember Him keeps us spiritually alive. But remembering Him implies accepting Him totally and without reservation as our Lord and Master. If someone instead seeks to establish this relationship on the basis of convenience then the link to the root is very difficult to establish. When we bow in acceptance if it suits us, but then in defiance raise demur when we do not find something to our liking, then the relationship is seriously flawed. In this case, we are not accepting Him as our Master but are only pretending to do so, and we seek the relationship to exist on our terms and for our own selfish material benefits. Thus is the link with our root destroyed. No relationship with the Lord is possible when we are even occasionally in defiance of His commands.

In line 2 the Guru says both, the acceptance and the defying, are false and will take us nowhere. The *salām*, the acceptance, is tainted when it is conditional and may quickly turn into dissatisfaction if the selfish desires of such a one are not fulfilled. If the acceptance is marked by the expectation of reward then also it is but a false pretence. The questioning and the defiance are without doubt going to take us further from Him. Both such actions are wrong and will result in our not reaching the Lord. Dada Chellaram sees this line slightly differently and says, "Nanak, false ones have both these. They have no place anywhere." The meaning is clear enough, however, and the Guru is exhorting us to ensure our acceptance of the Lord's Will is total and unconditional.

In this, the 21st, *pauṛi* the Guru tells us to remember that the Lord is the only bestower of peace and we must keep in mind our long term aim, of attaining liberation. He says:

ਪਉੜੀ ॥	Pauṛi
ਜਿਤੁ ਸੇਵਿਐ ਸੁਖੁ ਪਾਈਐ ਸੋ ਸਾਹਿਬੁ ਸਦਾ ਸਮਾਲੀਐ ॥	Jit seviai sukh pāiai so sahib sadā samālīai
ਜਿਤੁ ਕੀਤਾ ਪਾਈਐ ਆਪਣਾ ਸਾ ਘਾਲ ਬੁਰੀ ਕਿਉ ਘਾਲੀਐ ॥	Jit kīta paīai āpṇa sa ghāl buri kiu ghālīai
ਮੰਦਾ ਮੂਲਿ ਨ ਕੀਚਈ ਦੇ ਲੰਮੀ ਨਦਰਿ ਨਿਹਾਲੀਐ ॥	Manda mūl na kīchyi day lami nadar nihālīai
ਜਿਉ ਸਾਹਿਬ ਨਾਲਿ ਨ ਹਾਰੀਐ ਤੇਵੇਹਾ ਪਾਸਾ ਢਾਲੀਐ ॥	Jiu sahib nāl na hārīai teveha pāsa ddhālīai
ਕਿਛੁ ਲਾਹੇ ਉਪਰਿ ਘਾਲੀਐ ॥੨੧॥	Kicch lāhay uppar ghālīai [21]

Glossary:

ਸੇਵਿਐ	Seviai	Serving
ਸਮ੍ਹਾਲੀਐ	Samālīai	Contemplate
ਘਾਲ	Ghāl	Activity, deed
ਨਿਹਾਲੀਐ	Nihālīai	Watch
ਪਾਸਾ	Pāsa	Game
ਲਾਹੇ	Lāhay	Profit

Simply translated this *pauṛi* says always contemplate on the Lord serving whom we gain peace and joy. When we know we will have to reap what we sow then why plant the crop of bad deeds. Do not indulge in bad actions and take the long term view of what will benefit you. Play the game so that you do not have to go before the Lord as a loser. Earn some profit from your actions. Let us look now at it in detail.

In line 1 the Guru says, always contemplate on the Lord serving whom we gain internal peace and lasting joy. The theme of fixing one's mind on the Lord is here intertwined with the message that the joys of this world are ephemeral. If we go seeking contentment in worldly things, we will soon find that we are but chasing a chimera. Temporary ease may occasionally come, and some of the things may even occasionally seem especially satisfactory. But in reality we will find that these joys will vanish soon enough. The only joy that is permanent is to be found in serving the Lord. And what does service here imply? The Lord is after all not lacking for anything at all, nor does He in any way need any help that we mere mortals could offer through our service. The only service we can offer to Him is to fix our minds on Him, live a clean life as prescribed by the Guru and sing His praises, and live in a state of complete surrender. Thus is He served; and simultaneously we are uplifted through these efforts and of course by His grace.

In line 2 the Guru says when we know we will have to reap what we sow, then why plant the crop of bad deeds. The concept of our own selves being solely and totally responsible for our own actions is inbuilt into the Sikh belief system. Repeatedly are we told this in the *SGGS*, for instance, in *Rāg Āsa*, *Mahla* 5, page 406 and also *Rāg Māru*, *Mahla* 5, page 1098, "aih kar karay tay aih kar pāye" – what you do with one hand will come back to you on the other. We were also told in the *Japji Sahib*, *pauṛi* 4, that, "karmi āvay kapṛa nadri mokh dwār" – our actions will determine the body, the birth we are allotted. Again the Guru says in the *Japji Sahib* in the final *slok*, "karmi āpo āpṇi kay neṛay kay dūre", meaning by the merit of our actions is determined our proximity to the Lord. In spite of these clear injunctions, deluded by the false glitter of this world, or misled by our own ego-driven ways, men do err and so actions happen that are wrong or hurtful to others. The Guru is reminding us not to be under any illusions on the subject; he says that if our deeds are bad then the accountability is entirely our own. So, refrain from sowing evil lest you be compelled later to reap it yourself. It will of course always be in the Lord's hands as to when to grant us His grace.

In line 3 the Guru elaborates this further and says do not indulge in bad actions, and take the long-term view of what is good for you. If we do not show the foresight to recognize that our own bad actions of today will tomorrow become the millstone round our necks, then are we doomed to suffer. This balance sheet of the good we do and the bad we perpetrate will travel with us across births. Even if are unable today to visualize what those births will be, the Guru has made it clear often enough that the consequences of the evil done today will appear soon enough, often within this lifetime. Do not cause injury to others, or take what is not honestly earned by your own hard work. Let all your actions be governed by the realization that the effect of each action is going to stay forever with us.

In line 4 the Guru says play the game in such manner that you do not have to appear before your Master as a loser. If our actions are evil, then the purpose for which the Lord granted us this invaluable human form would have been defeated. The Lord sent us here to give us an opportunity to win back our place by His side. For that He gave us free will to choose the right path; and He sent us enlightened Masters, who showed us the right path, and brought His word to us. Their message is ever available to guide us out of this earthly web of entanglements. We have the option to follow any Master we choose. For a Sikh the Master is the *SGGS*, the ever present visible form of the Gurus. If we sincerely follow the prescribed path, and discipline and purify our inner selves so as to be ready to receive Him, then success in the game is ours. If we choose the opposite path we may succeed in giving ourselves some passing moments of sensual pleasure or momentary delight in a sense of ownership and power; but the game would have been lost. Do not play it in this wrong fashion, says the Guru.

In line 5 the Guru concludes by saying that we should earn some profit from our actions. As Dr. Gopal Singh puts it, "And strive only for that which brings thee True Profit". What is this true profit the Guru is saying we can hope to gain? It is the greatest of all possible rewards, union with the Lord and the shattering of the chain of rebirths into which all beings are bound. So we must follow the roadmap the true Guru delineates for us and through controlling our wandering mind, and ever singing His praises we can hope to be one day granted liberation, of course only if and when it pleases Him. Even if the chains that tie us into the cycle of births are not destined as yet to be broken, we will at least be assured of a better, higher more godfearing next incarnation where we will be better oriented towards godliness. As the Guru said in the *Japji Sahib*, "**ਕਰਮੀ ਆਵੈ ਕਪੜਾ**" – "karmi āvai kapṛa", meaning through our actions is the incarnation determined. There is thus profit in playing the game this way. So fix your mind on Him and recite His Name.

PAURI 22

This, the 22nd *pauri* has five *sloks*, all by the second Nanak, and relate mainly to the subject of the relationship between the human and his God. The first *slok* says:

ਸਲੋਕ ਮਹਲਾ: ੨	Slok Mahla: 2
ਚਾਕਰੁ ਲਗੈ ਚਾਕਰੀ ਨਾਲੇ ਗਾਰਬੁ ਵਾਦੁ ॥	Chākar laggai chākri nālay gārab vād
ਗਲਾ ਕਰੇ ਘਣੇਰੀਆ ਖਸਮ ਨ ਪਾਏ ਸਾਦੁ ॥	Galla karey ghaṇeria khasam na pāye sād
ਆਪੁ ਗਵਾਇ ਸੇਵਾ ਕਰੇ ਤਾ ਕਿਛੁ ਪਾਏ ਮਾਨੁ ॥	Āp gavāye seva karay ta kicch pāye mān
ਨਾਨਕ ਜਿਸ ਨੋ ਲਗਾ ਤਿਸ ਮਿਲੈ ਲਗਾ ਸੋ ਪਰਵਾਨੁ ॥੧॥	Nanak jis no lagga tis milai lagga so parvān. 1.

Glossary:

ਚਾਕਰੁ	Chākar	Servant
ਗਾਰਬੁ	Gārab	Pride
ਘਣੇਰੀਆ	Ghaṇerīya	Thick, plentiful
ਸਾਦੁ	Sād	Enjoyment
ਗਵਾਇ	Gavāye	Loses
ਪਰਵਾਨੁ	Parvān	Accepted

Simply translated this *slok* says that if the servant while serving is also disputatious and haughty he will not find the approval of his Master. The one, who selflessly serves, suppressing his ego, will find honour. He should so serve the Master to whom he is attached that his service is accepted and he is united with the Master. Let us now look at it in detail.

In lines 1 and 2 the Guru says if the servant while serving is also disputatious and haughtily argues, he will not find the approval of his Master. The allusion really would cover practically each one of us. We may deem ourselves faithful servants of the Lord and try to dutifully observe the discipline laid down by the *Satguru*, by way of prescribed devotions. But simultaneously most of us will also be raising demur and questioning whenever something we deem unpleasant happens to us. This is because our egos tell us we are wise and we know what is best for us. Our efforts then are to seek from the Lord what we deem to be good for us. In other words, we seek to have events moulded closer to our own desires. When our wishes remain unfulfilled, we question the Lord. Such behaviour obviously shows pride and a lack of acceptance of His Will. This is not true service, says the Guru, and such a servant will not win the Lord's favour. The example given by the Guru is from everyday life. A servant who while serving is arrogant and disputatious, and chatters a lot proclaiming that he is the true servant, is not an acceptable servant. The same is the position of the devotee in relationship to His Lord.

In the concluding lines, the 3rd and 4th, the same point is further spelt out. The Guru says the one who selflessly serves, suppressing and overcoming his ego, will find honour. Such a servant, who has won the battle against his ego, attaching himself to the Lord will find acceptance with Him. In other words, the sign of the value of such service, if it is selfless, will be that the devotee's conduct meets with the Lord's approval and he finds himself on the road to God-realization. As Dr. Gopal Singh puts it, "For approved is he who merges in whom he loves". Prof. Talib says, "By union with Him to whom is the devotee attached, shall such find approval". Simply put, the service is acceptable when we selflessly attach ourselves to the Lord, and it shall be rewarded with union with the Lord.

In the next *slok*, the second Nanak speaks to us of the need for humans to have a clean mind, and then only to expect good to come to them. He says:

ਮ: ੨	M: 2
ਜੋ ਜੀਇ ਹੋਇ ਸੁ ਉਗਵੈ ਮੁਹ ਕਾ ਕਹਿਆ ਵਾਉ ॥	Jo jīa hoye so ugvai muh ka kahia vāo

ਬੀਜੇ ਬਿਖੁ ਮੰਗੈ ਅੰਮ੍ਰਿਤੁ ਵੇਖਹੁ ਏਹੁ ਨਿਆਉ ॥੨॥	Bijay bikh mangai amrit vekho eh niāo. 2.

Glossary:

ਜੀਇ	Jīa	In the mind
ਵਾਉ	Vāo	Wind, air
ਨਿਆਉ	Niāo	Justice

In this brief *slok* the Guru says whatever is in the mind will bear consequences for us. The words we utter differently from what is really in our minds are nothing but empty air. The Guru points to the irony of how some of us sow poison yet expect that it will bear fruit from which nectar will be obtained.

The learned ones have rendered the 1st line broadly on similar lines though with small differences in nuance. Thus, Macauliffe puts it as, "what a man hath in his heart cometh forth; lip worship is of no avail." Prof. Talib renders it similarly as, "whatever is in the mind alone has effect: mere outward utterance is of little worth." Dr. Gopal Singh, Bhai Vir Singh and Prof. Teja Singh also follow the same line. Prof. Sahib Singh paraphrases it to the same effect, saying that the fruit that man reaps depends not on the words he utters but on what was really in his mind.

The Guru is telling us that putting up a show and uttering nice platitudes may work in this world but when we appear before the Lord our posturing will be seen for what it really is, empty wind. It is the intention within that determines in the divine court the worth of our actions. The fruit that we gain will be sweet if the intention behind the action is pure – for in the Lord's presence no camouflage will work and our inner reality will be seen for what it is, regardless of what show we may be putting up for the benefit of the world of men.

The irony however is that all too often our intentions are less than pure; so regardless of our efforts to hide behind nice words we are in reality planting poisonous weeds through such actions. It is ironical but a fact of life that we nevertheless will wish that the fruit should be beneficial to us. The lesson we are being given here is that the fruit of poisonous seed is never going to be anything but poison; it will never be nectar, however much we may wish it. The wish to reap nectar when we have sown poison is not justice, says the Guru. Be aware that only when the intention is pure will the fruit be good; words alone, however sweet, will produce no desirable fruit, and are merely like the wind.

In the third *slok* the second Nanak speaks to us on another everyday reality, while delivering to us a deep spiritual lesson. He says:

ਮ: ੨	M: 2
ਨਾਲਿ ਇਆਣੇ ਦੋਸਤੀ ਕਦੇ ਨ ਆਵੈ ਰਾਸਿ ॥	Nāl eyāṇay dosti kaday na āvai rās
ਜੇਹਾ ਜਾਣੈ ਤੇਹੋ ਵਰਤੈ ਵੇਖਹੁ ਕੋ ਨਿਰਜਾਸਿ ॥	Jeha jāṇai teho vartai vekho ko nirjās
ਵਸਤੁ ਅੰਦਰਿ ਵਸਤੁ ਸਮਾਵੈ ਦੂਜੀ ਹੋਵੈ ਪਾਸਿ ॥	Vastu andar vasat samāvai dūji hovai pās
ਸਾਹਿਬ ਸੇਤੀ ਹੁਕਮ ਨ ਚਲੈ ਕਹੀ ਬਣੈ ਅਰਦਾਸਿ ॥	Sahib seti hukam na challai kahi baṇai ardās
ਕੂੜਿ ਕਮਾਣੈ ਕੂੜੋ ਹੋਵੈ ਨਾਨਕ ਸਿਫਤਿ ਵਿਗਾਸਿ ॥੩॥	Kūr kamāṇai kūṛo hovai Nanak sipht vigās. 3.

Glossary:

ਜੇਹਾ ਜਾਣੈ	Jeha jāṇai	What the understanding is
ਨਿਰਜਾਸਿ	Nirjās	Judgement
ਸਮਾਵੈ	Samāvai	Merges
ਪਾਸਿ	Pās	To a side
ਵਿਗਾਸਿ	Vigās	Development

Simply translated this *slok* says that friendship with the unwise will never be of avail, and it can be tested that one's conduct will only be as sound as one's understanding. A thing will merge in another only when the previous thing is kept aside. In other words, godliness enters when the ego is kept aside. In dealing with the Lord not command but only prayer can work. Falsehood will beget falsehood, but lauding the Lord will bring joy. Let us now look at it in more detail.

In lines 1 and 2 the Guru says that friendship with the unwise will never be of avail and it can be tested that one's conduct will only be as sound as one's level of understanding. Bhai Vir Singh renders it as, "Friendship with the ignorant is not befitting, for he is limited in his conduct by the limits of his knowledge. This can be easily judged by anyone. If you want to remove the ignorance then give him knowledge which will gradually drive out the grime of ignorance." He then renders the 3rd line as, "When knowledge enters ignorance will be expelled as a stream of fresh water will drive out dirty water gradually from a vessel."

Prof. Sahib Singh's rendering is similar, but he adds to it by saying that as the friendship with the ignorant is useless, so is listening to our minds. He says the mind is foolish and always goes chasing after worldly attractions. If we try to be friends with it, if we follow the dictates of the mind, we will wander fruitlessly always. Bhai Vir Singh also, in the footnotes of his commentary in the *Panj granthi* gives this as an alternate view. Prof. Teja Singh also says, "Attachment to the infantine self does never come right. With it man acts only so far as it enables him to see; let anybody test it." In the context here the view taken by Prof. Sahib Singh and some other learned ones seems more appealing, that the Guru is telling us to beware the dictates of our minds which are always fickle. When we act from ego we will be distanced from the Lord, for, as the Guru said in *Rāg Vadhans*, *Mahla 3*, *SGGS*, page 560, "**ਹਉਮੈ ਨਾਵੈ ਨਾਲਿ ਵਿਰੋਧੁ ਹੈ ਦੁਇ ਨ ਵਸਹਿ ਇਕ ਠਾਇ॥**" – "haumai nāvai nāl virodh hai doye na vaseh ik tthāye", meaning that the ego and the 'Name' are mutually exclusive; if one comes the other goes. The Guru, while imparting to us a spiritual lesson, that becoming a slave to our capricious minds is a losing proposition, is also here referring to the oft-tested reality we would all have at some time experienced – that attachments to the unwise lead only to sorrow.

In line 3 the Guru says a thing merges in the other only when the thing previously filling the space is kept *pās* (aside). There are differing interpretations of this line among the learned ones. We discussed Bhai Vir Singh's view in the first line above. Prof. Sahib Singh and Macauliffe share a similar view. Prof. Talib, however, says, "In the supreme reality is the self absorbed when duality gets smashed." Thus, he reaches roughly the same conclusion even though, unlike most others, he takes *pās* to be a form of *pāsh* which he says means smashed. Some other learned ones see it as, "Worldly love has first to be cast aside then only the love of the Lord enters," which is close to what Prof. Talib has said. Only Dr. Gopal Singh sees it a bit differently and renders it as, "Yea the like merges in its like, but unlikes stand apart." The view taken by Bhai Vir Singh stresses on not only the cleansing out but also on the method thereof, which is to gradually insert fresh, clean matter which will push out the unclean stuff within until all is pure. This concept is important because the other way of removing the existing matter envisaged by the ancients was to empty the mind altogether, creating a vacuum into which divinity can flow. This in real life terms would indicate a withdrawal from everyday life. This concept, however, is not consistent with the life affirming, participative nature of Sikhism. Indeed does the existing soiled matter have to be removed from our inner selves, but this has to happen steadily with the infusion of the fresh water of the Lord's devotion. Then will the mind become pure and merge into the One Reality. All this happens while we live fully involved in the life of the householder, earning an honest living, sharing with others and constant recitation of His Name.

In line 4 the Guru says in dealing with the Lord, it is not command but only prayer that will work. Obviously if we accept someone as our master then the only relationship we can have with them is that of a servitor. For that relationship to hold, the only proper form of addressing the master is prayer. There can be no question of a servant issuing commands to a master. The moment that rule is broken the relationship would stand repudiated. So, says the Guru, approach the Lord as a servant would his master.

In the last line the Guru says falsehood begets falsehood, or evil, while lauding the Lord shall bring joy. In this, and to an extent in the previous line, the Guru is summing up for us the lesson of this *pauṛi*. He tells us to free ourselves from the diversionary pleasures and thoughts that our mind is always leading us into. We must form instead a relationship with the Lord, which will gradually cleanse our inner selves. If we practice falsehood, under the control of our egos, then the outcome can only be evil. Our selves will get more and more embroiled in worldly delusions. But if the mind is fixed instead on the Lord and His praises are sung then evil starts departing from within us, and what ensues is spiritual growth. Ultimately we can on this path hope for liberation and eternal bliss.

In the next *slok*, on the same theme the Guru says:

ਮ: ੨	M: 2
ਨਾਲਿ ਇਆਣੇ ਦੋਸਤੀ ਵਡਾਰੂ ਸਿਉ ਨੇਹੁ ॥	Nāl eyāṇay dosti vaddāru siu neh(u)
ਪਾਣੀ ਅੰਦਰਿ ਲੀਕ ਜਿਉ ਤਿਸ ਦਾ ਥਾਉ ਨ ਥੇਹੁ ॥੪॥	Pāṇi andar līk jiu tis da thau na thheh. 4.

Glossary:

ਵਡਾਰੂ	Vaddāru	One higher than oneself

This brief *slok* refers to everyday life and gives us some practical wisdom, that friendship with the ignorant, or immature, and love for the one higher than us is ephemeral like a line drawn on water. For a relationship, like friendship or love to exist there has to be some compatibility and some parity of status and capability. Absent, these the relationship will never be long lasting. *Vaddaru* here can be understood as referring to higher in either of the important parameters such as age or wealth, or learning, or wisdom. Any great disparity in these will ensure the relationship is short lived. The subject of relationship with the *eyāṇa* (immature or unwise person), we have of course discussed at length in the previous *slok* where the Guru had said in line 1 that, "nāl eyāṇay dosti kaday na āvai rās", meaning friendship with the immature will never be suatisfactory. Here also it could be taken to be referring to not only the immature human but also our minds. Thus, if we form too deep a fondness for our foolish mind and start following its wayward dictates we will have nothing to show for it at the end of the game. Bhai Vir Singh says *vaddaru* is also taken by some learned ones as 'traveller' and by some also as 'woman', but he says the correct meaning here should be elder or greater. This is the sense in which most of the learned ones take it. Thus, Prof. Talib renders it as "of a higher status". Macauliffe calls it "great man". Dada Chellaram puts it as "big folk", and Prof. Sahib Singh has translated it as "someone of higher status." However, Dr. Gopal Singh renders it as "egotist," and Prof. Teja Singh puts it as "the grandiose Pride". In the context here the view taken by most of the learned ones rendering it as "of higher status" seems more appealing.

In the next *slok* there is more on the subject of *eyāṇa*. The Guru says:

ਮ: ੨	M: 2
ਹੋਇ ਇਆਣਾ ਕਰੇ ਕੰਮੁ ਆਣਿ ਨ ਸਕੈ ਰਾਸਿ ॥	Hoye eyāṇa karay kamm āṇ na sakai rās
ਜੇ ਇਕ ਅਧ ਚੰਗੀ ਕਰੇ ਦੂਜੀ ਭੀ ਵੇਰਾਸਿ ॥੫॥	Je ik adh changi karay dūji bhi verās. 5.

Glossary:

ਵੇਰਾਸਿ	Verās	Wrongly, ineptly

This brief *slok* is again on the subject of our interaction with the immature one. The Guru says should the immature one attempt to do something he will not succeed. A stray success may come his way but the next effort will surely go awry.

The warning against the ignorant, the immature continue here. Should such a one undertake any task of some import he will normally mess it up. Yes, an occasional success may be noted but that will usually be an exception and soon the results will start going wrong again. The Guru is again asking to us to avoid the ignorant and the immature. Simultaneously, the Guru is implicitly conveying the message that the human mind is not a good guide since it is like the immature human, wayward and fickle. We must, therefore, overcome its control and fix our attention ever on the Lord.

In this, the 22nd *pauṛi*, with which these *sloks* were attached, the Guru speaks to us further on the relationship between man and his master, or the devotee and his Lord. This *pauṛi* is slightly different in structure from the rest in that it has six lines unlike the other 23 which have five each. The Guru says:

ਪਉੜੀ ॥	Pauṛi.
ਚਾਕਰੁ ਲਗੈ ਚਾਕਰੀ ਜੇ ਚਲੈ ਖਸਮੈ ਭਾਇ ॥	Chākar laggai chākri je chalai khasmai bhāye
ਹੁਰਮਤਿ ਤਿਸ ਨੋ ਅਗਲੀ ਓਹੁ ਵਜਹੁ ਭਿ ਦੂਣਾ ਖਾਇ ॥	Hurmat tis no agli oh vajoh bhi dūṇa khāye
ਖਸਮੈ ਕਰੇ ਬਰਾਬਰੀ ਫਿਰਿ ਗੈਰਤਿ ਅੰਦਰਿ ਪਾਇ ॥	Khasmai karay barābri phir gairat andar pāye
ਵਜਹੁ ਗਵਾਏ ਅਗਲਾ ਮੁਹੇ ਮੁਹਿ ਪਾਣਾ ਖਾਇ ॥	Vajoh gavāye agla muhay muh pāna khāye
ਜਿਸ ਦਾ ਦਿਤਾ ਖਾਵਣਾ ਤਿਸੁ ਕਹੀਐ ਸਾਬਾਸਿ ॥	Jis da ditā khāvṇa tis kahīyai sabās
ਨਾਨਕ ਹੁਕਮੁ ਨ ਚਲਈ ਨਾਲਿ ਖਸਮ ਚਲੈ ਅਰਦਾਸਿ ॥੨੨॥	Nanak hukam na chalyi nāl khasam chalai ardās. [22]

Glossary:

ਖਸਮੈ ਭਾਇ	Khasmai bhāye	According to the Lord's Will
ਹੁਰਮਤਿ	Hurmat	Respect
ਅਗਲੀ	Agli	Much
ਵਜਹੁ	Vajoh	Wages, stipend

ਗੈਰਤਿ	Gairat	Estrangement, shame, also pride & dignity
ਪਾਣਾ	Pāṇa	Footwear

Simply translated this *pauṛi* says that service to the Lord consists of acting according to His Will. The ones who do so will get much respect and double the wages. The ones who do not accept such service, but instead, deem themselves the equal of the Lord will only earn disgrace, lose their wages and get a shoe beating on their faces, meaning they will earn disgrace in the Divine Court. Praise always the Lord whose benevolence sustains us. Let us now look at it in more detail.

In lines 1 and 2 the Guru says service to the Lord is to act according to His Will. The ones who do so get much *hurmat* (respect) and double the *vajoh* (wages). The stress is on the humility in thinking and demeanour throughout these hymns, especially where the Guru is talking of our interaction with the Lord. Be like a servant, suggests the Guru. How does one become a servant to the Lord who is all powerful and the ultimate Bestower of all that exists? There is obviously no physical or material offering we can possibly make to that greatest of all Powers. The only service we can offer to Him, the Guru makes it clear once again here, is to live in total surrender to Him. Accept without demur or question whatever He may choose to give us. Do not indulge in both *salām* (salutations) and *jabāb* (argumentation); and do not indulge in *gārab vād*, as the Guru told us in the previous *slok*. Such a total and willing acceptance of His Will is the only service we humans can offer to the Omnipotent Lord. The Guru says if we do so we will get *hurmat* – respect and honor of a high degree. We will get also double the *vajoh* (wages), meaning that whatever we may have been entitled to on the basis of our *karam* will be added to by the Lord and, so to say, we will get a bonus. This term *vajoh* is used for a stipend, wages, and means of earning a living. The allusion is to the material rewards we seek in this world, as also to the level of acceptance in the Lord's court. The respect in the Lord's Court apart, the level of the earthly reward is also doubled, says the Guru, for one who wholeheartedly accepts the Lord as his master.

In lines 3 and 4 the opposite situation is described, of the one who does not accept the Lord as truly his master, the one who seeks not to serve Him but instead deems himself the equal of the Lord. The Guru says if someone dares vie with the Lord, he will only earn disgrace and lose his wages. The term *gairat* is from the Arabic meaning estrangement, alienation, shame or disgrace. It is also used for dignity, rightful pride or modesty. The appropriate meaning in the context here, however, has to be taken as 'disgrace', which is also how Prof. Sahib Singh renders it. Bhai Vir Singh sees it as "duality from the Lord", which also carries the same connotation, because the one who is estranged from the Lord is doomed to face disgrace. The other renderings by the learned ones are: "provokes the master" as Dr. Gopal Singh puts it; "will excite His jealousy" as Macauliffe says; "provoketh indignation" as Dada Chellaram and Prof. Teja Singh view it. The rendering as the Lord showing indignation or jealousy or provocation does not quite fit in the context. The Lord is supreme, the ever benevolent and it is unthinkable that traits and attributes like jealousy or indignation could be attributed to Him. The Lord of all that exists is not going to show annoyance or react with hurt pride just because some human has not shown Him due respect. The Guru says the one who accepts not the Lord will lose hope of any recompense. He gets no respect in the Lord's presence and little enough rewards on this Earth; Instead, he will be "beaten with shoes on his face", as the Guru says, meaning thoroughly put to disgrace.

In line 5 the Guru says praise that Lord by whose benevolence we are sustained. As Prof. Teja Singh says, "We should offer thanks to Him who gives us what we eat," or as Dr. Gopal singh says, "He whose sustenance sustains us, unto Him let us say 'All Hail'." This is how most learned ones have rendered this line. Accept that all we have in this world is but a gift from Him, and do not raise demur. Rather, always sing His praises.

In line 6 the Guru concludes with reiteration of the message that with the Lord not command but prayers only will work. Thus, in another way are we told to be humble and accept our position as the servant of that One Lord. Do not seek to claim equality with Him, or to seek to demand that He act according to our wishes. It is always the other way around. Mould yourself to His Will, accept and then success in this world as well as the next will come to us.

PAUṚI 23

There are two *sloks* attached with this *pauṛi*, both by the second Nanak. Here again he speaks to us on the subject of man's relationship with his Master. In the first *slok* he says:

ਸਲੋਕ ਮਹਲਾ: ੨	Slok Mahla: 2
ਏਹ ਕਿਨੇਹੀ ਦਾਤਿ ਆਪਸ ਤੇ ਜੋ ਪਾਈਐ ॥	Eh kinehi dāt āpas te jo pāīai
ਨਾਨਕ ਸਾ ਕਰਮਾਤਿ ਸਾਹਿਬ ਤੁਠੈ ਜੋ ਮਿਲੈ ॥	1] Nanak sa karmāt sahib tutthai jo milai. 1.

Glossary:

ਦਾਤਿ	Dāt	Gift, donation
ਕਰਮਾਤਿ	Karmāt	Gift, benediction

The Guru here touches upon a very important aspect of a seeker's approach to His Lord. He says that when a person is striving for something, whether material or spiritual, his attitude and his approach to the endeavour is a vital and important determinant of how fruitful the outcome will be. When he succeeds in such a mission, if he thinks the success is the result of his own prowess then he is indeed lost, he has not achieved real success. This is so because such an attitude would indicate that he undertook the task governed by his *haumai* (ego). And as we discussed in the *slok* with the previous *pauṛi*, the Guru has said, **"ਹਉਮੈ ਨਾਵੈ ਨਾਲ ਵਿਰੋਧੁ ਹੈ ਦੋਇ ਨ ਵਸੈ ਇਕ ਠਾਇ॥",**"haumai nāvay nāl virodh hai doye na vasai ik thai" meaning that *haumai* and spirituality cannot co-exist. So, the Guru is here telling us, if you have attained something and you think it is purely the outcome of your own exertions then obviously you are not willing to accept that it is a gift from the Lord. Then such success will only have further fed our ego and taken us down the wrong path, away from the Lord.

We have really achieved success when we fully accept that whatever we achieve is a gift from the Lord; a measure of His pleasure, His grace. When our actions are governed by the consciousness of the Lord as the all pervading, the only Reality, then will those actions be deemed as pleasing to the Lord. Then will our ego be under control and we will treat the fruit of the efforts as a gift that He did bestow on us. We will know that what He gives is for us the best possible endowment, the gift that He deemed to be suitable for us. When we recognize that what we have gained is not the result of our efforts but is a gift from the Lord then is our approach to the Lord, and to our own upliftment, the correct one. In simple terms when we undertake any action we must not worry about the result but concentrate only on putting in our best effort, leaving to the Lord to grant us what results He will.

In the next *slok*, the second Nanak tells us more about the relationship between man and his Lord. The Guru says:

ਮ: ੨	M: 2
ਏਹ ਕਿਨੇਹੀ ਚਾਕਰੀ ਜਿਤੁ ਭਉ ਖਸਮ ਨ ਜਾਇ ॥	Eh kinehi chākri jit bhau khasam na jāye
ਨਾਨਕ ਸੇਵਕੁ ਕਾਢੀਐ ਜਿ ਸੇਤੀ ਖਸਮ ਸਮਾਇ ॥੨॥	Nanak sevak kāddhiai je seti khasam samāye. 2.

Glossary:

ਚਾਕਰੀ	Chākrī	Servitude
ਖਸਮ	Khasam	Master
ਕਾਢੀਐ	Kāddhiai	Are said to be, pick

It is often the practice among some religious preachers to try and instil fear of the Lord into their audience. Some belief systems of course have the concept of hell where unthinkable tortures are inflicted on the erring soul, sometimes for eternity. These concepts came in handy for religious leaders to help keep their flocks on the straight and narrow path. The Lord in Sikhism is, however, viewed as the benevolent Creator, who permeates His creation and loves what He has wrought, the sustainer who sees His children through every difficult moment, and the bestower of the gift of His grace on His children. He is by no means a fearsome hard tyrant who will punish severely the slightest transgression. The Guru here says no, we must not dread the Lord, and our service is defective if fear dominates the relationship.

So, our relationship must not be dominated by a sense of fear. Humans may have cause to fear those who are oppressive and would hurt them, the tyrant, the killer, the aggressor. Why should we fear the Lord who is Love personified, who is the Creator, the Benefactor, the one who sustains? Our relationship with Him requires that it be full of love, respect and adoration, and when we must be in awe of His vast majesty. Respect and awe, and not fear, have to be the bedrock of our relationship. Yet do we find people frightening us with talk of different types of hell where we will undergo tortures for our sins. The Lord God, a torturer? The very thought is repugnant. Rightly, the Guru says, you are no true servant if you dread your Master. The true servant is one who gets absorbed in Him. Absorption, love, regard is how we need to approach the Lord.

Fear does in a way enter the relationship but only to the extent we are afraid to do wrong lest we displease our Lord. The fear of committing a sin because He is watching us, and knows all we do. But never any fear of Him. Such is the true servant. Claims not equality with Him, does not hold Him in dread, but is rather always absorbed in Him.

The 23rd *pauṛi* with which these *sloks* were attached speaks to us of the might of the Lord and says all that happens is by His Will. The *pauṛi* says:

ਪਉੜੀ ॥	Pauṛi
ਨਾਨਕ ਅੰਤ ਨਾ ਜਾਪਨ੍ਹੀ ਹਰਿ ਤਾ ਕੇ ਪਾਰਾਵਾਰ ॥	Nanak unt na jāpni har ta kay pārāvār
ਆਪਿ ਕਰਾਏ ਸਾਖਤੀ ਫਿਰਿ ਆਪਿ ਕਰਾਏ ਮਾਰ ॥	Āp karāye sākhti phir āp Karāye mār
ਇਕਨਾ ਗਲੀ ਜੰਜੀਰੀਆ ਇਕਿ ਤੁਰੀ ਚੜਹਿ ਬਿਸੀਆਰੁ ॥	Ikna gali janjīrīa ik turi chaṛhe bisīār
ਆਪਿ ਕਰਾਏ ਕਰੇ ਆਪਿ ਹਉ ਕੈ ਸਿਉ ਕਰੀ ਪੁਕਾਰ ॥	Āp karāye karay āp hau kai siu kari pukār
ਨਾਨਕ ਕਰਣਾ ਜਿਨਿ ਕੀਆ ਫਿਰਿ ਤਿਸ ਹੀ ਕਰਣੀ ਸਾਰ ॥੨੩॥	Nanak karṇa jin kīya phir tis hee karṇī sār [23]

Glossary:

ਸਾਖਤੀ	Sākhtī	Making
ਜੰਜੀਰੀਆ	Janjīrīa	Chains
ਤੁਰੀ	Turi	Horses
ਬਿਸੀਆਰ	Bisīār	Many
ਕਰਣਾ	Karṇa	Doing, creation

Simply translated this *pauṛi* says that we cannot know the limits or the ends of the Lord. He creates and He Himself destroys. Some created beings are in chains while others ride horses. He is the prime Mover; He is the Doer, then to whom shall we appeal. He who created all this is the one who will take care of it also. Let us now look at it in detail.

In lines 1 and 2 the Guru says we cannot know the limits, the extent or the ends of the Lord. He Himself creates and He Himself destroys. *Pārāvār* means 'this end and that'. When we cannot see the two ends of a thing then obviously we are unable to determine its size. The Lord's extent, says the Guru, is not within human capacity to measure. He creates and He, at His Will, destroys. This mystery is also beyond human ken. Bhai Vir Singh tells us that some learned ones have also rendered the word *sākhti* as hardness, cruelty and, thus, interpret the line as, "The Lord Himself makes us act in hard fashion and He punishes us," but this does not fit in the context here. The word *sākhti* is from the Persian *sākhtan* (making), so the proper rendering would be "He makes and He destroys," which is how most learned ones have rendered it. The mysteries of the Lord's actions – why He creates, why does He then destroy, how big is His extent are spoken of here. The answer, as elsewhere in *Gurbani* also, is that these are totally beyond human capacity to comprehend. The message then is to stop wasting energy on trying to decipher the Lord, and instead just acknowledge, and take pride and satisfaction in doing so, that He is your Master. Accept without question whatever He may choose to bestow on you; Fix your mind on Him and with the guidance of the Guru, uplift yourself by constant recitation of His Name and always sing His praises.

In line 3 the Guru says some are in chains and others ride horses. This touches on that other mystifying reality, of how human beings are apparently enjoying such differing degrees of comfort in this world. Why do some have chains round their necks while others ride high above them on horses? The unspoken answer here is that it is all in the Lord's hands. The Guru has given these examples from the everyday life of those times to show how some of us in this world always remain in deep trouble while others have all material comforts. The implicit lesson here again is that all this is part of His mysterious plan, and the reason is known only to Him. He alone knows who of us should be in what condition. Also, we have to remember that troubles are not always a punishment. Rather, as the Guru said in the *slok* with *pauṛi* 12, sometimes, "dukh dāru sukh rog bhaya", meaning troubles are the remedy and joys the disease. We have to therefore gladly accept in whatever condition He chooses to keep us.

In line 4 the Guru says that since the Lord is the prime Mover, and He is the Doer, then to whom we shall appeal. All the good and the bad things that we may in our limited wisdom think are happening to us are emanating from Him alone. Whether we have chains around our necks or whether we have the luxury of having many horses to ride on, is in either situation His doing; so do not go looking for another to appeal to. In other words, accept what we are given, with equanimity, and do not in restlessness go searching for any human or other agency to change our condition. Only He has the power. Therefore, go only to Him and above all learn to accept His judgement.

In the concluding line the Guru says, He who created all this is the one who will also take care of it. This, read with line 4, leads to the inescapable conclusion that, the Guru is telling us that we must look only to the Lord for whatever we want, because as the Creator He is also the sustainer, and also the sole court of appeal.

PAURI 24

This pauri has two *sloks*, one by Guru Nanak, and the other by the second Nanak, Guru Angad. Both touch upon the Creator and us, upon how the human condition manifests in reality in this world. In the first *slok* the Guru says:

ਸਲੋਕੁ ਮਹਲਾ: ੧	Slok Mahla: 1
ਆਪੇ ਭਾਂਡੇ ਸਾਜਿਅਨੁ ਆਪੇ ਪੂਰਣੁ ਦੇਇ ॥	Āpay bhāndday sājiyan āpay pūraṇ day
ਇਕਨੀ ਦੁਧ ਸਮਾਈਐ ਇਕਿ ਚੁਲੈ ਰਹਨਿ ਚੜੇ ॥	Ikni dudh samāīai ik chulhay rahan charay
ਇਕ ਨਿਹਾਲੀ ਪੈ ਸਵਨਿ ਇਕਿ ਉਪਰਿ ਰਹਨਿ ਖੜੇ ॥	Ik nihali pai sawan ik uppar rahan kharay
ਤਿਨ੍ਹਾ ਸਵਾਰੇ ਨਾਨਕਾ ਜਿਨ੍ਹ ਕਉ ਨਦਰੁ ਕਰੇ ॥	1] Tina savārey Nanaka jin kau nadar karay. 1.

Glossary:

ਭਾਂਡੇ	Bhānday	Vessels, pots; here, human beings
ਪੂਰਣੁ ਦੇਇ	Pūraṇ day	Completes, fills
ਸਮਾਈਐ	Samāīai	Filled
ਚੁਲ੍ਹੈ	Chulleh	Cooking hearths
ਨਿਹਾਲੀ	Nihāli	Quilts

Simply translated this *slok* says that He Himself makes the vessels, meaning human forms, and then gives them final shape. Then in some milk does He store while others stay ever on the cooking hearth, meaning some are in comfort while others suffer agonies. Some sleep in comfort on soft beds while others stand unsleeping at their service. Only those are raised in honour on whom His glance of grace falls. Let us now look at it in detail.

In line 1 the Guru says He Himself makes the vessels and completes them, giving them such final shape as He has prescribed for each. The process of creating human beings is referred to here by comparing the Lord to a potter and the humans to the vessels a potter makes. The potter shapes the vessel from clay, fashioning it on his spinning wheel, and then he fires the product in his kiln which completes the process and produces the finished vessel. Similarly are humans made in this universe, fashioned in the mould the Lord ordained for us, and then sent to exist on the worlds created by Him. The term *bhāndday* (vessels), is used for the human body elsewhere too by the Guru.

In line 2 the Guru says some of these vessels are then used to store milk, while some others stay ever on the cooking hearth. This is meant to indicate the human condition, just as in the previous *pauṛi* the Guru had said, "ikna gali janjīrīya ik turi charay bisīyār", describing how some humans are in chains and some have many horses to ride. Just as the potter's vessel, once it is ready, it may be used for storing a very desirable thing like milk, or it may forever be kept to simmer on the fire; the humans created by Him also have varying fortunes. Some are ensconced in apparent comfort and enjoy all material pleasures, while others are metaphorically forever burning in unfulfilled desires.

In line 3 the Guru describes another contrasting state of the human being. Some, he says, sleep comfortably on soft beds under quilts, while others stand unsleeping in guard over them. As in the previous line, the differing fates to which humans may be subject are indicated here. Some are destined to have comforts all their lives while others are destined to have hard times and will struggle against adversity.

In line 4 the Guru says only those are raised in honour on whom His glance of grace falls. The point the Guru is driving home to us is that the Lord is the fashioner and He is the One who will bring the created beings to completion. He keeps us in differing states of comfort or otherwise as it pleases Him. These states of apparent state of joy or sorrow, pleasure or trouble through which we transit while on this Earth are, however, not really relevant to our ultimate fate. These are temporary situations caused by our actions through the various incarnations on this Earth. Our actions will have their effect on our condition because as the Guru said in the *Japji Sahib*, *pauṛi* 4, "karmi āvay kapṛa", meaning our actions determine the sort of birth we will have to take. Above all, however, it will depend on the Lord's determination of the worth of our actions. This is not yet the final completion of the making process. That final finish will come and the process will be completed when the Lord's grace is granted to us. Who will be the beneficiary and when, is known only to the Lord. The ones comfortable in soft beds and quilts, or the ones riding high today are not necessarily assured of His ultimate grace; nor are those, seemingly in servitude today, doomed to be forever deprived. Any one of these could be the lucky one who finds completion or salvation through His mercy.

The second *slok*, by the second Nanak, is on the same theme. He says:

ਮ: ੨	M: 2
ਆਪੇ ਸਾਜੇ ਕਰੇ ਆਪਿ ਜਾਈ ਭਿ ਰਖੈ ਆਪਿ ॥	Āpay sājay karay āp jāyi bhi rakhai āp
ਤਿਸੁ ਵਿਚਿ ਜੰਤ ਉਪਾਇ ਕੈ ਦੇਖੈ ਥਾਪਿ ਉਥਾਪਿ ॥	Tis vich junt upāi kai dekhai thhāp uthhāp
ਕਿਸ ਨੋ ਕਹੀਐ ਨਾਨਕਾ ਸਭੁ ਕਿਛੁ ਆਪੇ ਆਪੇ ॥੨॥	Kisno kahīai Nanaka sabh kichh āpay āp. 2.

Glossary:

ਜਾਈ	Jāyi	The created things, the earth
ਥਾਪਿ	Thhāp	Create
ਉਥਾਪਿ	Uthhāp	Destroy

Simply translated this *slok* says that the Lord creates, fashions and He keeps all created things, the entire Universe, in their assigned places. Having created the world, He creates the beings therein and then watches the creation and the destruction. To which authority can we turn when He is everything Himself. Let us now look at it in detail.

The argument of the previous *slok* is restated and reiterated by the Guru here. In line 1 he says the Lord creates and fashions and he keeps everyone, each created thing in their assigned places. The phrase used in the previous *slok*, "āpay bhānday sājīyan" is here restated as *āpay sājay*, meaning 'Himself makes'. The

Lord creates and it is His Will that animates His creation. Then by His power are all parts of this vast creation kept in their appointed places. Dr. Gopal Singh has rendered the phrase *rakhay āp* as, "… gives it a habitation" which also has essentially the same connotation. Most learned ones though, have preferred the rendering as, "appointed or appropriate place". In the context here this is a more appealing interpretation.

In line 2 the Guru says having created the world He creates beings therein and then watches over the *thhāp* (creation) and the *uthhāp* (destruction). Bhai Vir Singh in his commentary says that *uthhāp* is also used for 'raising', 'lifting' and also 'inciting' but, usually in Punjabi, and in the context here, it has been used in the sense of ending, destroying. Many other learned ones have used the translation 'makes and unmakes' for *thhāp, uthhāp* which also is close to the sense of the message. The Lord alone is above this entire process; and all the created beings within this creation are subject to this constant process of *thhāp, uthhāp*. And the Lord watches over it all.

In line 3 the Guru concludes by asking to which other authority we can turn when He is everything Himself. In the previous *slok* Guru Nanak had told us, "āp karāye karay āp hau kai siu kari pukār". The same thought has here been restated. The sole authority in the created universe is the Lord, and to Him alone must we look for anything we seek.

In the 24th *pauṛi*, the last one in the *Āsa di Vār*, the Guru speaks further on the same theme that the Lord is beyond human ken. He creates and we all are subject to what He has prescribed. The Guru says:

ਪਉੜੀ ॥	Pauṛi
ਵਡੇ ਕੀਆ ਵਡਿਆਈਆ ਕਿਛੁ ਕਹਣਾ ਕਹਣੁ ਨ ਜਾਇ ॥	Vadday kīya vaddiāia kichh kahṇa kahṇ na jāye
ਸੋ ਕਰਤਾ ਕਾਦਰ ਕਰੀਮੁ ਦੇ ਜੀਆ ਰਿਜਕੁ ਸੰਬਾਹਿ ॥	So karta kādar karīm day jīya rijak sambāhay
ਸਾਈ ਕਾਰ ਕਮਾਵਣੀ ਧੁਰਿ ਛੋਡੀ ਤਿੰਨੈ ਪਾਇ ॥	Sāyi kār kamāvṇi dhur chhoddi tinai pāye
ਨਾਨਕ ਏਕੀ ਬਾਹਰੀ ਹੋਰ ਦੂਜੀ ਨਾਹੀ ਜਾਇ ॥	Nanak eki bāhri hor dūji nāhi jāye
ਸੋ ਕਰੇ ਜਿ ਤਿਸੈ ਰਜਾਇ ॥੨੪॥	So karay je tisai rajāye [24]

Glossary:

ਵਡਿਆਈਆ	Vaddiāīa	Qualities, virtues
ਕਰੀਮੁ	Karīm	The merciful one (the Lord)
ਸੰਬਾਹਿ	Sambāhay	To collect
ਕਾਦਰ	Kādar	Creator
ਧੁਰਿ	Dhur	Ab initio, from beginning

Simply translated this *pauṛi* says that man cannot gauge the greatness of the Lord. He is the Creator, the Prime Cause, and the Benefactor who provides sustenance to all His creatures. Each creature performs the task the Lord has assigned to him from the beginning. Outside of Him there is no other shelter and whatever He wills, comes to pass. Let us now look at it in detail.

The Guru speaks further of the greatness of the Lord. In line 1 he says man cannot gauge the greatness. As Prof. Talib puts it, "The supreme Lord's might beyond our description lies." Bhai Vir Singh renders *kahṇa* here as implying that the Guru says he wants to express the greatness of the Lord, even though so lofty is He that we cannot describe Him in any way. The attempt to describe His greatness is impossible but in order to reach Him we have to make the effort. In Sikhism the basic lesson has been stated by the Guru right in the beginning of the *SGGS*, in the *Japji Sahib* in *pauṛi* 4. He said there, "amrit vela sach nām vaddīai vīchār", meaning contemplate His greatness at the ambrosial hour. The greatness of the Lord is beyond comprehension and the more we think on it the greater it will appear. But fixing our minds on it reminds us constantly of Him, and thus are we benefited. So important is this contemplation that the Guru also told us, again in the *Japji Sahib* in *pauṛi* 25, "jisno baksay sipht sālāh Nanak pātsāhi pātsāh", meaning he is the greatest king to whom He has granted the singing of His praises. Thus, we are enjoined upon to sing His praises contemplating His greatness. We do this knowing that we cannot fathom Him. But making the effort is essential. Bhai Vir Singh also sees it this way.

In line 2 the Guru says He is the Creator, the Prime Cause, the Benefactor who provides sustenance to all His creatures. Bhai Vir Singh says that *Sambāh* is from the Sanskrit *sanvāh*, which has many connotations such as 'massaging', 'collecting', 'carrying', 'gathering'. In the *Gurbāṇi* it has been used more than once in the sense of 'providing'; thus, in *Rāg Gūjri*, *Mahla* 5, page 12 it says, "sirr sirr rijak sambāhay thākur", meaning "to each the Lord provides". Again in *Rāg Sūhi*, *Mahla* 3, page 1045 of the *SGGS*, the Guru says, "Sabhna rijak samāhay āpay", meaning "the Lord provides sustenance to each". Thus, the term here also has to be seen in the sense of 'to provide'. The reference here is to the Lord as the one who creates the means of sustenance, reaching it to every created being.

In line 3 the Guru says each one performs the task the Lord has assigned to him from the beginning. Each being, each thing when created is also given a place, a task in the divine scheme of things. So in this way does the entire system, vast and mysterious, move in total harmony, in fixed paths without any component or part trying to go its own way.

In lines 4 and 5 the Guru says without Him there is no other shelter and whatever He wills occurs. As Prof. Talib says, "Saith Nanak: other than the Sole Lord no place of shelter is for us." The learned ones are fairly agreed on the interpretation here. Bhai Vir Singh elaborates a little to say that the Guru implies that without the Lord there is none who could give us succour, and the Guru is happy in whatever the Lord has in store for him. The Lord is the Master whose Will ever prevails, or in other words He does whatever He chooses to do. As the Guru also said in *Rāg Āsa*, *Mahla* 4, page 13 of the *SGGS*, "Jo tau bhavai soi thīsi, jo tu[n] deh soee hau pāyi", what you please comes to pass, whatever You give that only will you get. The lesson here is to forget about any wordly or supernatural powers other than the Lord. Seek in Him alone any shelter that you think you need. Having done so then accept whatever He is pleased to assign you. The Lord's Will is supreme and what fate you are facing is because that is how He has prescribed it. That is how it is going to happen, even if you make serious demur. Wisdom lies in accepting and surrendering yourself completely to His Will. The miracle you will see is that the moment you do so your lot on this Earth will improve dramatically; peace and serenity will prevail inside and the passage through this mortal abode will become effortlessly easy.

SELECT BIBLIOGRAPHY

1. *Panj Granthi Steek*
   Bhai Vir Singh
   Bhai Vir Singh Sahit Sadan, New Delhi, Ninth Print, July 2005

2. *Sri Guru Granth Sahib Darpan*
   Prof. Sahib Singh
   Raj Publishers, 1972

3. *Shabdarth Sri Guru Granth Sahib ji*
   Sharomani Gurdwara Prabandhak Committee 2000

4. *Sri Guru Granth Sahib* (English)
   Prof. G. S. Talib
   Publication Bureau, Panjabi University, Patiala, 1988

5. *Gurshabad Ratnakar (Mahan Kosh)*
   Bhai Sahib Bhai Kahan Singh
   Panjab Languages Dept., 1974

6. *Adi Sri Guru Granth Sahib Steek (Faridkot wāla teeka)*
   Panjab Languages Dept., Reprint, 1989

7. *The Encyclopedia of Sikhism*
   Editor in chief: Prof. Harbans Singh
   Punjabi University, Patiala, 1998

8. *Santhya, Sri Guru Granth Sahib ji*
   Bhai Vir Singh
   Khalsa Samachar, Amritsar, 1981

9. *Āsa di Vār, Steek*
   Prof. Sahib Singh
   Singh Brothers, Amritsar, 2005

10. *A Popular Dictionary of Sikhism*
    W. Owen Cole and Prem Singh Sambhi,
    Rupa & Co., 1990

11. *Sri Guru Granth Sahib* **(English)**
    Dr. Gopal Singh, World Book Center, New Delhi, 1989

12. *The Oxford Dictionary of World Religions*
    Edited by **John Bowker**
    BCA, First Reprint, 2003

13. ***Sri Guru Granth Sahib***
Bhai Manmohan Singh

14. ***Sri Guru Granth Sahib***
Dr. Sant Singh Khalsa

15. ***The Sikh Religion***
Max Arthur Macauliffe

16. ***Āsa di Vār***
Prof. Teja Singh, Jan 1988

17. ***Āsa di Vār***
Dada Chellaram
Nirguna Balik Satsang, Saproon

18. ***Āsa di Var da gurmat teeka***
Dr. Gurmukh Singh,
Sikh Foundation, New Delhi, 2003

19. ***Āsa di Var da teeka***
Swami Anadghan,
Punjabi University, Patiala, 1990

20. ***Āsa di Var, Bahumukhi Adhyayan***
Ed: Dr. Jasbir Singh,
Guru Nanak Dev University, 2004

21. ***Āsa di Vār, Chintan Te Kala***
Dr. Bikram Singh Ghuman,
Waris Shah Foundation, Amritsar, 1998

22. ***A Treasury of Mystic Terms***
Science of Soul Research Centre, Radha Swami Satsang

23. ***Āsa di Vār,* audio-commentary**
Prof. Darshan Singh

24. ***Āsa di Vār***
Dr. Ajit Singh Aulakh,
Bhai Chattar Singh Jiwan Singh, Amritsar, 2005

25. ***Āsa di Vār,* audio-commentary**
Gyani Sant Singh Maskin

KEY TO PRONUNCIATION

	Gurmukhi Script	Roman script	Pronunciation
1.	ਅ	a	short 'a', as in 'normal', except at the end when it is long as in 'war'
2.	ਆ	ā	long a, as in 'war'
3.	ਇ, ਿ	i	short 'i' as in 'fit'
4.	ਈ, ੀ	ī	long 'i' as in 'meet
5.	ਉ, ੁ	u	short 'u' as in 'put'
6.	ਊ, ੂ	ū	long 'u' as in 'boot'
7.	ਏ, ੇ	e	sharp 'a' as in 'grey'
8.	ਐ, ੈ	ai	broad 'a' as in 'fat'
9.	ਅੰ, ੰ	[ng]	nasal, short sound, as in sing
10.	ਆਂ, ਂ	ā[n]	nasal, long sound as in brand
11.	ਸ	s	as in sad
12.	ਸ਼	sh	as in sharp, shut
13.	ਕ	k	as in kit
14.	ਖ	kh	as in *khālsa*, or silk hat (uttered quickly together)
15.	ਗ	g	as in good
16.	ਘ	gh	as in ghost, or log-hut (uttered quickly together)
17.	ਚ	ch	as in chat
18.	ਛ	chh	as in Chhatisgarh, or church-hill uttered quickly together
19.	ਜ	j	as in just
20.	ਝ	jh	as in *jhang*, or hedgehog
21.	ਟ	tt	hard sound, as in talk, or curt
22.	ਠ	tth	hard sound, as in thakur, or hot-house

23.	ਡ	dd	as in dark, or card
24.	ਢ	ddh	as in *dholak*, or in red-hot (uttered quickly together)
25.	ਣ	ṇ	as in *madhāṇī*
26.	ਤ	t	soft 't', as in *talwandī*
27.	ਥ	thh	as in thick
28.	ਦ	d	soft 'd', as in then
29.	ਧ	dh	as in *dhobi*, or breathe hard
30.	ਨ	n	as in nun
31.	ਪ	p	as in pup
32.	ਫ	ph or f	as in phone or fix
33.	ਬ	b	as in but, or tube
34.	ਭ	bh	as in *Bhagat*, or abhor
35.	ਮ	m	as in mat, or time
36.	ਯ	y	as in yet
37.	ਰ	r	as in rat
38.	ਲ	l	as in love
39.	ਵ	v,w	as in vent, with
40.	ੜ	ṛ	as in *pahāṛ*
41.	ਜ਼	z	as in zero

Maneshwar S. Chahal has an honours degree in English Literature, a degree in Engineering and a Masters in Public Administration. He has been an army officer, a senior bureaucrat in the IAS, CMD of the Punjab & Sind Bank, and a member of the State Human Rights Commission in Punjab. In the midst of these multifarious roles, he has continued to be a deeply devoted student of Spirituality, especially of the intensely humanistic Sikh Religion.

His series 'Way to God in Sikhism' offers a lucid and easy-to-understand delineation of the Spiritual path in the context of the Sikh belief system. Starting with the *Japji Sahib*, it has been warmly welcomed and much appreciated by scholars and lay readers alike.

Chahal lives in Chandigarh and can be reached at chahal37@hotmail.com.